KING SAUL

King Saul

A Novel

JOHN C HOLBERT

RESOURCE *Publications* · Eugene, Oregon

KING SAUL
A Novel

Resource Publications
An Imprint of Wipf and Stock Publishers
199 W. 8th Ave., Suite 3
Eugene, OR 97401

www.wipfandstock.com

ISBN 13: 978-1-62564-667-5

Manufactured in the U.S.A.

To Diana, who has now for 44 years been
companion, co-worker, wife, mother, lover, and friend
through all that a life can fling up, dredge up, offer up
to a pair of seekers after truth. She has been there
even when I at times have nearly fallen off
the edge of things, including this time
of attempted novel writing. Here it is, my love.
I hope it bears a tiny shred of what you
have meant to me for so, so long.

Foreword

> We are not always able to put ourselves in the place of someone from the past;
> but we always try to do so. Since our attempts are never rewarded (or tested)
> by the eventual appearance of the person in question, they proliferate boundlessly,
> nourished in their own unfulfilled hopes. We recapitulate what we already know
> or think we know, changing the sequence, hoping that somewhere in all of these facts
> a sudden illumination will offer itself, an inspiration be given us.[1]

THOUGH THE ABOVE QUOTATION comes from a biography of a very well known histori-cal character, the author's obvious humility in the face of such a famous person struck me as indicative of my own feelings as I sought to write a fictional life of Israel's first king. I certainly do not expect Saul to rise up and praise or bless what I have done—though Samuel's reappearance from the dead in the story does give one pause—nor have I awaited some "sudden illumination" to allow me to rearrange the "facts" in ways that will offer a new and uniquely inspired telling of Saul's story. Of course, the "facts" come from only one place, the Bible, and more specifically the book of 1st Samuel found in it. Such facts are literary facts only; whether or not they are fully or partially or not at all "facts" in the historical sense I leave to the battles among the biblical scholars, who always seem ready to enter the metaphorical ring, academic fists raised, ever anxious to strike a blow for their particular views on these matters. I choose not to don my trunks and join them. Saul's story for me has been and continues to be just that—a story.

I have written this novel of King Saul, based on the Bible's account of his life, because I have long experienced it as glorious and rare and strange. And I have been consistently disappointed by those biblical scholars who have not heard its richness and rareness and strangeness, but instead have reduced it to a crude propaganda wherein Saul is monster and Samuel is godly and David is godly beyond all telling. They seem to have swallowed whole the simplistic foolishness of the biblical author of Chronicles who summarily dismissed Saul by saying that he died "for his unfaithful-ness; he was unfaithful to YHWH in that he did not keep the command of YHWH; besides he had consulted a medium, seeking guidance, and did not seek guidance from YHWH. That is why YHWH killed him and turned the kingdom over to David, son of Jesse" (1 Chron 10:13–14). (Reader Note: I will throughout my story use the

---

1. Wolfgang Hildesheimer, *Mozart* Farrer Strauss Giroux: New York 1982, 279.

consonants YHWH when referring to the God of Israel whose name was later in their history deemed too holy for pronouncing out loud. You may, if you wish, try to pronounce out loud those letters, but I fear for your teeth and tongue if you do.)

I find this Chronicles reading chilling, a kind of Saul horror story. And too pat to be at all believable, either historically or literarily. Any even half-baked reading of the story found in 1st and 2nd Samuel ought to engender hoots of derisive laughter at the knuckle-head who wrote that claptrap. But amazingly, that absurd reading has been very influential when assessments of Saul and David are made. It appears that the actual *story* of the Samuel books, so marvelously rendered, so meticulously fashioned, has, until quite recently, rarely been taken with any seriousness by readers, religious or otherwise.

Fortunately, this has begun to change. Several scholars of the last two decades of the last century, have taken the actual story of the Bible with great seriousness. Each of these scholars of course has heard with their own ears the myriad subtleties that story brings forth, and has rearranged those discoveries to suit their own hearing which is at it should be in the world of scholarship. I have learned much from them, and I commend them to you if you are looking for that sort of thing, namely careful scholarship, finely delivered, with genuine literary sensitivity.

Other artistic efforts have been called forth by the story. For the music lover, you should get a copy of the wonderful and deeply moving opera, "Saul and David," by Carl Nielsen, perhaps Denmark's greatest composer. (I would recommend the CD on the Chandos label; I am still anxiously awaiting a promised DVD from a Danish National Opera production.) Though the opera is more than one hundred years old, it offers a remarkable reading of the character of Saul, not all of which matches my own. Still, his great aria at his death is well worth pondering. I have in fact borrowed and paraphrased a bit of it to place in the mouth of my Saul as he dies on Gilboa. Of the librettist of the opera I know little or nothing, but his reading of the story is plausible and highly dramatic, operatic in the very best way.

I, though a scholar of some gifts, albeit none to match those of the aforementioned writers, have finally decided that "that sort of thing," careful scholarship, finely delivered, is not enough for me. However fine the scholarship about the story, it is not the story. So I have concocted my own story, based squarely on the Bible's story, but imbued with whatever imagination and literary skill I possess. I have read and reread the biblical account in the ancient language, and I have followed the story's own shape in nearly every case in my own retelling, with an exception or two for my story's clarity. And, of course, I have taken liberties aplenty and have followed where the characters have lead on more than a few occasions. It was, however, let me be clear, my intention to tell Saul's story again, but to tell it new and to tell it "slant," as Emily Dickensen so memorably put it. I wanted to tell the story to get it out of the hands of preachers (though, God knows, I am one!) and scholars and back into the hands of real people who are ever thirsty for another great tale with which to shape their lives, practice their living, and learn more about themselves and others and the world they inhabit. Of course, if preachers and scholars care to become real people, they are most welcome to read the novel, too!

I want you, the reader, to hear this old story, not a sermon, not a morality play, not a bowl of religious pabulum, consigned to the boredom of a Sunday sanctuary, or to one's rocking chair old age.

This is hardly the only way to tell the story; if it were, it would not be worth telling in the first place. I can only hope that you enjoy the reading of it half as much as I enjoyed the telling. King Saul and his prophetic anointer, Samuel, and his chief rival David are each characters that have never died, though all three are quite dead indeed, and have been in their graves for nearly three millennia. But because they still are very much alive in their story, they remain worth hearing from. I can only hope that I have given them fresh voice once again.

John C Holbert
February 14, 2014

1

"Send in the next one!" Abior reached for the tankard of beer the better to ease the work of the day. It was that time again when the village elders had to review people who wanted to join the community of Gibeah. 12 men sat at the rough table, placed in front of a large and dusty space under a tamarisk tree to provide some shade from the fierce sun that shone, as always, on the hills outside the walls of the town. It was *Chislev*, the year's ninth month, and it was still hot. Abior stretched his right hand to grab the front of his best robe to pull it away from his sweating skin. "Best" was of course a relative term. His best was rude and rough, made hastily by his wife—she never was much when it came to the work of the needle, he thought. Pretty good in other ways, though, as a slightly lascivious smile creased his thin lips. Six children in ten years was not bad, he said to himself, as he sat up a bit straighter on the hard bench behind the council table, demonstrating for any who cared to see his obvious virility. He looked down the table at his fellow villagers.

There was Shmuel, too small, still unmarried. How did he ever get on the council, he wondered? Oh, yes, of course. He was rich in flocks and herds, and had just built a fine new house of four rooms, four! Such a palace was the largest in Gibeah; one could hardly deny such a formidable man a seat. But without children, well, there was talk of an unsavory sort. Still, Shmuel's vast and healthy herds shut many a gossiping mouth.

Next to Shmuel was Carmi. Abior liked Carmi perhaps best of the councilors, because they were so much alike. Carmi had a productive wife, not so beautiful, but a superb mother of seven, including five sons, to insure the future of the village. And Carmi was a magnificent hunter, the village's best. He went out with Abior regularly and almost never failed to bag a bear or a lion, or at least a deer to flavor the simmering pots that steamed and bubbled every evening. The thought of the pot around his own cooking fire made his mouth fill with spit and sent his stomach on the growl. Carmi's piercing voice brought Abior back to the council table.

"Well, who is next? These last three candidates were a sorry lot, ill-clad, poorly-spoken, foul-smelling, clearly unacceptable. We need more people for the village, but they need to be respectable, productive in the fields and in the home. Big families, bigger families! Bring us more children, more sons!" It was ever Carmi's cry when he spoke in council; more sons, more sons! Of course, whenever Carmi made his familiar speech, Shmuel blushed and looked down at his fine leather sandals, knowing that he

1

had not done his bit to keep the community growing. Yet, even he could not disagree. After all, so many women died on the birth stools, and so many children, too. A village always needed children, and especially sons who could harvest and fight and hunt. The rest of the council grunted their agreement. They were generally good men, thought Abior, though the one at the end, Doeg, always sent a chill up Abior's spine.

Doeg was tall, swarthy, brittle as a stalk of field thistle, and just as useless, said many in the village. He lived in a filthy hut with one disgusting room, surrounded by many children, which spoke well of him, and was tended to by a tiny woman who may or may not have been his wife. No one had seen the two marry, since they themselves had stood before the council many moons ago, having come from no one knew where. Some whispered Edom, but no one was certain. Doeg was elected to council after his heroic stand against some thieves who had threatened Gibeah sometime in the month of *Sivan*, the third month of the year, just six months before. It surprised the whole village to witness the ferocity of the man whom few had given a second thought to before the attack. But all knew that without Doeg's courage, many of those who now found life and success would have surely been dead and forgotten and the village destroyed. He had been chosen for the council straight away. But Abior was hardly the only man of the village to keep a wary eye out for the activity of Doeg and his family. His seat on the council had not cleaned his hut or stopped the rumors about his peculiar relationship with the woman who tended his fires. In fact, Abior had cast one of the negative votes when Doeg had asked to join the village. But he was now on the council, and that was just the way it was going to be—at least for now.

The delay in the proceedings was too long. "Well," shouted Abior, "Get on with it. My stomach is reminding me that council cannot go on all day!" Also, the sun rose higher and hotter in the blue sky; Abior's very name meant, "My father is light," which never failed to remind him of the ever-present sun, rather more present than his father who disappeared from the village long ago, never again to be seen. Abior had plainly outstripped that worthless man in every way.

Murmurs of agreement with Abior's demand for action were whispered and hooted from every council member. Finally, a strapping man of some forty summers stepped forward.

Kish, a Benjaminite, hoped to settle in Gibeah, to him a miniature but pleasant hillside village, a short walk from Ramah, the city of Samuel. Though the history of the tribe of Benjamin was checkered, to say the least, Kish himself was industrious, clever, and ready to put all that concubine madness well behind him. After all, that had happened long before his birth, and he now was a modern man, ready to take his own place on a well-run farm, close to a successful and growing village. He was convinced that he could become a man of stature in the place, even though his ancestors were all complete unknowns as far back as four or five generations. A respected family was very important as a key to success, particularly for one who had come to a new city. If your immediate and even distant ancestors were suspect, well, you were also suspect, not to be trusted, never allowed finally to be one of the group. When Kish first introduced himself to the city elders, his recitation of his forebears impressed the dour elders not at all.

"My father was Abiel, and his father was Zeror, his father Becorath, and his father Aphiah."

The Gibean elders' eyes began to glaze over as Kish droned on about ancestors who were unknown nobodies, probably village drudges, certainly hicks without pedigree. Many of the names were not known at all by the men, many of whom could trace their own families back into a past so distant as to be nearly mystical.

"Yes, yes," Abior interrupted him, "enough of that." Abior's faint memory of his own father, and the man's abandonment of his family still rankled, and he had no intention of listening another minute to a recitation of unknown and useless ancestors. "Tell us about who you are. Have you done anything of value? Are your crops lush? Are your livestock sturdy?" "Tell us of your children!" And he added with a definite sneer, "What do you know of the concubine's story?" Carmi and Doeg were particularly keen to hear just how far this Kish might have been implicated in the monstrous tale of the concubine and the ancestral Benjaminites' foul behavior. Every member of the council of Gibeah had proven beyond doubt that they had no connection to the story and found the actions of their forebears in the story repulsive, unacceptable in every way. The thing had happened some time ago, but the memory was so vivid that it seemed like a very modern event. All of them wished to forget, but none of them could.

Anyone who wished to join a community had to first meet with the elders of the place to determine whether or not the newcomer was worthy of a home in or near the village. This screening was doubly important for villages in Benjamin. A few elderly Israelites still vividly remembered the outrage of the inhospitable people of Benjamin many summers ago that led to the shocking abuse and murder of an innocent concubine of a wandering Levite. The story seemed to be very old, but not so old as to diminish its terror one tiny bit. Mothers in the village would often scare their children into better behavior by telling this story; act correctly or the Levite may come for you! Whenever the tale was told, the Levite grew in size and strength, his nose became increasingly knobby and wart-marked, his eyes more blazing, more penetrating, his hair more frazzled and shaggy, his arms muscular, his legs powerful, his rage unchecked. In reality, the Levite was probably a small, ineffectual man, most priestly types were, but in many of the minds of the current children of Benjamin he had become monstrous. It was certainly a terrible tale, and the elders of Gibeah were inordinately concerned with any unknown newcomer with a Benjaminite background. The new man might have some distant connection with the story, might even be a relation of the concubine, or of her father, or, YHWH forbid, the nasty priest himself. They had no intention of allowing such a person, corrupted by these undying phantoms, to live among their respectable selves.

King Saul

Many versions of that story continued to make the rounds, but the facts were something like this. Many suns before Kish's appearance in Benjamin, a Levite, a land-less priest, was living in a very remote hut up in the hills above Gibeah. He had devoted himself to prayer and solitude, as many of his kind did in those days, but he soon tired of being alone. He left his hut and travelled to Bethlehem, a few days' journey east, in order to buy a concubine, a woman who had few hopes of a real marriage, to provide a companion for his days and warmth in his bed at night. She was not much to look at, but she was willing enough; her mother had died at her birth and her father was a poor and ignorant man. She thus had no dowry to bring to any marriage. She too at first seemed glad of the company, as they left Bethlehem to return to the hut above Gibeah.

But things went quickly wrong. Some said that she tired of the life of a Levite's companion, its poverty, its mumbled words and complex rituals, and became angry at the Levite's constant demands on her for food and cleaning, as well as his unbridled lust for her body. Others say that she found a more congenial partner, or two or three, in the village of Gibeah. For whatever reason, she left the Levite and returned to the poor house of her father in Bethlehem of Judah.

Four moons passed. The Levite wanted her back; he was lonely again, his hut was filthy without her cleaning, his member was hungry for her flesh. So, he went to Bethlehem in the attempt to woo her back with tender words. He even changed his tunic for the first time in many years. When he showed up at her father's door, the old and poor man was overjoyed to see him. After all, he barely had food enough to feed himself, let alone his daughter whom he thought he had seen for the last time those four moons ago. He was more than anxious to see the couple reunited so that his troublesome daughter would leave his life for good.

For three days the father and the Levite ate and drank together and told stories of their difficult lives. The father spoke sadly of the death of his wife who was a good woman, and a fair one. The Levite spoke of his calling as priest, of his lonely hut, of the brief time with the father's daughter, which he remembered with some fondness, though she had surprisingly left him alone for reasons he could not understand. But on the fourth day, when the daughter had not yet made an appearance at the table or in the house, the Levite decided to give up and go back to his hut alone. But the father said, "Why not sit again and have some more food; it is a long journey, and you will need strength? In fact, the weather is so foul today"—it was raining big cold drops—"why don't you stay one more night? Perhaps she will soften her heart and go with you." The old man was more than anxious to be rid of his daughter, whom he loved not at all. The Levite was willing to give it another day, so he stayed. And he stayed again.

The daughter knew well who was sharing her father's table, and she hid in her room, hoping that the execrable Levite would go back to that miserable hut that she had no desire to see ever again. As the days passed, one, two, three, she could not believe that the priest had not given up. But, of course, she heard all too clearly how anxious her odious father was to get her off his dirt-caked hands, how he cajoled and pleaded with the Levite to stay, and stay, and stay! Would he never leave? She did, however, remember the lusty fun she had had in Gibeah with a supple young boy or two, when the priest was taken up with his weird mumbo-jumbo, so as the days became four and five, she thought that perhaps she could reacquaint herself with one boy or another, or perhaps even a fresher one or two if she could survive the priest's incessant demands on her for constant work and unpleasant sexual needs, both of which she had no interest in at all. Maybe, she thought, life with the Levite, with its potential for some joy and fun on the side, would be better than her current life with a loveless father and few local fleshly attractions.

So, finally, on the sixth day, the girl came to the table to eat with her father and the Levite, and the two men convinced her to go back to the hut with the eager priest. Well, unbeknownst to them she had already made up her mind to go with the man, so she needed little convincing. But there was little use in telling either of the stupid men about that.

She was hardly overjoyed to be going back to her lonely life as priest's companion, but her father clearly did not want her with him, and at least the Levite showed some sign of caring for her, however selfishly, however crudely. The woman was trapped between an inattentive and uncaring father and a dangerously demanding and too attentive man, who smelled of goat and often acted like one. Well, she sighed, at least he had changed his filthy tunic! Scant hope for a changed life, but more hope than life with father. And there were those nubile Gibean boys!

So they left to return to Gibeah. But since they made such a late start, they only got as far as Jerusalem before the sun was about to slip below the mountains of the west. "Let us stay here in Jerusalem tonight, and we can complete our journey tomorrow," said the servant, Lemuel by name, whom the concubine's father had loaned to them for the trip. But the Levite said, "We will certainly not spend the night in a city of foreigners; it is hardly safe to bed down with these foul Jebusites!" Levites were often very particular about those they rubbed shoulders with. It always struck the concubine as very odd how haughtily the man acted, given his tiny hut, his pathetic resources, not to mention his foul odors. So they pushed ahead, moving quickly toward Gibeah. By the time they reached the village, the sun had been down for some time, the stars were out in full, and a bright moon bathed the familiar city square.

It is customary in Israel that when strangers appear they are to be treated as honored guests, to be brought into someone's home, to be fed and housed for the night and sent safely on their way in the morning. In modern Gibeah a stranger was assured of a warm and congenial welcome, partly because of the memory of this tale. But when the three travellers entered the square of Gibeah back then there was only silence; no one came to care for them or their beasts. Well, they thought, it is very late, though they had rightly expected someone to appear to offer them help.

Finally, after almost deciding to leave the village and trudge on to their remote hut, though they were nearly asleep standing up, an old man walked slowly into the village after a long day's work in the fields. They were in fact amazed to see a single man returning from his work so late and so alone. His back was bowed with the hard labor of farming, his hands caked with the mud of the field. He was less than eager to spend another minute away from his waiting fire and simple food, but when he saw the strangers, the ancient and hallowed demand for hospitality overcame his exhaustion. He politely asked them where they were from. The Levite told him their story, saying that they needed no food either for the donkeys or themselves, but they did desire a roof for the night. The old man replied, "Shalom to you! I will care for all of your needs, but you must not spend the night in this square!" His tiredness dissipated and his back straightened when he uttered the last part of his sentence with real vehemence, shuddering as he glanced furtively around the village center, bathed in the lovely, soft moonlight. The travellers felt very uneasy as they watched the old man's eyes dart in the light. He urged them to follow him quickly to his house, and moved off much more swiftly than his age would have suggested.

His hut was small but neat. His aged wife, or sister, or companion, YHWH alone knew which, had tended the small fire well, and it crackled with a cheery flame, nicely heating the tiny space. It was a farmer's house, various implements of that life leaning against the shadowy walls, two hoes with metal tips, an old bronze sword, dull and ill-used, several clay jars, poorly made and weathered with cracks, leaking liquid down their sides. A wooden bench served as the only place for a seat, and the old man fell heavily onto it, the woman scurrying to bring the food to the large wooden table, three rough boards held together with what looked like camel ropes, replacing the metal clamps that had long ago rusted away.

As they were eating a small meal, bread from gritty flour, a few dates and olives, meat from an unknown and stringy animal, the people of Gibeah encircled the house of the old man and began pounding on the door. "Bring that man who is visiting you outside now. We wish to have our way with him!" But the old man bravely confronted the mob, and said, "My neighbors, do not act with such wickedness. This man is my guest; you well know the demands of hospitality. When a stranger comes, the custom stipulates their complete protection and safety. I have a virgin daughter and this man has a concubine. I will bring them out to you, and you can do with them whatever your filthy imaginations can conceive." The crowd was plainly a depraved lot!

But the mob would not listen, so the Levite pushed his screaming concubine out to the mob and slammed the door after her. The old man, his daughter, and the Levite retired to bed, while the cruel mob of Gibeah, the men, the women, and even some children, attacked the concubine all night long, raping her and assaulting her in ways too appalling to recount. (At this point in the telling, how graphic the details became was dependent on the character of the teller and on the number of cups of wine consumed.) As the sun rose, they let her go, throwing her down on the ground, not knowing or caring whether she was dead or alive. The poor woman crawled feebly toward the house, stretched out her hand to grasp its threshold, and collapsed unconscious.

King Saul

And in the morning, the Levite got up and opened the door. There, lying on the threshold, was the concubine, bloody and bruised, her tunic ripped, most of her body exposed to the sun's first light. "Get up," he said to her, "We are going." He offered no comfort; he expressed no surprise; he showed no anger at the monstrousness of the deed. He merely wanted her to get up and go with him to his hut.

But she did not answer. Was she dead or just nearly dead? Some say one, some the other. In any case, the Levite lifted her limp body onto his donkey. And then he did the thing that so terrifies young and old whenever the story was told. When he arrived back at his hut in the mountains, he grabbed the concubine, and taking a huge knife, the one with which he regularly butchered his meat, he cut her into 12 pieces, limb by limb, and sent the bloody chunks throughout all the land of Israel. He commanded each man who carried a piece of the concubine as follows: "Say this to all Israelites; 'Has such a thing ever happened since the day the Israelites came up from the land of Egypt until this day?' Consider well, take careful counsel, and then act!"

With every telling of this unforgettably brutal story the Levite became larger, uglier, more terrifying. But the upshot of the Levite's action was particularly well remembered. Israel had nearly descended to outright civil war, its tribe of Benjamin almost wiped from the earth. Because of all this it was crucial that any would-be member of the territory be closely investigated; it would hardly do to be neighbors with anyone who did not ascribe to the very highest standards of morality, and morality was identical to village custom. They needed no more mobs to deny the sacred rights and agreed upon customs of a respected Israelite village. It was that story that lay behind the elders' careful questions of any newcomer.

So they questioned Kish closely as he applied to join the elders in Gibeah. Carmi wanted him to repeat that long list of unknown forbears, but Abior quickly rejected the idea as unnecessary, thinking to himself that he simply could not listen to the vapid names one more time! Shmuel asked about Kish's religious beliefs, although one could always say the name YHWH enough times to convince anyone that he was safe enough as a believer. Abior asked if there were any more questions, and hearing none, asked for a vote. On certain occasions, when the council was badly divided they would cast lots, ancient animal bones that the priests said could reveal truths that simple humans could not, but in the case of Kish, there was no need for the rattle of the bones. They finally accepted him, nearly unanimously, but, as usual, some with reluctance. The elders always acted with reluctance whenever anyone asked to live in their Gibeah, clearly the best village in all of Benjamin, if not in the whole land. But Kish was accepted at the last and found a good plot of land quite close to the village, no more than half a morning's walk. Kish , his wife, and young sons, soon made their way to their new farm and settled in to a fresh life on the outskirts of Gibeah.

2

The decision worked well this time for both sides as Kish's flocks and herds expanded and his fields were thick with grain at the times of harvest. He had numerous sturdy sons, all of whom were strapping boys, strong workers, devoted to Kish and to Kish's God, YHWH. It was particularly important that Kish and his family prove themselves devotees of YHWH, the mysterious God of the far-away mountain who had created everything and who offered to the faithful the riches of the land. The elders had built a shrine to YHWH at the highest place near the village, and all were expected to bring appropriate offerings to the God as well as to learn of the many demands that YHWH had laid on those who would be the God's followers. It was no problem for Kish to be regular in his sacrificial practice for in truth he grew deeply devoted to YHWH, the often hidden deity, in response to the increasing successes of his farm. Kish was careful to speak often of YHWH to his family, and easily had YHWH's name on his lips whenever any of the elders came for a visit to Kish's farm. And Kish and his sons made regular trips to the shrine, bringing with them gifts of ripe grain and on special occasions like spring lambing season, a pure animal for sacrifice. Kish and family soon became respected members of the village, and he was elected to the council of elders as quickly as any new comer ever had.

One of Kish's sons stood out from his brothers in nearly every way. He was very good-looking, any girl in Benjamin could tell you that. Years of hard farm labor filled out his arms and shoulders, and since his particular job was plowing behind the yoked oxen, his legs became heavily muscled as well. Walking in the muddy fields, trying to keep the huge oxen straight in the rows, forced arms and legs to strain almost every minute, so the boy became a chiseled figure of a man. All commented that this boy, Saul, was very pleasing to the eyes of all who saw him. But that was not the most noticeable thing about him. He was no doubt handsome, but most of all he was magically tall. No one could remember seeing a man as tall as he; four cubits (that is the height of a very tall camel, a cubit representing the distance between the middle finger and the elbow) at least he was. It was something of a joke as the boy grew, how he first towered over his mother by age ten, and then dwarfed his father by age fifteen. Carmi and Doeg took bets on just how tall Saul would finally become, while Abior wagered with Carmi, ever the one for a wager, on just when he would stop growing. When he grew nearly a span (the space between last finger and thumb) in his fifteenth year, he would cry out in the night because of the pain in his legs, the bones and sinews stretching and stretching.

Old Kish, his father, first beamed with pride at his enormous and handsome son, but as his growing continued, he became fearful that perhaps his boy was some sort of freak, a misfit in a shorter, more normal world, a monster to terrify little children, the stuff of scary stories in the night. Saul was special, all right, but he was also odd, peculiar, and could not be treated quite like Kish's other children. He could not share a sleeping place with anyone else, since he took up the whole of any normal sleeping rug. His appetite was prodigious; Kish's wife had to cook more and more food for the family as Saul ate enough for three or four children, and eventually enough for three or four adults. Of course, he was very handy about the farm; only Saul could handle alone the great team of oxen that was so essential to the work of plowing and planting; only Saul could lift the enormous stones that the plowing always turned up. It was often said that stones were the finest product of the fields of Israel, so stone moving was a central job when working the land. And no one could move stones like Saul.

Stories about Saul were told far and wide in the land. One described the day that he killed a lion in the field with his bare hands; another spoke of the time he grabbed two eagles right out of the air, the eagles apparently not aware that even they could not overtop the towering Saul. Many wags in the alehouses whispered that Saul must be endowed with a member the size of a bull, and they told tales of a prodigious sexual appetite that had put smiles on the faces of many willing Israelite women. Though Saul was not yet twenty summers, his fame spread as fires sweeping up the canyons of the hill country.

It is not likely that any of these stories were true; or if they had a grain of truth, they had been expanded well beyond validity. In fact, Saul was a simple boy, a capable farmer, and a dutiful son to Kish. Oh, he was a huge man, no question of that. But he was a man, not a monster, not a freak, not sexually or emotionally extraordinary in any special ways. Quite the opposite. Saul was rather a loner and quite shy; his size cut him off from others; he had little interest in being the center of attention. Saul just wanted to fit in, have some friends, some simple fun, love a fine woman, marry and have children. That's all he wanted really. But everywhere he went he stood out, a full head and more taller than anyone else had ever been, as people liked to say. Whether he wanted to or not, Saul was special, unique, more physically gifted than any man. More powerfully handsome than all other men, too.

On longer summer days, after the farm chores were done, Saul loved to climb one of the hills that bordered Kish's land, sit on the top, gazing at the meadows down below. He wanted to be alone. Here on the top of the mountain, he could feel small in the face of the great land of mountain and valley spread all around him. Here he was not singled out for size; here he thought about his life and YHWH, creator of earth and sky. His father taught his boys well the stories, laws, and poems that made up the traditions of the ancestors. Saul loved all religious things; he reveled in the sacrifices the family made, especially when they took the day-long journey east to Gilgal and its hallowed shrine, a much more impressive place than the small shrine in Gibeah. He rejoiced in the singing of the psalms of the faith, some new compositions, and some borrowed and changed from the ancient Canaanites whose descendants still lived in the hills to the north. Saul, himself, loved to sing, his rich bass regularly heard above the smaller voices of his brothers and friends. He studied the laws of Israel carefully, attempting to understand their modern applications. He especially loved the account of the Exodus from Egypt, how YHWH had defeated the vast armies of pharaoh after saving the chosen people from certain defeat at the Sea of Reeds, a marshy lake of uncertain location far in the west. He thrilled at the exploits of the great Moses who had led the reluctant and often terrified and foolish Israelites to that sea, through it, and beyond it toward the land of promise, part of which Saul now was seeing and living in. He loved the tale of the gift of the law at the smoking and heaving mountain of Sinai, how Moses brought the tablets of that law down from the mountain, only to shatter them in anger when he witnessed the orgy of idolatry centered on the molten calf, created by Aaron, and worshipped by those same people, who had been saved from bondage by YHWH. He shook his great head always when he heard these stories; he just could not imagine how his ancestors had so quickly rejected the freedom of YHWH, turning instead to a ridiculous pathetic little calf of gold. If he had been there, he thought, he would have joined Moses in melting that disgusting idol and would have readily force-fed the golden liquid down the throats of those ingrates!

Saul often felt that he was closest to his God when he was alone on his favorite hill, remembering the stories of the past. And he was convinced in his heart that he had a special destiny from that God; why else would YHWH have made him so tall? Why else could he eat and work like four men? Perhaps he was to be a priest in some shrine or other? Perhaps he should wait to see if he received a word as a prophet? The prophet Samuel was very old, and Saul had heard that Samuel's sons were not going to succeed their father in the tasks of ruling Israel. Why not he? Why not the tallest and most handsome man in the land? Yet, Saul knew he felt most free, most contented when he was alone, away from staring eyes, away from the foolish stories that his size or his good looks had spawned. How could he lead anyone when he felt uncomfortable in the presence of even a few people? Whatever God's plan for him was, he hoped it would not include being looked at by a crowd of gawking strangers. And after he had sat alone for some time on the hill, he hurried home to his family before the sun set, because he had no wish to trouble Kish or his mother or his brothers. Saul was a good boy, and could be trusted to be at the place he said he was going to be at the time he had said. Even if YHWH did not have any special task for him, he would be perfectly content to live out his days on the farm, perhaps taking over for Kish when his days for rough work were over.

One day, Saul's younger brother, Asaph, who was responsible for the pack animals of the farm, the donkeys and the two golden Egyptian camels, had forgotten to reattach the gate rope, and all of the donkeys, all eight of them, had wandered off in the night. This was a catastrophe for any farm, for without the donkeys the grain sales in the nearby towns would be impossible. The grain would rot in the barns, and the family, deprived of the proceeds of the sale, would go hungry in the winter to come. They had to be found! But Asaph, who felt miserable for his mistake, was far too young to send on such a trip. Donkeys could have wandered many miles in any direction. The light rain in the night covered their tracks, making the possibility of quick discovery unlikely. It could be a trip of many days, and one always had to be concerned about bands of thieves quick to take advantage of a poorly defended group of travelers. Also, columns of Philistine warriors were always searching for new ways to breach the defenses of Israel and were a constant danger. There was only one of Kish's sons who should go on the search, and that was Saul. His size was an obvious advantage; few thieves would risk a confrontation with such a man, and the cowardly Philistines would think more than twice before attacking Saul. They had a champion of their own, named Goliath, who was reputed to be even taller than Saul, which was probably an exaggeration, but perhaps suggested why they would be reluctant to take Saul on. Saul, the very tall and powerful Israelite, like Goliath, the very tall and powerful Philistine, would be difficult if not impossible to defeat in open combat. So, Saul was chosen by Kish to go hunt for the donkeys. The plan pleased Saul, since a journey into the wilderness promised some possible adventure and released him, however briefly, from the sometimes monotonous drudgery of daily work on the farm.

Kish also chose an especially clever slave named Joseph to go with him. Joseph had been named after the wily son of Jacob, the trickster, and over the years of his time with the family had proven to be a great help to Kish when it came to keeping accounts straight, assuring that crop yields remained high, and running the everyday upkeep of the farm with skill and absolute trustworthiness. Joseph did talk a great deal; one could quickly weary of his interminable stories. Still, he was a worthy man, very short, balding, but honest in all things. Saul and Joseph left the next morning at dawn, Saul riding one of the camels, towering high over the diminutive Joseph who lead the other one, laden with supplies good for many days. Such an odd pair they made! The giant Saul, riding high over the desert landscape and Joseph, walking behind, often hidden in the huge shadow that Saul and his camel cast on the ground. But that shadow was often to Joseph's advantage. He paced his walking to use Saul's immensity to block out the blazing sun. It made the journey considerably more pleasant, and Saul did not know that he was the source of such ease for the clever slave. Joseph walked in Saul's shadow with a smile on his face.

Donkeys are not fools, so they will not simply wander off blindly in any direction. Saul well knew the story of Balaam, an ancient prophet who was saved from acting against the chosen people by, of all things, a talking donkey! Saul had obviously never heard Kish's donkeys speak, but he never underestimated their natural cleverness. Unlike the absurd sheep, they had more in mind than the next blade of grass. During those times when Saul sat alone on his favorite mountain and thought about the stories, laws, and songs of his tradition, he could not help but laugh when he remembered some priest piously intoning "YHWH is my shepherd." If YHWH is shepherd, then I am sheep, thought Saul, and that makes me about as smart as a hill of slippery shale! Religion and its ideas were not always so serious!

Donkeys were surely smarter than sheep, but they, unlike the wondrous camel, must drink every day, so Saul reasoned that the eight strays would move toward familiar water holes. And since Saul and Joseph knew all the watering places for many days' walk around, they figured that the search would not last long. They first moved in a northeasterly direction toward the territory of Ephraim, higher in the hills where there were several places for water, but the donkeys were not there. They pushed on ever higher and found themselves in the part of Ephraim known as Shalishah, now nearly three days from home. The walking and riding were hard, the footing difficult on the dry shale that covered the hills. Joseph's camel was often reluctant to continue, and needed to be coaxed and goaded over and over. Camels may be very helpful beasts, but they are not known for their easy willingness to follow orders, so Joseph shouted himself hoarse on the second and third days of the trip, urging, pleading, demanding, begging the filthy beast to get going. Too often, its four thin legs would splay out in a rigid position and it would not budge. There was nothing for it at those times but to take a break and wait for the shaggy thing to make up its own mind to carry on. This slowed the search, and made both Saul and Joseph anxious and frustrated the further they got from Gibeah.

Saul was a basically silent boy, while Joseph knew a thousand stories and was always anxious to share them with anyone who would listen and even with those who cared not to listen at all. He especially loved to brag about his namesake, the great Joseph, son of Jacob, savior of Egypt and ultimately Israel, too. So on the fourth day of the search for the lost donkeys, and after Joseph's disgusting camel had once more refused to continue up a steep and slippery slope, dropping onto its belly with its four legs akimbo, Joseph screamed in frustration, "Get up, you smelly beast! I have had it up to my eyeballs with your actions. I am master here, not you! If God had given me four legs, and you two, then you could tell me what to do. But YHWH, praise be, made you to carry and work and me to lead. So, let's go—now!" This brief lesson in the wondrous ways of God had no effect on the camel whatever; it lay on its hairy belly and spit its cud on the ground, which was also the way YHWH had made it. And, of course, it bellowed that camel bellow, which to Joseph sounded all too much like a laugh, a laugh directed at him and, he thought, at YHWH. Not only did the creature smell and refuse to move, it was a blasphemer against the Almighty, too, thought Joseph, as he tugged and cursed and shouted. The camel just bellowed. With a final fruitless pull, the rope snapped and Joseph fell hard on his very clever backside. And Saul broke into a broad grin, which for him was like a very great howl of laughter indeed. But it was only a grin after all.

King Saul

There was nothing for Joseph to do but laugh at himself. He had learned to do that quite well, realizing that the ability to laugh at oneself always helped those around to appreciate his company more. Joseph, unlike Saul, had many friends. Obviously, they would have to rest in their search, because the camel was not going anywhere for a while. So Joseph reached into his rich store of tales and pulled one forth. Saul looked as expectant as he could look, though he would have much preferred to get on with the work of donkey finding. He sat heavily on the side of the hill, and leaned his huge back against the cool of a large rock. And Joseph, seeing he had a relatively attentive audience, launched into one of his favorite family stories.

"My ancestor, the mighty Joseph, after whom I was named, (as if Saul did not know that!) became the great and terrible vizier of Egypt." (Though Saul did not know exactly what a vizier was or what such a person did, he did not question his servant, not wanting to appear foolish.) "And there was a monstrous famine in the lands of Jacob, so bad that he was forced to send his sons back to Egypt to get food from the rich stores of that fabled land. Well, of course the sons were less than eager to go back there and face the mighty vizier—they did not know that he was in fact their long-lost brother, Joseph, my ancestor (yes, yes, get on with it, thought Saul!). You see, on an earlier trip to buy food, the vizier had sold them food, for which the brothers had paid a fair price. But on the way back to their father, they had opened their sacks and had seen all the money they thought they had given to the man pouring out on the ground! They were horrified, convinced that the great man would call them thieves and throw them in prison or might even have them killed. They did not know what had happened, but they had little desire to go back and find out.

But Jacob insisted and they went. This time when the vizier allowed them an audience—he always had an interpreter between them, making the brothers think that he could not understand Hebrew—he asked after their youngest brother, Benjamin. The lad had not come with them, since Jacob doted on him, seeing in him the replacement for his original favorite, Joseph, who he was sure was long dead, devoured by one of the cruel beasts of the wilderness. Strangely, the vizier had insisted on seeing Benjamin, saying that if he did not come with them, they would get no food from him. So they made yet another long trip home. Jacob was adamant that his new favorite would not leave his side, but the brothers convinced him finally that they would all starve if Benjamin did not show his face to the terrifying Egyptian.

So the young Benjamin went with them, leaving the father weeping at home and fearing the loss of another favorite son. Once again, the brothers appeared before the powerful official whose all-seeing eye fell on the young boy. 'Is this Benjamin, of whom you spoke?' he asked. Joseph could hardly get the words out of his mouth, so moved was he when he saw the boy; it was like looking in a mirror that miraculously showed an image of what used to be. So, my ancestor left the audience chamber and wept alone for his love for his brother.

King Saul

He soon recovered himself, dried his eyes, and came back to continue his discussion with his brothers, though they did not know he was their brother." (Saul was only half-listening now, becoming very tired of Joseph's way of telling things he did not need to hear to understand the story. He had always hated excess words, something the servant had a surfeit of.) "Well, to make the story shorter ("thank YHWH," muttered Saul), Joseph finally revealed who he was to his brothers, and they were so shocked that they could not speak." (Would that you were the same, thought Saul!) "And the result was that they all lived happily together in the land of Egypt, and all thanks to my clever forebear, Joseph, the cleverest man in all our history. And of course YHWH, too, led him to act so." Saul was glad that Joseph had put YHWH into the story, but still thought that it sounded suspiciously like an afterthought.

Saul sat in silence, thinking about this story that he had heard Joseph tell too many times. It sounded simple—the rejected Joseph becomes a great man and thus saves his family and his people from starvation. But Saul always wondered why Joseph, that supposedly good and wise and wondrous man, had played with his brothers so, putting the money back in their sacks and demanding that his father release Benjamin to him, thus wounding him grievously at the thought of losing his favorite. Who better than Joseph would know just what pain Jacob would feel at the loss of a favorite son? And why would he pretend for all those moons to be what he clearly was not? Why not just reveal himself to them? Was Joseph just a good and clever man or was he also a man who wanted revenge against his brothers who had wished him dead those many years before? And what about YHWH? What had the God to do with all this trickery and deceit and revenge and pain? Saul wondered all these things, but did not speak them to Joseph. He had little wish to cross verbal swords with his servant, knowing all too well that in such a battle he would likely lose, and would hurt the feelings of Joseph who imagined that his namesake could do no wrong.

Well, after the happy ending of the long story, the camel had decided to rise again, like some reborn plant, and it appeared that he had agreed to allow Joseph to lead him up the steep hill. Saul rose, and grabbed the rope of his beast and helped Joseph retie it, that ripped thing that had left him on his backside. They headed up the hill, hoping that they would see the accursed donkeys at last.

But they did not, and turned back southwest, back into Benjamin, passing Baal Hazor and ancient Bethel, the shrine of Jacob the clever, on their right. Saul wished they had time to stop in Bethel and worship at the sanctuary which was said to contain within its weathered altar the stone that Jacob had chosen for a pillow, and finally for a monument to YHWH who had appeared to the patriarch at that very place. But they had been gone nearly five long days now, and their supplies were running low. Besides, Saul thought, a visit to the shrine might trigger still another long story from the loquacious Joseph. He vowed to return here another day, alone. Saul had his own familiar and helpful way to remember that story of Jacob and his stone pillow. What had always been important to him about that tale was the fact that Jacob had looked up from his place of sleeping at the magic place of Luz and had actually seen YHWH! That was the way the story was always told to Saul. Jacob, the wily trickster had seen YHWH! Saul had been told again and again that no one could see YHWH and live. Yet, Jacob had done so. What would it be like to see YHWH? What would YHWH look like? Tall like me, thought Saul? Bearded? Could YHWH be a woman, sweet and helpful like Saul's mother? Unthinkable! Or perhaps not human at all, a cloud, a fire as in the Exodus wilderness, a giant dragon as one of the psalms said? Saul often had these silent ruminations, but he seldom shared them with anyone. Others might think him foolish or stupid or blasphemous.

On the sixth day they found themselves near the village of Zuph, a tiny place close to the larger village of Ramah. More recently, Ramah had been the scene of contention between Samuel and some men of Beer Sheba over leadership in the land after Samuel's eventual death. Saul and Joseph had heard of the struggle against Samuel's leadership on account of his two unworthy sons, but there had apparently been no resolution, since those who had gathered at Ramah had simply left the place at Samuel's command. No leader had been chosen, and Samuel had remained alone in the city—or so it was rumored. Information was difficult to come by after the shock of the angry confrontation with YHWH's prophet.

They were now only about a day from home again, and Saul was anxious to see Gibeah and his father.

He turned to Joseph, and said, "We need to get home, because my father has now probably stopped worrying about the donkeys, which can be replaced by others, and will now be worrying about us, who cannot really be replaced in quite so simple a way."

Saul rarely joked, so Joseph missed the tiny witticism how humans could be considered more worthy than donkeys. The servant had an idea that might solve their problem and was somewhat surprised that his master had not thought of it, too. It came to him that they were barely a short walk from that Ramah, Samuel's hometown. If the prophet was still in Ramah, as some said he was, he perhaps had gone to his house to recover from his harrowing fight about his future, the future of his sons, and the future of the land. If he was there, Joseph knew what they could do. Joseph played coy with Saul at first as he revealed his plan.

"A small way ahead is the town of Ramah. There is a man of God there who is greatly honored by everyone."

Well, Saul of course knew at least by reputation whom Joseph meant—the man of God was Samuel—and the fact was that not everyone did honor him as before, as the recent conflict there had made all too clear. Though Saul had never actually seen the prophet, he like all Israelites, scattered throughout the hill country, knew his power and his great actions for all the people. Samuel was far and away the most famous man in the land.

"Everyone knows that whatever he says always comes true."

King Saul

Saul knew that to be so; Samuel had long claimed that his words were in fact YHWH's words, and Saul had no reason to doubt the prophet in this; he had been leading the land in every way for well over fifty winters, long before Saul had been born.

"Let's go into Samuel's city; perhaps he can tell us about this journey we have been on."

Saul thought it was an odd way to say that they should ask the great Samuel to perform some divining trick to help them find the lost animals. Did not the famous man have more important things to do than find lost objects for anyone happening to wander by his town? Still, Saul would gladly receive help with the dumb beasts, since he was heartily sick of the chase.

"Even if Samuel is in the city, what can we bring in the way of payment? I assume that mighty soothsayers like Samuel do not do their magic for nothing. We have no food, no present, no gift of any kind. I suggest we move on to Gibeah, and tell Kish that the donkeys are nowhere to be found."

But Joseph fumbled in his robe and produced, very surprisingly, a tiny quarter-shekel silver piece. Saul at first was irritated that Joseph had not mentioned this bit of money earlier, since Saul had thought they had spent all they had in the fruitless search. His second thought was that no decent seer would work his wonders for such a paltry sum, but he decided that they had little to lose in the attempt. The famous man, both seer and prophet, might be insulted; but, then again, after his recent confrontation with an increasingly divided people, he might be anxious for the simple task of divining a few strayed beasts. Success might help his reputation and soothe his bruised ego.

"Very well, " said Saul, "let's go," and with that the two of them entered the gates of Ramah.

The town was typical in design. Its walls were a mixture of undressed stones and mud, slightly higher than the height of a normal man; Saul, of course, could see over them easily. The streets were a warren of shorter and longer passageways, dotted on both sides by minute mud-brick huts, roofed with palm and large tree branches, doors covered with woven rugs among the richer places, sheep's hides on those meaner hovels. The dry streets were thick with dust, dotted with the dung of many sorts of beasts, peopled by shouting children, harried women, and sweating men, a great mass of confusing smells and sights, all familiar to anyone entering a village in the poor land of Israel. Ramah was built into the side of a hill, the better to protect itself from attack from the rear. The wall needed only to be built around half the place, the other half well guarded by the rocky outcrop that formed both its backdrop and its rear guard. The lowest part of Ramah was at the entrance gate; all who came there found themselves immediately walking uphill into the city.

Saul and Joseph moved directly toward the city center, as always marked by the well, the gathering place, the community center, the origin of news and gossip along with the life-giving water that made the city possible at all. Of course, cities live on more than water; news and gossip are as life giving and important as the fresh liquid that flowed forth from the ancient well that supplied water even in the driest of seasons. As the strangers approached the well, some lively girls came to draw some water. There were three of them, two veiled, but one whose dark eyes flashed in admiration at the sight of the giant and handsome young man, accompanied by his much smaller, and much less interesting, servant. Saul smiled at the dark-eyed one, appreciating her own beauty and energy, drinking in the obvious flirting, with its not-so-hidden promise of future pleasures. Kish's lost donkeys briefly clip-clopped from his mind, as his vision filled with those dark eyes and the striking face from which they gazed.

"Is the seer here?" he asked, not attempting to hide his obvious pleasure at the woman and her companions. Saul imagined that these young women would not be all that interested in the magic of the soothsayer, but the reputation of Samuel made it certain that they would know whether or not he was at home today. As Ramah's most famous resident, his activities would be known by nearly everyone.

But the answer he received from the women was certainly different than he had expected. They fairly bubbled with excitement and let loose a torrent of words, many of which had little to do with the simple question he had asked.

"Yes! There he goes just ahead of you! (They pointed vaguely toward the hill.) He has come to the city just today, because the people have a sacrifice today, and, of course, the great Samuel is the only one who can lead the ritual. Close to the entrance to the city, back from where you have just come, you can find him, before he goes up to the holy high place to eat. (Now they pointed the other direction!) The people will not eat until he comes, because he alone can bless the sacrifice. After that, those eat who are called. Now go up there! You will meet him right away!"

And with a gaggle of giggles the three hurried away, though they had forgotten completely to fill their water jars. Saul was very confused by what they had said. They first said that Samuel could be found up at the high place of sacrifice but had then gone on to say that he was at the moment near the gate of the city, the place from which Saul and Joseph had just come. And, anyway, why would they bother to tell Saul, a complete stranger, anything about the protocol of the sacrificial event? What did he care about who was invited to the sacrifices of Ramah? What interest did he have in the order of the events, who participated and who did not? He only wanted his donkeys, and the powerful magician might hold the key.

Saul and Joseph headed toward the sacrificial place, guessing that the great man might be there, walking deeper into the town, moving ever higher up the hill. Just then, they saw Samuel move directly toward them. Though neither Saul nor Joseph had ever seen the famous prophet, they knew him immediately. He seemed impossibly old, his face marked by deep crevasses, his beard nearly white, though somewhat yellowed now, his notorious eyes still sharp, albeit growing milky and clouded. Though he was on his way to the high place, as the girls had said, when he saw Saul and Joseph he came straight toward them. And he had a noticeable frown on his deeply weathered face, for unknown to Saul, Samuel knew all too well who he was. The prophet would gladly have searched for the stupid beasts, even if it took a whole moon, rather than do what he now felt forced to do.

3

How the great Samuel had been chosen prophet by YHWH became legendary, though his beginnings were far more ordinary. Indeed, the thought that Samuel of all boys would one day be Israel's great prophet and priest and judge, and would both make and depose the first of Israel's kings, and would crown the second, would have brought gales of laughter from those who witnessed his start in the pathetic village of Ramathaim-Zophim in the remote hills of Ephraim. He had been born to a long-barren woman named Hannah, the second wife of a minor landowner named Elkanah. Elkanah's first wife, Peninnah, was marvelously fertile, always an important attribute in a woman, and gave her husband son after daughter after son, almost yearly. But poor Hannah could have no children. As a barren wife, her status dipped lower and lower until the community looked with more fondness on some of their productive livestock than on the increasingly sad and frustrated Hannah. Elkanah, too, was increasingly frustrated. YHWH knows he had tried to give Hannah a child, but it had simply not happened, and he was ready to give her up as an empty vessel, a dry tree, a woman without a future with him or anyone else.

Hannah could barely leave her house to perform the daily chores. Cooking on the outdoor fire was unbearable as the women would snigger behind their hands, and gesture to their bellies, miming flat and round. Washing at the stream was worse, since when she waded in to retrieve the clothes, the water accentuated her thin body, devoid of a child, and muffled laughs would rise behind bushes. Her life was made even more miserable by Peninnah, her fabulously fertile co-wife. With a haughtiness born of success at the birthing stones, Peninnah would ask Hannah to watch her expanding brood while she and Elkanah would slip quietly into the tent for what Hannah knew was a sweaty act that would result in still one more child for the woman. More than once Hannah thought of running away or wading far enough into the river to cover her flat body forever.

One year, Hannah had had enough. Enough of nasty Peninnah's children, enough of nasty Peninnah herself, enough of the pitiful attempts of Elkanah to coddle her, and mollify her, and cheer her up. She had had enough of the whole sort of life she was being forced to live. She decided on her own to go talk to her God at the sacred shrine of Shiloh. Shiloh was a holy place, the holiest spot in the area. The great Joshua, after he brought Israel into the land, had chosen the site of Shechem, near Shiloh, as the spot from which the rest of the land was to be viewed and finally won for YHWH. It was even rumored that those who lived in the land had worshipped their gods of field and stone here long before Israel had come. "Choose this day whom you will serve," the great Joshua had demanded at Shechem, and the first generation of Israelites had readily enough responded, "We will serve YHWH!" Well, Hannah mused, they and we had not always done so, despite the General's call. But so it is with those who claim allegiance to anything; constancy is at a premium. But Hannah was determined to have a child, so to Shiloh she went.

There was a uniqueness to the place, a kind of hushed and hopeful mystery that made a desperate woman want to find communion with that deity who ruled here and everywhere. She walked early one morning in the direction of the central shrine, a low stone building of one room, lighted dimly by an oil lamp set in one wall. The priest of the place, Eli by name, was sitting in his seat near the entrance, but he barely noticed her as she rustled quietly by him into the innermost part of the dark sanctuary. Small puffs of incense added to the gloom and somewhere in the shadowy distance a holy voice was chanting words in some ancient dialect she could not understand. She stood in the center of the room, quite alone, unable at first to discover the words she needed to say. She desperately needed a child. She desperately wanted to shut the mouths of all those who had made her life an unspeakable horror. Tears coursed down her sunken cheeks. Finally she knew what she had to say to this hidden God.

"O YHWH of the armies! If you will closely look at the misery of your servant, and not forget me, but remember your servant, and give to your servant male seed, then I vow that I will give him to you all the days of his life; no razor will ever touch his head!"

She knew what she meant by this vow to the God of Shiloh. She had just promised to give her desired son to the shrine forever as a priest, to have him only for a few short years, and then to relinquish him to YHWH's life-long service. He would never get a haircut, because the vow of a Nazirite, one fully given over to God, insisted that his hair was God's alone and should thus be forever uncut. Nor would he ever drink wine and live and work around grapes or their vines. Nor would he ever touch or stand close to a dead body. The vow was strict and demanded courage and commitment and complete determination. It could be for a short time or for a whole life. Hannah was desperate; she vowed the service of her son-to-be for his entire life.

Everyone knew the old story of the most famous of Nazirites, Samson, the bull-headed hero of old, who had killed many more people when he died than when he was alive. He may have been a hero in the story, but Hannah had always found the over-sexed man nothing more than a brute. And besides, he had been a miserable example of a Nazirite. He had drunk barrels of wine at numerous parties, had touched and created more dead bodies than anyone before or since, and had received an infamous haircut from that brazen woman, Delilah. And though the hair had grown back, lead-ing to that dramatic destruction of the Philistine temple of Dagon when Samson had pulled it down with his massive strength, Hannah had been horrified by the fantastic loss of life far more than she had been thrilled by the great hero's actions. She had no intention of allowing her son to become such a wretched example of service. No. Her son would be a Nazirite beyond compare! But, of course, first she had to become pregnant. But somehow she felt, after the energy of her vow in the darkened sanctuary of Shiloh, that this time she would lose her flat belly at last.

As she was concluding her prayer, and meditating on what she had vowed, the rough voice of the priest broke the silence of the moment.

"How long will you make such a drunken mess of yourself! Throw away your wine, you filthy woman!"

Hannah realized in an instant that she had prayed her prayers silently but had moved her lips all the while. The foolish priest had concluded that she was drunk! Did he not expect faithful and desperate people to come to his sanctuary for prayer and to commune with God? Would he not be open to the supplicant, offering words of support rather than shouts of condemnation based in ignorance and stupidity? Still, he was the priest no matter how poorly he understood the role. And it would probably be this wretched priest to whom she would have to entrust her future son. So she tried patiently to explain.

"No, my lord. You are mistaken. I am a woman in great pain; I have been pouring out my life to the God who resides in Shiloh. I have drunk no wine this day nor any strong spirits. Do not treat me like some sort of foul creature, because I have been speaking to God out of extreme anxiety and frustration all this time. Can you not see my pain? You have been far too hasty in your conclusions about what you have witnessed."

But the priest did not apologize, nor did he feel chastened at all. He merely mumbled a rote blessing to Hannah, as she turned to leave.

"Go in peace, and may YHWH grant whatever it was you asked YHWH." He did not even ask Hannah what it was she wanted so desperately! She had thought a priest of all people would at least have asked that. Still, she responded appropriately and traditionally enough.

"May your servant find favor with you," and bowed courteously.

But when she left the temple, she smiled sardonically, wondering to herself how such a fool could ever have thought he could serve the great YHWH at all. But no need to waste time with that. She had to find Elkanah now, because she just knew that a son of her own was going to be born in about nine moons!

And so it had happened. Hannah and Elkanah had made such love as they had never made before, and she had gotten pregnant, much to her vast delight and relief, and much to the surprise and chagrin of her many detractors. He was a beautiful child, healthy and strong, and Hannah herself named him, although the custom was that the father had that right. But Hannah would have none of it. When the naming day came, she stood proudly, even defiantly, in the circle of her neighbors, among those who had laughed at her and scorned her, and joked about her, raised her son up to the sky, and shouted for all to hear.

"This boy shall be called Samuel, because I asked YHWH for him!"

Then she fiercely held Samuel to her breast, while he screamed his welcome to the world.

But the community looked at one another in surprise and confusion. The naming had been decidedly odd. The name "Samuel" means "God listens," and they expected Hannah to explain the name by announcing that YHWH had heard her cry for the child. But that had not been her explanation for the boy's name. She had said that the reason for the name was that she had "asked" YHWH for him. But "asked" is from another verb altogether, as they all knew. The boy should have been named something more like Saul, since that is a possible name from that verb. Had Hannah made a mistake? Was she being deliberately mysterious or confusing? Was she somehow making fun of those in the community who had made fun of her? Whatever Hannah had meant by her peculiar naming rite, no one ever forgot what had happened that day, especially after the appearance of king Saul so many years later. Had Hannah known about Saul? But how? She was long dead by the time he was born. Was Hannah somehow privy to the workings of the wonderful YHWH? Everyone looked at her very differently after the birth of Samuel, and Hannah herself was a completely different woman. She held her head high when she appeared at the well; she proudly made her way to the place of washing, carrying her son on her hip with shoulders squared and back straight, though she was surely not the youngest woman in the village.

When the time for the yearly pilgrimage to Shiloh came around, Hannah told Elkanah that she would not go with him this year! She actually defied her husband in this!

"When I wean him, he will go with us to Shiloh, but not before," she said with a withering glance in the direction of Peninnah and her many children.

And she strode right back into the tent, not bothering to see them off.

Elkanah, much impressed with his formerly despondent wife, said to her retreating back, "Do what seems best to you; wait until you have weaned him. May YHWH establish his word!"

But those who heard him say that were not clear whose word he meant, YHWH's or Samuel's. Given what the boy became, it could have been either.

Of course, Hannah knew that when she took Samuel to Shiloh, she would have to leave him there to fulfill her vow to YHWH. She was in no hurry to do that, so delayed the weaning as long as she comfortably could. But in the boy's fourth year, it was time for them to go. There was no doubt that she was going to do what she had promised, but her preparations for the trip were slow and as deliberate as she could make them. The lively Samuel played nearby with his favorite toy, a carved wooden bear, while his mother packed some simple food into her bag of skin, finally scooping Samuel into her arms. He was not old enough to know that this would perhaps be the last time he would see this village and its familiar smells and sights, but Hannah vowed silently that she would see her son as often as possible. She had already devised a plan to do so.

In addition to the lunch of bread and dates, Hannah selected the finest of the family's best bulls—a huge and expensive offering—along with an entire bushel of flour and a full skin of wine and began the trip to Shiloh. Little had changed since her last time there, that time when she had been favored by YHWH. The temple had not changed at all; it was still unimposing on its tiny rise and still dark and smoke smelling within its one room. But this was to be the place of her son's new life, so she went to it immediately. Outside, at the spot of sacrificial slaughter, she killed the bull, prepared it for proper sacrifice, and mixed wine and flour into a paste. Then holding tight to her son's hand, she moved toward the dark room of the tiny temple and placed the sacrificial food on the crude altar, while she uttered the old words of thanksgiving to the God from whom she had asked the child, that same God who had heard her plea.

"Praise to you, O YHWH, ruler of the universe, who gives us fruit of the vine, grain from the fields, and children from our womb!'

The last phrase of the prayer she said with special energy and gladness. All the while, the young Samuel stood wide-eyed in the dim room, surrounded by the smells of meat and smoke and wine, mesmerized by the ancient words pouring forth from his beloved mother.

When the prayer ended, Hannah turned from the altar and led her son to the old priest, Eli, who was sitting in his usual place by the front entrance to the sanctuary. She wondered silently to herself whether the fat old man had moved from the spot in the many moons since first she saw him! His blind eyes were fixed on some horizon only he saw, his priestly robes filthy with spilled wine and blotched with grease stains of meat. He seemed no more alert to her now than he was all that time ago, but he was the priest and she had made the vow. She gave the speech she had practiced again and again but was still reluctant to say. She spoke loudly in case the old man's ears worked no better than his eyes.

"Oh, my lord! As you live, my lord, I am the woman who was standing with you here many suns ago, praying to YHWH. You said I was drunk, but I was not. For this child with me I prayed that day. YHWH clearly has given to me what I asked." The priest was startled from his reverie by the shouted words, his face turning toward the unwelcome sound.

But now came the hard words, nearly choking her as they came out.

"Now I offer him to YHWH all of his days; he is now offered to YHWH forever."

Eli was silent, pointing his withered hands toward the sound of Hannah while she and her son prostrated themselves before him, falling down in religious devotion before YHWH's priest. The truth was that the old man did not remember the woman, or her vow, or the fact that he had accused her of being drunk those moons ago. There were so many worshippers, so many desperate people. Eli had been priest for countless years, and his eyes were no longer clear, his mind no clearer. He rummaged around in his heart for some recollection, some clue that could remind him of what this obviously fervent woman was talking about, but he was blank. He decided to say nothing so as not to reveal his confusion.

Hannah expected something from Eli, some sign, some blessing or other. She did not expect that the aging priest would be overjoyed to be given charge of a young boy. And she had heard that Eli's own grown sons were scoundrels, bribe-takers, defilers of sacrifices in the sanctuary itself, even having illicit sex with some of the women who served the temple. She would not be surprised if Eli might be reluctant to assume the responsibility of another boy when his own were such a disgrace to him. But she had made her vow, and she would keep it. Eli would simply have to mentor her son.

She waited in vain for him to say something, anything, but he was mute. But Hannah had things to say; her heart was full both of joy for the gift of her son and sadness that she was about to leave him with this doddering priest. But her prayer welled up and burst into the dank air of the sanctuary, saying much more than even she expected.

> My heart exults in YHWH!
> My power rises up in YHWH!
> My mouth opens wide against my enemies,
>> as I rejoice in your victory.
> There is no Holy One like YHWH,
>> no one besides you,
>> no rock like our God!
> Warriors' bows break,
>> while feeble ones grow strong.
> Those who were comfortable have sold themselves for bread,
>> while hungry ones grow fat with spoil.
> Barren ones have borne seven,
>> while the one with many children fades.
> YHWH kills and brings to life,
>> sends to Sheol and raises up from there.
> God protects the feet of the faithful,
>> while the wicked shall be cut off in darkness;
>> surely not by strength alone is anyone strong.

The silent priest listened to her prayer in shock. This woman had taken her experience of the birth of her child and had turned it into a claim that YHWH was about to turn the world upside down! The strong are weak; the weak are strong. The warriors' bows become useless while the unarmed gain strength. The rich grow poor and the poor grow fat. What gives a simple, arrogant female the right to utter such nonsense in the house of YHWH? And why does she wish to saddle me with her brat? She has filled his ears with this twaddle since he was born, I wager, and how am I to train him in the ways of the priests if his mind is so muddled with these revolutionary thoughts?

Eli had half a mind to tell the creature to shove off and to take her sniveling child with her. But she had vowed to leave him, or so she said, so he was trapped. If he refused to raise the boy, he was, at least possibly, denying YHWH's word, a word that was always mysterious in any case. But if he accepted the child—well, what mischief might he bring? Eli was simply too tired and confused to say no, so when the family left, Elkanah, Peninnah and her many children, and Hannah, Samuel was left behind. Eli felt with his aging hands for the little boy and wondered whether he had made a mistake. Too late! He would have to deal with him now. He grabbed his tiny hand and half led and half followed him to the small priestly quarters at the back of the dark sanctuary. Samuel whimpered a bit, fearful of the terrifying and fat and blind old man, but he did not cry aloud. He sensed, even at his very young age, that crying would do him no good with Eli.

He got to his tiny room and reached for his wooden bear, stroking it with pleasure, feeling its solidity, its certainty, its reality. He lay down on the platform that formed nearly all of the room, and as Eli stumbled his way out of the place, Samuel did not move but lay quietly, impassively, rubbing the bear, gazing at the four clay walls, adjusting his eyes to the dim light. After a time, he slept and dreamt of Ramah and his mother. He felt very small, very alone, completely abandoned, and fear along with a knot of anger welled into his chest. One would expect fear from an abandoned child, but anger was unusual in one so young. Fear was understandable, but the origin of that anger was not at all clear.

4

The look on the old priest's face those long years ago swam into Samuel's mind once again, and he smiled a bitter smile as he moved toward the newcomer to Ramah. Eli was certainly not prepared to mentor anyone, the old fool! But, thought Samuel, I suppose he had done his best, given Hannah's absolute certainty that YHWH wanted the boy to be a priest and a Nazirite. With all these thoughts in his mind, swirling around inside his head, he had awakened that morning fearing that YHWH would present to him the prince he was to anoint. He feared that he, like Eli before him, was about to be forced to mentor his own replacement! He had hoped to get to the sacrifice, perform the rite, eat the sacred meal, and return home in silence. But now he saw the man he did not want to see. He was enormous! He was inordinately good-looking, and he was young, his face unlined and open. Samuel was afraid that he was looking at the first king of Israel. There was no way that he could avoid the duty that YHWH had thrust on him, and he knew that with the thing he must now do, his own family of Israelite leaders would end with his death. When Samuel anointed this extraordinary boy, his sons' futures were over, and his own memory as a faithful leader of the people was in the most serious jeopardy.

As Samuel deviated from his path toward the high place to meet the boy, YHWH's voice insinuated itself into his ears once again.

"This is the man of whom I spoke to you yesterday; it is he who will rule over my people."

Samuel now knew there was no escape. His replacement stood before him; his ruin was walking toward him; the man who had the power to displace him in the hearts of the people he had loved and cherished and protected for fifty seasons of years loomed up like a mountain in his very own city. With all that was within him the mighty prophet of YHWH wanted to shout out for all to hear that he would have no part in anointing a ruler or prince or king over Israel, since only YHWH was king and only Samuel was YHWH's prophet. But with YHWH's unequivocal words ringing in the air, he saw no way out; he was going to have to anoint this man prince over Israel. But, he thought, I do not have to like it! Nor do I have to be quietly comfortable with the deed or the man. "Ruler?" "Prince?" "King?" We will see, thought Samuel. We will see what sort of ruler this huge boy may be. We will see.

His reverie was broken by Saul's first words to him.

King Saul

"Please tell me exactly where is the house of the seer?"

Was this huge boy so thick as not to know whom he was addressing? Who in Israel did not know Samuel? Had he been born in a cave? Just what sort of fool had YHWH chosen to be prince over Israel? Could it be that YHWH had chosen just such a one to satisfy, on the surface at least, the demands of the people, but at the same time to demonstrate that rulers, kings, were finally no good, that they were incompetent, that they were dangerous? Samuel's eyes brightened, his mood lightened. YHWH was ever mysterious! Could it be that the great God had chosen just such a fool as this to demonstrate to the people that only YHWH could be king, after all? He thought of all of those years of leading Israel, all of those years of doing the work of YHWH. Who better than he knew the mind of the God? Who better than Samuel, the one who had been uniquely called for leadership of the people, whose words had been God's word for moons beyond counting? It had begun with that amazing call from his God. He stood mute in the square of Ramah, gazing at the uncomprehending man, and his aging mind wondered back again to a distant time when he was very young, back to that tiny room in Shiloh's temple.

He had whimpered quietly as he had watched his mother turn her back on him for the first time in his life and to leave him with the smelly old priest whom he had not liked the first time he saw him in the dimness of the temple. His smoky clothes, his straggled hair, dully yellowed by sacrificial fires and cheap lamps, hung in uneven strands down his face and into his eyes. And those eyes! They had once been a green of some sort, but now the cruel march of milky white clouds was invading both so that complete blindness was not far off. The young boy shuddered in terror to look into those eyes that seemed more dead than alive, ghostly, beastly, inhuman. The first few days of his time with Eli, Samuel could not get the look of those eyes out of his thoughts; they followed him as he explored the puny world he had been assigned—the barren, rocky ground around the temple, the temple itself, forever dark and dank and usually silent save the hum of prayers and the crackle of the sacrificial fires. Outside in the animal pits, there were the near constant screams of frightened creatures having their unwilling throats slit for offering to YHWH—birds for the poor and destitute, sheep for the less poor and especially desperate, and for the rich and the nearly hopeless even a cow, though cattle were rare and hard to keep alive in the lean years of bad pasturage.

All these beasts shed their blood for the God, day after day and week after week, until the ground was red with it, and the pits for slaughter were full of rotting corpses with flesh-picked bones sticking out of the ashes. One of Samuel's earliest tasks in the temple compound was to shoo away the multitudes of carrion birds that gathered thick as flies around that pit, all too ready to gorge on carcasses either before sacrifice or after. The birds were not picky. Their bloody beaks were not attuned to the technicalities of divine sacrifice; they swooped and cried and dove on the pit despite the five-year-old boy's valiant attempts to scare them off into the sky. Some always managed to get through Samuel's cries and screams, accompanied by wild wavings of a stick, said by Eli to have been the very rod of Moses that he used to part the waters of the Sea of Reeds. What would the great lawgiver have thought to see his wondrous rod reduced to a defense against birds, not to mention to witness its wooden sides marked increasingly with bird leavings and sacrificial ashes?

As Samuel grew older, his work in the temple changed as his understanding of the workings of YHWH matured under the teaching of the priests assigned to the task. He learned primarily the stories of Israel's past; how the world was created by the mighty YHWH; how humanity was made and given a garden, but how they had disobeyed the command against eating the fruit of a certain tree and had been expelled from the garden; how the first murder in history was committed by a brother against his own brother; how the flood had come to wash the evil away, but how that evil persisted even after the waters had dried up; how Abram became Abraham and Sarai, his wife, became Sarah; how they had given birth to a boy called "laughter" (Isaac) when they were far too old; how Laughter had had twin sons, one foolish and the other clever; how the clever one (Jacob) had had many children, one of whom (Joseph) had through marvelous adventures become a powerful man in Egypt and had led Israel there; how they had been enslaved by cruel pharaohs for a very long time; how the great Moses had led them forth from there with the power of YHWH, had given to them the law by which they would live, had led them to the very edge of the land of promise; how he had died before entering the land, after handing the leadership of the people to Joshua; how they had now lived in that land for many years, close to the former owners of the land in uneasy alliances and tentative neighborliness; how the sea-faring Philistines had appeared from the west to populate the coastlands and to threaten again and again those living in the central mountains of the promised land.

The priests were an insulated group of men, little familiar with the world outside of the temple and its restricted compound, but they knew of the Philistines, of their iron chariots and swords, of their designs on the fertile pasturelands of the central highlands. The priests taught that vigilance was always needed to guard against Philistine raids and Philistine deceptions and especially Philistine religious beliefs in the god, Dagon, a god of grain who was of course no god at all in the eyes of the priests. Samuel heard daily that the only God was YHWH, the mountain monarch who had chosen and saved Israel time and again, and who would deal with these blasphemous heathen in YHWH's good time. By the time of his adulthood, when he had seen fourteen summers, Samuel had no doubt that YHWH was the only God in the universe, and that other gods were useless, mute, powerless, and finally did not exist at all.

These beliefs were underscored by the yearly visits of his mother, Hannah, who made sure that his robes always fit and were well cleaned. She had seen the filthy rags worn by Eli and his priests and did not wish for her son to emulate such disgusting models. Also, the priestly garment, the ephod, was tiny, barely covering their manhood. Cold winters in Shiloh made those strips of cloth around the waist absurd, however holy they were purported to be. So each year she herself would sew him a new garment, each year taking careful measurements to be certain of the right fit. When she came to deliver the new robe, she and Samuel would talk late into the night about YHWH and divine things. She would remind him over and over that his very existence was due to her fervent prayers and to YHWH's joyful answer. There was little doubt in Hannah's mind that her son was destined for greatness. The manner of his conception and birth, the prayer that she had spoken in the temple the day she left him there, the ways in which he had grown in knowledge and diligence during his years at Shiloh, convinced her that Samuel would soon enough burst the tiny bonds of the poor village and would be known throughout the land. Each year she would assure him of his destiny and each year both of them would pray to YHWH to bring it about.

Hannah had come with the spring, but Samuel began to see that her hair was no longer dark, her gait no longer easy, her back no longer straight. She always asked him first, "Are you eating well enough, my son?" He imagined mothers had asked such a question of their departed children since children first were born to them. And he, as others before him, always replied with a small chuckle, "Well enough, mother, well enough," though she looked askance at his too small frame, his spindly arms, his greasy hair, uncut to fulfill the vow, the hair of a priest too long near the sacrificial pyre. Finally, in the final year of her coming, he saw she could barely walk, her eyes dim, her face deeply lined. And her first question that last time had been, "Will you bury my withered self when the time comes, my son, in the hallowed way?" His throat had closed however briefly, but he knew that priests were not expected to weep in the face of death, no matter how unwelcome it was. Besides the vow of the Nazirite, made by Hannah herself, forbade Samuel from touching her dead body himself. But he said, "I will be certain that your body is well treated, mother. Do not be afraid." He added this last, since he had learned from the older priests that such words were to be said to the dying, and Samuel knew that his mother was dying. And not long after her final visit to Shiloh she did. And Samuel made certain that she was well and rightly buried near her home, but not too near her long-time rival Peninnah. He was sure she would be glad of that.

He did wonder about where his mother was now that she no longer saw the light of the rising sun. The usual answer, of course, was Sheol, that shadowy place far below the surface of the soil, somewhere deep in the earth, far away from any living thing. The priests regularly warned the people about Sheol, picturing it as a great maw, ever ready to swallow down the unsuspecting fool who failed to follow the ways of the great YHWH. Yet, every dead one went to Sheol, they said, whether wise or foolish, whether fat or thin or short or tall, whether known for goodness, like his mother, or known for wickedness, like numerous greedy and grasping people living around Shiloh. There was no shortage of greedy fools, so far as Samuel could tell. Did they too go to Sheol? Were they also there with his lovely mother? What did they do there? The priests said they did nothing, that they were shadows, wraiths, ghosts, floating and moving in the place of darkness, darker than the caves of Ein Gedi, more silent than the Salt Sea. Yes, all went to Sheol; the goal was to delay the trip for as long as possible, and Samuel felt no desire to join his mother there. He planned to live a long time, because he knew that YHWH had plans for him that were still to be revealed.

Yet, Samuel, who had imbibed the religious language of Eli and his priests for all this time, and had listened carefully to the words of his mother, had not yet had any personal experience of YHWH to prove to him finally that the God was in fact his God. His need for such an experience was great, because the terrible sons of Eli, Hophni and Phineas, had proven as bad as they had been rumored to be. It had long been known that they were not fit to be priests of any kind, let alone high priests in the land, so when Eli reported to Samuel that a messenger from YHWH had come to him to warn him about the appalling actions of his sons, their bribe-taking and sexual immorality, and how he, Eli, had not done enough to restrain them from their foul behaviors, Samuel began to realize when Eli died, he would need to take the role that Eli's sons were not equipped to take. But he wanted a sign. The stories of Israel were important and exciting and regularly filled his mind, but he needed an experience of his own. He needed his own story with YHWH.

But with the aging and increasingly incompetent Eli, experiences of YHWH were very rare, if they existed at all. His two nauseating sons and his own now complete blindness had led the priest to despair and profound depression. He sat day after day on his seat by the doorpost of the temple, sometimes failing to move for hours at a time, forgetting to eat, lost in a trance of prayer or confusion; it was hard to tell which. Each evening Samuel would lead the pathetic man to his room behind the temple and help him get into his filthy bed. However often Samuel cleaned the room and the bed, both remained unspeakably rank, with small white insects scurrying in and under the bedclothes and the acrid smells of rotting flesh permeating the fetid air. Eli saw and felt and smelled none of it; he just collapsed into the bed and stared unseeing into a place only he seemed to know.

After getting him settled one night, which was just like so many other nights, Samuel went out to tend the temple light that by custom was never to be allowed to go out. The people were convinced that the light somehow represented the presence of God, and if it ever were extinguished God would disappear with it. So Samuel's job, one of many, was to be certain that the light was always seen. As he approached the lamp, a small poorly made clay vessel, with an uneven point on one end and a loop at the other, by which it was hung on the wall with a peg, he noticed that the light was sputtering more than usual, threatening to go out. He hurried to the vat of olive oil that rested under the lamp and quickly dipped out a ladle of the oil and poured it carefully into the bowl of the lamp. The flame sputtered a bit more and then caught strongly; the light briefly illuminated one of the corners of the dark temple. But after that surge of light, the flame settled back down to its usual dimness, being less the source of light than a source of comfort for the few worshippers who were wandering through the place.

Samuel shooed out the few desperate souls still in the place of God and locked the large wooden door, placing the bar into the slots on either side of the doorframe. At last, he thought, I can finally go to my own bed. Though the room was smaller than Eli's, at least it was clean and neat, devoid of the nasty bugs and upwind of the rotten animal smells. The room opened right out into the larger temple room. From his bed, Samuel could look directly into that room at the mysterious box of YHWH, the holy Ark of the Covenant. Samuel thought how strange it was that such a fabled object had ended up in this dank and rather pathetic room in a miniscule village in the highlands of Ephraim. Given what was believed about this wooden chest, Samuel thought that it deserved a more splendid context, a brighter, larger temple, with gold curtains, or-nate lampstands, huge images of power and splendor all around. It was nothing less than embarrassing to see the holy thing sitting on the dirt floor, shoved without any real ceremony against the back wall of this miserable room, nearly forgotten, usually avoided by worshippers intent on bloody sacrifice at the altar.

The Ark of the Covenant had a colorful, supernatural history. When the people of Israel had escaped from Egypt, led by the hero Moses, they had moved toward the sacred mountain of Sinai where God was said especially to live. At the mountain God had given to Moses the Ten Commandments, incised on two tablets of stone by God's own fingers. While that gift was being given, at the base of the mountain, Aaron, Mo-ses' priestly brother, was creating with his own fingers a splendid golden calf as a way to calm the terrified Israelites who had become certain that Moses had abandoned them to the horrors of wilderness. Moses carried the precious tablets down the moun-tain to offer them to his people, but instead of seeing people anxious to receive the law of God, he witnessed scenes of complete wanton debauchery, as they worshipped their little bull with unspeakable acts. Aaron was nowhere to be seen. When Moses finally found Aaron, and had demanded he explain the monstrous things his eyes beheld, Aaron calmly lied that he had not made the calf at all, but had merely tossed the gold brought to him by the people into the fire, and the calf had magically popped out! Moses was so enraged that he shattered the two clay tablets of God into a thousand shards. He then had rushed back up the mountain to ask forgiveness of YHWH for the people's evil and had even offered his own life in their place if God demanded such a sacrifice. God did forgive them, and even made for Moses another set of the ten laws for him to take with them as they moved toward the land God had promised.

It was then that the Ark was made, as a receptacle for the tablets of God. It was made to the exact specifications of YHWH, big enough to contain the two divine tablets of the law, but not so big as to be unwieldy to carry the long distances through the wilderness. It was wooden, nothing special to look at, oblong in shape with leather loops at the four corners on the top through which long wooden poles could be passed so that it could be carried by two men on their shoulders. Carved on the top, too, was the monstrous figure of an ancient Cherubim, a winged creature with cruel claws and sharp beak that warned away those who would abuse the Ark or even touch it. The carving was surprisingly crude, but again, thought Samuel, if it were too ornate it might rival the God who was thought to be enthroned upon the Ark, seated somehow on that Cherubim itself. The Ark possessed a wondrous power, nothing to be trifled with, bearing as it did the tablets of the Almighty YHWH. Samuel had learned as one of his first lessons the Song of the Ark. When the Ark was made to appear, this was said:

> "Arise, O YHWH; let your enemies be scattered!
>   May those who hate you flee from your presence!"

And when it was returned to the temple, the people would say:

> "Rest, O YHWH; may the thousands of Israel increase!"

Samuel had memorized these ceremonial words that were uttered whenever the Ark was moved in and out of the temple. But those exciting days were few now; he could not remember the last festival day for the movement of the Ark of the Covenant. So it sat, silent, neglected, gathering dust, the memory of its vaunted power fading with its cracking varnish and splitting wood. In every way the boy Samuel could see the glory of Israel was something far less than glorious, the temple of Shiloh was a crumbling hulk, and the future of the land was as uncertain as the flickering lamp on the wall. He closed his eyes with these dark and hopeless thoughts clouding his mind, and tried to recover that first excitement that his early days in this place had given. He was as close to despair as the day his mother had left him here so long ago.

Suddenly, a voice shattered the silence.

"Samuel, Samuel!"

Immediately and automatically, the boy replied,

"Here I am!"

This was the correct way to respond to a summons, and Samuel leapt out of his bed to rush to Eli's room. Perhaps the old man was ill. Perhaps he had had a bad dream, as was common as he aged. There was some irritation in Samuel's reply, however much he tried to keep it polite; he got little enough sleep as it was without the interruptions of a foolish old man.

"I'm here; you called me."

Samuel waited for the instructions to get Eli some water, or to soothe his troubled mind, or to clean up his bed after still another accident; he could hardly control his body anymore. But instead the man said,

"I did not call; go and lie down."

Samuel trudged sleepily back to his bed.

But the voice spoke again.

"Samuel, Samuel!"

This time, without replying, a disgusted Samuel stomped toward Eli's room, ready to berate the slobbering idiot, but before arriving he calmed enough to say again, "I'm here; you called me."

But Eli, turning his head in the direction of Samuel's voice, said with genuine surprise, "I did not call, my son. Go and lie down."

Samuel wanted to add that he thought Eli was so addled as not to know what he was saying, but left the rank room in silence.

But no sooner had he settled into his bed when the same voice came a third time. "Samuel, Samuel!"

And a third time, Samuel got out of his bed and with real anger walked to Eli's room. And through clenched teeth, he glared at the blind priest and said, "I'm here; you called me!"

But this time Eli paused before responding, as if he were thinking, as if his muddled brain was attempting to come to some sort of conclusion about what appeared to be happening.

This time he said, "Go and lie down, and if the voice comes again, say exactly this: 'Speak, YHWH, for your servant is listening.'"

Samuel stared in shocked silence. Could YHWH be calling him? Could this be the experience he had hoped and prayed for? It seemed completely unlikely that YHWH would announce the divine presence in the dead of night to him, a boy, not a man, in the failing temple of Shiloh, calling his own name again and again.

He rushed back to his bed and waited…and waited…and waited. There was no sleeping now, no ruminations on past glories and present disappointments. Samuel's ears strained to hear the voice again. All was silent. The voice must have been Eli's, the priest's confused mind manifesting itself in incoherency. Samuel had about convinced himself that the explanation for the nighttime voice was Eli's uncontrollable shouting after all, when the voice spoke again just as it had before.

"Samuel, Samuel!"

Samuel was terrified, but not really believing that this was in fact the voice of YHWH, he did not quite respond as Eli had told him to.

Instead, he said, "Speak, for your servant is listening," not identifying the ghostly voice as YHWH.

But to his amazement and horror, it soon became clear that it was the voice of YHWH, and that Samuel had been singled out for a terrible task.

"I am about to do something in Israel that will make both ears of anyone daring to hear it tingle. On the day when I act I will do everything I said I would do to the house of Eli. I am about to punish him and his family and all his relations, because he knew all the evil of his disgusting sons, who spend their lives blaspheming me, and did not do enough to restrain them. As a result, there are not enough sacrifices, not enough prayers, not enough vows to assuage my fury against all of them, and that fury will never be quenched but will forever rage and rage and rage!"

And with that final "rage" echoing in the air, or it seemed to be in the air, the voice was stilled. And Samuel was stunned.

YHWH was infuriated beyond calming! God had announced to Samuel that he was coming to punish Eli and all of his house. But how? When? And what was Samuel to do? YHWH had not told him to do anything. YHWH had just vented fury, warning about coming judgment. The boy-man lay on his bed trembling all night. Was he to tell this monstrous news to Eli? Why should he, an apprentice to the priest, be called to announce such things to a pathetic old man? And just why was God so enraged against him? Samuel had heard Eli attempt to censure his two boys, but they were incorrigible, untrainable, unchangeable. Surely, a doddering and enfeebled father could not be fully blamed for the actions of two wayward sons. Surely he could not be held so culpable that his entire future, and the future of his family, were now forfeit? Is YHWH so demanding as all that? Could there not be forgiveness from God for all the faithful priestly service, for all the prayers and all the sacrifices Eli had offered in the little temple at Shiloh? This YHWH was a hard taskmaster, a demanding God who brooked no argument, whose mind when made up was not to be changed. Samuel wrestled all night with his love and respect for Eli, who however weak and confused, had mentored him as well as his limited gifts could do, and he wrestled with the harsh pronouncement of YHWH who was determined to obliterate the house of Eli for all time.

But how was YHWH to act? The anger was clear but the means of that anger were not. Was this the way that YHWH charged chosen servants with divine work? Was it up to the servants to choose just how the divine work was to be carried out? Samuel struggled all night with what he should do. This YHWH was stern and demanding, but not as clear as the boy had hoped or needed.

As the sun rose, Samuel got up off his bed, removed the bar off the door, and flung the door to the temple wide. The bright sun streamed into the dim room, and the lamp flared with the morning breeze. But still he hesitated. He feared to tell the news to Eli; such news could easily kill him. He thought he might reveal only part of it, just the part about God's anger, that God wanted him to reprimand his two sons to bring them back into line with God's will and way. Perhaps that would suffice. He went about his morning chores—the lamp, fresh water for the animals and for him and Eli and the priests, rekindling the fire for the daily sacrifices. He went out of his way to avoid Eli as long as he could.

But he could not avoid him forever.

Soon Eli's voice, he knew it was his voice this time, crackled through the air, "Samuel, my son."

And Samuel could do nothing else than respond, "I'm here."

Eli drew him down to sit on the edge of the filthy bed and with surprising strength demanded, "What did God tell you? I know it was God. What exactly did God tell you? Do not hide it from me! May God strike you dead if you hide anything God said to you last night!" The old man spoke with a vehemence born from a divine silence too long endured. If God had spoken to this boy, the priest had to know what was said. Samuel noticed that Eli had not called the God YHWH. Perhaps he was too fearful to utter the divine name for fear that what had been said was too terrible to hear?

And Samuel had to decide. His youthful mind weighed again what he felt he was called to do. The whole truth of God? But what exactly was the whole truth of God? Was it God's truth to destroy the future of an old and faithful man whose life was about over in any case? Or was it God's truth to protect Eli from the full horror of God's fury against him? In an instant, Samuel chose, and the choice was fateful for the rest of his life and for the life of Israel. He saw himself here and now and for as long as he lived as God's avenging messenger, God's hammer, called upon by a harshly demanding deity over and over to correct the ever-sinning people, to correct them without question or pause, to speak the full truth of God as Samuel discerned that truth in every place and in every time. Samuel now knew he was God's agent, God's prophet, and that when his words were spoken they were without doubt and without contradiction the words of YHWH.

And so with that resolve he told Eli all that he had heard the voice say in the night, how Eli's priesthood was over, how his sons were doomed, how his family had no place in the ongoing life of Israel. He spared nothing; he spoke with the harshness of the voice that had spoken to him. He was no longer pupil, no longer student. He was now the master, and the old master was deposed and rejected by the mouth of the new master. Eli reeled under the blows of Samuel's words, uttered without pity. He lay quietly for a time on his bed.

Finally he said with as much dignity as he could muster, "It is surely YHWH who does whatever YHWH wishes to do." He had now named the God as the YHWH he had loved and served all his life.

Eli had never said anything more true. Samuel knew he was right, and also knew that he would stake his prophetic life on that truth; YHWH did whatever YHWH wanted to do. He remembered the poem his mother had sung right after his birth; she had sung it to him often enough when he was a child. "YHWH kills and brings to life, sends to Sheol and brings up from there." This God acts in ways only this God could act, and there was nothing for it but to be YHWH's messenger in the world. And so Samuel had resolved that day to be.

But that was then, and this was now, and Saul, the powerful one YHWH had demanded for ruler, stood before him. Why was it that YHWH had chosen this one when Samuel was still fully capable of leading the people and the land? Surely YHWH would not cast him away from the leadership of Israel after all these years! He was old, but his mind remained clear, his body slower but still useful, his experience unmatched, his devotion undimmed! YHWH had deposed the vastly diminished Eli but Samuel, while somewhat old, retained his vigor, his voice, his ability to interpret what the mighty YHWH wanted for the people. I am no feeble and doddering Eli, he thought, and God would surely not reject me yet from service!

He must think! He must ponder again the thing YHWH had called him to do.

"Stay here, boy. I will return soon."

Samuel left the square and sought a shady spot, out of Saul's sight, where he could think undisturbed. There must be a way to avoid this day! Samuel hoped to find the way, as he again plunged down the well of the past.

5

After Samuel's nighttime visitation by YHWH, he had remained at Shiloh for a time, but YHWH's promised vengeance against Eli soon appeared. The Philistines began their attacks on Israelite outposts in the west, overrunning them with comparative ease. News of their advance soon reached Shiloh, and a call for the Ark of the Covenant to be displayed on the enlarging battlefield went out. A group of soldiers came to get the Ark from the temple, and the people gathered for the ceremony for its coming forth. All sang the Ark's song, waving banners and bits of old clothing, shouting so as to split the earth. But triumph soon turned to horror. Incredibly, the Philistines captured the sacred Ark, after destroying the army that bore it, and took it to their pagan temple of the corn god, Dagon. Both Hophni and Phineas, Eli's wastrel sons, were among the battle's dead. When news of their deaths reached him, Eli was generally unmoved, but when the news of the Ark's capture came, the longtime priest, as usual sitting on his familiar seat near the entrance to the temple, fell over backwards and died. He was an incredible ninety-eight summers old, completely blind, and grossly fat. Samuel rushed to Eli, but it was too late; the priest was gone. His great weight had caused him to shatter his neck so that he had died instantly. And Samuel had remembered God's fury at Eli and his house and knew that YHWH's word had come true through his own mouth. He was more than ever convinced that he had been anointed God's prophet.

Samuel had gotten up from the body of Eli and had gone to his room in the temple to pray for his old mentor. But his prayers had not come easily. The face of Eli floated in and out of his mind, as he lay prone in front of the altar. The din outside the temple was nearly overwhelming. The people of Shiloh were weeping and wailing for the dead Eli, for the loss of the ark, and just as much for themselves as their terror of the advancing Philistines consumed them. Several of them had removed the corpse of the priest and had begun the burial ritual. In the hot climate of the hill country, it was important to bury the dead quickly, since putrefaction was swift and the carrion creatures came rapidly in enormous and hungry numbers.

As he trudged slowly behind Eli's body, carried aloft by six strong and straining men—the ancient priest had truly been enormously fat at the end—Samuel found some time to think of what needed to be done. Eli's entire family was dead. None of the lesser priests of Shiloh was at all worthy to be considered for the role of high priest.

King Saul

There was little doubt in Samuel's mind that he should be the new priest at the shrine. After all, he thought, it was my prophecy from YHWH that had brought calamity on Eli and Hophni and Phineas. It was I whom YHWH had chosen to deliver that hard word, and I delivered it at God's command. It had come true in all particulars! The evil sons were dead; Eli was dead. I am alive, and I am the agent of God. Amidst the wailing and shouting of the Shilonites, a small smile played just briefly over Samuel's lips, though his face was nearly consumed in an outward show of deep grief over the loss of his mentor.

Eli's huge corpse was wrapped in cloth after being smeared with oil. And his old rod, that one he had first told the very young Samuel was the rod of the great Moses, was buried with him. Samuel spoke the customary words of blessing and thanks. But he added the following prayer as many eyes in the crowd, first bowed in piety, soon lifted in surprised wonder.

> "O YHWH! You have spoken your word and had your way through your servant Eli for many years. He was your faithful slave for his whole life. Even at the end, he did what he thought best, however weak he was, however blind, however muddled in mind. So now, YHWH, here I stand, your servant Samuel. It is I you have chosen to speak your eternal word of truth. It is I who delivered the word of your judgment against Eli and his family. It is I who speak this day to you and for you. Make my words always your words. Make my mouth always your mouth. Let no words of mine fall to the ground unfulfilled. I give myself to you alone, O YHWH!"

Samuel's youthful voice had risen in volume as he spoke so that the entire crowd could hear him with ease. His face grew red, the veins stood out in his neck, his thick shock of uncut brown hair was whipped by the wind. When he last invoked the name of YHWH, his long arms were raised in ecstasy. Incredibly, dark clouds rushed into the sky, and the strong wind freshened with what felt like an augury of rain. The people instinctively lowered their heads in awe, as the new prophet of God went on.

> "O YHWH, the pagan enemy has captured your sacred box, your holy Ark. Show forth your power through it, O God. Bring to foolishness and emptiness their designs for its abuse. You alone, O YHWH, have power and strength! You alone, O YHWH, are creator and sustainer of the world! You, O YHWH, turn the plans of our foes to nothing. They are as nothing before you. We are your servants, the people of your pasture whom you chose for yourself, to be the fire of truth in your world, to become the hammer that breaks the rocks into pieces. Shatter your enemies, O God! Raise us up to be your agents of their destruction! We are yours, O God! We are yours! Give us your power. Give us your victory!"

Samuel's eyes were closed, but his mouth was twisted into a screaming hole from which poured prophetic language, urgent words that brewed those who heard into a frenzy of foaming fury. The tears for the dead Eli were gone from every face; the fear of the Philistines had drained away in the flood tide of Samuel's oratory. The cries of the crowd drowned whatever further words the prophet spoke, but no further words were needed. On the day of Eli's death and on the day that the Ark of God was captured in the defeat of battle, a new prophet had been born publicly in Israel. The temple student had disappeared and in his place there now stood an oracle of God.

And Samuel knew it, knew it even as the words poured forth from his cracked lips. God had chosen him for this role. His mother, Hannah, had been right; he had a special destiny from YHWH. As the clamor of the people broke over him like the waves of the sea, he bathed in it, accepted it as his due. He was for now and always the prophet, Samuel, mouthpiece of the terrible God, YHWH of the Armies, and he did in fact speak for God on this earth. He fixed every eye he could see in the crowd with a stare as if to tell them that his face should accompany them wherever they went. He, Samuel, should guide their feet in the ways they should go. He, Samuel, should inhabit their dreams, as they searched for the future of their lives. Samuel was supreme; Samuel was the prophet of God!

He had felt at least a cubit taller as he strode with absolute confidence from the burial place and back toward the temple. Those in front of him parted as quickly as they would in the presence of a king, and those behind surged to follow him wherever he was going. He thought it important to return to the temple for one last time in order to lead a worship of YHWH and then to gather his few things for a journey. Samuel knew he needed to leave Shiloh. It was the past now; its day had gone. He needed a new place of his own, a place identified as the new hope of Israel, a place known as the place of Samuel. What better place than his hometown of Ramah? Both of his parents were dead, as was the fertile Peninnah. Elkanah, Samuel's father, had died as a victim of the Philistine attacks in the west. Samuel had respected his father, but had not loved him. After all, Elkanah had doted on Peninnah at the expense of his own mother; no young boy enjoyed watching his mother slighted by a father who had little time for still another son.

Ramah was centrally located, well fortified, and well protected from the dangerous Philistines. He would return there and would create a center of power to rival any in the land. Israel and YHWH and Samuel were now ascendant!

6

His fame had grown quickly throughout the land. From his new base at Ramah, Samuel began to extend his influence. His startling return to Ramah after all his years in the temple at Shiloh became the stuff of an enlarging legend. Soon he was issuing proclamations from Ramah for the people to join him at various places for worship of YHWH. He held rallies for YHWH at Geba, Beth-aven, and Michmash, tiny villages only a few miles from Ramah. At each successive event the crowds grew. More and more Israelites were eager to hear the new prophet, to bathe in his confident words, to be moved by his puissant declamations. At every place, Samuel's message was the same: YHWH was a God who demanded exclusive loyalty; worship of the gods of those who lived in the area, but who did not share Israel's memory of YHWH's deeds with the first families and Moses and the event at the Sea and the giving of the law at the mountain and the gift of this very land, was rejected completely. No matter how comforting it was for Israelite farmers to erect a sacred pole in their fields, a pole representative of the goddess of fertility, Astarte, in order to ensure a plentiful crop, those poles must be torn down and burned for fuel. No matter how often Israelite villagers found themselves worshipping with their Canaanite neighbors in the many shrines of Baal dotting the countryside, offering up prayers in their neighbor's tongue to the storm god who in their belief brought the rains to the land, they must stop such behavior immediately.

In increasingly large and colorful festivals, Samuel preached that it was YHWH alone who made their fields fertile; it was YHWH alone who was the bringer of the rain. There was no need at all for them to waste their breath on prayers to beings that, if they existed at all, which Samuel deeply questioned, had no power in a world that was owned completely by the mighty YHWH. He spoke often of the commandment that Moses had carried down from Sinai, on those tablets that rested silently in the Ark of YHWH, the one that said, "You must not have any other gods in my presence, nor must you worship them or bow down to them." Even if the words implied that other deities might exist, they had no significance whatever in the presence of YHWH, who was creator of skies and earth.

And every one of Samuel's powerful and demanding sermons ended in the same way: rejection of these so-called gods, and exclusive devotion to YHWH, which would lead inevitably to the defeat of the threatening Philistines. Had they not already seen how the power of God had been made real in the very cities of the Philistines them-selves, how the Ark had made a mockery of Dagon, who in the end was no different than Baal or Astarte, finally no god at all? Had their Dagon image not fallen on its face before the holy Ark, the throne seat of the unconquerable YHWH? Had not the very hands and feet of Dagon been cut off by the power of the Ark? "Put away your worship of these no-gods," Samuel thundered, "and YHWH will be with you to the consternation of your enemies." In all of the cities of the hill country, in the territories of Benjamin and Ephraim, Samuel spoke words like these. At last, after many years of such potent oratory, and after occasions of judicious listening to an increasing group of fervent followers, he felt himself ready to take the word of YHWH to the greatest place in the area, Mizpah.

By this time, Samuel had amassed a large retinue of persons and things that had become the means by which he could proclaim his message to ever larger groups of Israelites. There were the provisions to feed those who came to listen. There was the large tent that was erected to shelter the crowds from the heat and the infrequent rain. There were the musicians, players of lute and harp and tambourine, along with the singers who energized the people in preparation for the words of the great prophet. When Samuel came to a place, all who lived there were eager to see and experience him and his words, as well as the music and dancing that delighted the eye and titil-lated the senses. In the remote and stolid villages of the hill country, Samuel's visits were eagerly anticipated as occasions of excitement. But Mizpah was far from a remote village. It was the real center, at the very heart of an emerging Israel.

Though Mizpah was only a brief journey north and west of Ramah, it was at the same time very important and darkly notorious. In the not too distant past, Israel had had a ruinous civil war centered at Gibeah, very close to Mizpah, a war that had threatened the future of the tribe of Benjamin and thus the common future of the entire land. The story was well known, and its point was remembered by all those who heard it. And the ending was always the same. The cruel Levite always was made to say, "Has anything like this ever happened in the land since we came here from Egypt? Think carefully, talk it over, and get ready to act!"

At this point in the telling of the story, a good teller would pause and allow the listener to ponder about just what the "this" in the command of the Levite consisted of. Of course, it included the horrors of the marauding people of Gibeah and their destruction of the concubine. But was it not also the disgusting offer by the old man of his own daughter to those perverts? And was it not also the abandonment of his concubine by the Levite himself? Was not the whole sordid affair filled with the most appalling abuses of human against human?

In response to the bloody message all the tribes assembled at Mizpah. They brought significant numbers of fighting men to root out the evil from the land of Benjamin. So the civil war began. Hundreds, even thousands, were killed on each side, until Benjamin nearly disappeared as a people. Only 600 or so of the fighting men managed to escape from the last battle and went to hide in the mountain range known as the Rock of Rimmon, cowering there for four moons while the much larger army of the eleven tribes burned Gibeah and the surrounding cities of Benjamin, slaughtered their livestock, and cut down those remaining Benjaminites unable to escape to the mountains. They gathered at Mizpah and vowed that no woman would be given to any Benjaminite under any circumstances, thus insuring the tribe's complete extinction. The surviving and desperate Benjaminites at last captured some women for wives, and the tribe was saved.

As the storyteller ended the story, he would pause and wait for the comments and questions that always came.

"What an appalling story," some woman listener would say. "Rape and abuse and murder and theft and brutal war! What sort of time was it? What sort of people were these ancestors of ours?"

"Well," the storyteller would respond, "there were no real leaders in those days; everyone did what was right for themselves."

The stories of the concubine of Gibeah and of the attempted decimation of Benjamin at Mizpah always bred terror and horror and wonder when they were told. One had only to mention Gibeah and Mizpah to send a shudder down many an Israelite back.

But now a leader was emerging in Israel, and Samuel called all who would to meet him in Mizpah. For Samuel, it was essential that Mizpah be the place of his largest gathering. The horrors of the civil war between Benjamin and the rest of the tribes, and the brutality with which it started and with which it was conducted, were still all too fresh in the minds of the people. Samuel knew that a gathering at Mizpah would conjure up all those blighted memories. But he also knew that the memories of Mizpah would speak a word of truth to all who were there. When he stood in front of them and announced that they were a sinful people, in the most desperate need of God and God's trustworthy prophet, not a single one of them would be able to deny the truth of what he said. All would cry out for God's mercy, and Samuel would be the conduit of that mercy on earth. Mizpah's monstrous deeds would serve as a springboard for Samuel's advancing career as YHWH's prophet. Mizpah would no longer be known as the place of human arrogance and lust and greed and brutality, but henceforth it would be the place of God's extraordinary mercy, and just as importantly, a place of Samuel's prophetic power. His patient waiting and working for all these years were about to bear fruit. So Samuel's people took special care in setting up the great tent, and brought extra food and gifts for those who would come to listen, fine figs and dates, extra jars of the best wine and rich beer, fresh loaves of bread, all ready to be handed to the worshippers. And, of course, there was always the anticipated smell and tastes of the sacrificial meat that capped the worship. But since the day was fine, and not too hot, Samuel decided that the tent was not appropriate this time. Instead, he chose to use the natural cliff-face of the city to serve as the backdrop for his service.

King Saul

As the sun moved just past the mid point of the sky and headed to its place of rest in the west, like a bridegroom moving toward his marriage bed, Samuel strode toward the amphitheater's cliff. The milling crowd soon caught sight of the prophet, known to some by sight and to others only by reputation, and moved to the rocky grotto in expectation of the main event of the day's activities, a speech from the now famous Samuel. Many of the people were not sure what to expect. Those who had heard him speak before, those from his home in Ramah and the nearby villages of Beth-aven and Michmash especially, imagined that it would be something of what they had already heard. He was, they knew and he never tired of saying, YHWH's prophet, so he always recounted the great history of that God's works for the people of Israel, the creation of the world, the parting of the sea, the gift of the law and the land. He would surely speak of that. And he deeply detested the foreign gods, Baal, Astarte, Milcom, Dagon and all of their little godletts, often so beloved of the people of the hills and of the foreigners still living among them. They could safely bet that there would be a verbal annihilation of the lot of them, and a companion demand for exclusive devotion to YHWH who was God without peer or rival. But the prophet was also unpredictable, and would spice his oratory with unexpected stories and harsh words against any who dared disagree with him. For, above all, Samuel believed completely that he was speaking the word of YHWH directly; thus, any contradiction of his words was a rejection of YHWH, worthy only of scorn and abuse. Such a belief made for verbal fire at times, and the people were often anxious for some courageous, but ultimately foolish, listener to challenge Samuel's claims and demands. That made for a lively time, and in the middle of the afternoon, and after a rich period of snacking on bread, dates, and flavorful beer, and anticipating the flavorful meat to follow, a sparring match was just what was needed to enliven a sleepy day.

The sun finally set, and the elders of the city of Mizpah lit the huge torches to illuminate the grotto and to light the path toward the sanctuary for those who wanted to pray before the evening meeting with Samuel.

The prophet made his way toward the stone grotto, led and followed by two blazing torches that outlined his face and hair in fire and gave his person an almost spectral look, unearthly somehow. As he climbed up on the platform, the shadow of his body shown enormously on the face of the cliff, dancing hugely with every one of his movements. He had hoped that his shadow would match the thunder of his voice as it boomed out of his bearded face and out of the dimly lighted darkness. All seemed to have worked perfectly, and Samuel waited for the crowd to hush. He called them all to prayer.

> "YHWH of battles, full of mercy and forgiveness, but always demanding righteousness and truth, we, your people, come this night in fear and in hope. We fear your power, but we hope in that same power. You have acted for our ancestors in the past in Egypt, at the Sea, at the holy mountain, at the city of Jericho. Act for us now, for we are great sinners in your sight, and our enemies

43

are nearby. Our enemies are your enemies, so defeat them, O YHWH, and defend your name in their sight. Speak your truth this night through the mouth of your servant. Let your people know that my words are yours, and that your people can trust in me. For as you love your people so do I love them and give my life for them. Speak, YHWH, speak. Call us all to serve and love you! Bind us together here at this place of shame into a people of unity and power, supported and led by you, our help and our God."

The final word "God" resounded throughout the grotto and into the ears of everyone there, and a great shout of "Amen" rent the night air. Then other shouts were heard.

"You are YHWH's prophet, great Samuel!"

"We will follow you to victory over those hated Philistines!"

"Our lives are in your hands and in the hands of our God, YHWH!"

And many other affirmations were expressed until Samuel held up his hands for quiet. Finally a hush returned. And Samuel spoke again.

"You are not the only ones listening to the sound of my voice, my brothers and sisters! Yes, the Philistines have heard of our meeting and even now they are lurking just outside these shadows, waiting for the time to strike us and to kill us."

Immediately, the people were in an uproar of terror. They began to shout to be saved from the warriors of the iron weapons and flying chariots. They felt helpless against them here at Mizpah, so close to the Philistine lands, a mere one-day walk to one of their largest cities, Ekron. How could they have been so foolish as to expose themselves and their families here at Mizpah? How could they have allowed this upstart prophet to lure them so far west, and to increase their vulnerability to their enemies? The crowd, so supportive of the prophet, began to turn against him and to demand that he protect them. If the Philistines were now so close as to hear Samuel, as they were hearing him, how could they hope to escape? Again, Samuel raised his hands for quiet. He lifted that great voice and spoke into the murmuring crowd.

"Have you no faith in the power of YHWH? Even as I speak YHWH is beginning to deal with these pagans. Just as YHWH tossed the wretched Egyptians and their vaunted chariots into the Sea of Reeds, so YHWH will again attend to the chariots of these Philistines. We have only to wait and watch and see the power of YHWH!"

And with those words, Samuel produced on the platform a snowy lamb, a pure sacrifice to YHWH. At his command two men built a fire on the platform, just to the left of the prophet, who proceeded to raise the lamb high over his head and to slit its throat so that the blood flowed down Samuel's thick beard and onto the flaming altar. With a small squeal the lamb died, and with a mighty shout Samuel dropped the carcass onto the roaring fire. As the smell of the lamb rose up, and as the grease popped and crackled in the fire, Samuel shouted again to YHWH.

"YHWH, we give our best to you, so now do your best for us. We give you this lamb so now return to us the power of a lion so that our enemies may see and all your people may see and all the world may see that you are God alone and that we are your people!"

Suddenly, there was a scream from the crowd! Several Philistine soldiers had appeared on the top of the cliff behind the enormous shadow of Samuel. Then several more appeared at the sides of the grotto, and the crowd began to panic, rushing here and there in a vain attempt to get out of the space that now was about to become their slaughterhouse. Then there was another sound, much larger than the screams of the people, even larger than the voice of Samuel. It sounded to some like thunder, but of course there were no clouds in the night sky. But at the sound, all the Philistines who had appeared on the top of the cliff suddenly fell off to their bloody deaths on the rocks below. And those other warriors who had appeared to have the Israelites surrounded found themselves attacking one another instead and falling on top of one another in ghastly piles of death. The confusion of the Philistines was complete, as they rushed at one another instead of at Israel. At another command of Samuel, unseen by most of the crowd, several hundred Israelite warriors, who were well-armed and obviously well-prepared for battle, ran after the confused remnant of the Philistine force and pursued them for several days, all the way back to their coastal cities. All who were there that day were astonished and so confused by what they thought they saw that many different tales were told in Israel ever after.

But all agreed on one thing; Samuel was without doubt God's special prophet. It was his prayer, his sacrifice, his call to YHWH that had saved the people from a massive slaughter at the hands of the Philistines. To be sure, he had prepared some soldiers before the gathering to engage the enemy, but more happened that day than a battle between Israelite soldiers and Philistine soldiers. No, God was there, too, some-how, and Samuel it was who had called YHWH forth.

7

Suddenly, he was back on the dusty street of Ramah in the shade of a building. He shook his aged head to clear it of that astonishing night at Mizpah before he moved again into the square of the city to face the incredulous boy and his servant, both of whom were still waiting for Samuel to say something to them. As he had aged, the prophet noticed how much harder it had become for him to stop his restless mind from sliding back and forth in time, from the present to the past. He spent much more time in the past now than he had ever done before. But in the past Samuel knew that he would find things very important for his present and future; in the events of his life, he could discern the ways YHWH wanted him to turn. Perhaps he could not fully understand just what YHWH had in mind for him and this boy, but he trusted that if he recaptured the right events in his past, if he reflected upon their meanings in the correct ways, he would know what YHWH wanted from him. He needed more time to think.

"Boy, I cannot speak to you now," he said commandingly to Saul. " Meet me here by the well before the sun brushes the mountain."

And with that, Samuel headed back to the cool of his room, leaving Saul and his companion with mouths open and questions on their faces. He needed time to think and to grasp the moment. He needed again to search what had brought him to this place.

He settled on his rugs, lifted the cool beer his servant had brought, and allowed his memory free rein.

No matter how far his tireless work had taken him, he always had made his way home to his beloved Ramah. He had established an administrative center there for the dispensing of justice in the land. And just before his fortieth summer, he surprisingly took a wife. All thought he was in effect married to Israel, but a rather young maiden, Ziah by name, caught the aging bachelor's eye, and they married in Ramah and set up a household there. Soon two boys were born to the couple, Samuel called the first Joel—"YHWH is God"—a most fitting name for a child of the prophet, everyone immediately said. And very soon Ziah was pregnant again, and her second son was named Abijah—"YHWH is my father"—and the people were overjoyed to see that Samuel had now two heirs to carry on the work he was doing in Israel.

King Saul

As the boys grew, Samuel taught them the ways of YHWH, as he had been led to understand them. Each night there were prayers, the prayers that Hannah, his mother, had taught to him when he was small and had repeated to him each time she had come to Shiloh to bring to him a new tunic. There were prayers of thanksgiving for food and drink and safety and warmth. There were prayers of request when YHWH was needed to protect and guard the people when the enemy drew near, when the harvest failed, when the wasting sicknesses fell on the land, attacking cattle and human alike.

And there were the sacrifices of many kinds, all of which had to be mastered if real leadership was to be practiced and accepted by the people. Samuel had no doubt at all that his two boys would follow him as leaders in Israel. Who else could possibly have the experience, the training, the authority from God that Samuel had? He was unique, alone in power and reputation. Of course his sons would succeed their father; they had only to be reared up in the right way, the way of YHWH, the way that only Samuel knew fully.

Sacrificial practice was intricate and subtle. On the surface, it looked quite simple; kill the unblemished beasts in the accepted way and hoist them on the altar to be offered completely to the God who awaited the pleasant odor. Though the pagan Babylonians had foolishly imagined that their gods (who were of course no gods!) actually lived on the sacrifices of their created people, Israel believed no such idiocy. No, YHWH was pleased with the people's animal gifts and especially enjoyed the rich odors of sheep and goat as they arose into the skies from the faithful altars. Had not YHWH said precisely that when Noah had first sacrificed a clean and pure beast right after the land had dried up from the flood? The very ancient Babylonian story of the flood, a story they told out of their complete ignorance and which the Israelite historians had narrated correctly, claimed that the gods who brought the flood, because they were terrified of their own human creations, had forgotten that without human sacrificial gifts the gods themselves would die of hunger! Samuel loved to tell this ridiculous story to his boys so that they could readily see how nonsensical the pagans were and, in contrast, how glorious were the stories and traditions of Israel.

But YHWH demanded sacrifices rightly done, so Samuel had spent long hours teaching Joel and Abijah the intricacies of the rites: which knives to use in the ritual slaughter and just where the knives were to be applied to the throats of the beasts; how to tell which animals were truly pure and unblemished and just which sort of spots were and were not acceptable in the search for purity; how grain offerings were done, which grain to use and how much; whether animal or grain sacrifice which motions were done and when, right hand up, left hand down, then reverse. There was so much to learn, but Samuel was eager to teach.

Unfortunately, Joel and Abijah were neither one eager pupils. When they were young, under the age of ten, they still stood in considerable awe when their aging father, now past fifty, performed the offerings at the temple in Ramah, employing his still thunderous voice to fill the room with the ancient prayers. Their eyes would grow

King Saul

wide as the squalling beast was killed, then heaved onto the rock altar, on the roaring
fire, to disappear in smoke up to the ceiling and out the hole in the roof, snaking its
way to YHWH, who awaited it with eagerness, as their father had always said.

But when they grew old enough to wonder, to ask questions about the ancient
and hallowed practices, their boldness made the prophet angry.

"Why not kill the bad creatures, Papa," asked the 13-year-old Joel "and save the
best for yourself? Burnt up beasts smell and taste the same whether they are blemished or not. Who will ever know?"

"Just how do you know that YHWH wants burnt flesh anyway," asked Abijah;
"does the God eat it? How? Does YHWH have a mouth? How big is it? Why can't we
have the roasted flesh? I'm hungry!"

Abijah was always hungry, and Joel was always questioning. Samuel would snap
out a response.

"Both of you need to worry less about your stomachs and your ridiculous questions and more about your future work for the people of Israel!"

And he would fume and rage and storm out of the temple, rushing back to his
wife, demanding that she take a firmer hand with the boys.

But she did not. She loved them to distraction, and could see no wrong in them.
Samuel was often gone to the surrounding towns, dispensing justice, offering the sacrifices, since he was seen as the only one who could really lead in the services, since he
was the only one who was God's prophet, God's priest, God's judge. In short, Samuel
was the leader in Israel of all facets of their lives, and thus was on the road as much
or more than he was home. Ziah was as much in awe of her husband as was everyone
else, so she tried her best to ride herd on the growing boys, but without Samuel's presence they defeated her with their increasing arrogance and secrecy and lying.

When Joel turned eighteen and Abijah sixteen, Samuel thought it would be valuable experience for the boys if they were given leadership over the far-away region of
Beer-Sheba in the southern deserts of the land. Though it was distant from Ramah,
some six or seven days' walk, it was hallowed as the final place where Abraham and
Sarah had camped during their first trip to the land promised by YHWH inumerable
winters ago. Though Samuel was intent on having his boys take over the whole land
when he died, the old priest did not know his boys at all. Just like the two boys of his
mentor Eli, his boys were foul and rotten and unworthy of leadership of a pig sty,
let alone the whole people of YHWH. But Samuel could not see, however clearly he
claimed to see the word of YHWH. And Ziah was much too afraid of her husband to
share with him her growing misgivings about their sons. For she had seen them with
young women and heard their bold-faced lies when she asked them about it. When
she had demanded that they say their prayers before meals, they would look at each
other and laugh, tearing into the flesh, gorging on the bread, and loudly slurping their
beer with unclean hands and lips silent to YHWH, who had supplied the feast. And
she knew that they had far more money than she ever gave them, and often wondered

to herself where it had come from. But none of this did she tell Samuel, whose doting old age fatherhood blinded him to the truth. She had heard of the real blindness of the dead priest, Eli of Shiloh, but ruefully thought that her own husband, Eli's pupil and successor, was just as blind as Eli had been.

So, Samuel sent Joel and Abijah to Beer-Sheba, the so-called "well of the seven." It received that name when Abraham of blessed memory offered seven pure lambs to Abimelech, who was then king of that distant place, and swore an oath with him. In fact the name could also mean "well of the oath," but one never knows the meanings of these ancient names exactly. Perhaps it means both. After all, Isaac, Abraham's son of his very old age, later went to the same place and dug some wells there, after the Philistines had stopped up the wells his father had dug. A part of both of these old stories is the lie both Abraham and Isaac told about their wives, Sarah and Rebekah. It seems that both father and son were fearful for their lives in this foreign place, so they told the two Abimelechs that their wives were really their sisters. So quite innocently, the two kings, themselves father and son, took the women into their harems and richly rewarded their "brothers" in the bargain. Fortunately, neither kings had gotten around to exercising their kingly sexual rights with the two before a dream told the first Abimelech the truth, and the second Abimelech saw with his own eyes the intimacy between Isaac and Rebekah that was not the intimacy of a sister and brother. So lies were long connected to the southern Beer Sheba.

But Joel and Abijah brought lying and wantonness and debauchery to new heights very soon after their arrival in the deserts of the south. They quickly established their absolute authority in the whole territory, invoking the holy name of their father as surety for their power. They demanded a percentage of all trade done in the cities, the main one of Beer Sheba, but also Aroer, Arad, and other villages dotting the countryside. All travelers, bound for Egypt and returning from there were steeply taxed as they passed between the Judean hills. And as they watered their donkeys and camels before the long trek through the vast southern deserts, Joel and Abijah were certain to get a huge cut of the services rendered. In less than a year, the boys had grown wealthy and began to have built a larger house than any other one in the area.

But large taxes and service fees were not enough for the two. They established competition for tax collecting and water services and traveler assistance, pushing aside those families who had long controlled these activities. And with competition came bribes in order to secure the rights to perform the services, so Joel and Abijah got money first from those who would win the contracts and money from those who received the services. And after another six moons, they decided to build a larger house still with a central fountain and an upper story to catch the evening desert breeze.

Justice disappeared from Beer Sheba. Or better said, the only justice was justice as determined by Joel and Abijah that was in fact no justice at all. And the people of the territory grew angry and frustrated, and no one, save those who shared in the bribes and kick backs, cared for Joel and Abijah and wished that the great Samuel would do something about his greedy sons. For however far Beer Sheba was from Ramah, news of the evil boys soon got back to the father. The news came at a most inopportune time. Right in the middle of a magnificent whole-burnt offering of an unblemished sheep, honoring the feast day of Abraham, a messenger rushed into the temple to whisper to Samuel, now nearing the fantastic age of sixty winters, that there was trouble in Beer Sheba and that a contingent of the people of that place were on their way for a confrontation. Samuel, rather too quickly, concluded his part of the ritual and handed over the final words to his assistant, and then hurried from the sanctuary.

Stripping off his priestly robes, he demanded further information about what was happening in Beer Sheba.

"My lord," stammered the messenger, choosing his words with great care, "your sons are not as successful in their work as you had hoped. Many in the territory are confused about their leadership, and are hopeful that you will be able to help them by giving them the guidance and direction only the chief priest and prophet in the land can give."

Sweat was forming on his neck under the colorful tunic that southerners often wore. He stood waiting while Samuel pondered his words.

"Why are my sons not successful? What exactly is confusing about their leadership? I have already provided to them all the direction and guidance they need to be good leaders for their people. Just what exactly is the problem?"

The famous thundering voice began to sound as Samuel continued to ask his questions. The messenger regretted the day he had been chosen to speak on behalf of the people of Beer Sheba.

"O Samuel," he began, "I cannot say what is the problem; I myself have never had any problems with your sons, who are, as far as I know, excellent community leaders."

This was less than the truth. The messenger had abundant evidence of Joel's extortionate demands and Abijah's insatiable sexual and material desires. The boys were monsters, but he had no intention of ever using such a word with their father.

"I pray that you ask the delegation of citizens that will arrive before the setting of the sun; they will be able to answer your questions."

He hoped that Samuel would release him before he drowned in the rivers of sweat now cascading down his back.

"You may go," Samuel said irritably, "but if you see this so-called delegation, tell them I eagerly await what they have to say."

The messenger backed out of Samuel's presence as slowly as decorum dictated but as swiftly as fear demanded. He ran to the local inn for a tall jar of beer to settle his nerves. He did not envy those who would meet with Samuel this night to bring to him news of his terrible sons.

King Saul

Samuel brooded in his chambers. *What have my sons been up to? They know the proper sacrifices and prayers. They have my authority to do what needs to be done. Surely no one in that backwater Beer Sheba would have the nerve to challenge my authority as prophet and priest of YHWH? Surely no country rube would have the gall to question any interpretation of YHWH's law that I have been called to give? My sons are extensions of my own self; they are my heirs! To question them is to question me! We will see what these grumblers, if that is what they are, have to say.*

And just as Samuel continued to reflect on this unexpected turn of events, the citizens of Beer Sheba appeared on the threshold of his house. He gathered himself, tamping down his fiery fears the better to listen carefully to what these country folk had in mind.

"Welcome, my brothers. I trust my servants have offered you appropriate hospitality. I would not want it said that Ramah was a latter-day Sodom!"

He said this attempt at a joke rather too loudly and laughed rather too loudly at the jest. He noted that few smiles lighted the faces of the men of Beer Sheba.

"Come, you have travelled such a distance. How many days is it to your home?"

No one replied to Samuel's jocularity. Their faces were hard, determined. They were on a definite mission. Samuel ceased his banter and waited for one of them to speak. Finally, one who appeared the eldest among them, stepped forward, looked at Samuel without a trace of apprehension, and began.

"Samuel, you are old, and your sons are not anything like you. They are bribe-takers, extortionate lovers of too much wine and too much food and too much intimacy with too many women. Since they came to our home, our lives are a misery, our pockets lighter by half at least, our girls unsafe, our neighbors suspicious one of another. We demand that you act. First, remove your cankered sons from us; lance them like the foul boils that they are! Second, choose a king who will rule over us, like the Philistines have, like all other powerful and successful nations have."

The man was brutally blunt, and the demands of these people were equally clear. Depose his sons and choose a king. Samuel was speechless. His rheumy eyes opened wider as the man talked, the veins in his neck, now folded and refolded like the discarded skin of a snake, bulged red as he listened. His tangled beard shook briefly as he attempted to assimilate what this madman wanted. *Reject his own sons? Choose a king? A king in Israel? Like the other nations around, all those pagan nations?* Slowly he turned his back on the group and said nothing. Time stopped as the wall torches sputtered their intermittent flames. Finally, the men of Beer Sheba quietly left, not knowing what the priest would do, how he would respond to their demands. But they were prepared to wait in Ramah until the old man did something; they had had their bellies full of Joel and Abijah, and since Samuel would surely die soon, there seemed no alternative to a king. They dreaded the horrific possibility that one of the prophet's sons would claim his mantle of leadership. Samuel the great prophet of YHWH could use his near-divine power and anoint a king for them now before that monstrous possibility could occur. Anything was better than this slow death and humiliation at the hands of his offensive sons!

Samuel did not notice that he was alone again in his room. A king? A king! The idea was perverse, an abomination, ultimate blasphemy against YHWH who was the only king Israel would ever need, and the only one they would ever have, as long as Samuel was the one in charge. Old, was he? They would see how old he was, ungrateful wretches! He had poured out his life for the people in the service of YHWH, nearly all sixty springs of it, and the reward was this insane demand for a king from a rabble of hicks from the desert who knew nothing about service of God, nothing about the unceasing demands of that service, nothing about the demands that the God placed upon chosen servants? Their demand for a king was nothing but a repudiation of his whole life, of his hopes for a future of leadership for his family and their families and their families after that, for a future with YHWH as king of a land ruled in justice and right, as that was defined by Samuel and his countless heirs after him.

The more he thought of the demands he had heard, the more he felt they were directed at him personally, at his sons. Perhaps they were not as talented or as committed as he had been, but they were good boys deep down who knew God and who wanted to serve God with their whole hearts. Yes, he was old, but he had some good years left, and however many or few those years would be, his sons were waiting, and now experienced, to keep the flame of YHWH alive in the land. There could be no king in Israel. There would be no king in Israel! And with that thought resounding in his head, Samuel had headed back to the temple.

Samuel needed time with his God. He had fallen prone in front of YHWH's rough altar, his face nearly touching the blood stained earth, and he had shouted at his God.

> "YHWH! Your people have rejected me and my family from leadership! They want a king instead, an earthly king who is just like all the other earthly kings around them, a human king puffed with power, swollen with false authority, claiming to do what only you, O YHWH, can do. But they have rejected me, me, who has poured out his life in your service and theirs, who has led them from the altar and the justice seat and the place of the prophetic word for sixty years, sixty years, longer than most of your people have ever lived since the hallowed days of the patriarchs and matriarchs of your people. YHWH, I cannot make them a king. I refuse to make them a king! Only you are king over us. Only you can ever be king over us!"

And Samuel's furious words stopped as he could think of nothing more to say to his God. He was quite overwhelmed with his feelings of betrayal and rejection and denial. He felt shunted aside, deposed, denied, thrown away, discarded. He felt like the ancient worthy Job, sitting alone on his heap of ashes, deposited like an orange peel on a pile of refuse outside the walls of human habitation. He felt like the concubine of the Levite in that horrible old story, tossed out to a raging mob to be abused and tortured and finally forgotten, left for dead, awaiting the carving knife to end his life as it had ended hers.

The temple was silent; there was no sound save the scuttling of creatures in the shadows, the far-away hooting of a hunting owl, the triumphant baying of a coyote with a fresh kill. Samuel never felt so alone, never so old. What was he to do? He briefly thought that he would ask YHWH to end his life, to ask some chosen woman to drop a millstone on his head, like that fool would-be king, Abimelech. Or maybe God could chose an Israelite murderer, a latter-day Cain, who would ask Samuel to go out with him to some field and fell him with a large stone. Sixty years! Sixty years! Enough, he thought; more than enough!

But from some distant place in his brain, he heard again that voice that had spoken to him all those years ago in Shiloh, that voice that called him to service in the first place. But the voice spoke words that Samuel did not want to hear.

> "Listen to the voice of the people in all that they say to you, Samuel. They have not rejected you at all; they have in fact rejected me from being their king, just as they have done from the very days when I brought them out of Egypt and into this land. They are forever serving other gods and rejecting me. You are just now getting a tiny taste of that rejection that I have swallowed for centuries. I repeat: listen to their voice. Make them a king! That's right; you heard me. Anoint for them a king! But warn them, Samuel. Warn them about kings; tell them clearly what kings are like."

Yes, thought Samuel, that's it! YHWH is king and does not really want a king for the people. But he wants me to anoint one anyway! So I know what I am to do. But, most important of all, I am to tell them about kings, warn them about kings, tell them about the practice of kings, how they operate, how they rule. YHWH and I agree completely as we always do! God hates kings as much as I. YHWH wants me to describe kings as YHWH would describe them. So, they want a king, do they? Well, after I get through with them, they will certainly not want one. I may be old, but YHWH's words are my words, YHWH's thoughts my thoughts! YHWH said for me to listen to their foolish demands for a king, but YHWH also said for me to warn them. This means that YHWH really does not want a king at all. And neither do I!

Thus armed with divine certainty, Samuel commanded that the delegation from Beer Sheba join him and the rest of the people of Ramah at the field in front of the temple immediately. The sun was just coming up as the city awoke and responded to the command of their trusted leader. Samuel felt just as he had felt all those years ago when the voice of YHWH had called him to the prophetic work. He knew precisely what he had to do, and he stood in front of his people, YHWH's people, and told them what he was convinced YHWH had told him to say. The men from Beer Sheba expected Samuel to announce his search for a king, after he had admitted that his two sons were failures at their appointed tasks. The citizens of Ramah, as well as any visitors to the city, assembled with curiosity, many having no idea what Samuel was about to say, but ever ready to listen to the one who had led them for so long. He was more stooped than some remembered, his beard more gray and frayed, his fantastically long hair matted and tangled, his eyes clouded, covered, with the beginnings of the blindness that had afflicted his mentor, Eli. But the voice had lost little of its power and terror. After waiting for absolute quiet, Samuel began and was immediately in full prophetic flood.

> "So, you want a king, do you? Let me tell you about kings. In my long years of travel around our land, I have myself witnessed the ways of foreign kings, and I have heard what they are inclined to do. Listen carefully to what I just said. I spoke of the "ways" of these kings, and I used the word that also means "justice" for us. But I warn you that there is only one sort of justice for kings; it is the justice they decide for themselves!"

At mention of the word "justice," the grumbling of the delegation from Beer Sheba grew quite audible.

One of them shouted out, "We have not seen the justice of kings, but it can hardly be worse than the so-called justice of Joel and Abijah, your polluted boys! So make us a king—now!"

Samuel pretended not to hear the arrogant interruption of his speech; he was not used to interruptions, since they all knew he was God's only prophet, did they not? With a shrug of his shoulders, and a repositioning of his priestly robe, Samuel went on, convinced that words from him would always trump words from any other human being.

> "I repeat! The ways of the king you want will be as follows: he will conscript your sons for his armies, forcing some of them into his chariots as drivers and the rest to be foot soldiers running in front of the chariots, easy targets for any enemies' bowmen. A very few lucky ones will be commanders of thousands, thus escaping the first onslaughts of the battle, but many more so-called "lucky ones" will be commanders of fifties who will lead their charges into the very jaws of death. You all know how many of those leaders return to their homes after conflict. Those sons found unfit for battle—those lame or halt or weak or diseased—will not escape his service. They will plow and sow and reap the kingly harvests or they will make his weapons, his swords and bows, his chariot wheels and armor.
>
> You think your daughters will be spared the all-seeing eye and insatiable greed of the king? He will take them to make the fruity perfumes for his many wives as well as the sweet lotions to mask his human smells when he chooses to lie on his bed or in his bath at any hour of day or night. Some of your daughters he will send to his huge kitchens where in the roaring heat of the many ovens' blast they will bake his bread and dress his meat and create sweet cakes to adorn his groaning table.

King Saul

Those of you blessed with fine fields and vineyards and orchards, listen! He will take them and hand them over to his indolent friends at court. Your vines and your olive trees will never be safe while the king's appetites are in need of satisfaction. And if he does not confiscate your lands, he will demand a tax on all of it, stealing 10 percent of it all, giving it to his fat, lolling cronies. He will, whenever he wants, take outright any of your male and female slaves that he chooses, as well as the very best of your livestock and pack animals to do whatever work his whims urge him to do. And what he does not steal, he will tax whatever you may have left. My fellow Israelites, you will be his slaves and no longer free. The freedom that YHWH gave to your ancestors at the great sea will disappear, and you will once again return to the slavery of Egypt. And, like of old, you will cry out to YHWH, because of this king whom you have chosen for yourselves. But unlike the days of Egypt, YHWH will give you no answer on that day of your new slavery. You will cry for God until your lips are cracked and your tongue sticks to the roof of your mouth, but the heavens will be silent. Silent on that day!"

Samuel was exhausted after this furious speech; his words stopped, his still large chest heaved with the exertion, sweat poured from his face like the fall rains, his thinning hair stuck to his pate in clumps. His priestly garment had slipped from his right shoulder and hung down, touching the hard-packed soil of the speaking ground. He was spent, but also knew that he had delivered a fatal blow to any possible thought of a king for Israel. YHWH had told him to listen to their demands, but YHWH had also said to warn them about the disasters that having a king would surely bring. He had done as YHWH had commanded, as he always did. Once again, Samuel's words were YHWH's words; YHWH's words had poured out of Samuel's old mouth. The exhausted prophet waited in silence for the people to admit the foolishness of their request for a king. His ears ached for confirmation that his speech had won the day for him and for YHWH, that he would remain as God's only spokesperson and that YHWH would remain as Israel's only king.

But Samuel's words had sounded rather different to some in the crowd, those men of Beer Sheba who had raised the desire for a king in the first place. Everything that Samuel had said were the evils of a king was in fact the evil of his own sons! They had stolen and bribed and taxed and paid off their friends and lain about in increasing luxury, almost from the first day of their coming to Beer Sheba. But they had no armies or chariots or weapons while the Philistine threat was once again increasing all around them. At least a king would establish a standing army for necessary defense of the land against the cruel pagans. At least a king would be a reliable bulwark who could lead the people as needed. At least a king, unlike these noxious sons of Samuel, would demonstrate real authority, have real power to make decisions that needed making, not would-be likenesses of their much greater father. For the men of Beer Sheba, Samuel's speech, far from turning them away from their desire for a king, had rather reconfirmed that desire.

King Saul

They did not listen to the warnings of Samuel, but listened to the implications of his words for them and their situation. The same man who had voiced desire for a king the previous night in Samuel's room now spoke again.

> "No! We will not be turned aside! We are now even more determined to have a king over us. That way we will be like all the other nations, solid in leadership, fixed in government, firmly established for the future. Our king will actually lead us, go before us, fight our battles with us! Samuel, you are too old to do all these things we need for the future of our land. Make a king for us, and do it now!"

This stirring speech fired the rest of the delegation of Beer Sheba to unrestrained shouting, and the citizens of Ramah, and all visitors, soon joined the uproar. The indiscriminate voices quickly coalesced into the cry, "A king! A king for Israel! A king! A king for Israel!" Every face was streaked with joy, both young and old, both man and woman. The word "king" thundered from every throat; it arced into the morning sky; it echoed down the valleys and up the mountains that surrounded the city.

Only one voice was silent. The great voice of Samuel was stunned in his throat, and though he willed it to cry out against the madness of the crowd before him, he could not summon it to the task. As the bedlam continued, he retreated into the temple, defeated and alone. No one in the crowd saw him leave. Samuel went to the one who had always spoken exactly what he needed to hear, exactly what he himself knew to be true. He entreated the mysterious YHWH. Throwing himself down before the familiar altar, with pain wracking his aging knees and feet, the prophet repeated to YHWH the words he had just heard from the mob outside.

"They still want a king, O YHWH. I did just as you said. I warned them in the strongest terms I could muster about the horrors of kings, but they still want one. Tell me, my God, what am I to do?"

And he waited for YHWH's reply. He fully expected YHWH to commend the work of the prophet, to reiterate God's feeling of rejection at the hands of the ungrateful people, to command Samuel to go back out and try again to convince the idiots that YHWH was king, and that Samuel was alone YHWH's prophet. But Samuel this time heard the unexpected from his God. The words were brief and the words were clear, sounding in his head.

"Listen to their voice; set a king over them."

There was this time no talk of warning, no talk of rejection, no commendation for the lifetime ministry of God's faithful prophet. YHWH said for the third time, "Listen to their voice." Well, Samuel had listened, but what he had heard had sickened him, infuriated him, disgusted him. Surely, YHWH was just as angry as he about being replaced in the hearts and minds of the people! Surely, YHWH would show forth divine rage against any who would dare to choose a king over YHWH, God of Israel! But the words of YHWH that Samuel heard contained no rage, no disgust, no anger.

King Saul

"Set a king over them," YHWH had said. Set a king over them? After Samuel's speech of dire warning against the dangers of kingship, how could he simply go out to the delirious mob and calmly pick a king from among them? They would think he was a fool, he, Samuel, prophet/priest of YHWH! No, he was still Samuel; he still was leader in Israel. He still had two sons who would be his heirs, despite some rumors of their bad behavior in Beer Sheba. Those rumors would quickly be proven false, and the hotheads who spread them would be dealt with severely. Samuel had no intention of setting a king over Israel. Perhaps he had heard God wrongly; perhaps God had really said for Samuel to continue to resist the would-be kingmakers in Israel. Surely that must be it; he had simply not heard God clearly.

And with that conviction, he strode out of the temple with new assurance about the course he must follow. He was Samuel and while he was leader in Israel, there would be no king, ever! The crowd had quieted down considerably while Samuel had been in the temple, and when many of them noticed the priest signaling for silence, they passed the word to their jubilant companions that Samuel had something else to say. All of them fully expected him to announce his choice of king among them, or if not that, at least he would say that the process for the selection of their king would begin now with a final decision made in due course. Their silence was eager, and they became eerily quiet in anticipation.

Samuel waited for absolute calm, and then said, clearly and loudly, "Each of you may go home."

He turned and moved back into the temple without another word, but if any of them could have seen his face as he turned, he would have seen a satisfied smile crease his lips.

Rage burst from every throat in the crowd; they demanded that Samuel return and do what they asked. They commanded him to come back and to face their anger. They shouted after his retreating back, but he seemed not to hear the din. As he disappeared into the sanctuary, the crowd was reduced to impotent fury, breaking apart into knots of people, all talking at once, wondering now what they should do. The men of Beer Sheba in agitation saddled their animals, and left Ramah for the long journey back to their city and their repulsive leaders. Nothing had been solved. Nothing had been decided. Israel was in limbo, a long-time servant near death, two sons unworthy of his legacy, and no leadership in a time of advancing dangers. Beer Sheba and Ramah and all the cities of the land were filled with anxious hearts that night as all wondered what they were to do. What was the word from YHWH? What was the word from Samuel? No one could answer either of those questions.

8

Samuel finished the cup of beer with a satisfied smacking of his lips. He was glad that his life-long Nazirite vow only prevented him from products from grapes, and not grain. This beer was so good and relaxing. Yes, they had all awaited his words, which were the words of YHWH for Israel. Samuel was more than ever convinced that YHWH did not want a king—not really. YHWH wanted him to choose a king who was so weak, so pathetic, that once Israel saw a king in action, they would crawl back to Samuel and demand that he depose the monstrosity and give them again his great leadership skills, and after his death, the skills of his sons. It was time to return to Saul, who, as the pliant boy he appeared to be, would be waiting politely by the well. I will give them a king all right, he thought, and smiled confidently as he tossed his cup aside and returned to the well of Ramah.

He could now see very clearly the game YHWH was playing.

"Anoint a king, Samuel," YHWH had said, but "warn them about kings."

Samuel had done so in the strongest terms he could muster. But he had also resisted the promptings of his God. But now God had thrown a candidate for prince in his face, had forced him to anoint, had given him no escape. Yet, the man, though impressive to be sure, seemed slow, unaware, naïve. Samuel could anoint this one, and after a time, perhaps a very brief time, the people would see the mistake they had made, would reject the man as their prince, and would return once again to their real princes, YHWH and Samuel, and finally to Samuel's sons. Yes, Samuel could see what YHWH had in mind.

He walked up to the well, and looked high into the handsome face of Saul.

"I am the seer."

If the idiot thought of him only as a seer, a kind of soothsayer, a finder of lost things, why should he enlighten him that he, Samuel, was in fact the mighty prophet of the creator of heaven and earth, YHWH of the armies? Still, he would tell this so-called prince exactly what he would now do, down to the finest details. Samuel was still master in Israel, and no young pup, no matter how big, no matter how handsome, would get in the way of that mastery.

He turned his massive voice full on, and pointed it at the towering boy.

"Go up before me to the high place, for both of you must eat with me today. Then in the morning, I will send you away, Saul, right after I tell you everything that is in your mind and heart."

King Saul

Samuel lessened the power of his voice as he spoke this last sentence, emphasizing his ability to play the role of seer if he wanted to; he did not exactly whisper the words but he did utter them with a particularly portentous tone. He was not after all above a bit of playacting when it served the purpose.

In a more common way, he then said, "As for the donkeys that were lost those days ago, drop them from your mind, for they have been found."

Saul's eyes widened as he heard the wizard not only tell him why he had come but announce that he had solved the problem before being told what it was! He turned to Joseph in wonder, rather like a child with a clay boat, and smiled broadly at him, and then looked back at the magical Samuel. But the old man had one more thing to say, and this time he mustered his best prophetic voice, not loud but cavernous, as if the words were coming from long ago, from deep in the ancient earth.

"And who is in fact the whole desire of Israel? Is it not you and the house of your father?"

The words nearly choked in Samuel's throat, but he had worded them carefully. If this was the prince-to-be, so designated by YHWH, then Samuel wanted him to know it. But he also wanted him to know that this thing was the desire of Israel, not his desire. Nor, did Samuel believe, that it was really the desire of God. This silly boy was going to play the dupe for God and Samuel, and after he was shown for the fool he was, the people would come to their senses and return to Samuel, the only prophet of YHWH. Still, he could not bring himself to say the word "king" or "prince" or "ruler" or any word remotely resembling them. "Desire of Israel" would do, because the people's evil desire for a king started all this mess, and Samuel was about to give them what they wanted, however insane he thought the whole thing was.

Saul was first puzzled by the words he had heard from the ancient man, the man who had solved his donkey problem, and looked at Samuel with a completely blank stare. How in God's world could I be the "desire of Israel," he thought; I cannot even keep track of a few silly donkeys? And why should my "father's house" be any sort of a desire for Israel? Kish had some land and property but no distinction, no gifts, no notoriety or reputation of any kind. Kish and Saul were not even the desire of their village, let alone all Israel! Perhaps the seer had misspoken; perhaps he had become slightly unhinged in his vast old age; perhaps he had confused him with someone else.

"I am only a Benjaminite, the very least of the tribes of Israel."

Saul, like everyone else in his tribe, knew the terrible story of the Levite and the concubine; his mother used to scare him with it when he was a small child. She too vividly told the part when the poor woman was dismembered by her master, her pieces sent throughout the land. Saul trembled slightly even now as that scene tumbled back into his memory.

"And my family is the most insignificant family of that most insignificant tribe."

Saul almost said "cursed" but he feared a rebuke from the holy man who stood silent before him.

"Why have you spoken to me like this?"

He strongly emphasized "me" in his response. He waited for the old man to speak again. But he did not.

Instead, Samuel stood between Saul and his servant, and led them up to the high place and into the small hall that served as the spot where worshippers ate after the close of the sacrificial rites, that is, if one was invited. To his shock, Saul sat at the head of the table, in front of some thirty people who were obviously the significant people of Ramah. Many mumbled as Saul sat in front of them, some smiled but some giggled in derision, wondering how this huge oaf had gotten into the party of the important. In the general hubbub Samuel summoned the cook for the feast.

"Bring that portion I pointed out to you, the one I asked you to save."

The cook, used to obeying the orders of Samuel without question, rushed to get a superb piece of roasted meat, the richest part of the lamb, cooked to perfection, and set it down before Saul. The aroma was intoxicating, and Saul reached for the meat eagerly, saliva forming pools in his mouth. He had eaten very little during the last days of the search for the cursed donkeys. He needed this lamb joint desperately! But Samuel stopped his first bite with another oracular announcement, spoken again in that tone he had used earlier down the hill.

"Behold! What was kept back has now been set before you. Eat, for it was kept back for you for this appointed time. It was I who invited these people. It was I who invited you."

Even if Saul had understood what Samuel was saying, which he did not, he was not listening too closely, since the smell of the food was heavenly, and his ears were far less interested in words than his stomach was in meat. When he saw that Samuel seemed finished at last, Saul tore into the meat with relish, and washed it all down with some of the finest wine he had ever tasted. He hardly looked up from the meat and the wine to see the bemused faces of those who were sharing the table, and if he heard the cluck-clucking comments about his ravenous devouring of the meal, he cared not at all.

But the excitement and wonder and confusion of the day finally sapped Saul's remaining strength, and he longed for sleep. The meal at last ended, and Samuel sent all the guests to their homes, while he led Saul and Joseph down from the high place into the city. A bed had been prepared for Saul alone on the roof of Samuel's own house, since the night was hot, and the roof tended to catch the breezes from the great sea, if any were to stir. Saul lay down and fell instantly asleep as though he were dead. Joseph was also given a palette for sleeping in another part of the house, while Samuel retired alone to his room. But he was not tired but agitated.

He knew he had to do what he did not want to do; he had to anoint Saul prince publicly to satisfy the demands of the people and the call of YHWH. He was still somewhat uncertain about his reading of YHWH's demand. Why had YHWH implied that the people needed saving from the Philistines, when Samuel had played that role for decades? Why had YHWH said that the people had cried out for respite from their suffering when Samuel could see no real suffering among the people? As he thought these painful thoughts, he began to understand all the more how Eli must have felt toward the end, his eyes dimming with age, his belly growing so vast that even simple movements became nearly impossible. No wonder at the end of his life he mostly sat immobile on his priestly seat, unaware of the events swirling around him, of the capture of the holy ark, of the terrible defeat the Israelite armies. Samuel no longer saw as well as once he did. Perhaps he too was not as attuned to the times? Could it be that YHWH was grooming him for displacement and grooming Saul to succeed him, choosing Saul to destroy the future of his sons, his line, his dynasty? No, it simply could not be! He was still YHWH's prophet, YHWH's man, YHWH's mouthpiece. He was not fat, blind Eli; he was Samuel, the chief man in the land of YHWH's choosing!

Samuel fell down on his aching knees, heard the bones crack as he painfully lowered himself to the floor of his room. And he prayed.

> "YHWH, I have served you since I was a boy, much younger even than this Saul whom you have brought to me. I have done your bidding without question all my days. I have led your people selflessly, courageously, energetically. All know that I am your man and your special prophet. Do we really need this new man? Do you really want him to do my work? He is young, none too bright, desperately inexperienced, naïve in the extreme. How can he possibly rule your people? YHWH, reconsider this action, I pray! Remember my sons, Joel and Abijah, your good servants whom I have trained to follow in my footsteps as your new men. Why not have me call them back from Beer-Sheba? I will anoint them instead of this nobody, this upstart, this absurdly large boy from the awful tribe of Benjamin. Answer me, YHWH, answer me!"

And Samuel waited for YHWH to answer, assured that an answer would come as it always had in the past. But YHWH was silent. And Samuel waited until the light of the dawn kissed the dark of the night. But there was no answer, and Samuel found himself alone in his room with aching knees and trembling hands and lips. To his shock he felt the salt of tears staining his mouth. Crying? Why was he crying? Had YHWH abandoned him? He refused to believe that after all these years. Well, so what? So what? He rose, resolved in his mind about what needed to be done. He would anoint the boy, but he would also tell him where to go and what to do. And whenever Saul did or said anything that Samuel had not told him to say and do, as he was sure that he would, well, we would just see. We would just see.

The sun rose, and Samuel slowly hobbled up to the roof.

"Get up," he said, rather more gruffly than he intended. "I need to send you on your way!"

Saul stretched his giant arms to the sky; Samuel thought that the massive boy could have squeezed the life out of him without a moment's thought. Sleepily, Saul stood up, uncoiling his frame fully, shaking the night's sleep from him, and silently followed Samuel down from the roof of the house. Joseph, aroused by Samuel's loud command to his master, joined them as they walked into the streets of Ramah and moved toward the city gates.

"Tell the servant to move on ahead of us, and when he has done so, you stand right here, and I will tell you the word of God."

Joseph went on right up to the gates, but looked back several times to see what his master wanted him to do. Saul's eyes were wide in fear and expectation. He was about to receive the word of God from the one man in Israel who had had the right to speak that word for years and years. Saul could not quite imagine what God's word had to do with him, much less imagine what the content of that word might be. He rooted himself to the spot and waited. Words would pour from Samuel's mouth as surely as the spring of Jericho gushed its flow into that city. Saul remembered his nights on the hills near his farm and his hopes that YHWH had some special plan for him and his life. He trembled slightly as Samuel moved closer to him.

Before Saul realized what Samuel was doing, he felt a sticky stream of olive oil slide down his face and into his beard, as the dry and cracked lips of the prophet kissed his cheek. The prophet had stood on a rock to enable him to reach Saul's head and face, and still had had to reach up with his scrawny arms to direct the stream of oil from the jar. He was on the tips of his toes, making quite a spectacle in the morning sun. But no one saw the action of the anointing or heard what he said next.

"Is it not true that YHWH has today, this instant, anointed you over God's inheritance, Israel, prince?"

The hollow tone of the old man's cavernous voice, and the awkward syntax of the sentence he had spoken, stormed into Saul's anxious ears like waves of the Great Sea. The word "prince," fairly shouted at the end, echoed in Saul's head, as if he had a large shell affixed to his skull, resounding with the word. Prince. I am prince over Israel; I, Saul, who failed in my attempt to find my father's donkeys, have been anointed prince over all Israel. How could this be? What am I to do? Where will I go? How am I to be a prince?

These sentiments filled Saul's brain as he stood in hushed silence, feeling and smelling the oil, swimming in the astonishing words just spoken by Israel's greatest man. But the speech had not stopped, and Saul broke out of his reverie and attempted to focus on the words.

> "When you leave me today, you will meet two men near the tomb of Rachel in the territory of Benjamin at Zelzah. They will say to you, 'The donkeys that you went to find have been found, but now your father has stopped worrying about the donkeys and has started worrying about you, saying, "What shall I do with my son?"' Then you shall leave there, go on further, and come to the oak of Tabor; three men you will find there going up to the God of Bethel, one carrying three young goats, another carrying three loaves of bread, and

another carrying a skin of wine. They will give you a hearty 'shalom' along with two loaves of bread that you will take from their hands. After that, you will come to Gibeath Elohim, the hill of God, where the Philistine outpost is. Just as you come to the town, you will meet a band of prophets, coming down from the high place, preceded by musicians playing harp, tambourine, flute, and lyre. They will be in a prophetic frenzy! Then the spirit of YHWH will possess you, and you will fall into a prophetic frenzy with them, becoming another man."

Saul tried his best to follow this tumbling pile of demands and instructions, but the astonishing events of the past few hours were too much for him. The regal meal with its choicest cut of meat. The honor of sleeping in comfort in Samuel's own house. The portentous words about Israel's desire. And now the feel of the oil on his face and the sound of "prince" ringing in his head left Saul bewildered, amazed, shocked, overwhelmed, confused, terrified. As Samuel rambled on with his demands and predictions, Saul simply could not hear what the man was saying, and stared dumbly at him, gazing emptily at the fixed gaze of those unforgettable eyes. What was he saying about goats and bread? What was that about prophets and their frenzy? Saul had avoided the weird men known as prophets his whole brief life. They lived on the highest mountains, usually out in the open, dancing, singing, shouting words or sounds only they could find the meaning of. Had Samuel just said that he, Saul, would not only meet a gaggle of these madmen, rushing down some mountain or other, but would become like one of them, uttering nonsense, saliva flecking the corners of his mouth? Ridiculous, thought Saul; he would never allow himself such public humiliation!

Visions of himself as a bedraggled fool with filthy hair, linking arms with such offensive people filled Saul's inner eye, but Samuel's sudden shout dragged him back to the present.

"Now pay special attention, prince! Heed my words well! After all these signs occur, and occur they surely will, do for yourself whatever your hand decides to do, because God is with you."

Saul stood even taller as he heard those words, the first thing Samuel had said that registered fully in his cloudy heart. God was with him, and as a result, he could do whatever he felt needed to be done. Perhaps he really was the prince of Israel! He was free to act in ways that a prince should act. Free! But exactly what that was, the actions of a prince, remained a mystery. He was free to act, Samuel said, but just how to act had not yet been made clear. Saul waited for further instructions, hoping that Samuel would start to reveal to him just what it was that he and God had in mind.

"You will go down to Gilgal ahead of me, and then I will go down to you to offer whole burnt offerings and to sacrifice gifts of peace. Seven days you will wait, until I come to you. Then I will let you know what you are to do."

Abruptly, Samuel's speech ended, and he turned away from the new prince of Israel and left without another word. But if Saul had seen Samuel's face, he might have

seen a slight smile play on his lips, whether of satisfaction, scorn, or hidden pleasure he would not have known. But Saul probably would have been unaware of any
of Samuel's facial expressions in any case, because he was now thoroughly mystified
about what he was to do. After those bread and goat signs and promises of prophetic
frenzy, few of which he could actually remember, happened, which seemed highly unlikely as he stood alone, outside the gate of Ramah, he was then to head off to Gilgal,
a lengthy journey back through the rugged mountains through which he and Joseph
had just come. Then he was supposed to wait seven days for Samuel to come to lead
the sacrifice at the high place there. That seemed clear enough, but then Samuel had
added "until I come." Well, which was it? Was he to wait seven days, or was he to wait
until Samuel came? Did the old man mean he was going to come in seven days, or was
Saul to wait for him if he did not come for eight or nine or twenty days? However that
confusion was to be untangled, the last thing Samuel had said was that he was going
to show Saul what to do. But that too was confusing. Had Samuel not first said that he
could do whatever his own hands found needed doing, because God was with him?
But he had ended by saying that Samuel was the final authority, just as he had always
been. What then did it mean to be prince over Israel, when the real "prince" with the
real power had not changed at all? Saul's understanding of Samuel's demands of him
was as distant as Mount Tabor, as absent as his father's donkeys.

He turned to leave the shadow of Samuel's city and felt the power of God move
through him. Samuel had been right, thought Saul. God was with him, and though
he was far less than clear about the road ahead, he walked toward Gilgal with energy
and hope, his giant frame erect, his long legs swallowing the distance with ease. Joseph
scrambled to keep up with his massive master, whimpering more than once that Saul
might slow down just a bit, since the day was hot and his legs were short. And all happened as the prophet had said. Men with bread and goats did meet them, and Saul did
take some bread, but whether these things happened in the order predicted by Samuel
remained uncertain, since he just could not remember Samuel's exact words.

But Samuel was right about the prophetic band. A few short steps from Ramah, as
he and Joseph approached Gibeah, several wraith like figures loomed up from behind
a huge rock, babbling and shrieking, one even falling on the ground and writhing in
the dirt like a man possessed. Their dress was rags, their hair matted, stuck unwashed
to their skulls, their chests concave from lack of regular food. Saul at first drew back in
horror, and Joseph cried out, diving for cover from these supposed men who looked
rather more like animals or, even worse, demons come from the desert to drag him
into the maw of Sheol. But to Joseph's utter astonishment, Saul soon fell on his knees
at the feet of these beings and joined his huge voice with theirs, crying out, beating the
air with uncontrolled fists, rolling in the dust, his finest cloak torn to tatters, his knees
and elbows and hands scratched and bleeding, compelled by an unseen power even
stronger than Saul's own.

King Saul

The noise was frightening, its sound echoing from the rocks into the surrounding countryside. Gibeah was a popular spot to visit, and many in the area knew of Saul, the extraordinarily large young man from the family of Kish.

At the loud noise 20 or 30 people who had come to Gibeah for some food and fun, gathered at the site of the prophets' shrieking and groaning, and said to one another, "Is that one over there not Saul, son of Kish? Of course it is! Look at the size of him! I never took him to be one to join the prophets; he always seemed a sensible enough boy, not given to religious talk or peculiar ways."

But one sneering voice shouted above the din, "Just who is the father of these lunatics?" and the whole group burst into appreciative laughter at the clever saying; after all, questioning the paternity of anyone was not a nice thing to do, but it certainly was funny since they all knew who Saul's father was well enough.

All those who had known Saul before never forgot that day at Gibeah, and they passed an expression around the area so that nearly everyone knew it.

"Is Saul among the prophets?"

They would say it whenever anything very unlikely happened, since they believed that if Saul could end up foaming at the mouth with those mad people, anything at all is possible: two-headed cows, a pleasant Philistine, a truly generous priest. Given what happened to Saul, however, the saying took on a rather more sinister meaning.

As the crowd tired of the spectacle of prophetic frenzy, and returned to their food and games, Saul reclaimed his right mind and resumed his climb toward the high place of Gibeah. When he reached the summit, he met his uncle, Lemuel, Kish's older brother. Lemuel had always been a much more religious man than Kish, and as he aged, he rarely missed a day of sacrifice on some high place or other. So Saul was not surprised to see him standing near the stone altar, his hands raised in supplication to YHWH as the smoke of the sacrifice rose lazily into the azure sky. After he opened his eyes and returned in his mind to the mountaintop, Lemuel turned away from the roasted flesh and hobbled toward the path leading down the mountain. Immediately, his eyes found Saul, who was always the first person to be seen in any crowd.

"Where have you been, and what brings you here?" the old man asked in his quivery voice.

He apparently had been so consumed by his religious devotions that he had not heard the loud commotion at the foot of the mountain when Saul had joined the prophetic band in their unintelligible jabberings.

Saul debated within himself just how he should answer this quite innocent question. He could easily say that he had gone looking for Kish's donkeys and that they had been found. If he told Lemuel about his secret anointing by Samuel, how he had apparently been chosen by YHWH to be prince over Israel, and how confused he was about the whole astonishing business, he feared the old and deeply religious man would either fall down before him as a living sign of the presence of YHWH or, worse, he might accuse Saul of blasphemy, or lying, or both. Saul chose the way of least confusion.

"I went looking for the lost donkeys, and when Joseph and I could not find them, we went to see Samuel who has a reputation for finding lost things." "What did the great prophet say to you?" Lemuel asked. He knew that Samuel was far more than a local magician who spent his days in cheap conjuring tricks. Samuel was the most powerful man in Israel, and if he had spoken to his nephew, he surely had more on his mind than donkeys.

Saul looked down at his uncle's expectant face, and said, "He told us that the donkeys had been found."

Lemuel waited for more, but there was no more. Saul said nothing to him about oil or special portions of food or meetings with people with goats and loaves of bread, nothing about prophetic frenzy, nothing about the astonishing events of the past few hours. Without another word, Saul turned and rushed down the mountain; he did not exactly run, but his gigantic strides were lengthened so that no normal-sized person, let alone an old one like his uncle, could possibly catch up. Lemuel shouted after the retreating figure, but Saul either did not hear or chose not to hear.

"Was that all?" he said.

But Saul was gone.

As he hurried away from Gibeah's high place and headed for home, Saul thought about all that had occurred to him. What did it mean? Perhaps it was a dream of some sort. Why on earth would the great Samuel speak to him about leadership in Israel? He knew well the stories told to him by his mother about YHWH's amazing choices of leaders. The drunken Noah and his life-giving ark, the lying Jacob and his unending trickery, the arrogant Joseph and his manipulation of his brothers, the very reluctant Moses who had rather been anywhere than Egypt whence he was called by the ever-burning bush in Midian, uttering his lame excuses right in YHWH's fiery face. Given that history, it was certainly no surprise that YHWH could choose even Saul for a great work, but why? Why Saul? He knew that he was very handsome. Many women's eyes had devoured him since he was barely a young man. And of course he was very tall. But good looks were no criterion for leadership, were they? Joseph had been a handsome man, but no one ever commented about the beauty of Moses or Jacob or Noah. Were any of them tall? No one ever said so. But what else did he have to recommend him to YHWH? He was a nobody from a suspect tribe, a ranch hand without connections from a family little known in Israel. Why? Why? Who could he talk to about all of this? He needed help to understand. He needed someone to tell him what he should do now. He had done everything Samuel had commanded, and everything had happened just as the prophet had foretold. But what now? Saul could think of nothing. So he went home to Kish's farm and waited.

9

A week passed or was it two? Saul had said nothing to anyone about the events with Samuel. He had settled back into the routine of the farm, turning up the soil for the planting to come, lashing his hulking body to the wooden plow, attempting to keep the furrows straight as the two great oxen, Joachim and Boaz, plodded through the fields, dragging the plow in their wake. Each day he worked took his mind further from the bewildering events, and he thought less and less of princes and oil and magic goats and prophets. He began to feel again like himself. He was Saul, farmer and rancher, son of Kish, who expected to follow his father as farmer on this land. Samuel was the only prince and priest and prophet that Israel needed, and at each sunset Saul thanked YHWH that Samuel's anointing finally meant nothing and that Saul could once again be simply a very tall and handsome man, merely a citizen of Israel, living his life in quiet and peace.

His uncle, the deeply religious one, did visit Kish one day, telling him of his confrontation with Saul on the mountain the day after the boy had seen Samuel. He had suggested that Kish's son had not told him all that had happened with the great prophet; he just knew that something else had gone on, something momentous. Of course, Kish well knew that his brother was forever looking for things momentous, especially of a religious bent, so he dismissed his brother's surmise with a sibling's laugh. "Now, Megog," he said, (that was his nickname for his older and much more impressionable brother; it bore the whiff of condescension, though Kish usually did not intend it in a wounding way) "you know Saul. He is an inveterate truth teller; why should he lie to you? He went to Samuel, and the crusty old seer told him where to find our donkeys; I hear he is good at that sort of thing. That is all there is to the story. Why not have a another cup of beer?" Reluctantly, Lemuel took the jar, but maintained a questioning look as he slurped his brother's offering.

Saul of course knew that many had witnessed his prophetic frenzy—if that was really what it was—at Gibeah's mountain, and that people were whispering about him far more than once they did. But he trusted that time would change that; people were ever ready to talk of the latest thing, and soon Saul would be a thing of the past, forgotten and no longer discussed. He had only to stay out of the way, had only to farm the land, find a willing woman to join him in the farming life, raise some strapping sons and lovely daughters. Then he could die in peace, surrounded only by the family who

67

loved him, could return to the land that he had worked, become again part of the soil from which YHWH had created him. Saul knew there was a right time for everything, and the life he imagined would richly fulfill his simple dreams.

And life had quickly returned to normal. Kish was very glad to have his donkeys back safe and healthy; the crop was very promising and those donkeys would be needed to carry the grain and grapes to the markets of Ramah and Mizpah. And he was very glad to have his wonderful son back, too, plowing the fields, eating his prodigious meals, and sharing quietly the things that he said had happened to him and Joseph in their days of search. But Saul said nothing of the strange events, events that continued now to fade into the cloud of dreams, into the stuff of legends, of stories, of lies. Best to forget it all, thought Saul. Leave kings and prophets and leadership and public demands to others. "I am a farmer, a keeper of animals, a grower of crop, and that is all." His dreams soon were nearly bereft of kings and prophets and dripping oil.

One fresh morning, as he began to tie himself to the plow and finish the field's preparation, a messenger arrived at the farm. Samuel had summoned all Israelites to join him at Mizpah for a crucial announcement. There could be no question of avoiding Samuel's call; the prophet had guided Israel for more than sixty summers and had worked faithfully for the protection and betterment of the land. From Mizpah to Gilgal, from Beth Shemesh to Shiloh, Samuel had judged and led and defended his people. Though he was now old, supernaturally old, having lived far beyond the usual forty or so years of an average person, his vigor was undimmed, even though the booming and familiar voice was more often gravelly and rough than once it was. But Mizpah, only a brief walk from Samuel's Ramah home, was now his favorite location for assembling the people for sacrifice and for public events. Thus Saul reluctantly unhooked himself from the plow and called his father and the rest of the family to join him for the journey to Mizpah. Saul was of course less than eager to attend Samuel's called meeting. He feared that the announcement might have something to do with the events he had tried so hard to forget. But there was no avoiding this call of the most powerful man in the land. The messenger had said that Samuel would lead a sacrifice and speak to the people when the sun was straight overhead, so Kish urged his family to hurry.

They arrived well in advance of the time for the assembly, so hurried to get a good position in the growing crowd to hear what Samuel intended to say. Hundreds of people were gathering from the four corners of the hill country, farmers mostly, but also merchants with their richly loaded camels, and entertainers dressed in lavish and colorful costumes, ready to offer songs and dances after Samuel had had his say. As always, stalls sprang up like over night grain, offering fruit and wine and children's toys, fine carpets, tent supplies, cloth and stakes and rope, cheese and yogurt. All assemblies quickly became celebratory fairs, as isolated people welcomed the chance to see old acquaintances and to share the gossip, to curse the weather and the price of wheat.

King Saul

As Saul and his family moved through the tightly packed stalls, looking for some sweet figs to stem the hunger of the trip, he overheard again and again his name being mentioned, accompanied by furtive glances from the men and hungry, sometimes overtly lascivious, looks from the women. More than once he heard the dreaded word "prince," and even the word "king," as he passed through the mob. And each time he heard his name and those words in close connection, his heart sank, his hunger was forgotten, and he began to fear that he was the reason that all these people had come to Mizpah this day. As the crowd thickened, Saul found a way to separate himself from Kish and his family and soon disappeared from sight.

Just as the sun stood straight overhead, and the shadows of people and tents grew small, Samuel appeared at the high altar, followed by an unblemished goat, led by an under priest of the shrine. Samuel turned toward the altar, mumbled the words of blessing to YHWH, slashed the throat of the goat with one quick stroke from his flint knife, and allowed the much younger priest to hoist the carcass onto the blazing altar; the old man plainly could no longer perform the full sacrifice alone. The smell of roast meat quickly filled the air, and the people near the front of the vast crowd joined Samuel in the ritual words.

"Praised and blessed are you, YHWH, ruler of the world, who in your mercy gives us food from your hand. We are your people, the sheep of your pasture. Remember us, O YHWH, and rescue us in the time of our trouble. For you alone are God!"

By the time the last words were spoken, nearly every member of the crowd, now numbering in the thousands, spoke them together so that the hills rang with the sound.

Samuel waited for the echoes to stop, paused again with bowed head and upraised arms toward the sky, now filled with the smoke of the goat, and slowly turned to face the gigantic throng. He had thought for days about exactly what he would say to these expectant faces that had come faithfully at his call. The word "king" was much in the air; Samuel had heard it spoken as well as Saul. He also knew that YHWH had demanded that he anoint Saul king, and he had done it, however privately, however unenthusiastically. But now he felt he needed to do something more. The people's demand for a king had not been met, and their grumbling had increased to the point that angry words against Samuel were being spoken brazenly in the streets of every town and village. He feared open rebellion could not be far off. He simply had to find a way to assuage this budding anger as well as establish his sons as legitimate heirs to his leadership. However much he had prayed for them, cajoled them, and threatened them, the two rascals had not much changed their ways, remaining in Beer Sheba, despised by nearly all the people there. But Samuel felt that if he could buy more time, he could still straighten his boys out, bring them back renewed and changed to Ramah, and present them to the people as genuine leaders for the future. Once that was done, the so-called king would be forgotten and rejected, and things would return to the way they had been for so long. Samuel would be pleased, and he was sure that YHWH would be equally pleased and satisfied.

Still, Samuel was going to make Saul king, and he was going to do it publicly, right here, today, in Mizpah. But he was going to do it in such a way as to prepare the people who demanded a king to see what a terrible mistake the king would be. He knew he was taking a risk by doing this. It was possible that the people might embrace the king, might forget about Samuel and his sons. That would be a disaster. But Samuel was convinced that Saul was just the right sort of man to crown king, because there was something not quite kingly about the boy. Samuel had seen the weaknesses in Saul the first day he had met him: too reticent, too shy, too easily manipulated, too easily led, not quick to understand what was happening, not quick enough to adapt to events. He supposed there were other problems that would arise after the coronation, but these were more than enough to demonstrate that kings were a bad idea. Samuel gazed at the eager faces of his people, and began his very carefully rehearsed speech, the most important speech of his life. On it rested the future of his hopes for his sons and the eternal memory of his own greatness in Israel. He wished his once majestically sonorous voice were as it had been twenty summers ago, but what was left would have to do. What it lacked in pure power could be compensated for by range and distinctiveness of timbre. Samuel had spent a lifetime using his voice to get what he wanted, and what he was sure YHWH wanted, and he knew he would not fail today to succeed as he always had.

He would of course first speak in the prophetic voice of YHWH; though the words came through Samuel's throat, the voice was in fact YHWH's own. Thus it had been for nearly everyone's living memory.

"Thus speaks YHWH, the God of Israel."

The crowd tensed in anticipation, as even the crying of infants ceased at the sound of the aged but familiar voice. History was always the place to begin, thought Samuel, as he continued.

"I brought Israel up from the land of Egypt, and I rescued you all from the hand of the Egyptians and from the hand of all the kingdoms that oppressed you."

Why demand some earthly monarch, some head of a new kingdom just like all the other kingdoms around them, thought Samuel? What better way to begin than to remind them all of the absolute and unique mission and power of YHWH whose might was ever-directed toward the saving and prospering of Israel? And these truths were pouring out of the lips of YHWH's favorite and only spokesperson. The people listened gladly to the one they had known and heard their whole lives.

"But you have today rejected your God who is always saving you from your disasters and your distress. Instead you have said, "No!"

No to God, no to God's saving, no to God's rescue.

"Set a king over us," you have said.

King Saul

Samuel said this last with a snarl, sneeringly making fun of such a foolish and ridiculous request in the face of the truth of YHWH's sole kingship. But a king they would have. Oh, yes, a king they would see now. Samuel heard the grumbling rise in the midst of the crowd, but he knew he had them with him, as he had always known it.

"Now, gather yourselves before YHWH by tribe and clan."

Samuel prepared to cast the sacred lots, three cubes of animal bone, six-sided with a different symbol engraved on each side. The roll of the three cubes, and the resulting combination of symbols, would show the prophet, and through him the people, the proper course of action, determined and revealed by YHWH. Given what happened that day at Mizpah, some skeptical Israelites, always speaking in whispers in some tavern or other, wondered whether the sacred cubes had somehow been fixed to give the solution that Samuel had already determined on his own. Whether it was the will of YHWH or the will of Samuel would be much talked of, but whichever was finally true, the outcome was a fateful one for Samuel, Saul, and Israel.

As each tribe gathered together before Samuel, he would cast the cubes on the ground, examine their revelations, and announce the results. In this way the tribe of Benjamin was chosen. This choice brought murmuring to many in the vast crowd, since the notoriety of the Benjaminites was legendary, their bitter memory not much dimmed by the passing years since the cruel murder of the Levite's concubine and the subsequent civil war. But, Samuel shouted, the Benjaminites were chosen this day. Each Benjaminite family paraded in front of the prophet, and the family of the Matrites was chosen by the rolling cubes. Each member of the family of the Matrites, including the family of Kish, moved slowly in front of Samuel. And the cubes spoke again; Saul, son of Kish, was the choice of God!

Cries of joy arose from the Matrite clan, as they realized that one of their own had been chosen king over Israel. It was to be Saul, their huge and handsome kinsman, whom YHWH had selected. Shouts of approval rent the air, along with whoops of pleasure and more than a few taunts against the losing families and tribes. Among the losers, the joy was muted, and in the back of the crowd audible dis-ease greeted the choice. Had not this Saul been a failure in his donkey searching and therefore an untrustworthy guide, even for his own family? And many had heard of his surprising prophetic frenzy, joining with those mad men from the mountains. Some saw that as a sign of Saul's devotion to YHWH, his willingness to humble himself before God, to risk humiliation for a pious connection to the Divine One. Others saw such behavior as deeply suspect. Only fanatics would act like that, they thought. We need a king, a warrior to stand up to the Philistines, not some religious fool, who was subject to pious frenzies at the wrong moments. We of course want our king to be religious, a follower of YHWH, but all things should be done in moderation and good order. Prayers alone would not defeat the hated Philistines, but by necessity the force of arms.

Nevertheless, all the tribes gathered at Mizpah were ready to receive the choice of king from the hand of Samuel, their leader and friend, and from the sure sacred cubes of YHWH whose truth was eternal. Samuel called for Saul to join him at the sacred place and waited for him to emerge from the crowd. After all, he could hardly be inconspicuous for long; his heroic size made that a certainty. The susurration of the great assembly grew as all waited for the man to appear at the front. Just where was he? This was coronation day! Samuel and YHWH had spoken. Any man so chosen would rush to the front of the people to receive the crown. At last, the demands of Israel would be fulfilled, and they would have a king. Confusion ruled the crowd as many called out for Saul; messengers were sent to outlying villages, while others hunted in the streets of the town below.

Samuel, sensing the crowd's growing impatience and rising anger, turned his back on the mob, fell on his aged knees, and cried out to YHWH, "Is the man here?" A hush fell over the assembly to see whether or not YHWH would answer.

Samuel turned back around and announced, with a tiny chuckle, "God says that he has hidden himself among the baggage!"

Pandemonium broke out at this absurd statement. In the baggage, many shouted in derision? The baggage? On the day of your choice as king? What sort of choice is this? What sort of king might this one be?

One loud-mouthed wag in the back shouted, "I thought the surprise about him was that he was among the prophets? It looks like now he is among the bags instead!"

And peals of laughter rang out from every corner, and conversations broke out, questioning Samuel, questioning the sacred cubes, and more quietly, questioning YHWH. Meanwhile, several stout men rushed to the place where all the crowd's equipment had been stored, the camels and donkeys, the food for human and beasts, the extra blankets, the jars of beer and skins of wine. As they approached the tumble of things, suddenly Saul stood up to his full height, towering over the bags and animals, and looking down at the men who had come to get him. The look on his face was peculiar, and the men who brought him to Samuel argued for days about what the look meant.

"He was scared," one said.

"He was defiant, determined not to be king," said another.

"He looked like he did not know quite where he was," said a third.

But they all agreed on one thing; Saul had hidden himself at a time when hiding should have been the very last thing on his mind. He should have marched to the front with energy and power the very moment his name had been called out as the chosen one. The fact of his hiding that day, among the simple objects of everyday life, among the needed accoutrements of daily existence, was never forgotten by anyone who watched the enormous Saul being led from the baggage to the kingship of Israel. Even the jubilant family of the Matrites secretly wondered what sort of king their giant cousin would make.

As Saul finally stood next to Samuel, towering over the tiny, fantastically aged man, the prophet raised his leathered arms for quiet. Slowly, the people hushed.

King Saul

"Do you see the one that YHWH has chosen?" shouted Samuel.

As the people looked at Saul, his extraordinary height, his astonishing beauty, many were nearly swept away in a kind of rapture. Many women blushed in response to lustful urges, wondering what it would be like to bed this spectacular example of manhood. Many men became convinced on the spot that this young giant was just the sort of man needed to confront the Philistines. A roar of approval began to swell, and Saul's ignominious hiding in the baggage was quickly forgotten. But Samuel was not finished with his introduction. Again he called for quiet, and again it fell on the crowd.

"There is no one like him among all the people!"

The response to this statement was a general tumult; roars of "Long live the king!" were heard from many throats. Arms bearing swords, arms dangling with bracelets, hands filled with jars of beer, arms lifting babies for the new king to bless, joy suffused many faces. However, not everyone joined in the chaos. Not everyone had forgotten about Saul's prophetic frenzy, Saul's membership in the tribe of the repulsive Benjamin, Saul's hiding in the baggage when he should have taken control. These thought again about what Samuel had said. "There is no one like him among all the people." Perhaps Samuel said more than he knew, they thought; there is indeed no fool like this one in all Israel! How in Sheol can this man rescue us? And while streams of the new king's followers rushed to the front to offer Saul presents—gossamer carpets, exquisite golden cups, superb sheep and cows, sacks of wine, bowls of fresh flowers—some brought him no present, grumbling that this man was not the king they had in mind.

After the presents were piled high in front of Saul, the new king stepped forward to address his new subjects. But before he could say a word, Samuel stepped in front of Saul and spoke again. In a long and rather rambling speech he outlined the rights and duties of the king, and he made it more than clear that the king did not possess unlimited power, that the king could not make decisions strictly on his own, that the king of Israel was not in fact a king like those kings that were to be found in the other nations. Because YHWH was the true king and would always be the true king of Israel and the whole world. No earthly king was YHWH's rival, and no earthly king would ever be confused with the divine one. Painstakingly, Samuel himself, in a crabbed hand, inscribed these truths on a fresh piece of animal hide, scraped clean and dried for the purpose, and placed it on the altar of YHWH. He then led the great, now silent crowd in a brief worship and demanded that they witness the words just written and follow them to the letter. By this action he implied that the parchment was the real power in the land, and that the author of it, Samuel, with the help and approval of YHWH, remained firmly in control of Israel. And to seal that certainty, Samuel sent all the people back to their homes.

The new king, Saul, watched silent and passive as the prophet performed these various acts of political and religious power. The brief speech he had thought to utter, accepting the kingship, pledging his very life in the service of the people, asking them for prayer and YHWH for aid in the difficult days ahead, was unspoken. Saul doubted that the speech would have been a great one; he was hardly the orator that Samuel had been for so long. Still, it would have been a good thing for the new king to speak; it would have been helpful if the people had heard from their king so that they might know that Saul was going to do his very best to govern with justice, to lead them well in battle, to try in every way he knew to work for peace. But Samuel had stolen the moment; the prophet had given him no chance to connect himself with his people but had laid on them, and on Saul, rules of kingship, none of which Saul had seen or few of which he fully understood. He only knew that the day of his coronation had started and ended very badly.

He had hidden in the baggage, because he had feared that Samuel was going to crown him king, was going to make public what he had done outside Ramah some weeks ago. Saul was still basically uncertain about his fitness for kingship. And though he knew that the ways of YHWH were mysterious, and that the God had regularly chosen unusual people to serve the divine ways, he still was uncertain, hesitant, and deeply fearful. How was he any different from the devious Jacob, the lying Abraham, the sniveling Moses? Would the people now add to the list "the oafish Saul?"

And he was just as deeply distrustful of Samuel, of his motives for making Saul king, of his motives for choosing a king at all. Saul was perhaps not the most astute of the sons of Kish, but he was no fool, despite what some were saying. He noted the look on the prophet's face when he announced to the crowd, pointing a bony finger at Saul, "there was no one like him in all Israel." One did not need to be a learned scribe to recognize double-tongued speech, and though many had taken the words at face value, that Saul was a paragon of the people, and well deserved to be king, Saul had seen the scorn in the eyes and the slightly cruel upturned corner of Samuel's mouth as those words tumbled out. Saul knew that Samuel did not want an earthly king—that was clear enough from his many speeches ridiculing the very idea—and that he felt Saul was a particularly bad choice for king. In short, Saul was a king, created by a man of power who hated kings. Samuel's actions of the day added mortar to Saul's growing edifice of fear and uncertainty. How could he ever be king while Samuel was alive? Now standing alone as the crowd dispersed to their homes at the command of Samuel, Saul resolved to listen to the prophet carefully, but also resolved to be as much of a king as his fears, and Samuel, would allow. "Do whatever your hand chooses to do, for God is with you," Samuel had clearly said. Saul intended to do just that.

The new king gathered his belongings and prepared to return to Gibeah. He might be the king of Israel, but there remained the farm to attend to, animals to feed and water, fields to plow, crops to gather in. Being a king hardly relieved one of the responsibilities of life, and Saul was eager to get out of the limelight of Mizpah and to return to his rural retreat. He longed for the loneliness of his own thoughts, but as he moved to leave, he was joined by several stout warriors, some fifteen or so, men well known in the area for their fighting abilities and their heroism in the many skirmishes with the Philistines. They said nothing, but indicated by their quiet actions that they had decided to follow this new king. Among them was Abner, a seasoned warrior, with facial scars and sword cuts on his massive arms to prove it. His huge sword—for he was a very tall man, too, though still a span less than the enormous height of his king—rested easily against his muscled leg while his armor-bearer carried his leather shield, decorated with portraits of exotic animals incised on its face.

Abner was ready in his life for some new challenges. Hit and run struggles with tiny Philistine patrols were exciting but offered little long-term success. What was needed was a major battle, with all the appropriate preparations—troop recruitment, battle plans, equipment purchase, proper training—that would drive the blasphemers from Israel forever. Abner was betting that this giant of a man, now a giant of a king, would be just the focal point for such an undertaking.

So he joined Saul, as he made his way to Gibeah, and he brought with him some of his best fighters. They would be the core of the army to come, the army of Israel, led by their king, the army of YHWH that would drive their enemies into the sea, back where the creatures had come from in the first place! For Abner and his men, the day of victory seemed closer at hand than it had been in many summers.

But Abner's eager and jaunty steps were not matched by the actions of another group of men who had waited until most of the crowd had left. These were those grumblers who did not believe that Saul was the right choice for king. Among these were some who had first voiced their demands for a king in the face of Samuel, and who had left at first disappointed and furious when the old prophet had refused their request. They had waited impatiently for this day of coronation, and were as eager as Abner to squash the disgusting Philistines like the evil insects they were. But Saul's out of control, so-called prophetic frenzy, his family failures, his membership in the tribe of Benjamin, and most of all his cowering in the baggage on his day of triumph, had convinced them that a terrible mistake had been made. Such a man was not fit to be king of Israel! Such a man was not even fit to be a donkey driver, as his loss of his father's donkeys had shown. They detested Saul, and as the sheep-like crowd had poured forth their presents to the so-called monarch, they had stood at the back of the mob, glaring their fury, muttering their rejection of the whole mess.

And they muttered still, and pointed at Saul and his ominous band of warriors. Abner turned at the sound, and when he saw their obvious hatred, and heard their taunting oaths, he turned to his men and urged them to cut the sniveling rebels to pieces. But without a word, Saul laid a huge hand on Abner's arm and shook his head. He said nothing and did nothing. And though Abner knew that such slights needed action—all must bow to the new king or be destroyed—he and his men stood down, sheathed their swords and turned toward Gibeah. And Abner wondered at this, but for the moment kept his objections to himself.

10

To the east of the Jordan River sat an out-of- the-way village named Jabesh-Gilead. It was founded some years ago on a good water source right at the border between Israel and Ammon. The village had nearly been annihilated during the tribal conflicts begun by the notorious assault on the concubine. (How wide spread were the effects of that wretched event; just like tentacles of the wily and ink-stained octopus did it reach into every part of the land!) But the village had revived with new inhabitants that had moved in from the west.

Nobody knew where the bloodthirsty Ammonites had come from; they were just people from the east, part of the wild desert tribes who were forever rising from the wasted places on the far side of the mountains. How anyone could survive in such places was a mystery. But some decades before, they had established a capital of sorts at Rabbath-Ammon, a small town populated by rough tribesmen, shrewd traders, and the occasional desert tough who fancied himself a leader of people. Such a man was Nahash, so-called king of the Ammonites, although his would-be kingship was hardly recognized by a tenth of the peoples who lived spread out on the eastern slopes of the mountains and at the widely spaced watering holes of the wilderness, leading up to the Euphrates river, the ancient western boundary of the great civilizations of the Land Between the Rivers.

Just about the time when Saul was being crowned publicly at Mizpah, Nahash had tried to press his emerging authority on the village of Jabesh, about three suns north and west of Rabbath, the city Nahash had taken as his own base of operations. Nahash was a rough man, hardened by years in the desert, with wild hair and a scraggly beard to match. He was short, but stocky with tree-stump legs and arms deeply veined with cruelly roped muscles. Over the years of his rise, he had fought, intrigued, and murdered his way to power. On occasion, he would attempt negotiation with those who stood in his way, but in the end swords and blood usually had the last word. His code was victory at all cost, and the cost was inevitably violence and corpses. Having subdued every would-be Ammonite rival, Nahash now risked his rule by besieging Jabesh. As usual, he surrounded the place, cutting off all entry and exit, and waited for them to surrender before they all starved.

Under a banner of safety, the elders of Jabesh came out of their city, and made an offer to Nahash that they hoped would save their village and themselves.

King Saul

"Make a treaty with us, and we will be your slaves."

They felt they had no choice. Nahash had brought a rag-tag army of thuggish killers, numbering over 200, and the glint in their eyes suggested that beer and booty and women were their final goals. It was obviously what the whoreson dogs lived for, as any fool could see. Living slavery was to the men of Jabesh better than rape and slaughter at the hands of these so-called men, so they hoped Nahash would accept their desperate offer. He did, but with a terrible condition. Nahash was never one to give something for nothing.

"I will be happy to make such a treaty with you, but first you all must do one thing. Each of you, men, women, and children, must come out of Jabesh, one at a time, and I will gouge out every one of your right eyes! So, when all of you are maimed and helpless, unable to carry your shields, unable to shoot your arrows straight, unable to see to protect yourselves from attack from your right sides, then the land will feel your disgrace, will feel my power, and will tremble in fear before me. What I will do to you, I will surely do to anyone who dares to confront me!"

In horror, the elders filled the air with screams of anguish and retreated within the walls of the city, telling their fellow citizens what the foul Nahash was asking of them. Wailing and crying rose immediately, as they pictured the torture that awaited them all.

But one of the elders called out for quiet, and said, "Perhaps we can delay this monster long enough to find relief from some place. I suggest we send some messengers throughout Israel from Dan to Beer Sheba, asking if anyone could muster a force to combat these filthy Ammonites. As desert dwellers, they understand the code of honor that allows opportunity to send for help before they slaughter the innocent. It is our only hope."

So he, Mosheh by name, after the lawgiver, went back to Nahash and proposed his plan. Nahash, peering over his knife with which he was cleaning and paring his filthy nails, delayed answer to the plea a long time. Then he waved the knife in the face of Mosheh, and snarled a reply.

"I give you seven days," said the Ammonite, "but if no one comes after seven days, I will heat my iron rods, and you will present yourselves for eye removal, thereby becoming half of what you were before." If this was a stab at dark humor, Mosheh heard nothing of it, though Nahash chuckled through his blackened teeth. Mosheh hurried back to the city.

Twenty messengers were sent across the Jordan, ten going north, and ten south. Seven days was not long to cover the land, but the messengers traveled all day and all night, encompassing as much of Israel as their camels and legs were able. On the third day, one of the messengers reached Gibeah of Saul, and wearily related the deadly danger faced by his people. When the people heard his horrific tale, they wept aloud, wishing they could help their brothers and sisters, but they knew that Jabesh was a world away from them, and they had problems of their own. Besides, they could not possibly get there in time, and there was no one to lead them. So they wailed loudly, and cried to YHWH, and told the messenger that they would pray for him and his people, but that that was all they would be able to do. The messenger silently cursed these cowardly curs and rushed away from the city to search for more helpful souls.

At that moment, Saul was preparing his fields for harvest, and had just come to the end of the field closest to the town. He clearly heard the great sound of anguish rising up from the city and was very curious.

"Why is everyone weeping?"

He unstrapped himself from the yoke of oxen and came closer to hear the story of Jabesh from the people. Saul paused briefly after the story ended and then swung into furious action. The men and women of Jabesh watched in astonishment as Saul cut the ropes off of his oxen, and then with numerous strokes of his gigantic sword, sliced the oxen into many pieces. So quick were his thrusts into the animals, that they made no sound as they died and were dismembered. Saul handed great chunks of the bleeding meat to many of the men standing there, and demanded that they run the length and breadth of the land, shouting to everyone, as they held up their oozing trophy,

"King Saul of Israel commands that everyone who does not join the force of men called out by Saul and Samuel shall have his oxen turned to bloody bits like these you can plainly see!" Of course, those who carried the grisly trophies immediately thought of the awful story of the concubine and her dismemberment as a way of calling Israel together to right what was perceived to be a grievous wrong. Had Saul also remembered the story all knew so well? Had he chosen just this method to announce his first kingly act of leadership as a reminder of that story, casting himself as the avenging Levite, or had he done it to cleanse the people of Benjamin once and for all of the stain of their shame from that event? However Saul intended his demands, people swung into action.

The messengers rushed out of the city, some south, but more northward, since Saul had decided to gather his army at a place called Bezek, a long way north of Gibeah.

Over the next two days, fighting men from all parts of the land brought their swords, shields, and bows to Bezek at Saul's command. The towering king met them there, standing in front of nearly a thousand men from the northern regions—Ephraim, Jezreel, Asher—and several hundred from the southern tribe of Judah who had run nearly two full days to join the force.

In all of their hearing, Saul commanded his messengers, swift runners all, to hurry to the city of Jabesh, nearly an all-day run east across the River Jordan and the mountains, and announce to them, "Tomorrow, by the time of the hottest sun, you will be delivered!"

The new army thrilled to hear these martial words from their new made king, and when the messengers slipped into Jabesh just before midnight, the Jabeshites also sent up very quiet sounds of joy to YHWH, for their deliverance seemed possible after all. Quickly, the elders of the city devised a ruse to make the Ammonites confident of their victory. They sent out their intermediaries to announce that they had failed to find rescue from anyone in Israel, so tomorrow they would turn themselves in to Nahash, and he could do to them whatever he wanted. As they spoke, they noted the irons being heated in the fires, and shuddered. Nahash went to bed, hoping to dream of his triumph to come, including the screams of his victims that would be music to his large and hairy ears.

Saul force-marched his army of 1,500 warriors over night, and upon arriving in the vicinity of Jabesh, divided them into three companies of about 500 men each. Just as the sun slipped above the horizon, at the time of the morning watch, Saul's army struck the Ammonite camp from three sides, overwhelming Nahash's 200 warriors by superior force and by complete surprise. In less than two hours time, as the day's heat was settling on the land, Saul and his men had decimated the Ammonites so completely that no two of them were alive together, only a few stragglers surviving to be bound as prisoners, destined for the slave markets of Shechem. The victory was total, the Jabesh-Gileadites jubilant, the army of Saul, suffering few casualties, ready to follow their king into battle wherever he led.

While the men stripped the corpses to retrieve the booty, and while they found the wine of the Ammonite Nahash, Samuel was carried into the camp on a large and comfortable palanquin. It was a wooden platform, covered in several thick carpets, festooned with golden cloth curtains to blunt the rays of the sun. Four burly men carried it by poles thrust through loops on the four corners. In truth, Samuel hated to be carried around; it was demeaning, calling attention to his age and incapacity, but he knew his days of walking long distances over the hard land of Israel were over. If he were to maintain any control over events, he would need to suffer the indignity of transport.

He had of course heard immediately of Saul's brash act of mutilating his oxen to call the forces of Israel to battle, not half a day after he had done it. He had his spies in every city and village who reported regularly to him concerning anything that had to do with the welfare of the people and land. Quickly he had called for his guards to get the palanquin and had directed them to move toward Bezek as rapidly as they could run. The four men had kept a steady pace, an uncomfortable trot, for nearly all of the journey, arriving in the city before the rising of the moon, well ahead of most of the assembling warriors. Samuel sat silently in his moveable tent, curtains drawn, and listened while Saul summoned the troops, ordered the messengers to tell Jabesh that their deliverance was near, then, peeking through the curtains, watched him lead the troops toward the beleaguered city to certain victory. Samuel had almost admired the decisiveness of the new king, his resolve and conviction everywhere in evidence. In his younger days, Samuel mused, he could hardly have done better. Still, he knew he had to get to Jabesh as soon as he could while the victory was fresh, while the men were flush with success, and while Saul was receiving the plaudits of his soldiers.

King Saul

Samuel drew back the curtains of the palanquin, and was immediately accosted by several leaders of Saul's army, covered with blood and mud, their mouths wreathed in smiles of joy and fury.

"Who are those who said, 'Shall Saul be king over us?' Bring them to us so that we may kill them!"

But before Samuel could respond in any way, the shadow of Saul loomed over both the speakers and the prophet.

"No one shall be put to death today, for today YHWH has brought deliverance to Jabesh!"

It was an act of great magnanimity on the king's part. He had every right to punish those who said he could not be king after his amazing demonstration of royal power and leadership. It was of course easy to be magnanimous with the enemy nearly all dead and the remainder of them bound for the slave markets. But to leave alive those who openly despised and rejected the king on the day of his crowning was perhaps less than wise, however well it played with the victorious troops. To them, not only was Saul every span a king, he was also merciful like the YHWH who had given them victory. The joyous triumphal party was in full spate, as the men drank, stripped the dead, and at least occasionally, between great gulps of beer, offered thanks to their God.

Samuel was frankly amazed. The king YHWH had chosen as an example of the horrors of kingship, the one who was to be an example of all that is most wrong about kings, had surprisingly played the role of king to the hilt. He had been clever, displaying excellent battle tactics, superb preparation, and valiant leadership, rightly receiving the acclaim of the people. In short, Saul had become the king in nearly every sense of the word, and Samuel was deeply troubled.

While the drunken shouts of victory poured forth from every corner of the battle site, Samuel closed his curtains and thought, the chaotic sounds muffled by the heavy cloth. What should he do now? If the gigantic boy continued to find success as a leader in battles, what would stop him from founding his own dynasty of Israelite kings? Where would Samuel's sons and Samuel's memory be then? He could not sit by and watch such a thing happen. YHWH had not had this in mind, Samuel knew, and though he had not heard from YHWH on the matter of Saul's victory, Samuel felt called to act. He needed in some way to blunt the force of Saul's success. But how? Slowly, more slowly than in his younger days, an idea formed in his mind.

He threw back the curtains, and bid two of his bearers help him stand on his own feet. Then he raised his huge voice and called for the soldiers to cease their riotous fun and come to him. Once Samuel's voice had sounded, the men dutifully left off their drinking and looting and moved as one to the gilded litter. Samuel waited for quiet, and then said,

King Saul

"Come; let us go to Gilgal, and there renew the kingship! I anointed Saul first privately before anyone knew he was to be king. Then we all went to Mizpah and crowned him there, though there seemed to be some reluctance on Saul's part."

Samuel could not resist just a small reminder of Saul's hiding among the baggage at Mizpah.

"Now, after this great victory of YHWH, we will all go to the holy Gilgal and with sacrifice and feasting we will crown the glorious Saul again!"

It was after all important that the people see Samuel perform the act of coronation and thereby to put into their mind the clear idea that kingship needed the constant affirmation of the prophet if it was to have any legitimacy at all.

And what better place than Gilgal? It was there that Joshua first led the people Israel after their crossing of the Jordan, and from there that he began the occupation of the land YHWH had promised the ancestors. An ancient ring of stones was there, hence the name that means "stone circle." Gilgal had been a sacred spot long before any Israel existed at all, so it would be perfect as the place where Saul could once again be crowned and where Samuel could have a chance to speak to his people once more about the meaning of kingship, and about his role in its creation and maintenance. Also, it was some two days' journey from Jabesh, the site of Saul's triumph; the trip would offer time for the flush of victory to fade a bit, and in the presence of the awesome holiness of the place, Israel could turn its attention to YHWH, and to YHWH's prophet, away from their new and shining king.

Samuel had chosen the place well, but bid his bearers not to hurry this time as they carried their master south. Time and distance were both in Samuel's favor as he thought carefully about what he needed to do at Gilgal.

The place was indeed holy. It sat on a short promontory, looking over the Jordan River to the east, a brief walk from ancient Jericho, the city of palms, blessed with one of the greatest water sources in the land, pumping vast quantities of the sweetest and purest of water daily since the beginning of human time, and probably long before. The high place commanded a view of Jordan and Jericho as well as the flatter plains in all directions, including the forbidding Salt Sea to the south where nothing lived. Within the circle of stones at the high place rested an Israelite altar, made of undressed rocks, piled carefully on one another up till the height of a human waist. Samuel was carried there, was lifted out of his palanquin, and prepared to lead the sacrifices that preceded the coronation.

But the people would not wait for the proper rites to be completed. They, themselves, literally hundreds of them, demanded that Saul be brought forth even before the chosen animal was killed and burned. They crowned Saul king there at the altar of Gilgal, and then, and only then, offered the sacrifices of peace before YHWH. Exactly when the sacrificial rite ended, the cry of "Long live King Saul" resounded throughout the high place and echoed down the four sides of the hill. And a raucous party began; Saul and all the people of Israel were in a high festive mood. Drinking and singing and dancing were the order of the day, and all joined in with gusto until the sun set and the torches were lighted, giving a sparkling glow to the scene. The drinking and the dancing soon turned to even more sensuous pursuits as couples paired off, seeking darker corners to satisfy ancient calls to pleasure. Loud sounds of singing gave way to moans and cries of joy and lust, as the ways of men and women once more ruled the night.

One man did not join the fun. He did not indulge in great drinking or singing or dancing. He lighted the sacrificial fire, uttered the familiar words to YHWH, and then left the high place to the urges of the people and their king. Samuel knew he had to act and soon. The longer that the king was viewed as the guarantor of safety and of love and of hope, the more difficult it would be for Samuel to remind them of his work on their behalf, of his sons in Beer Sheba, of his deep connections with their God, YHWH. He decided that the morning would be best, but none too early. Many would sleep until the sun was full up, and when they awoke, their heads would throb with the remnants of drink and their bodies would ache from battle and travel and sweaty love in the night. When the sun was straight overhead would be soon enough, he thought. So he waited, sleeping fitfully, and pondered the coming speech.

Finally the time arrived. The camp was well awake, cooking fires were prepared, the smell of bread and meat saturated the air. Stretching bodies exhaled clouds of drunken breath, while slaves brought jars of water from the spring at Jericho with which to wash and cook. Men and women sat together, some still feeling the pleasure of the night between their thighs, others longing for that feeling again. The gentle hum of the morning was everywhere on the high place of Gilgal.

But the familiar great voice now overwhelmed the hum of the morning, as Samuel took his stand next to the altar of YHWH, and addressed the people as he had done so many times before. They always welcomed that voice, the voice that had served them as leader for countless mornings, the voice that had given his very life for them time and again in prayer, in battle, in numerous occasions of teaching and service. All respected Samuel, all were in awe of him, and many, though not all, even loved him. He was a hard man but a fair one, and he spoke for YHWH, the God of Israel. He demanded attention, and the people readily gave it. Though the face and form were withered with uncountable years, the voice retained still a great portion of its former power and energy. And so they listened to their prophet once again.

"For a certainty, I have listened to your voice, to all that you have said to me, and I have crowned for you a king."

All eyes went to Saul, that splendid man, resting easily on a massive smoothed stone. He lolled indolently, comfortably, after a long night of food and drink and his choice of women, all of whom had been anxious to explore the wonders of the new king. Saul lifted his right hand in a small gesture of acceptance of his regal role and smiled politely for his people, sending more than a few young women, and not a few men, into peals of pleasurable giggling. "Yes!" thundered Samuel, demanding their ears and eyes to return to his voice and face. "The king walks before you, while I am old and grey."

Samuel wished that he had arranged for a soothing group of harpists to accompany this part of his speech, but he knew that the wonder and familiarity of his voice itself would probably be sufficient.

"Still, though I am indeed old, never forget that my sons are with you!"

At the mention of Samuel's wasted sons, who had done their best to destroy the hopes of Beer Sheba with their foul behaviors of greed and lust, a dark murmur slipped from numerous throats, as one loud, but unrecognizable voice said, "May your disgusting sons find their wretched way to Sheol today!"

Cruel laughter accompanied the gibe, and Samuel's eyes narrowed; he knew they were right. His sons were no good, not fit for the role he had bred them for, not fit for life at all, he thought grimly. Well, I am still very much alive, he thought, and anger at those evil sons, and at those who knew how bad they are, empowered his next sentence.

"I have walked before you from my youth until this very day."

Samuel used the same verb he had used to describe what the king was doing, that is, "walking before" the people. In fact, it was and always had been Samuel who had walked before them, and was still doing so now. Several voices in the crowd cried out in approval of Samuel's faithful walking before them.

"You have been with us, Samuel. When we were fearful, you prayed; when we sinned, you asked God to forgive."

"Have I not treated all of you with justice and plain-dealing?" Samuel said. "Test me, test me! Speak now against me anything I may have done that was unjust. Tell it right here and now in the presence of YHWH and YHWH's king. Whose ox have I stolen, or whose donkey? Whom have I cheated or oppressed in any way? From whose hand have I accepted a bribe, thus blinding my eyes to what is right?"

Samuel's sons popped into his head as he spoke those words, his terrible sons who were addicted to bribery; he feared that many of his listeners would think of the boys, too, so he hurried on.

"If I have done any of these things, and I swear I have not, I will restore the things taken; I will make full restitution for any slight, however small!"

Samuel pleaded with his richest voice, commanding any whom he had somehow abused to speak now.

The reaction to his call was swift, as many spoke at the same time, "You have not cheated us or oppressed us or taken anything from any of us, Samuel. Why would you say such things to us; why would you bother to raise any such absurd possibility? Your hands are clean; your life is pure; you are a man of YHWH!"

And many more raised their hands to affirm what these speakers had said. Samuel allowed the noise to run its course and to fix in the minds of all those gathered that they believed him beyond any reproach. The sound slowly disintegrated in the air.

"YHWH is witness, and YHWH's king is witness today, that you have found absolutely nothing to accuse me of; my actions have been always clean like the winter's snows."

A quick glance over at Saul punctuated Samuel's inclusion of the king as one of his witnesses to purity. Saul offered a gracious smile, raised his hands to Samuel as a sign of his agreement.

The people nodded vigorously and shouted as one, "YHWH is witness!" But about the king, they said nothing. And so Samuel moved to the thing he had wanted to say from the very start of his speech.

"YHWH is a witness this day, that same YHWH who chose Moses and Aaron and who brought your ancestors up from the land of Egypt."

They all knew the story well enough that Samuel did not have to fill in the familiar details of just how the great exodus had occurred, but it was of course crucial that he remind them that the exodus story stood as the foundation of all discussions of the actions of YHWH for Israel. Out of pure love YHWH had chosen them out of all the nations of the world, so one could never tell that story enough as the basis of Israelite life and hope. However, Samuel had a special reason for reminding them of the central story today, as he was about to make very clear.

> "Stand tall now, because I am about to enter into judgment with you before YHWH who has done righteous deeds for you and for your ancestors since the days in Egypt. Remember what some of those deeds were. When Jacob was called into Egypt by his powerful son, Joseph, everything seemed well. But when Jacob, and then Joseph, and then all the early generations of that family died, our ancestors became slaves just like so many other peoples, and Jacob and Joseph were forgotten by the Egyptians and nearly forgotten by the oppressed Israelites. So YHWH sent Moses and Aaron, who brought them out of the slave pits of Egypt and settled them here in the land YHWH promised. But your ancestors had learned little from the long years in Egypt endured by their ancient relatives and quickly forgot YHWH, their and our God. So God sold them into the power of Sisera, the terrible commander of the army of the Canaanite king, Jabin of Hazor, and after another round of Israelite evil into the power of the king of Moab.
>
> Then that generation of evildoers cried out to YHWH. 'We have sinned, because we have abandoned YHWH, and have served gods of the Philistines and Canaanites around us, Baal gods and Astarte goddesses; please rescue us out of the power of our enemies and we will serve you!' So in response to their admission of guilt, and because of their recognition that only YHWH could finally save them, YHWH sent Jerubaal, Barak, Jephthah, and Samuel, all of whom rescued you from the hand of your enemies on every side. You were safe then!"

King Saul

The familiar history lesson from Samuel was just on the verge of tedium, and many in the crowd were no longer listening with both ears, when Samuel used his own name among the list of the great leaders of the past. More than a few eyes flew open in surprise, since the custom was not to include living persons in such lists, nor to mention your own name in the same breath with these ancient and venerated worthies. If Samuel's goal was to capture their attention, he had been successful.

"But!" A grand pause followed this tiny word, suggesting that the sermon's point was about to appear.

"When you saw that King Nahash of the Ammonites confronted you, you said to me, 'No! We will not wait this time for a savior from YHWH. We will have a king, and we will have him now,' though you know that YHWH, your God, is your only king!"

Saul was listening especially carefully to this part of the speech. Samuel had first mentioned his own name as one of those people who had been chosen by YHWH to rescue Israel, and after sixty winters and more of service to the people few would have disagreed. But then he had implied that Israel had only asked for a king when they were threatened by Nahash. He and Saul and everyone there today knew that was hardly true. Their request for a king had come for many reasons, but the threat of Nahash was not one of them. Samuel himself had twice anointed Saul king at the specific request of YHWH, first privately then publicly. Saul was already king before Nahash reared his ugly head. What exactly was the old prophet playing at, as he embellished and twisted the history they all knew well?

But some in the crowd knew exactly what Samuel had in mind, even if Saul could not immediately see it. If Samuel were one of YHWH's great deliverers, and if under the threat of Nahash, Israel had faithfully cried out for one of YHWH's deliverers, the only living one being Samuel of course, then their demand for a king was nothing less than a rejection of YHWH's kingship in two terrible ways: YHWH as king was usurped by the choice of the earthly king and YHWH's choice of deliverer was rejected by that same earthly king. Samuel had just convicted them all of the most grievous rejection of YHWH, and the very object of that rejection, Saul, had been reduced to a living example of the most appalling apostasy! The gigantic Saul appeared to shrink in the eyes of many that day, and as Samuel continued his speech, the king of Israel, having just won an enormous victory over a dangerous enemy, apparently sealing his kingship over Israel in the process, moved further and further away from the angry prophet. If the tallest man in Israel could be said to disappear into a crowd of his citizens, that is what Saul did that day at Gilgal. His triumph was turning into the beginning of his destruction.

Samuel now had them right where he wanted them.

"All right!"

His aging voice suddenly regained a youthful vigor, and his crooked spine straightened noticeably. All eyes and ears were squarely on Samuel.

"Here is the king whom you have chosen, for whom you have asked."

King Saul

He pointed in the direction of where Saul had been sitting, but the king had disappeared. Samuel was surprised, but the flow of his speech continued like a spring wadi. His sharp emphasis on "you" made it clear that Saul was their choice, not his.

> "Even though YHWH has placed a king over you, all actions finally being YHWH's actions, still you must listen very carefully: if, and I emphasize if, you fear YHWH and serve YHWH, and listen always to YHWH's voice and never rebel against any command of YHWH, and if both you and the king who rules over you will follow YHWH your God in every way, it will be a world of shalom for you. But, and I emphasize the but, if you will not listen to the voice of YHWH, but rebel against any command of YHWH, you can be sure that the hand of YHWH will turn against you and against your king."

Saul, now crouching toward the back of the crowd, could barely believe what he was hearing. This is the same man who some time before had anointed him prince over Israel and had promised him that he could do anything that he decided to do, because God was uniquely with him. Now this same man had just announced that the very action of creating a king was a slap in YHWH's face and that just because they had a king, and just because Saul was that king, all of the king's actions, all the king's decisions were strictly subject to the approval of the commands, the voice, of YHWH. And just who was it who determined what YHWH's will was? Who interpreted the meaning of YHWH's voice? Who explained what YHWH's command was? Was it not Samuel, the prophet? Was it not still all too apparent that Samuel was in reality, if not in fact, the real king of Israel? What was Saul to do now? How was he ever going to be a king? He felt as if his victory over Nahash meant nothing, and he longed for the life on his farm near Gibeah, the steady rhythm of the crops and the animals, the quiet evenings of firesides and stars. How could he be a king while Samuel remained alive? And for the first time, King Saul prayed that Samuel would die.

But Samuel did not die that day at Gilgal. His speech was not quite finished, however devastating its effects had been already. Everyone in the crowd now believed that their request for a king had been wrong, that Samuel, God's spokesman, was furious with them and that he might now do something monstrous to all of them. Terror filled every eye.

"Stand where you are and witness a terrible thing that YHWH will now do right before your eyes! It is today the wheat harvest, the dry season when our crops are secured for the winter ahead. I will now summon YHWH to send thunder and rain, and you will then know and see that the wickedness you have done in YHWH's sight by asking for a king is enormous and unforgivable!"

All eyes moved to the skies that were a dazzling blue. A hush fell over every mouth. Samuel raised his face toward the sky and bellowed something that sounded like a shout of command, but was spoken in a tongue no one living knew. Suddenly, as if the bowels of Sheol were disgorging its dead, the blue sky became black, lightening ripped the thickening clouds, followed by thunder such as had not been heard since the plagues of Egypt. And the rain came down in sheets, instantly turning the dry ground to mud, and then streams of water. The wheat crop was destroyed, and the people of Israel were filled with a horror beyond any they had ever felt. Samuel had demanded that they fear YHWH, and it was obvious at that moment that all feared YHWH, and, just as obviously, they feared Samuel, too.

Their feet covered in mud, their hair plastered to their heads by the pounding rain, their garments stuck to their shivering bodies like the skin of a donkey, they pleaded with Samuel to do something, to make the deluge stop.

"Pray to YHWH your God for your servants, so that we do not die! You are right, Samuel. We have added to our many sins this last one of demanding a king for ourselves!"

The prophet, hair and beard streaming water, eyes wild with religious fervor, looked at them with little recognition of their existence at all. He seemed to be someplace else, almost as if he and YHWH were somehow together, or as if YHWH had come to the earth, along with the rain, and had entered Samuel's crabbed body. The divine light flashed from his eyes, as he said,

> "Do not be afraid! You have done an evil thing, and it is good for you to confess it. I repeat what I said earlier: do not stop following the way of YHWH. Serve YHWH with your whole heart. Stop turning your attention to empty things that are always useless. Be assured that YHWH will not finally toss Israel aside but not for anything you have done or not done, but because YHWH was pleased to make you a special people. Also, you are and have always been my people, too. Far be it from me that I should ever sin by ceasing to pray for you. And I will continue to instruct you in the good and correct way. Only fear YHWH, for you have just once again witnessed YHWH's vast power. Serve YHWH faithfully with all your heart; remember the great things YHWH has done for you. But—need I remind you—if you still act wickedly, you will be swept away, like the crop of wheat, like the faithless ones in the days of Noah, like the Egyptian oppressors, both you and your king!"

As Samuel finally concluded his long speech, he looked around for Saul but could not see him. But Saul could see Samuel. The king had during the supernatural storm hidden underneath an outcropping of rock behind the high place but still within sight and hearing of Samuel. Saul watched Samuel throughout the storm, even while all the others were cowering in terror. Saul was not quite certain how Samuel had brought on the storm, but he did not doubt that Samuel and YHWH had some special bond that Saul would never have with his God. But he did know one thing for certain; he still was the king of Israel. Both Samuel and YHWH had determined it, and the people of Israel had confirmed it twice in public events at two holy shrines. As the storm slowed, and the torrent of rain became a light mist, Saul stepped out from under the rock. Just before he turned to go home, his eyes locked with Samuel's eyes. Neither man blinked for a long moment. Saul stretched to his full height, while Samuel's mouth turned up slightly in a brief smile. A token of friendship, thought Saul? Hardly. Saul knew that Samuel was his implacable enemy. Saul smiled slightly in return. Hatred, thought Samuel? Perhaps, but it made little difference to the prophet. He had reduced Saul to insignificance this day at Gilgal, and though he still might be king in name, his power was now subject to Samuel's own, and to YHWH's, for as long as he, Samuel, lived. And as ancient as he was, he planned to live a very long time.

11

The next years in Israel were a combination of fear, confusion, and anger. The Philistine threat did not subside; on the contrary, the peoples of the sea continued their relentless pressure on the western flanks of the land. Villages of the borderlands like Keilah, Socoh, and Aijalon were overrun on several occasions by Philistine warrior bands. And just as often the villages were retaken for Israel by soldiers aligned with Saul. The powerful Abner was especially active in these western skirmishes, and though he had great hopes for the towering Saul, he was not altogether clear whether the king was ever going to unite the people in a mighty force, significant enough to deal with the Philistine enemy once and for all. For Abner, as for many Israelites, the political situation had not been clarified after that mysterious day at Gilgal when Samuel had both reaffirmed Saul's kingship and had then immediately made a mockery of Saul as king, or so the prophet's words had sounded to many there on that day. Abner was a soldier, and not a theologian, and as such he cared little for the hair-splitting of priests and the details of sacrifice. He wanted support for battle; he needed troops and equipment and if prayers were effective for his men he would take them, too. Was Saul really the king or was Samuel still the power in the land? It had been nearly four winters since Gilgal, and the answer to that question was no more certain now than it had been then.

Saul had returned to Gibeah, to his first wife, Ahinoam, his second wife, Rizpah, to his eight children, and to his beloved farm. His sons were four: Jonathan, the eldest, nearly as tall as his father before he was twenty, Abinadab, as handsome as Saul, though not nearly as tall, Malchishua, who idolized his older brother, Jonathan, and Ishbaal, his youngest. He also had two daughters, Merab and Michal. Rizpah had two sons with Saul as well: Armoni and Meribaal (sometimes called Mephibosheth). The fact that Saul had named two of his sons using the hated name of "Baal," that filthy foreign deity of the ancient and irritating Canaanites, had always caused muttering in the village; many people simply refused to say the disgusting name of that so-called god out loud. Not that "Mephibosheth" ("shameful borders") was much better, but at least the dangers of idolatry were lessened by the nickname.

Abner and his eager warriors continued to look for the Saul who had roused the troops and defeated that animal, Nahash, so decisively with brilliant tactics and lightening decisions. But that Saul had been nowhere to be found these past days.

King Saul

While the Philistines threatened, Saul plowed. While the infidel brazenly looted Israelite villages, killed Israelite men and children, raped Israelite women, Saul built extensions on his house, a private room for him and Ahinoam, another for Rizpah and her sons, larger spaces for his other sons, more and bigger barns for his increasing herd of livestock.

Even the incredibly old Samuel, still living in Ramah, who had lived now longer than anyone had ever experienced, save the pathetic priest Eli, nearly four score and ten winters, had been quiet after Mizpah. He seemed content to live out his days in prayer to YHWH, leading daily sacrifices at Ramah's high place, regaling local children with stories of the old days, of the Ark of the Covenant, of his call in the Temple of Shiloh, of his early battles with and defeat of the Philistines, and most of all of his absolute faithfulness to YHWH, that part of his story that always led to a sermon demanding trust in the God in all things. The children and grandchildren of Samuel's foul sons, whom they had sired on YHWH knew how many women, had for some time now lived with the old man, since Samuel had finally realized that nothing good could ever come from them in Beer Sheba. When questions about his own sons arose, he very quickly changed the subject; Joel and Abijah were apparently still in that village in the far southern deserts, but whether they acted the parts of leaders of the town, whether they had been deposed in fury, or whether they were still alive at all, were subjects never broached in Samuel's presence. He was more often than not very sad as he talked, his eyes not nearly as sharp as once they were, his huge voice reduced at times to little more than a croaking whisper. His hair and beard were all white and thinning noticeably. He had only now to wait for death, for his trip to Sheol whence there is no return. What small pleasures he found now were in these young men and women and their children, and the conviction that he had saved them from corruption at the hands of his own lost boys. As Israel was still under threat, Samuel began to think that it was simply no longer his concern; it was far past time for his death and he could do little more than wait for it to come.

But Abner could not wait any longer, or was simply sick to death of waiting. He spent much time around Saul's farm, hinting that the time for action had come, pleading with Saul to leave his plow and to galvanize the Israelites to strike the Philistines a mortal blow so that all Israel could have the pleasure that Saul appeared to have of the comfort of a successful farm and a loving family.

But Saul was reluctant. He sat on many nights with Jonathan, Abner and his young fighters, drinking beer, gazing at the countless stars, listening to the restive warriors argue the case for war. But Saul had seen enough war and death to last a thousand lifetimes. His easy victory over Nahash, his army's slaughter of the Ammonite soldiers, had left a lasting impression on Saul. More than once he had dreamed of those dying soldiers, their arms and legs severed from their bodies, the blood trickling or oozing or gushing from wounds that would never close. But it was their screams that filled Saul's head, those piercing shouts that would be their last sounds, those high-pitched squeals, so like the cries of young girls at play, issuing from men's lips that would never again form understandable words. It was obscene, how living men could be reduced to such lifeless things by the swing of an ax, the rush of a well-placed arrow, the thrust of a gleaming sword. Surely, YHWH of Israel took no pleasure in the death of men, whether they were Israelite, Ammonite or Philistine.

Abner completely disagreed with this vapid philosophizing, and though he recognized Saul as his king, and began each speech to him with "my lord" or "my king," he believed that YHWH had chosen Israel for special work in the world, had picked them out from the slave pits of Egypt to be YHWH's special people. And since YHWH was the only true God in the world, the maker of all things in the world, anyone who claimed some other god, like the Philistine Dagon, or the Ammonite Shemesh, or the Canaanite Baal, could not be allowed to spread their lies any further in and around Israel. The only thing to be done with such people was to obliterate them, and the sooner that was done the sooner YHWH would be honored and the sooner there would be a lasting peace. No squeamish musings of an inactive king were going to blunt the furious righteousness of YHWH's champion, the brave Abner. Night after fruitless night, the budding general would plead his case with his king, and night after night, Saul would sit, pensive, quiet, undecided, in Abner's eyes the very shell of a monarch. But finally this night he had had enough of this infuriating waffling.

"My lord," cried Abner, "I cannot believe what I am hearing from you, if you will forgive my disagreement. The cruel Ammonites, lead by that beast, Nahash, had to be dealt with, and we did what needed to be done. These monstrous Philistines are no better and deserve the same blunt and swift destruction. They have killed us and robbed us and raped and abused us, and we have had enough. My king, it is past time for us to form an army and give these impious butchers the sharp end of our swords!"

By the end of this speech, Abner was looming over the seated Saul, his voice raised to a shout, the veins of his neck bulging with the exertion of his address, his face red in the torchlight. All those there shouted in agreement with their fighting leader who was fast becoming a general over what he hoped would become an expanding army.

Saul stood in order to regain the advantage of his height. He looked through the darkness at the eager faces of the men. Most especially he looked in the face of Jonathan and noted the blood lust of the battle in his eyes. And Saul wearily knew he could delay what had to be done no longer. He gazed longingly at the now-peaceful farm, the quiet animals, the soft birdcalls of the moonless night, and thought of his wives sleeping in the nearby house and of his other children. In his aching heart, he knew that what he was about to say would lead to much blood and much death. He had fooled himself to imagine that he could live out his days on his farm, surrounded by those he loved and who loved him. May the day be cursed when old Samuel chose him to be king or prince, or whatever he was, over Israel! But if I am king, then I will be king. Though the king looked as if he had thought not at all about war, these eager soldiers were mistaken. The thoughts of war had often been on his mind, and the details of how such a war might be fought had skittered in and out of his heart on more than a few occasions. That terrible option now seemed inevitable.

Fixing Abner with a face like iron, Saul said, "All right, if it is to be war, then war it will be to the full! I want three thousand men mustered as soon as possible. Two thousand will go with me and Abner toward Michmash, north and east, and Jonathan will take the other one thousand with him to Geba, further on in the mountains. We know that there is a temporary Philistine garrison at Geba which they are trying to make more permanent as a way to catch us between that group of fighters and their larger forces moving up from the west. They hope to crush us in a scorpion's claw, the better to sting us with their blasphemous tail. But they will soon see that there is poison in the Israelite tail, too! Send messengers now, tonight, and summon all warriors to meet us at the assigned places. May YHWH give us victory!"

A frenzy of activity began, as messengers scurried away and warriors ran to gather their weapons, some to meet in smaller groups to discuss strategy, others to saddle their donkeys and camels to go to the staging areas chosen for battle.

Jonathan began to join a group of young fighters when Saul stopped him by grabbing his arm.

"My son! I see the excitement in your eyes, your eager desire to spill Philistine blood. Take care that they do not spill yours! You have much life left, and I desire to witness your living of it."

Jonathan rushed off, saying, "Do not be afraid, father. We fight for YHWH, who is always our champion. YHWH will give us the victory over our enemies!"

Saul watched the retreating figure of his son. He was proud of his eagerness but saddened by the real possibility of his death. But there was little he could do now; the jackal of war was loose and would go unbound until there was some resolution of the fight. And whether the mysterious YHWH would give victory was not at all certain to Saul, however convinced these anxious men appeared to be.

Saul lead his two thousand men toward the pass at Michmash in order to cut off any possible retreat by the Philistines who were camped at Geba, a higher stony outcrop above the pass. Meanwhile, Jonathan led his one thousand soldiers up to the camp under cover of the moonless night. The surprise was complete. The Philistines, no more than sixty warriors, were completely unprepared for an assault, having become complacent in the face of Saul's inactivity. Their sentries were half-asleep, their swords and shields askew on the ground, their fires' embers still aglow, lighting the way right to the camp. Jonathan and his men had only to stand silently and grimly around the entire camp, and the Philistines surrendered with no loss of life, no wounds, on either side. They were tied up and their equipment, food and drink confiscated. The sixty or so Philistines would make lovely slaves, fetching good prices in the flesh markets close by. Jonathan thought how sweet it would be to take the battle gear gained in trade for these Philistine scum and kill other Philistine soldiers in future fights.

King Saul

News of Jonathan's easy victory soon reached Saul and his men near Michmash, nearly as quickly Philistine spies had reported the defeat and dissolution of the Geba garrison to the main Philistine city of Gath. They were enraged and alarmed at the loss of their outpost, a location that had taken some moons to situate and fortify. They had used Geba as a foothold in the heart of Israel, both as a means to announce to Israel that there was no place off limits to Philistine power and as the first stage of their future complete annexation of Israelite land. With the loss of the garrison, and all of its men, the Philistine plans had been thwarted and they had been humiliated by the upstart mountain people. Such an outrage could hardly go unpunished! The various city armies of the Philistines were mustered at Gath over the next few days. Thousands of warriors joined together, bringing with them horses and chariots. When the entire force was gathered outside the walls of the city, their number seemed no less than the sand on the shore of the Great Sea. Gath's king, still Achish, a man more given to art and food than to war, nevertheless stood on the city walls and charged the troops.

> "Men of Philistia! The time has finally come when these fleas, these moun-tain goats, these Israelites who hide in caves and holes in the ground like the locusts they are, need to be taught a lesson! They have destroyed our post at Geba, and they have enslaved our brave fighters there. Punishment for this foul deed must be swift, certain and devastating. Ride like the wind! Push your horses and chariots deep into their land and destroy them. Kill them where they stand! Root them out of their hiding places and annihilate them all, men, women, children and beasts. Take what spoil you can but leave no trace of these Israelites on the land. Their houses and fields will be ours, but all memory of them as a people we will bury in that soil forever!"

It was a grand speech, written for Achish by one of his scribes who had a way with martial words. Its effect was like the lightening on a stormy sea. The army turned to the east with loud shouts and the clank of iron swords and chariots. In actuality, of course, all knew that those fearsome chariots, so splendid on the flatlands of the shore, were of little use in the rocky lands of Israel. But they were a magnificent sight from the walls of Gath, arranged in ordered rows, lurching east with the phalanx of soldiers. The Gaddite citizens were overcome with the power of their army, with the terrible beauty of the battle flags of each city's troops, and with the prospect of the great vic-tory to come. For who could stand against such a force? The pathetic Israelites, with their rag-tag army, lead by a peculiar king, surely would be no match for this astonish-ing host now heading inexorably toward them.

Their destination was Michmash, where they had heard Saul had mustered the main force of Israel. However, Saul, immediately after he had heard that Jonathan had destroyed the camp at Geba, had ordered his son to bring his troops and join him and his army at Gilgal. He had also made a decree that all other able men of Israel should come to the sacred place, too, for the final struggle with the Philistine hoard, he hoped, was now to begin. Many soldiers had come, but news of the vast size of the Philistine force had made many reluctant to join. Then, too, it was well known that Saul, though king in name, had not offered much leadership for Israel over the past few summers but had preferred the farming life at Gibeah to the ongoing needs of a threatened people. Why should they come at Saul's behest to risk their lives against the terrifying and monstrous Philistines who were noted for their cruelty and beastliness? On the other hand, life under Philistine rule might be harsh, yet they were masters of the iron trade and had successfully colonized the coastlands, building impressive cities and sustaining an expanding population. The uncertainties of Israel, the confusion of leadership, the diminishing opportunities for trade with the rich Philistines, not to mention the inability of Israel to establish stable communities in the harsh territory of the highland mountains, made Philistine rule an intriguing, possibly lucrative, option. So, many did not join Saul at Gilgal.

For those who did come, one look at the Philistine thousands, winding their snake-like way up the passes into Israel caused them to flee further east, even crossing the Jordan River, seeking safety in Gad and Gilead. Those who did remain at Gilgal with Saul, searched frantically for places to hide in the area, behind huge rocks, in deep caverns, in abandoned water cisterns, even in old tombs full of ancient bones and molding clothes. All the Israelites, those in hiding and those who fled Gilgal entirely, were terrified of the battle to come, seeing no hope at all of survival, let alone victory.

Saul too was very much afraid of what was to come, and when he witnessed the people's terror at the sight of the Philistines, he knew he must turn to YHWH for help. Though he remained uncertain about the God, unclear about YHWH's activities and demands, Saul plainly knew that YHWH had wanted him to be king—Samuel's public double crowning of him had made that fact certain. So he imagined that Gilgal, the place of his most recent kingship renewal, was the right place to come to begin the struggle for Israel's future. He had never forgotten what Samuel had said to him on the occasion of his private anointing those years before: "Go to Gilgal, and I will come there to offer the right sacrifices to YHWH. You shall wait for seven days until I come to you to show you what you must do." He remembered the words all right, but their exact meaning had not been clear then and they were not clear now. He should wait for Samuel, and he should wait for seven days. But the old prophet had also added, "until I come." Would he come within the seven days, or might he come on the eighth day or the ninth, or the fiftieth? How long must Saul wait?

He waited for the seven days, the time specifically commanded by Samuel. The wait was an agony for Saul. Each day more soldiers slipped away from him. Sometimes individually, more often in groups of twos and threes. His force, once numbering upwards of five thousand, began to diminish rapidly as fear and confusion depleted the will and softened the spine of the would-be fighters. The time to strike was now, but Saul would not go to battle for YHWH without proper sacrificial respect; he believed that ritual demand if he believed anything about YHWH. Each day, he hoped for

Samuel's appearance. He set guards at every possible way that Samuel might come to Gilgal. With the Philistines encamped at Michmash, north and west of Gilgal, Saul knew that Samuel would have to travel the longer southern road from Ramah to avoid a possible Philistine advanced patrol. And, of course, his travel would not be quick, since he needed to be carried in his traveling tent by four men who would need much rest along the way. But as each sun set, Samuel did not come and more soldiers left the camp. When the seventh day dawned, and there still was no sign of Samuel, Saul's army had diminished below the initial three thousand he had first called to Michmash. Jonathan was impatient to bursting, like a wineskin in the sun. Abner was beside himself and had to harangue and threaten his anxious men to keep them in line. The grand confrontation with the enemy that seemed to be imminent seven days ago was now promising to be a slaughterhouse for Israel rather than a triumph.

But Saul could not be moved to change has mind about waiting for Samuel to offer the sacrifice.

"He is the high priest, the man closest to YHWH in all the land," shouted Saul at Abner's latest attempt to get the king to act before it was too late. "Speak to me no more of this, Abner. We will wait!"

Abner left the presence of Saul in disgust and wondered whether his reservations about the hulking king had been right after all. The seventh day dragged by with the Philistines continuing to ready their army for the struggle, though confused about the lack of Israelite activity. More and more Israelite soldiers snuck out of the camp, until barely a thousand remained. Those old soldiers who stayed, and who knew the ancient stories of Israel's glorious past, told one another of the judge Gideon who had defeated an overwhelming force of Midianites with no more than 300 warriors who had no weapons save clay jars and lanterns along with a few loud trumpets. Such stories were designed to buoy up sagging spirits, but as what was left of Saul's army gazed grimly at the Philistine host, an army that had not diminished by so much as one man, ancient stories seemed cold comfort indeed.

As the sun went down on the seventh day, and no report of Samuel was heard, Jonathan asked to speak to his father. He found Saul sitting alone in his tent, his colossal head in his hands, his eyes staring blankly at the cup of beer balanced precariously on an uneven rock on the floor of the tent.

"Father," said Jonathan, and Saul started in surprise, returning to the tent from a place far away.

"Yes, my son," he whispered listlessly, not caring whether his son heard the reply or not.

"You must act, my father. The army has decreased four-fold, and those who are left are in no mood to fight and die against a force many times its size. That wretched Samuel is not coming, no matter what he promised those years ago. Surely you are aware that that foul prophet has no love for you. He wanted his own legacy in the land, but his disgusting sons thwarted his plans. So he crowned you as a way to satisfy the longings of many in Israel, but he took no pleasure in the deed and has tried in every way to undermine your work as king. Father, his day is past. His fantastic age is fully upon him, and the future of Israel is now in our hands. It is up to us to defeat these Philistines with or without the nagging Samuel. Act now, for soon there may be no Israel for you to rule."

Saul was silent for a time, weighing his son's words carefully.

"I must sacrifice to YHWH," he finally said. "Battle for YHWH without sacrifice to YHWH will lead to disaster and defeat. Samuel has always led the sacrifice, and he must do so today!"

Saul stood up, his head brushing the top of the tent, as he towered over his son. Jonathan refused to drop his gaze from the eyes of his father, and replied,

"But you are king, father; he is merely an old man with darkening eyes and frail limbs who must be carried everywhere. You are king, prodigious and powerful, whose immensity of body and heart are inspirations to your people. Play the role of the king you are! You must act now, and I will always stand beside you!"

Jonathan held the flap of the tent open so that Saul could exit. But Saul hesitated still.

"If I offer the sacrifice, will YHWH accept it from my hand?"

"YHWH made you king; surely as king YHWH will readily receive your sacrifice!"

Saul was convinced by this, and strode out of the tent.

As he appeared, silhouetted against the blazing sunset, a great cry rose from the army.

"Saul has come," they shouted. 'The king has come to lead us once again, and his glorious son, Jonathan, is by his side!"

Energy returned to the soldiers, a deep spirit that led to that most important commodity for any group of people: hope. Saul called out to one of his retainers,

"Bring the burnt offering here to me along with the offerings of peace. We will honor our God and then we will defeat our enemies!"

With enthusiasm and joy, the whole army followed Saul up to the ancient high place of Gilgal, that same place where Saul was crowned king among them. The un- blemished goat was dragged bleating and crying by two young holy men, its stick-like legs grabbing the dirt desperately for a hoof-hold against forward movement. But in vain. Upon reaching the altar, Saul began the ritual, thanking YHWH for great deeds in the past, for provisions for the present, and for uncounted hopes for the future of the land. All echoed Saul's "amen," and expertly he killed the goat with one pass of the knife. By himself, the king hoisted the goat over his head, its lifeless body seeming to float high over the crowd in Saul's hands, and tossed the carcass onto the flaming altar. The peace offerings of grain and corn were added to the blaze. Saul called for silence, and the entire army hushed. The familiar smell of the sacrifice wafted over them as they all fixed their eyes on the sky, silently imploring YHWH to hear them and to accept the sacrifice so freely given by the king and his subjects. Many felt a peace that had eluded them for days.

The silence was shattered by a voice as familiar as the smell of the roasting goat.

"Saul," bellowed the voice!

Samuel's palanquin had appeared at the edge of the hill and was placed down on the first flat spot near the altar. The wizened face, yellow now with age, filled with dark spots such as the very old possess, was nearly red with fury, as the veins of the flapping neck jutted out like camel ropes.

"Saul!" the prophet repeated.

The king calmly moved toward the palanquin to meet the prophet and to welcome him to the camp of Israel. Without a greeting of any sort, without asking to be helped out of his traveling carrier, Samuel spluttered,

"What in Sheol have you done?"

The king's calm response to this furious question was unexpected. Many of the soldiers wondered how they would have responded to an apoplectic question hurled at them from the mouth of God's prophet? They listened to their king with wonder.

"When I watched the people slipping away from me, and saw that you had not come within the appointed time, and that the dreaded Philistines were mustering their army at Michmash, I said to myself, 'The Philistines will fall upon me at Gilgal, before I have entreated YHWH's good favor.' So I took it upon myself to offer the burnt offering." It was a splendid reply, all thought, who heard it that day. The facts were clear. The time of battle had drawn close as the Philistines were about to force the issue, and the army of Israel was dwindling, mostly out of fear and also out of frustration at the too-long delay. Saul had dutifully waited the full seven days for the prophet-priest to come to Gilgal and to offer the sacrifice. But he had not shown up. So the king of Israel, the chosen one of Samuel and YHWH, had taken it upon himself to do what needed to be done, and had done so out of deep religious devotion. No one could fault the actions of Saul in this matter, no one!

But all who were there that day were quite wrong. Samuel found fault with everything that had happened and proceeded to assault Saul in the most shocking ways. It was on that day at Gilgal, in the face of the immediate threat of Philistine attack, that Samuel began his complete rejection and humiliation of the king of Israel, that king he himself had created. Samuel asked to be lifted out of his palanquin, and standing on his feet now, with the help of two of the carriers, he looked up at Saul through his dim eyes, and shouted through his cracked lips.

"You have played the fool!"

He used a word that was the complete opposite of wise actions, right behaviors, or laudatory ways. In effect, he had just branded Saul, the king of Israel, a dolt with the brains of a donkey.

"You have not obeyed the commandment of YHWH your God, that was so clearly commanded of you!"

King Saul

And with that Samuel labeled Saul a blasphemer, a religious apostate, who knew what YHWH wanted but who deliberately had not done it. In two biting sentences, the prophet had called the king fool and heretic!

Only Saul knew how unfair and false both charges were. Samuel had based his charges on his own memory of his and Saul's first meeting those summers ago at Ramah. Saul had not remembered all Samuel had commanded him to do: to meet men with goats and bread, to fall into a prophetic frenzy with the wild prophets of the mountains. But he had remembered word for word about the sacrifice at Gilgal: to wait seven days for the prophet to come to tell him what to do. That is what Samuel had said to Saul alone at Ramah, and Saul had done it all, down to the last tau. And he also remembered clearly what Samuel had *not* said that day. He had in fact not mentioned YHWH a single time, save when he said that God was with him in all that he decided to do. No! Saul was not following YHWH's commands in his actions; he was following Samuel's commands, and apparently those commands had been given a new interpretation over the time since they first were uttered. Saul had waited seven days, the time expressly appointed by Samuel; he could hardly be accused of not following that command to the letter. But that is exactly what the prophet was now saying!

Saul's head swam as he tried to focus on the remainder of Samuel's assault on his actions, as he tried to remind himself that he had done nothing wrong in all this.

"But for this, YHWH would have established your kingship over Israel forever. But now that kingship will not continue, because YHWH has searched for a man whose heart is just as YHWH's heart, whose will is YHWH's will, whose goals are YHWH's goals. YHWH has already appointed him prince over the people, because you have not listened to what YHWH commanded you!"

With a slight movement of his eyes, Samuel signaled to those holding him erect that he wanted to get back into his carrier. Without a sound they lifted the old man up and returned him to the palanquin. Then all four carriers grabbed the poles thrust through the four corners of the conveyance and trotted away from the high place.

The hill was wreathed in silence. Saul and the army were stunned. Samuel had called Saul fool and heretic, had claimed that after his kingship there would be no more Saulides on the throne of Israel, and had said that YHWH had already chosen a successor to the king. Jonathan looked at his father in horror. Was he a fool? Hardly! It was Jonathan who had urged the king to take charge of the disintegrating situation, and the king had done so with energy and commitment. Saul was decidedly no fool. Heretic? Of that Jonathan was less sure. He had not heard what the prophet had first said to Saul. Perhaps Samuel had specifically warned the new king against offering sacrifice; perhaps Samuel had warned Saul against any number of acts that had been direct warnings from YHWH? But what effects would such actions have, however evil in Samuel's eyes, on future prospects for Saul's sons, especially for Jonathan, his eldest son? And just who was this mysterious "prince" that YHWH had chosen? Where was he? When had this choosing occurred? When had the ancient prophet left his house in

Ramah to make such a choice? Could he be talking about one of his own sons, Joel or Abijah, the "Beasts of Beer Sheba," as they were now universally called? Maybe Samuel had found a way to get one of these creatures on the throne of Israel after all.

Saul had wanted to respond to the ridiculous things he had just heard from Samuel. He was forming the right reply as the man had been carried away. Saul began to rush after the disappearing litter, but sensed any reply he might give the furious prophet would count for nothing. He wanted to shout that Samuel had said nothing about YHWH in his first commands to Saul. He wanted to say that he had in any case broken not one of the commands that Samuel had set for him. He had been a king; he had led the people to a great victory over the Ammonites; he was about to engage the hated Philistines in a battle for YHWH; he had waited the time Samuel said to wait. As for this other prince, now the new chosen one of YHWH, Saul thought Samuel was bluffing. He imagined that there was no other prince, that Samuel had invented him in order to make it more possible to reject Saul, and perhaps to force Israel to accept one of his own sons as king, as a better alternative to the fool and heretic who was currently their king. The whole scene at the high place at Gilgal had been a show, an act put on by Samuel who had always been a fine actor with an actor's voice and an actor's exquisite timing. Was it not amazing that Samuel had appeared at Gilgal right after Saul had offered the sacrifice, at the very beginning of the eighth day? He had crowned Saul king, and now he had uncrowned him, and had branded him fool and blasphemer at the same time. Oh, it had been a successful play all right; it had worked to perfection for the wily old monster. But he had neglected one thing; for better or for worse Saul was still king, the only visible king that Israel had. And the Philistines were still an immediate threat, their army still encamped not far from where Saul and his men were. He still had an army to lead, a battle to fight, and Samuel or no Samuel he intended to do just that.

12

Saul turned with fresh resolve and demanded that all the troops left on Gilgal present themselves for battle. After all were mustered at the high place, Saul counted some 600 men. Samuel's absurd delay, followed by his stinging rebuke of the king's actions, had done their worst as many more Israelites had deserted the camp. Saul quickly decided that remaining at Gilgal, so close to the huge Philistine army, was dangerous in the extreme, so he force-marched his remaining troops to Geba, the former camp of the Philistines, liberated by Jonathan some time before. He did this under cover of darkness, so that the army of the Philistines stayed in Michmash, unaware for several days that Saul and his men were no longer within their easy reach. Once they discovered that Israel had abandoned their camp, the Philistines sent out three patrols of ten men each to find them. One group headed due north from Michmash to Ophrah, another went far west toward Beth Horon, near the border of Philistia at Aijalon, and the third went south and east toward the Salt Sea. They failed to look in the place that might have been the most obvious, that is, their own former encampment at Geba, only a short way south and west of Michmash.

So the army of the Philistines spread itself through the hills around Michmash, and established a more permanent garrison at the pass. This pass was a gateway to the plain of the River Jordan, and could serve an important strategic purpose in a later struggle to conquer that plain and the cities beyond the Jordan. And with this move, the Philistines began a significant change in their tactics, since their vast superiority in numbers had not given to them the complete victory they craved. Hence, it seemed far easier to them to avoid direct, big-army confrontations with the Israelites, and focus instead on skirmishes here and there, leading to the creation of outposts throughout the land. Soon, there would be so many of these outposts that Israel would be effectively surrounded within and without, and the Philistines would simply annex the whole of the land as their own. This tactic was in part necessitated by the very hilly terrain of the central highlands, places were Philistine iron chariots, the weapons most feared by Israel, were not effective. The passes through the mountains were too narrow, the ground far too uneven for the chariots to operate. Time was on the Philistine side. They had a significant and growing base of operation on the sea coast, easily defensible by their ring of large cities facing east and protected by the vastness of the Great Sea on the west. In contrast, Israel was separated by the very hills in which they lived; unity was extremely difficult due to the isolating hill country. In effect, the terrain that saved them from annihilation at the same time made unified action nearly impossible. So the Philistines had decided to act slowly, deliberately, as they infiltrated the land.

It was again Jonathan who saw clearly what the enemy was about and who decided to act against them. He thought the Philistines were fools not to take advantage of their superior numbers; a great thrust into Israel with the full force of their army could have decimated the puny Israelite forces, making their defeat inevitable. But Jonathan also knew that Achish, the king of Gath, the leader of the Philistine forces, was a cautious man who deplored death and bloodshed and would prefer a slow, less dangerous course of action. He was certain that Achish was the reason that the large Philistine army had dispersed and become many much smaller forces throughout Israel. Jonathan decided to test the resolve of one of these outposts, and the one he chose was the one he knew best, the post at Michmash. The myth of the invincibility of the Philistines had begun to grow among the Israelites, and Jonathan took it upon himself to give the lie to that myth as soon as possible.

He was resting for a brief time with Saul and the 600 soldiers who had escaped Gilgal and had gone to the village of Geba, south and west of Michmash pass. After two uneventful days at Geba, Jonathan felt it was time to strike.

He whispered to his armor bearer, his personal body guard, "Let's go see what these Philistines are really made of; I suggest a short trip to their camp."

The armor bearer, Ephron by name, a distant relative of a famous Hittite land owner of the same name who had sold the first piece of the promised land to Abram many years before, was shocked that Jonathan had decided to act in this dangerous way. Two soldiers against . . . how many? Twenty? Thirty? It was foolhardy in the extreme, but Jonathan had never been reluctant to take dangerous risks. Silently, the two gathered their weapons and slipped out of the camp, moving toward Michmash pass.

While his soldiers had set their tents in Geba, Saul had gone further west, closer to his farm in Gibeah, and had established his royal camp near a famous pomegranate tree just east of the town. There were countless stories concerning this tree, which always produced the finest fruit in the area, rich and red and filled with seeds for future plantings. It was said that thousands of trees in the region were direct results of the seeds of this one amazing tree. Israelite ancestors had eaten the fruit of this tree during their long-ago sojourns in the land, Abram as he first moved through the land from north to south, Jacob on his flight back to Haran, Joseph as he was taken to Egypt. It was hard to imagine that any tree could live so long, but the tree was old and the stories persisted through the years.

With Saul in his camp were Ahijah, a great grandson of the disgraced priest, Eli, Samuel's mentor. This young man had taken up the priestly life of his great grandfather and had brought new honor to it after the death of Eli and his two sons in the fiasco of the Ark's capture by the Philistines many years before. Ahijah brought with him the sacred ephod, a special cloak, finely made with gold thread, which when worn was a means of discovering the will of YHWH. Saul was ever intent on seeking the will of his God, and had invited Ahijah to join him wherever he went. However, as intent as Saul was to discern YHWH's will in all things, he was completely unaware that his son and his bodyguard had left the camp. Indeed no Israelite knew that Jonathan had gone to stir up Philistine trouble that day. It was night, and there was no moon.

Jonathan led Ephron upwards into the pass, right towards the Philistine garrison. On both sides of the pass there was a large rock outcrop, forming a kind of canopy over the pass at its narrowest point. At this very spot, only one soldier at a time could squeeze through the pass. Thus was Michmash easily defended, but also thus was confrontation of many against one very difficult. Indeed, the narrow notch in the trail in essence took away from the Philistines the value of superior numbers. Jonathan had noticed this fact the day he had first taken Michmash. And he planned now to use that fact of topography against those who were perhaps less clever than he.

As he and Ephron scrambled up the pass, attempting to move as quietly as the scree and the darkness would allow, Jonathan whispered, "Up ahead there is the garrison of the uncircumcised. It could well be that YHWH will act for us; absolutely nothing can stop YHWH from works of power whether there are many or few to do them." Jonathan well remembered the stories of miraculous Israelite victories that his parents had seeded his youth with, and he called them to mind now as a way to strengthen him for the uneven struggle about to begin.

Those stories calmed his own thumping heart as much as he hoped they lifted up the courage of his companion. But he need not have worried about Ephron who was as eager to strike a blow for YHWH as his master.

"Do whatever is in your heart to do, because I am with you. You and I are one mind, Jonathan."

Jonathan smiled at the words and imagined that Ephron smiled, too, although they could see very little of one another in the thick darkness of the night, under the overhanging rocks of the notch. Jonathan drew Ephron close to his mouth in order to reveal the plan he had formulated.

"Let's climb up the notch to the camp and show ourselves openly to the Philistines. If they see us and say, 'Wait there until we come down to you,' we will stand still and wait for them. But if they say, 'Come up here!' then we will go up. Those words, whichever they are, will be a certain sign that YHWH has given them into our hand."

Ephron found the plan almost laughable. It seemed to him that the Philistines were certain to say one or the other of these phrases, or something very similar, so it was hardly a test of the promise of YHWH's victory, as Jonathan imagined it to be. But it was not uncommon for Jonathan, just like his father Saul, to speak the name of YHWH as support for actions he had already decided to do. Ephron knew how important it was for highborn leaders to invoke the divine name; it was good for morale and kept the priests and prophets happy, too.

So he smiled at the language game that Jonathan was about to play with the Philistines. Really, Ephron cared nothing for any of these tricks; all he wanted was to return to his wife and their bed and to kill as many of the insect enemy as he could. He was terrified to show himself to the vermin right out in the open, but he trusted that his daring master somehow knew what he was doing. Silently, Ephron invoked the presence of YHWH just to be on the safe side; why not? YHWH might actually come to be with them; after all it had happened in the past, or so the priests liked to say over and over. Even a tiny pillar of fire would be welcome in the close quarters of this narrow pass, just big enough to scare the Philistines and to hide Jonathan and him.

But before he could get a decent prayer lifted to YHWH, Jonathan had vacated his hiding place and was loudly drawing the attention of the sentries in the Philistine camp. He was shouting and waving his arms, so Ephron, his prayer stuck in his dry throat, joined in. The Philistine sentries were nearly asleep, but when they heard the human shouting, they leapt to their feet with genuine alarm, thinking that the Israelites perhaps were beginning an assault on the garrison. Some reached for their swords and hoisted their spears, while others notched their arrows, drawing their bows back in a position of readiness. There were six of them; sweat broke out on their brows as fear of battle consumed their guts. One of them, the youngest, let go a stream of urine, but tried to hide the shame of it by quickly wiping the wet with a corner of his tunic, hoping none of his comrades would catch the smell on the wind. Each man froze, looking furtively to those right and left for support.

But the young one, covering his shame with bravado, when he saw that only two soldiers stood below them in the notch of the gorge, laughed derisively,

"Look at that, will you! The Hebrews are finally coming out of those holes where they have hidden themselves!"

The other sentries joined him in laughter at the sight of Jonathan and Ephron, shouting and waving like fools, exposing themselves to the arrows and spears of the men. All Philistines knew that the Israelites were peculiar, but these two were decidedly stupid! What sort of soldier is it who stands in the face of a superior enemy, fairly inviting an arrow in the face or a spear in the groin? The Philistine fears turned immediately to relief. One of them said, a smirk on his now relaxed face, "The two of you come up here, and we will show you something." What he had in mind to show them was the sharp edge of his sword, and he now gripped it hard, readying himself for the pleasurable feeling of Israelite blood spattering his feet and Israelite flesh gone cold. His fellow guards gripped their weapons, too, and awaited some sport with these ridiculous men.

At the sound of the Philistine's invitation to come up to their camp, Jonathan whispered to Ephron, "It is a sign! Follow me up! YHWH has handed them over to Israel!"

Without another word, he turned to scramble up the gorge, climbing on his hands and feet; Ephron followed in the same way, fearing the worst at the hands of the fully prepared Philistines. Exactly what happened then has become the stuff of legend. Before the six sentries could release their arrows, hurl their spears, or even get their swords out of their belts, Jonathan and Ephron were on them, slashing and cutting and shouting and kicking. The six were killed and mutilated in what seemed an instant, along with about ten more soldiers who appeared from deeper in the garrison. The bodies that lay strewn about were pocked with arrows, heads and trunks smashed beyond recognition by rocks and stones. Jonathan and Ephron somehow slaughtered nearly twenty Philistines, and neither of them received a scratch.

When the rest of the garrison ran to help their fellows, they saw only dead Philistines, arrows protruding from them, faces become mockeries of humanity, bodies mangled into mounds of flesh. Jonathan and Ephron were gone, disappearing like wisps back down the gorge. The silence was palpable, and the living Philistines were shocked, their hearts shaking within them. They looked at one another and at their broken comrades, and panic seized them, tightening its grip on their throats to make breathing labored, fastening itself to their legs to make flight slow. It seemed as if the earth itself began to move, little avalanches of stones tumbled down the two sides of the gorge, and at the sound the Philistines, even their most hardened warriors, ran up the notch in horror and jumped into their tents, hoping that the two monstrous men who had done this thing to their friends were not about to return to kill them, too.

The panic in the garrison became so wide-spread that the lookouts in Saul's camp in Gibeah, some way down the valley, could see the strange activity in the Philistine encampment, soldiers rushing here and there, leaderless, purposeless. Tents were being struck, and donkeys loaded with goods as if they were about to abandon their strategic location at the top of the pass. One lookout ran to report the activity to Saul who was completely unaware of the change that had overtaken his enemies. Quickly, he demanded that the roll of the soldiers be called to discover who had left the camp, against his express orders. All were accounted for, save Jonathan and Ephron. Saul was for a moment unclear about what he should do. The Philistine panic was obvious, and it seemed safe to say that Jonathan, always a rash and unruly son at the best of times, had had something to do with it. It could be that Jonathan was a hero, and had made it possible for the Israelites to strike a mortal blow against the Philistines. But it was also possible that Jonathan, rather like a hungry bear after honey, had thrust his hand into the Philistine hive, and had stirred the camp into a desire for revenge, a revenge they were about to deliver against Israel.

Saul needed to consult YHWH. He demanded that the sacred ephod be brought out by the priest, Ahijah. Saul trusted Ahijah, though his ancestors, Eli and his sons, were worthless and justly forgotten, their sons and grandsons had served Israel well as priests for some years now. The ephod was a special robe, worn only by those deemed worthy. When it first became important in the worship of Israel, it was a short, rather crude garment, made from simple material to match the rough and simple stone altars of sacrifice, but as the priestly class grew in numbers and influence, the ephod became more elaborate, finally becoming a loose-fitting, beautifully colored tunic, covering the whole person and marked by a front pocket, containing the sacred lots, Urim and Thummim. Ahijah strode majestically into Saul's presence, the blue and gold thread of the elaborate ephod shining in the early morning sunlight. Saul was in awe of the ephod, as he venerated all objects connected to his God. He waited silently as Ahijah stood still before him, allowing the full effect of the glowing ephod to still the Israelites. Deliberately, he reached into the pocket to draw out the Urim and Thummim, the bones of fate and destiny that revealed the will of YHWH, and all bowed their heads to await the announcement of the oracle. But Saul's eyes drifted from the ephod and the bones back to the Philistine garrison. The panicked soldiers showed no signs of calming or ordering themselves once again; in fact, they seemed even more confused and terrified than when Saul had first looked.

He was so convinced that the time to strike his enemies was now that he turned to Ahijah and stopped the ritual of the oracle in mid action.

"Pull back your hands from the ephod's pocket," shouted the king. "There is no need of that now; the Philistines are like ripe fruit in the orchards of Aijalon. There is no doubt that YHWH has bidden us to attack! Swords, spears, bows and arrows at the ready! Up to the garrison of the uncircumcised!"

The king moved up the gorge at Michmash, more rapidly than his size would have predicted, and more than a hundred soldiers followed his lead. When the Philistines saw the Israelites moving up the pass, they tried to rally themselves, but their leaders had fled, and the stench of their dead friends filled their noses and deflated their lungs and hearts. Even the few Israelites who had defected to the enemy now rejoined the forces of Israel, and the rout was on. Swords whistled, arrows sang through the air, spears flew, and many died, more than a few at the hands of their own people. When fighting hand to hand, jaw to jaw, swords more than once severed the head of a friend or even a brother, while arrows launched at enemies too often found targets familiar to the shooters, and stones crushed the skulls of acquaintances.

And when many who had hidden themselves from the Philistine incursion into the hill country heard the roar of the battle, they came out of their hiding places and joined the fray, doing a bit of killing and more than a bit of looting of the dead. The victory that day was enormous, and the Philistines were pushed out of the pass at Michmash and back beyond Beth Aven, back toward the great sea. Israelites appeared from many places and joined Saul's army until several thousand men were under arms. Most were farmers, unused to the rigors of armed conflict, but all knew about death and killing, and all knew that Israel, including their lands, was under threat by the murderous and heathen Philistines. So they came to fight and to drive the invaders back toward the sea. As the Philistine garrison was destroyed, and many of its soldiers were killed or captured, the battles spilled over into other areas of the hill country of Ephraim. Saul saw that the time for the defeat of the Philistines was now, and he resolved to remove from Israelite territory every Philistine soldier and farmer and every vestige of Philistine presence from the land of YHWH. Saul was still the king of Israel, and he dreamed of a complete defeat of the hated Philistines, thus wiping away the public humiliation he had suffered at the hands of Samuel at Gilgal. The old man would finally have to admit that he, Saul, was king, and was the leader of Israel. Perhaps then he could live with the ancient prophet in peace.

13

After all, Saul considered himself a sincerely pious man, strict in the ways of his God, as difficult as that God was to understand at times. He never sallied forth to battle without some proper respect for YHWH, the Lord of Battles. No quick prayer from Ahijah was enough for Saul. He regularly demanded the ephod be worn and consulted, and a full burnt offering be given. His actions at Gilgal had made his deep devotion more than clear. He knew that he had risked a great deal by offering the sacrifice in the place of the ancient high priest, Samuel, but he had had to act, and act he did with what he felt was the full approval of YHWH, whose heart was always warmed by an accurately performed sacrifice. And this recent victory over the Philistine garrison, and the beginnings of a more complete Philistine defeat, had proven Saul right; YHWH was with Israel in power and Saul was YHWH's king.

It was thus second nature for the king to devise an oath before continuing the struggle against the heathen, an oath by which YHWH would be greatly honored. He knew that his soldiers found the oath distressing, saw that they grumbled at its rigor, but Saul further knew that YHWH was often a demanding God who challenged the people by strict commands that needed following to the letter. Only such complete adherence could pass the test that YHWH set, and Saul was convinced that YHWH had led him to this particular oath. Saul knew well the history of his people and his God, who more than a few times had made what appeared to be absurd demands of them. Had not YHWH commanded the great Moses to fling his shepherd's staff on the sand, whereupon it became a foul and slithering snake? If that were not enough, YHWH had commanded the trembling shepherd to grab that snake by its tail, a foolish act no man of the desert would ever have done. But he had done it, and the viper had become ramrod stiff again. Had not Joshua confronted and destroyed the giant city of Jericho, so long impregnable to would-be attackers, with only well-tuned trumpets as weapons?

This oath was small when compared to those magnificent ones. The oath had merely demanded that no soldier should eat anything until Saul had secured the victory over the Philistines on that one day.

Just before Saul had mustered the troops for the morning, he had stood before them and said, "Let anyone be cursed who eats food before evening, before I have taken vengeance against my enemies!"

King Saul

The soldiers were used to such oaths. It was an ancient tradition that before battles they were to avoid their women's beds; they all knew the languor they felt after a vigorous sexual tussle. But because they knew that fact, it was customary to eat heartily before the hardships of the day of battle. They would need all of their strength to survive their well-armed enemies, so Saul's oath, however well intentioned, however religiously motivated, went down hard with the soldiers. How were they to maintain their sharp eyes and muscled arms without the strengthening of the morning meat? But the king had spoken on behalf of YHWH, and they would obey. Still, some of them remembered the mighty Samuel's rebuke of Saul's attempts at sacrifice at Gilgal, and they feared that he might not be fully aware of what YHWH's demands actually were. But in the end, every soldier complied with the oath, however much they did not like it.

As they ran up the pass at Michmash and routed the garrison, as they spread out throughout the hill country of Ephraim, defeating the enemy in every place, many soldiers saw ready food, honeycombs on the ground fairly oozing the sweet nectar, bushes filled with berries, trees heavy with late fruit, but no one touched a thing. They had heard the oath made to their God by their king, and they were afraid to risk the displeasure of either one or the possibility of defeat that such displeasure could bring. Most of the time the thrill of victory made them forget their gnawing hunger, but the honey and the berries and the fruit seemed to mock them, their stomachs growling and yearning, their anger rising against the king.

Jonathan and Ephron had not heard the oath uttered by Saul, since they had left well before the camp had awakened. So quite naturally, as the morning's fighting intensified, as Jonathan dove again and again into the fleeing groups of screaming Philistines, he saw some honey shining in the sun, stuck his spear into the sticky sweetness, and brought the dripping and golden matter up to his mouth. Almost immediately, his flagging spirit revived, and he turned back to pursue still another knot of the heathen.

But a soldier, who had joined Jonathan and Ephron in their pursuit of the Philistine retreat, tried vainly to stop Jonathan's eating, shouting, "No, my lord! Your father strictly charged all the soldiers this morning, 'Let anyone be cursed who eats any food today!' That is why so many of us are nearly faint with hunger."

And it was all too true. Jonathan looked at the soldiers and saw that many were falling well behind the fleeing Philistines. And Jonathan was furious.

"My father has brought trouble on the land! Just look how this bit of honey has revived me. How much better it would have been if we had eaten freely of the heathen spoils, lying all around for the taking. Our victory has been far less than it should have been!"

And the Philistines fled further and further west, their running figures becoming smaller in the reddening disk of the setting sun. One after another, groups of Israelite soldiers gave up the chase as they became ever fainter with hunger. Jonathan's anger was soon well known to them all, as well as his rejection and breaking of Saul's oath.

And his suggestion that they fall on the Philistine spoils freed them to do precisely that. Without hesitation, the troops pounced on the leavings of the heathen, but they cared little for the gold cloth, the fine wrought cups, the elegant shields and swords. Their stomachs overruled all else; they grabbed the remaining cattle and sheep and oxen by their bleating, baaing and lowing throats, plunged their swords deeply into the warm flesh, and scooped out hunks of blood-drenched meat by the handful, stuffing the chunks into their maws, barely stopping to chew. Several horrified soldiers rushed away from the scene, their religious sensibilities overcoming their churning stomachs, and rushed up to the king.

"My lord, the people are sinning against YHWH by eating the blood!"

Saul was shocked into momentary silence. Not only had his oath been shattered by the rabble of his soldiers, but they had also failed to prepare the food properly, devouring the blood of the meat, blood that belonged only to YHWH. They all knew that the blood was the very life of all creatures, and that all life was God's. How dare they! They were no better than the heathen they had partially defeated this day! Saul marched to the place where the sacrilege was occurring, and the sight that met his eyes was repulsive. His men were sprawled all over the ground, their mouths smeared with blood, their bellies distended with too much food. Some were retching the raw meat they had devoured, staining their tunics with bile and blood. Saul's eye fell on Jonathan, his son, whom he knew had had a hand in all this, but before he dealt with the boy, he was moved to address the sacrilege so obviously displayed before him.

"Traitors," he thundered, and a hush fell, punctuated with a heave here and a belch there.

Saul fixed his eyes on each soldier individually, as he walked slowly around the place, being careful to avoid the gore scattered on the ground.

"Roll a huge stone over here!"

Those men who had alerted Saul to the disaster of eating chose a gigantic rock, nearly round, that lay buried upright in the soil. With a tremendous effort, three powerful men dislodged the stone and, sweating profusely, rolled it to the king and forced it to fall on its larger side.

"Now watch," Saul shouted.

He grabbed one of the goats that had been missed by the gluttonous men and with one stroke of his knife cut its throat. He held the lifeless animal over the stone while the blood poured out onto its jagged surface. Saul waited while the blood flowed until only the merest trickle came from the huge wound in the neck. He then lighted a fire on the stone and tossed the carcass onto the flames. When the odor of the goat meat permeated the air, Saul took his spear and pushed the roasted animal out of the fire and onto a waiting cloth, held by one of the soldiers still able to stand.

"That is how it's done! That is the way YHWH demands the preparation of food. You simply must not eat the blood!"

King Saul

And one after the other the men came close to the stone, dragging or carrying an animal and did as their king had done. After all the animals had been rightly roasted, Saul did something he had not yet done in his life: he himself built an altar to YHWH. He picked up many stones, none of which had been tainted by the blood of the gluttony, and piled them as high as his waist. And on the altar, he sacrificed a lone remaining animal he had saved back for the purpose, calling on YHWH to forgive his men for their transgression of divine demands and urging YHWH to remain with them in their struggles against the Philistines.

Jonathan stood by, a silent witness to this scene. He had not eaten any of the tainted meat, had not swallowed any of the sacred blood. He watched when his father had upbraided his men for their lax behavior, for their inappropriate actions with the meat. But Jonathan was furious, too, but not at the men, but at his father, the king. The oath had been absurd! No matter how much Saul had wanted to honor YHWH, a fast before a battle was not the way to do it. The men could hardly be blamed for needing sustenance for the fight! How could they be expected to perform for their God and king when they had had no food! It was in fact Saul's mistake, not theirs. If he had not demanded such a fast, they never would have acted as they did, would never have devoured meat and blood together. What right did Saul have to treat his valiant men like criminals, like the heretic Philistines? It is he who should repent of evil actions, not they. He can sacrifice all he wants, roast the meat just so, drain out all the blood, but that will not atone for his stupidity, his misplaced religiosity. The Philistine victory should have been complete, their soldiers slaughtered, their morale deflated. Instead, because of Saul's ridiculous oath, they were running to the safety of their cities and would soon be back to harass Israel again!

Jonathan looked carefully at Saul. But this time he saw him differently. He saw the great warrior, the huge spear and shield, the commanding presence, of course. But he also saw in him a fear he had not seen before, a fear of YHWH and a fear of something else, of something else he could not name. What sort of king was he, what sort of commander? Since his anointing some years before, there had been many who had only very reluctantly given their allegiance to the man, and there were still others now who felt the same. Just who was he? Jonathan looked at his father as if for the first time, almost as if he did not know who he was. Perhaps he didn't.

Saul finished the sacrifice. The men rose up from their gluttony and waited for the king to tell them what to do.

"Let us go right now, tonight, and destroy these disgusting Philistines! Let not one more sun find any of them breathing!"

Saul grabbed his spear and shield and began to leave, and the rattle of sword and ax announced the preparation of the troops to follow. But Ahijah's high-pitched voice stopped the king in his tracks.

"Have you forgotten God?! Let us keep close to YHWH here!"

King Saul

Saul flushed, because in fact he had for an instant forgotten that he must consult YHWH before embarking on a battle. The altar he had just constructed lay smoldering with the remains of the goat, but he still needed to consult YHWH directly concerning the upcoming clash.

He put his sword and shield on the ground, moved close to the altar, raised his hands high over his head, and implored YHWH, "Shall I follow the Philistines, and will you give them into the hand of Israel?"

Saul's eyes and the eyes of Ahijah searched the glowing coals of the fire on the altar. They raised their heads to observe the movements of the smoke of the sacrifice against the twilight sky, and examined the entrails of the goat that remained on the altar. But they saw nothing; YHWH was silent. Saul looked at Ahijah, but the priest had nothing to say. The soldiers waited anxiously to be told what they were to do, rush after the Philistines or make camp here.

Saul could not believe that YHWH had chosen not to reveal the divine will. Something was wrong, and Saul intended to find out. Perhaps YHWH had not forgiven the misused blood? Perhaps the badly prepared sacrifices, devoured right in YHWH's angry face, had closed the God's mouth? And then another thought came to Saul: perhaps someone had earlier broken his oath. He had to find out. There was obviously some sin in the camp; YHWH would surely respond if all were well among the people. And they could not go out to battle with evil lurking in their midst.

"All leaders are to appear before me now! We will find out exactly how some sin has arisen today."

Saul snarled this last sentence, filling his mouth with bitterness and rage. And then he said something that he would wish had never entered his head.

"By YHWH, the savior of Israel, even if the sinner is my son Jonathan, he is a dead man!"

It was still another rash oath from the king. No food all day and now the prospect of murdering his own heroic son! The assembling leaders looked at their king in horror and wondered, some of them not for the first time, just how this enigmatic man could ever lead them.

But the oath had been uttered, and there was no retracting it. Saul fixed them all with a stare and began the ancient process of discovery.

"All of you, leaders and soldiers, stand on one side of this altar, and my son Jonathan and I will stand on the other."

Saul glared at Jonathan who obeyed his father's direction, and the rest of the troops reluctantly moved toward the other side of the altar. They all knew immediately that Saul suspected that his son was the culprit, and they also knew that the king was fully prepared to slaughter his son for the sake of YHWH and YHWH's implacable rejection of all sinners. Though all said what the ritual demanded they say, "Do whatever you think is right," the possibility of Jonathan's imminent sacrifice filled them with dread.

King Saul

When all were in place, Saul lifted his eyes to the sky and began the prayer.

"YHWH, God of Israel, why have you not answered your servant today? I am your anointed king, the leader of your armies, the master of the land. I have sacrificed to you in the way you command, and yet you remain silent to my pleas. I sense guilt in my camp. If this guilt, whatever it may be, is in me or in my son Jonathan, choose Urim. But if it is among your people, then choose Thummim." Ahijah stepped forward to cast the sacred bones. He pulled them from the breast pocket of the ephod and tossed them onto the top of the altar. They rolled through the ashes of the fire and stopped at the back edge of the great stone. The bone Urim was the clear choice. YHWH had pointed to Saul or Jonathan and the rest of the people were found innocent. There was an audible sigh of relief among the soldiers, but the tension of the camp tightened.

Jonathan and Saul looked at one another, neither blinking, neither looking away from the other.

Saul said, "Cast again, Ahijah, between my son and me."

Once again the bones were tossed on the altar, and Jonathan, son of Saul, was selected. An anguished cry rose from many of the soldiers. Several moved toward Jonathan as if to shield him from his father's rage. But Saul was strangely calm.

"Tell me what you have done," said the king quietly, but since the camp was completely silent his words were heard in every corner. Jonathan responded directly and without a hint of fear or regret.

"I tasted a bit of honey with the tip of my spear. I am prepared to die for it if I must. Your oath is binding, and I am the guilty one!"

Jonathan nearly shouted the last line in as much as to say that Saul's oath was absurd, that his father was a fool to make such an oath on the day of a battle, that he had not even heard the oath spoken. He was prepared to die, all right, but death because of such a ridiculous oath would be a foul and useless death indeed.

With a great roar, Saul drew his massive sword, and shouted, "May God do so to me, and even more terrible things, if you are not a dead man, Jonathan!"

He lunged at Jonathan, clearly intending to decapitate his son. Jonathan ducked below the sweep of the sword just in time, and the people shouted out with one voice that Saul should stop the execution.

"Should Jonathan die, the hero of the battle, who began our great victory over the heathen today? By YHWH, No! Not one hair of his head shall fall to the ground, because he was the one who acted for God this day!"

While these words were shouted, several of the larger soldiers stood between Saul and Jonathan to prevent the king from pursuing his intentions. Saul was aflame with fury at Jonathan, knowing that he had to execute the wrath of YHWH against the sinner and knowing too that if he did not do so, his stature as king would be diminished in the eyes of his people. His mind clouded with rage, his heart filled with humiliation as his eyes hooded over with impotent desire. If he murdered his son, he would be following the clear will of YHWH, but if he murdered his son, his troops might leave him, reject his leadership. But if he did not carry out the demanded execution, his oaths would mean nothing, his words empty, his leadership severely compromised. Damned if he does; damned if he doesn't. Saul was trapped in his own oath, caught in a net of his own devising.

Everyone stood silent on the hill. No one quite knew what to do. Without a word, the king sheathed his sword and walked away. His face was a storm of emotion, anger, fear, shame, but finally unreadable. Jonathan watched his father leave, and knew that never again could they have any sort of genuine relationship. He was still Saul's son, perhaps the future king of Israel, in spite of the vituperative words of the ancient seer at Gilgal, but Saul was now a stranger to him, his willing executioner, his ready murderer.

His mind harkened back to the terrible story of Abraham and Isaac that his mother, Ahinoam, used to tell him. She told it, she always said, to teach Jonathan about the grace of YHWH and the need for Jonathan to have deep faith in the mysterious God, but Jonathan always shuddered when that story was told. He did not hear grace in that story or the call to faith; he heard of an abusive father who would have murdered his son at the whim of his God but who was saved from the slaughter by a last-minute reprieve. Surely this was not faith, he thought, but foolish and blind obedience, leading to an irreparable breach between father and son. The story, as his mother told it, never revealed what Isaac had thought of his father after the old man had bound him to that altar on Mount Moriah, and had been ready to plunge his flint knife into his son's throat. He had wondered about that every time the story was told, but now he thought he knew. Watching his father lunge at him with his sword with the certain desire to murder him, convinced Jonathan that he was not fully Saul's son, but only his tool, an object readily sacrificed if it be his father's, or his God's, inscrutable will. Jonathan watched his father disappear down the hill and knew that his father was in fact disappearing from his life forever.

14

The troops dispersed from Michmash, and the hoped-for complete victory over the Philistines dispersed with them. The leaderless rabble of Philistines who had escaped the Israelite onslaught all returned to their towns on the seacoast in safety, preparing to regroup to fight another day. They had been ripe for the plucking, like figs in their season, but the harvest had been missed. Saul had gone to his tent alone and would see no one, and his army had faded back into towns and villages. The moment of victory had come, but the moment of victory had been lost. A sort of non-war ensued where small skirmishes broke out here and there, but no concerted struggle between armies took place.

There were plenty of enemies to worry about of course, enemies on every side. And Saul mustered his forces against Moabites and Ammonites and Edomites to the east, tiny princedoms that were more irritants on Israel's flanks than full-blown adversaries. And there were always the filthy Philistines, ever anxious to plunder and raid from the west. Saul fought them all, and did well against them all, as well as his rather scattered forces could do. But instead of a final victory, all Saul could muster was a shaky truce with other peoples east and west, north and south.

Saul, when he was not on some short campaign or other, mainly stayed in Gibeah and farmed his land. His sons, Jonathan, Ishvi, and Malchishua, always were ready to help their father in the work, although Jonathan, since that day at Michmash, stayed away from his father as often as he could. Saul also had two daughters, Merab and Michal, both of whom were good girls, attractive and lively, both pleasing in their father's eyes. His wife, Ahinoam, was mother of six of his children, an excellent woman, skilled in all the womanly arts who kept the household ordered and active whenever Saul went out on his frequent raids. Rizpah, Saul's other wife, also lived in the household, helping Ahinoam with the children, and on occasion sharing his bed.

Abner was the commander of Saul's forces, a fully dependable man, always trustworthy in his dealings. Saul's father, Kish, a very old man now, lived close by so that his son could care for his every need as he aged. Saul was without rival king of the land, and always did his best to secure the safety of his people, but Israel was ever threatened by the Philistines throughout his reign. For several years very little changed in this small corner of the Middle East. Indeed, it might have gone on forever just as it was, but the now incredibly old Samuel was still a force to be reckoned with in the land, and his desire to exert his authority still burned bright within him. He and Saul had not seen the last of one another, however much the king had hoped it was so.

One clear morning in the early spring, when the winter rains had ended, and the flowers were bursting in the fields around Gibeah, Saul and his second son, Ishvi, were mending fences in the back pasture. The fierce storms of two moons before had caused much damage on the farm, and the fence mending was only the beginning of a vast amount of work that Saul and the family had ahead of them. Ishvi was a fine son, thought Saul, as he watched him hoist a large stone and drop it on the rising pile that would stop the gap in the fence. Several valuable animals had escaped through this hole before Saul was aware of its existence, and he had no intention of allowing any more of his livestock to wander off to their doom and his impoverishment. It was such a pleasure to watch the growing Ishvi work on the farm. He had always loved the land, nearly as much as Saul did, and had been a willing worker since he was very small. Saul remembered with a smile those times when, as a tiny boy, he had tried to help around the place, picking up little rocks and clearing a few branches of the stinging nettles that plagued the soil. Even when the nettles tore into his baby flesh, he would not cry, but would merely lick the bleeding places and work on. Ishvi was an easy son to love, so different from the eldest, Jonathan. Jonathan had grown large, almost the size of Saul himself, and there was no questioning his bravery and cleverness. But he was wild and unruly, and took orders poorly, preferring to strike out on his own, whether in work around the farm or in battle, as the debacle at Michmash had proved all too well.

And Jonathan had become sullen, too, since Michmash, seldom interested in the large family gatherings so beloved of Saul and Ahinoam. He always seemed to find some excuse that took him away from the farm, to join his friends in some escapade or other, or to woo still another local girl. Saul wished he could forget about the oath, that oath that had nearly forced him, because of religious honor, to kill the boy, but apparently Jonathan could not, or would not forget. He had no more smiles for his father, no more easy laughter, no more intimacies of any kind. He was son in name only, but rarely in practice. If only he were more like Ishvi, or even like the youngest, Malchishua, a fun-loving lad who craved the outdoors, and would rather hunt than eat, would rather play than listen to the tutor priest who tried to teach him his aleph-bet. Saul loved Malchishua especially; he was so free, so unassuming, so open-faced about life, so amazingly optimistic about the future of his life and the life of Israel. Saul envied his son that optimism, for Saul too had once been optimistic about Israel's future and the future of his kingship. He was now hardly so certain. He had strong sons, two charming daughters, two loving wives, but threats were constant, and YHWH's ancient promises of land and a huge population for Israel seemed at these times the dreams of an idiot child.

Saul's mind wandered between dashed hopes and fears for the dark future, between the quiet life of the farm and the shadows of the heathen all round. But his mind was jerked back to the present by a familiar sound. Four powerful men walked purposefully toward the fence where Ishvi and Saul were working, bearing on their shoulders, glistening with sweat even in the cool morning, the palanquin of the prophet. The labor of carrying the old man shown in their faces and was mirrored in the grunts of effort that were torn from their throats as they put their burden down onto the flower-bedecked field. From inside the curtain of the palanquin the familiar voice called forth, crackling now with great age and made at last smaller by the vast number of years it had boomed the words of YHWH into the land.

"Saul, Saul," croaked Samuel from the regal conveyance, "are you there, Saul?"

"Here I am," replied the king, forcing himself not to bow before the prophet.

After all, he was king, and if anyone should bow it was Samuel, the anointer of the king.

"Lift me out of here, now," Samuel commanded, and Saul felt himself pulled toward the palanquin by the power of that voice, a power he had never been able to resist since first he heard it.

He threw back the curtain, and was stunned at what he saw within. Samuel had shriveled like a dark plum too long in the sun. Lines tracked his face from his wispy-haired forehead to the few stray old-age spots that ringed his jaw. His back was so bent that he could not stand on his own, his legs so gnarled they appeared less like human limbs than like twisted branches of dead trees. And his eyes, those unforgettable eyes, that had fixed themselves on Saul all those years ago at Ramah and Gilgal and other places too numerous to name or remember, were now completely clouded with white so thick as to swallow the once-dark eyes that had poured their power into the land for so long. Samuel was obviously blind, like his old mentor Eli had become in his vast old age.

No one could guess how old this wreck of a man was, but his mind seemed not affected by the useless thing his body had become. The stench of the aged assaulted Saul's nostrils, and he had to beat back the unbidden urge to retch in Samuel's face. Immediately after Saul had picked him up from the palanquin—he weighed practically nothing— and placed him on a blanket carried by one of the bearers, the voice insinuated itself into Saul's ears. "Me YHWH sent to anoint you king over the people of Israel." Saul suppressed a smile as he heard Samuel put himself first in the sentence, a very peculiar way to express what he wanted to say; he was sure that the grammarian priest trying to teach his sons the rudiments of Hebrew would not be pleased. However, it was just like the prophet to first remind the king, as if he needed any reminding, that Samuel was YHWH's choice to do the anointing of the first king of Israel. Of course, Saul also knew all too well that the prophet would rather have pulled off one of his arms than have done the anointing of Saul at all, but this was no time to engage in that old debate again. For good or ill Saul was king. Samuel hurried on, speaking as rapidly as his dry and cracking throat would allow.

"Because you are king, now listen to the sound of the words of YHWH!"

King Saul

It was again a strange way to word the sentence. The familiar way that other prophets had spoken was "thus says YHWH;" that was neat and short and to the point. What did Samuel mean by bidding Saul to listen to the *sound* of YHWH's words? Did the old man know that Saul had been having a difficult time hearing from YHWH, so now promised him the very sound of the divine voice? Or did he mean that the words about to be uttered were nothing less than the very sound of YHWH, as if YHWH were standing in this field speaking directly through the mouth of Samuel? Perhaps he meant both things; Saul would hardly be surprised if that were true. The prophet was ever fond of double-tongued speech, and the clever Samuel certainly had Saul's full attention this time.

"Thus says YHWH of the armies, 'I am about to punish what the Amalekites did to Israel when they opposed their passage during their escape from Egypt. You, Saul! Strike Amalek and obliterate all that they have; do not spare a thing! Kill man and woman, young child and infant, ox and sheep, camel and donkey!"

That said, Samuel signaled for one of his bearers to lift him from the blanket and put him back in the palanquin. Saul started to comment, to ask for clarification, to discuss the terrible charge he had just been given, but Samuel was quickly back in the dark confines of his personal cart, and the four men were bearing him back to where he came from. Ishvi spoke up only after the prophet had gotten out of earshot.

"What does all that mean, father? Exactly what are you to do?"

Nearly everyone in Israel had heard of *cherem*. How could they not have heard of it? Joshua, Israel's storied general, had been charged by YHWH to perform *cherem* against the peoples of the land of promise in order that Israel would have a safe place in which to live. The stories were conflicting about whether he had done so, or, perhaps better, had been able to do so. It was a fact that the central hill country of Israel had been cleared for the Egyptian escapees to live there, but it was also a fact that the great northern ring of Canaanite cities—Meggido, Taanach, Beth-Shean, among others—cities old by the time of Israel's coming to this land, had not in any way been destroyed by Joshua or anyone else. The purpose of *cherem* was to avoid the contamination of heathen influence, the danger of foreign ways. Israel was always ready, it appeared, to give in, or to sample, the ways of the peoples among whom they lived, and often this "sampling" (a polite way to put it, Saul thought) had led to the most repulsive heathenisms, better left unremarked upon.

"Samuel has just charged me to annihilate the Amalekites, because when our sacred ancestors were led out of Egypt by the great Moses, these Amalekites, I assume, had somehow impeded their progress toward this land on which we are now standing, and of which I am king."

Saul thought privately that he could not clearly remember the part of the Exodus story when and how the Amalekites had done something so terrible as to warrant their complete destruction, but he had no doubt that Samuel could enlighten him if he asked, something he vowed never to do. Nevertheless, Saul once again felt trapped by

Samuel. Just as at Gilgal when Samuel had commanded that he wait the seven days for Samuel to come to lead the sacrifice, so now Samuel had demanded that he slaughter all Amalekites, including innocent women, children and babies. But there was a difference this time. He had clearly claimed that the words just spoken were the direct words of YHWH, whereas at Gilgal those years before, he had not claimed any such thing. YHWH had spoken, said Samuel, and Samuel had been from time out of mind the spokesperson of YHWH. Saul had to act.

"I have no choice, my son," he said to Ishvi. "I am king, but it is finally YHWH and the prophet who rule over Israel."

This last he said with no little bitterness, a fact not missed by Ishvi.

Father and son went back to the house to inform the family that Saul had been sent on a mission by the great God YHWH, a mission he intended to fulfill to the letter. Ahinoam was used to her husband's sudden departures for battle, and knew what needed to be done. She gathered up the extra change of clothes he and her sons would need, since they could be gone for weeks. She demanded that her servants pour extra wine in the leather sacks and to collect the dried meat and the freshest loaves of bread, taking them to the camel stalls for loading. Soldiers of course lived mainly off the land, but in the early spring not all the fruit would be ripe enough for eating, and the food would stave off starvation far from home. And in the southern deserts of the Amalekites, there would be scant food to scavenge. Saul and his sons went to the family armory, selecting the stoutest shields and spears, as many arrows as the quivers would hold, and the sharpest swords. Leather helmets would offer some protection against long-range arrows and blunt swords, but were better protection against the sun, which even in spring could wither a man in the desert in a brief time. And the Amalekites were desert dwellers, masters of the hit-and-run warfare that the desert demanded. Saul knew it would probably be a war of attrition, with many pitched struggles of a few against a few, rather than a large conflict of army against army. Saul also knew he had the superior numbers; the Amalekites would soon realize it, too, and would avoid direct confrontation as long as they could.

Saul and three of his sons mounted their horses, large beasts bred from ancient Hittite stock, those long-ago warriors who had been mighty horsemen of the northern steppes, but whose empire had collapsed and dispersed in the fabled past. Their descendants could still be found among many of the peoples of the Near East. In Saul's own army, there were Hittite warriors who traced their names back far into the distant past; Jonathan's armor bearer, Ephron, was one. The army commanders rode fine donkeys, Abner mounted on the finest of all. They were trustworthy animals that could run all day and carry loads many times their weight. The camels were mainly used for the larger loads of weapons and tents; their ability to go up to a full seven suns without water was crucial for desert warfare. Then too a phalanx of twenty-five camels, running at a group of soldiers at full gallop, was a terrifying sight, and Saul hoped that at the end of the struggle against the Amalekites, he would finish them off with a glorious camel charge.

By just past mid day, the army was ready to depart, some 300 warriors, most on foot, walking in front of and behind their leaders as protection for them. After the advanced guard of seven, the largest and swiftest of the foot soldiers, came Saul and his sons, proudly astride their prancing horses, followed by Abner and the commanders on their sure-footed donkeys. Then came the pack camels, nearly thirty, followed by the main force of 250 men, backed up by the rear guard of twenty or so, watching carefully for any possible sneak attacks. It was a magnificent force, and as they spread out over the plains near Gibeah it appeared that many thousands had assembled to fight the battle for YHWH and Samuel. The news of the coming battle against the Amalekites had spread to the south, and some Judean warriors joined the march. After all, Judeans hated the desert-dwelling Amalekites, since they bore the brunt of Amalekite incursions among their farms and homes. More than a few of these Judean warriors had scores to settle with them, and they were eager to shed some Amalekite blood. Saul's powerful army was just what they had been waiting for. They were welcomed gladly by the Ephraimites, since more good warriors, whatever their original homes or their reasons for fighting, meant the possibility of victory was all the greater.

The army, now numbering over 400, wound its way southward, passing the heathen stronghold of Jebus on the left with its high promontory and deep valleys, a nearly impregnable fortress, unconquered and seemingly unconquerable. They then came to Bethlehem, "the house of food" the name meant, since it was surrounded by fields of grain and pastures for sheep. It was too early for grain harvest, so the army passed by without asking for provision. After two days march they reached Hebron, the site of the burial place of the patriarchs and matriarchs of Israel, Abraham and Sarah, Jacob and Leah, all laid to rest in the cave of Machpelah, bought from the ancient Ephron, a Hittite man of long ago. One of Saul's soldiers, Hattusilish by name, claimed relation to Ephron, but many thought him lying. After a rest stop at Hebron, offering time for remembering the great worthies who lay dead there, the army continued south, passing Debir on its right, then Goshen, and finally arriving at Beer-Sheba, now several days from Gibeah. This was as far south as the majority of the soldiers had ever been, as far from home as nearly all had been. As they had traveled, the sun had become hotter, the desert more empty, the vegetation more sparse.

They were very happy to see the short walls of Beer-Sheba, yet nearly all knew that the masters of the desert city were the two foul and now quite elderly sons of Samuel, Joel and Abijah. The sentries on the walls had spotted the large army some miles before their arrival and had alerted the two men. Both were, as usual, drunk, even though it was early in the day. Their tunics were spotted with grease stains of meat and the juice of figs, their beards were tangled with filth beyond telling, their speech slurred by excess of beer. After the gates were opened to receive the king and his men, Joel and Abijah staggered out for the formal greeting. Joel spoke first.

King Saul

"Such a delightful surprise to receive the mighty Saul and his glorious army!"

He had in his condition quite forgotten the formal greeting for a king or perhaps his bitterness at being left here in Beer-Sheba, abandoned by his father, forgotten forever in this YHWH-forsaken hole, got the better of him, the drink seizing his addled tongue.

"What brings you to our humble city, O king of Israel?"

Abijah then added, "Why would any sane man come to this refuse dump in any case?"

The people of the city, those who had bothered to come to the center of the town to greet their king, muttered at the insulting remarks of their two leaders, both of whom were marked for murder as soon as a satisfactory plot could be devised. But the elders of the city had not dared act while the powerful Samuel remained alive. They had long ago determined that Joel and Abijah would die excruciating deaths on the very day of the death of their father, although many had begun to believe that the ancient prophet might be immortal.

"I am grateful for your welcome," boomed Saul, with a wry smile and a wink shared with his sons. "We are on a mission from your father and his God to obliterate the Amalekites once and for all. YHWH is enraged at their behavior long ago when they impeded the safe passage of our ancestors as they escaped from the clutches of pharaoh of Egypt. We propose to annihilate them from the earth, man, woman, child, camel, donkey. And we will then sow salt in their soil, and no green thing will grow for them ever again!"

The inebriated pair smirked grimly at one another as they heard this news, trying to determine what value it had for them and their wasted lives. Joel thought that at best Saul might be killed in the battle, along with his three sons, thus clearing the way for Samuel to bring him back to Ramah and make him judge over Israel at last, as he had promised him so many years ago. Abijah mused that with the pesky Amalekites out of the way, he might fulfill his dream of taking over all of the southern deserts, right up to the borders of Egypt, then forming an alliance with the pharaoh of the day, whoever he was, against Israel. With the powerful Egyptians on his side, he would attack the Israelites, depose this fool Saul, kill his ridiculous father, the man who had stuck him in this desert to rot, and finally become king of the land, his rightful role in the first place.

The two sots plotted in their beer-soaked hearts, but they said aloud, "May YHWH protect you on this sacred quest! You are God's chosen, and surely you will be victorious!"

Saul looked at the drunken fools with disgust. Meeting the sons of Samuel for the first time, it was now clear why the people of Israel had rejected completely Samuel's plan to install these nasty idiots as judges over Israel after his death. No wonder that Samuel had anointed him king at the request of YHWH, no wonder that YHWH had rejected them. But the filthy judges were speaking again to him.

King Saul

"King Saul, we welcome you to Beer-Sheba, and hope that you will spend some time with us here in our city. We have few visitors in this desert and would be glad for news of the north. How goes the struggle with the Philistines? What are the finest men of the place wearing now? Are the women compliant, fully subservient to their men, as the custom has it?"

Joel and Abijah leered as they asked these absurd questions. They asked nothing of their aged father, a fact that did not escape Saul's notice, a fact that did not surprise him in the least. He had in fact thought to spend a day or two in the city, but seeing and hearing these drunks, dressed in their repulsive robes, unwashed for YHWH knows how long, jabbering on about fashion and women, made him eager to leave the place as soon as the animals had been watered and after the briefest of respites for his men. Since Joel and Abijah had greeted him with rudeness, Saul felt no need to act otherwise.

"We have no intention of staying in this goat pen you call a city. The two of you disgust me beyond telling, and if I were not in a hurry to fulfill YHWH's call, I would clap both of you in prison, choose a more worthy leader for the place, and tell your father, the prophet, just how repulsive you are. You can count yourselves fortunate that my time is not my own. Let the two of you rot in the desert, and may the jackals lick your bones!"

As Saul's curse echoed through the square, the commanders remounted, and the army walked directly out of Beer-Sheba. Joel and Abijah stood mutely, increasingly unsteady on their feet, as the sun beat down on their heads. Several elders of the city glanced knowingly at one another and retired to an inn to talk. Perhaps the time had come to act. These two imbeciles needed to be dealt with now. The judges, blissfully unaware of the plots swirling around them, called for their servants to help them back to their homes where several nubile and comely girls were awaiting their masters to soothe them after such a trying confrontation. But a cup of beer and some time in bed with one or two or more of the girls would wash away the bad experience of the last hours.

The army continued south, finally reaching Aroer, the very southernmost village in Saul's land. Ahead lay the Amalekite territory, spread west toward the mountains of Sinai and east up to Edom, the territory directly south of the Salt Sea. The desert now was at anvil heat, and the army had to move more slowly to preserve energies for the coming conflict. As it passed the border of Israel, the advanced scouts came across an encampment of Kenites, workers of metal who always caught wind of coming battles, and knew that their technical services would soon be needed, sharpening blunted swords, refitting arrows, strengthening shattered shields, reheading broken spears. When Saul was told of their presence, and how they had been hired by the Amalekites for their expertise, Saul called their leader to his tent. A wizened man of indeterminate age, with the massive hands and wrists and arms of a worker in metals, came humbly, and greeted Saul in the appropriate manner. Saul quickly thought that Joel and Abijah could learn much from this man about the correct way to greet a king.

"My Lord king," he shouted, perhaps a bit too loudly, the ring of metal working always ringing in his ears, "what would you say to me?"

Saul liked the man immediately.

"My friend, I have been sent by my God, YHWH, to annihilate the Amalekites, to wipe them off the face of the land. I know you have been hired by them to work on their behalf, and I do not begrudge you that work. However, in my zeal against them, stirred up by YHWH, I might accidentally kill you along with them. I cannot every moment control the soldiers and their charge to kill all they see. Because this is true, listen to me carefully. Withdraw from these Amalekites, because they are only dead people walking. In the stories my mother told me about the great Exodus from Egypt at the behest of YHWH, your ancestors showed great kindness to mine. Thus, I have no quarrel with you, but I cannot guarantee your safety. I will strike the Amalekites at first light tomorrow, and I give you and your people until then to move away from the place of battle."

The man was quick to reply.

"My Lord king, I hear your words and sense your resolve to do what your God has called you to do. I and my people will leave immediately."

And with a quick series of bows, the Kenite backed out of the tent. Saul was greatly relieved to hear that the man was accepting his offer of safety; he had no desire to slaughter innocent people, but he was resolved to kill the Amalekites. But he had not quite yet decided just how he intended to effect the killing. He had no doubt that his superior force would prevail over them, whether they were foolish enough to confront him directly or whether, as Saul imagined they would, they chose to fight him piecemeal, a small skirmish at a time. He was completely confident of victory, but he wanted to please Samuel and YHWH with the kind of victory he achieved. Obliteration on the field of battle was simple enough, and had a certain neatness to it. But, he thought, why not something more grand, more memorable?

YHWH gloried in right sacrifice; Saul had been taught that all his life, and Samuel had tried to humiliate him over that very thing at Gilgal. Saul frowned as he remembered that day and still firmly believed that what he had done was correct. He had waited the seven days and had offered the sacrifice before the battle. The fact that Samuel had not understood the events in the same way still rankled, but it did not deter Saul from his conviction that he needed to sacrifice to YHWH in the right way and at all available times. A plan formed in his mind. He would annihilate the Amalekites, but he would save all the very best of the animals of the Amalekites for sacrifice to YHWH. Yes, better still! He would offer them at the sacred Gilgal, the place where Samuel had abused him. This grand holocaust would clear up that confusion, as the prophet would see that Saul loved YHWH so much as to provide the greatest of sacrificial rituals for God at the most sacred of places.

And then another idea came to Saul. What would be the very greatest sacrifice of all? A king! That was it! The king of the Amalekites. If Saul could manage to capture the king alive, he would offer him too, along with his unblemished beasts, to YHWH at Gilgal. His heart thumped with the genius of the plan and with the sheer excitement of it. No sacrifice like this one had ever been conceived in Israel! Israel would talk of it for generations, how Saul, first and greatest king of Israel, had not only defeated and destroyed the Amalekite heathen, but had also offered to YHWH an all-day burning sacrifice of a countless number of the purest beasts, topped off with the immolation of the enemy king. The enormity of the plan overwhelmed Saul, as he moved to share it with his sons.

Ishvi and Malchishua were enthusiastic about the planned great sacrifice, but Jonathan urged caution.

"My father," he said, "I know you have not forgotten what Samuel said and did to you at Gilgal after you offered the sacrifice before the battle. And even though I agree that you did wait the right amount of time before doing so, still the man accused you of breaking the commands of YHWH. Why risk it again? We all know that Samuel has no love for you and still holds out hope for those monstrous boys of his, although after meeting them at Beer-Sheba, I cannot imagine how he thinks those sots could rule an ant hill, let alone the land of Israel. It is clear that family blood has completely blinded his blind eyes. Why not just allow the troops to obliterate the Amalekites on the field of battle and be done with it? Samuel will have no choice then but to proclaim that you are the king of Israel, rightly chosen by YHWH, and always ready to follow the will of YHWH to the letter."

What Jonathan did not say, but what he clearly thought, was that if Saul went ahead with this sacrificial plan, he was not only risking, again, his kingship, but also Jonathan's future kingship after him. There was no reason to run such a risk, for all of their sakes.

But Saul was not convinced, however reasonable Jonathan's arguments were. Saul saw that the impetuous, action-oriented boy had become a thoughtful and clever man and would make a wonderfully able king after Saul's death. But Saul needed a public victory and a public honoring of YHWH to atone for that humiliating day on Gilgal. He was certain that his plan would work beautifully—a great victory followed by the greatest of sacrifices would please both YHWH and Samuel, and Saul would secure his place in Israelite history and his dynasty over the land. Such a grand event would even help everyone in Israel to forget about the food oath he had made that had led to his near-murder of Jonathan and then to his further humiliation when he had been forced to back down. Perhaps even his son would finally forgive him for that. An unmatched sacrifice was the only way, and Saul had resolved to do just that. His mind was made up, so the word was passed to the troops to save all the unblemished animals from the total annihilation.

King Saul

Once the directions of the king for the battle were clear in the minds of the troops, Abner divided his force, now numbering over 500 with the addition of local tribesmen eager for revenge against the marauding Amalekites, into five separate patrols. The advanced scouts had located several Amalekite raiding parties of ten or fifteen fighters, and Abner sent two of the patrols to destroy them and their animals and families. Amalekite raiders always traveled with their whole kinship groups, since they had few permanent homes in the desert but survived by bartering and trading at the best of times and theft and plunder at the worst. The two patrols would be more than sufficient to take care of these small bands of desperate thieves. Before sending them on their way, Abner sternly reminded them that any pure, unblemished animals located in these camps were to be spared and brought back to Saul's enclosure. The other three patrols moved out together toward the central city of Amalek, a slightly larger encampment deep in the desert where the king, Agag, could be found in his large hide-covered tent, surrounded by stacks of plundered goods, served by slaves, some of those Israelites who had been captured in some raid or other. Abner knew that surprise was on the side of Israel, since Agag's defenses were lax, his guards few, his village walls little more than tiny haphazard heaps of stones, not fit to restrain a goat let alone repel a force of 300 determined soldiers. He was surprised that the Amalekites were not better prepared, but was glad about the fact; perhaps the victory would be all the easier.

He planned to attack the encampment from three sides to insure panic and certain defeat. He would lead the frontal group, while Jonathan and Malchishua led the two flanking patrols. Saul himself insisted that he ride with Abner, even though the general urged him to take special care, since his enormous size, perched high on his magnificent horse, was always a clear target to any skillful archer eager for the glory of the killing of a king. But Saul was nothing if not courageous to the point of foolhardiness , and would not be deterred. Before approaching Amalek, Saul assembled the 300 for a final word.

"Fine fighters of Israel," he began, "today we are fighting the battles of YHWH who has called us to a divine service. Let me make clear my commands to you. You must spare the very finest livestock you encounter. Look carefully at each one. If it is in any way blemished or deformed, kill it quickly and leave it to rot. But if it is pure, without mark, capture it and bring it back to our camp. For every pure animal you capture alive, I will reward you with a fresh sack of beer and a new loaf of bread. And for the one who brings the greatest number of pure animals, I will give him a feast fit for a king, served up by my two lovely daughters in my own tent!"

A huge roar split the air as the troops heartily approved the largess of their king, the massive Saul who was splendid in the morning air, even though he had seen well more than forty springs in his life. Many soldiers dreamed of a night of feasting in Saul's tent and perhaps a night of something more pleasurable with one or both of Saul's daughters, comely women both, though most pined for Michal more than her older sister, Merab. It was Michal whose ripe body and full lips disturbed the dreams of Saul's soldiers. But several said that they would not kick Merab out of bed in any case, since she was after all a woman in her prime and the daughter of the king. Only a fool would avoid such a chance, if it presented itself. With many such thoughts and others no one of the men would share with another the troops awaited the command to march on Amalek. But Saul had one more stipulation.

"Men, if you fight your way to the center of Amalek, and enter the tent of Agag, you must capture him alive. I repeat! Agag must be spared and brought to me bound and ready for sacrifice at Gilgal. For after we have dispatched these squalid Amalekites, we will go straight to Gilgal for the sacrifice to YHWH, who will give us this day the victory. I warn you, all of you. If Agag is killed today in battle, and if I discover who did the killing, I myself will bury the killer up to his neck inside a hill of ants, and I will pour honey over his exposed head, and he will die a most unpleasant and lingering death. Am I understood?"

Saul fixed his army with an unblinking stare, and no one was the slightest bit confused about the life of the king of the Amalekites.

"Grab your swords and spears! Check your arrows and bows! The sooner we dispatch these vermin for YHWH, the sooner we will see our homes and our wives."

Saul turned his horse toward the southern desert, and Abner followed him on his donkey. The several commanders joined in the line of march, followed by the rest of the troops, on foot and in great high spirits.

It was a short walk to Amalek, and Saul's force arrived near the village before the sun was straight overhead. Agag had made his camp in a deep and dry stream bed, whose two walls were some twenty cubits high, affording him a measure of safety from large packs of animals, but also making easier the approach of a force of soldiers, since they could be hidden well by the high earthen walls until they were nearly right on top of the camp. Abner had trained his men to approach silently, creeping low in the sand. The scouts had revealed clearly the layout of the camp.

There were perhaps thirty tents within the heaped up stone walls with the king's prominent tent in the center of the thirty. Outside of the tents were simple pens for the animals, a few donkeys of a low quality, goats for milk and sheep for meat and clothing. Agag had no battle camels, nor camels of any kind. It was a typical assembly of impoverished thieves whose king was a petty tyrant and whose future was very uncertain. Abner's plan was simple and fool proof. The three patrols of one hundred men each would swoop down on the camp from three sides, one down the earthen wall to the east, one from the west, and the third would rush down the gorge, emulating a late summer rainstorm. But this time the storm would not be life giving, but death dealing. The signal was Abner's clever imitation of the call of a hawk. He waited until all was quiet save the few sounds of a camp preparing for the hot afternoon.

He ensured that the patrols were in place, then he put his fingers to his lips, and the sound of a circling hawk filled the blue sky, though if any of the Amalekites had looked up at the sound, they would have seen only empty air. One old man did gaze upward, but he saw no hawk but the flash of a sword catching the sun, followed by the monstrous sound of screams as the first of the patrols rushed over the side of the dirt wall and plunged into the gorge from the west. Meanwhile at the same time another patrol poured over the other wall and, screaming, streamed into the camp from the east. Just two beats later, the third patrol ran toward the camp from the open end of the gorge, and there was created a heaving mass of soldiers and unarmed men and women and children and panicked animals straining to break free from their ropes. Shouts of excitement were matched by screams of terror, as the swords of the Israelites cut heads from necks and limbs from shoulders and feet from legs, spears flew to impale Amalekite men as they reached in vain for their weapons, and showers of arrows stopped other men from joining the fray. The rout was swift and complete, and blood soon made the sand slippery, while cries of anguish and horror struggled with shouts of triumph for first place in the ears of all in the gorge. It took only minutes for several Israelites to reach the tent of the king, and once there, they rushed in, killed the few guards where they stood, and pointed eight swords at the heart of the king before he could rise to attempt a defense.

The lead soldier, Cushi by name, shouted at Agag, "Put down your weapon, Agag, you are captured, your men are dead, and your town is destroyed! The fight is over; you must surrender in the name of YHWH!"

Agag was no fool; he had not survived in the southern deserts all these years, growing passably powerful and rich, by struggling when struggle was futile. He had been defeated before, and had lived to rule a rabble of tribesmen again. This time would be no different.

"I readily submit to superior arms and tactics. You are clever men. Just who are you?"

The king quickly had regained his composure; he knew he had to remain in control of himself if he were to live on.

"We are Israelites and servants of King Saul, the great monarch of the northern mountains, and we have come on a mission of YHWH, our God, to destroy your people."

Agag thought the simple soldier insolent and ill mannered in his presence, but his claim to have destroyed his people deeply disturbed him.

"You have come to destroy the Amalekites?" he asked. "Surely we can come to some agreement between us. I am not a poor man, and I have many things that any great king would long to possess. Please lead me to this Saul, and he and I will make a treaty with one another."

Sly smirks crossed the faces of the soldiers, as they thought that no treaty was in fact possible between one people and another when one of the peoples no longer existed. They roughly tied Agag's hands behind his back, and pushed him outside into the carnage of the day. The king gagged as he saw what his camp had become, a slaughterhouse of blood and bone and ruined flesh. All of his people were dead, every last one. They had been slashed and impaled and abused beyond recognition; the men, the women, even the tiny children were broken like cloth images, like smashed pottery, like discarded refuse on a nightmare heap of trash. He could not walk in any direction without stepping in gore, without tripping over a part of a body, without slipping in blood. He had seen death, more dead people than he cared to number, but death like this, complete, monstrous, total death he had not seen. Such death was unspeakable, unimaginable, obscene.

Just then, a gigantic man strode toward Agag, his massive arms spread wide, a manic grin on his face. Agag thought this must be the king of these crazed warriors.

"Well," shouted the huge man, "Here is the king, the infamous Agag, alive and well!" Agag knew it was important to show deference to the victor, so he immediately fell on his knees before this Saul, in the process dropping his right knee directly into the entrails of a dead man, whose head had been struck from his trunk during the insane battle. In momentary horror the king struggled to extricate himself from the mess that was once human, but his pinned arms made getting out of what was left of the man difficult; Saul reached down and helped Agag to stand clear of the corpse.

"No need for servitude now, Agag! I have great plans for you."

And with a hard-edged laugh, Saul turned his back on the king, signaling for Abner to take care of him, and moved quickly toward his great horse.

Abner grabbed Agag by his bound arms and began to drag him toward his donkey. As he stumbled awkwardly along, the king spoke to Abner, who seemed a reasonable soldier.

"What was the point of the wanton slaughter of all my people? What need did you feel to dismember babies and old men? Why disembowel perfectly good goats and sheep? Just what sort of people are you?"

"We follow the hard commands of our God and that God's prophet, the immortal Samuel, who sent Saul and us on this mission. We were to annihilate the Amalekites, and we have done just that."

Abner had no interest in further discussion of things theological, things beyond his soldierly interest. But Agag persisted.

"The commands of the gods are strange, to be sure, but surely no god would ask for the slaughter of babies and the waste of good livestock, especially in the blasted desert where babies and livestock are precious things."

"I do my duty to my king," growled Abner, "and I have no more interest in this subject."

Agag wanted to ask what his own fate was to be, but because he was now in the grip of seeming madmen, he chose not to speculate further.

Saul was thrilled with the victory. All had gone just as he had planned. He had a fine selection of pure beasts for sacrifice, and he had Agag, the king, to culminate the service in glorious fashion. And the Amalekites were annihilated; Jonathan and

King Saul

Malchishua had done their duty and had destroyed all persons and unclean beasts among the small Amalekite encampments that lay scattered in the deserts. The Amalekites were no more; all living traces of them were gone and soon the reliable carrion of the desert, bird and insect, would complete Saul's work. (Of course, further south and further west more persons calling themselves children of Amalek still lived and later would become the targets of another king of Israel.) Only a fading memory would remain of these thieves, and after the great sacrifice of their clean beasts and their king at Gilgal soon to come, even that memory would in time disappear. Perhaps a few descendants would persist for a time, but like the Hittites and Sumerians, ancient peoples once great, the Amalekites would become merely names without faces. YHWH must be pleased with the work of Saul, YHWH's servant. And Samuel, who seemed to hope for Saul's failure, would now be forced to admit that his choice of the son of Kish was the right one after all. With a light heart, and a flashing smile, Saul mounted his horse and faced his troops again.

"My great warriors, as I knew it would be, so it has become! YHWH has given to us a magnificent victory over the Amalekite scum, and all we now need to do is bury our few dead and march back to Gilgal. There is little need for hurry in the face of so enormous a success, but I am eager to conclude the matter in the way it must be done. We will offer a sacrifice at Gilgal such as has never been offered, a sacrifice that your grandchildren will speak of with awe. Let us move back north and home. And this time we will even wait for the aged Samuel so he too can see that we will honor his God, and ours, and that YHWH has smiled once again on the chosen people!"

And with a great shout of joy, Saul raised his spear, the very sign of his power and kingship, high into the sky as if he wanted YHWH to see it and smile along with him. Fewer than twenty Israelite soldiers had died in the slaughter, so deft had been the plan and the surprise, so only a scant few graves were needed to bury those dead. Soon, the force moved off north, with Saul and his three sons and Abner leading the march. The spring air had never been more lovely, the flowers in the valleys of the north more lush, the grass more plentiful. The pure beasts ate with gusto, and Saul did not hurry them along, so full was his heart of his success and his future. He had never felt better, and had never been so convinced that he was indeed the king of Israel.

15

While the forces of Israel were on joyous return to Gilgal and a colossal sacrifice, Samuel brooded in Ramah. He had sent Saul on YHWH's mission to obliterate the Amalekites, and had only scant hope that the gigantic king would be able to perform the task. He had after all failed before at Gilgal, failed to wait until Samuel had arrived, failed to offer anything like an appropriate sacrifice. And then there was that ridiculous oath that had nearly cost the king the life of his first-born, Jonathan. Samuel smiled to himself when he pictured the great oaf towering high over his troops, ready to murder his son due to his confused notion of YHWH's demands. Why had YHWH forced him to anoint this Saul? It had been a monstrous error from the beginning, and Samuel was exhausted in his attempts to keep the king in line and to keep the hopes of his sons alive. He was so old! His body was a shadow of its former vigor, his legs useless, his eyes darkened, his voice a dry crackle, like the flames of a bramble fire. He had to admit to himself that he was very glad that YHWH had asked him to send Saul against the Amalekites. Surely, YHWH knew what Samuel knew: Saul was doomed to fail, and with that failure, it would be time to get rid of the giant man once and for all. His sons' time had come at last! As poor as the boys had proven to be, they were Samuel's only sons, and they would be his heirs in the land he loved.

The idea of ridding himself of Saul finally and completely fixed itself in his brain. Two of his slaves appeared to bathe their master. They heated the water for the basin and gently picked Samuel up and laid him into the large bronze pool that he had had brought to Ramah from the metal worker in Beth Shemesh. Samuel felt its smooth sides with deep appreciation for the workmanship. On the outside of the tub there were artistic portrayals of palm trees and water birds, great fish and crocodiles with huge mouths, studded with rows of terrifying teeth. Samuel of course could see none of this, but his slave, Etan, had carefully described the pictures to him, and Samuel had many times over the past weeks lain pleasantly in the tub and allowed his hands to play slowly over the raised etched pictures. But today his mind was only filled with one idea: Saul had to be deposed soon. If Samuel were to die with Saul on the throne, his sons would be left in Beer-Sheba and forgotten. And what would happen if, against all expectations, Saul managed to fulfill the command of YHWH, and was able to annihilate the Amalekites? What then? The people would never allow Samuel to act against the king; he would be too popular, and in Samuel's incapacities they would forget him, too. What must he do? If he were only younger, more vigorous, more able to act now, decisively on his own!

Suddenly, he was convinced that YHWH was speaking. It was not quite as clear to him as that wondrous voice in the temple of Shiloh those uncountable years before, but he felt it was the God. As he lay in his bath, luxuriating in the heat of the water, his ancient bones held up by the delicious buoyancy, YHWH's words were clarified in his brain, as if the water had cleansed them of their opacity. Samuel knew that YHWH felt about Saul exactly as he did! And he was glad beyond all telling of it.

"I am sorry that I made Saul king!" said YHWH, and Samuel was in full agreement with that sentiment; he was sorry too that he had ever raised that horn of oil over the fool's head outside the gate of his city.

"Saul has turned away from following me, has not established my word!"

Yes, it was true, thought Samuel. Saul had rejected YHWH's commands at Gilgal by not waiting for him, YHWH's prophet, to perform the sacrifice. Samuel vaguely remembered that when he had asked Saul to wait, he had said nothing about YHWH's command, but that mattered little; he, Samuel, was the very voice of YHWH, and to disobey one was to disobey the other. Was YHWH talking only about that earlier apostasy, or had the so-called king done something else to anger the demanding God? Samuel did not know, but he imagined that Saul had probably acted foolishly in some way, because it is all one could expect from him.

Samuel croaked as loudly as his voice allowed.

"Etan! Etan! Hurry in here and get me out of this tub! I have work to do. Call the bearers now!"

The slave was always ready to serve, and rushed into the bath chamber with his assistant at his heels. The two men reached into the water, now fetid and cold with the old man's dirt and body fluids floating on the surface, and lifted him out onto the waiting blankets, freshly washed expressly for the occasions of the great man's bath. Once Samuel was safely seated on the blankets, his wasted body wrapped in cloths of sheep's wool, Etan rushed from the chamber to call the bearers. The sun had not yet risen fully over the horizon, and the bearers would be asleep. Etan shook them awake and demanded that they wash their faces, don their finest tunics, and come quickly to the master's house, prepared to work. They did as they were told, and not much time had elapsed before the four large and muscled men stood holding the palanquin, ready to carry mighty Samuel wherever it was he asked. They were prepared to bear him from Dan to Beer-Sheba, since that is why they were chosen for this work. Secretly, each hoped the trip would be short, but they would never say such things aloud. It was an enormous honor to bear the glorious, if now shriveled, body of Israel's greatest prophet. Each bearer stood at rigid attention, waiting Etan's orders.

Samuel's spies in Saul's army had been busy. They knew well that the victorious force was marching slowly toward Gilgal, and were less than a day's distance from the shrine. Samuel met one of them as he was carried by Etan and the assistant toward the palanquin.

"Where are they exactly?" said Samuel to the man.

"My lord, the army is in the highest of spirits, and they are not one sun's walk from Gilgal. If I might add, my lord, they have not come from the Amalekites alone. They have any number of fine sheep and goats with them, and I thought I saw, although I am not completely certain, an Amalekite nobleman in the company as well. It might even be the king, but since I have never seen the man, I am not certain. Forgive my ignorance, great Samuel!"

"Sheep and goats? And perhaps the king? What can this mean?" croaked Samuel, his face flushed with increasing rage.

But while his face flushed outwardly, his mind rejoiced. He thought to himself, "Well, the fool has done it now! Livestock and the king! This is no *cherem*! This is no obliteration! Saul has hanged himself on these goats and sheep, and he will not escape my fury. YHWH is right; Saul needs to die!"

He motioned Etan to carry him out to the bearers, but again he was stopped by another of his spies.

"My lord," the man said breathlessly, "Saul passed Carmel on his way to Gilgal, and he there built a shrine to himself to commemorate his victory over the Amalekites. He is now closing in on the sacred place of Gilgal."

A shrine for himself! He adds to his apostasy by declaring himself greater than YHWH who gives the victory! What sort of king is this who thinks himself greater than the only king of Israel! Spittle formed at the corners of Samuel's mouth as fury overtook him. He did not bother to ask the man whether this monument building had actually occurred, but he was convinced that it is precisely the sort of thing that the fool Saul would do.

"Take me to Gilgal" he shouted, "and run all the way!"

The bearers lifted Samuel into the palanquin, raised it to their shoulders, and began a forced march run to the shrine. Behind the curtains of the palanquin, Samuel seethed and raged and knew that his upcoming meeting with Saul would be his last, and that Saul's kingship had come to an inevitable end.

Meanwhile, the army had arrived at Gilgal, had pitched their tents at the base of the hill where the shrine stood, had tethered the animals for sacrifice, and had made certain that Agag was securely guarded for his starring sacrificial role to come. Saul's spacious tent had gone up first, and the king and his sons and commanders were soon lounging comfortably on soft rugs and furs, sipping fine wine, plundered from the Amalekites and kept cool by submerging the sacks in a nearby stream, swollen with snow melt from Mt. Hermon in the far north. The conversation was lively, sprinkled with stories from the victory just past.

King Saul

"Did you see how those Amalekites' eyes widened when we slipped over the two sides of their supposed protective hills? They never would have dreamed they were vulnerable as stupid lambs in that place!"

Ishvi howled with derisive laughter as he recounted the foolishness of the enemy.

Malchishua added, "That so-called king is a shifty man. Did you see how he first thought he would fight with us, but then just as quickly changed his tune toward some sort of bargain, as if he had anything to bargain with!"

And Abner said, "The whole thing was like a summer's bird hunt, and not a battle. Except the birds are more clever!"

The whole tent rocked with laughter, and Saul looked at his sons and his general and glowed with genuine pleasure at these wonderful comrades. He felt his complete vindication in the eyes of the people, of his son, and of Samuel was at hand. He leaned back comfortably and took a huge swallow of the sweet wine. Life was good when you were a victorious king with adoring people all around and a sack of wine at your lips!

Just then Jonathan burst into the tent; Saul had not noticed that he was not in attendance at the gathering, and his irritation clouded his joy.

"Father," his oldest son shouted," Samuel is outside and requests leave to speak with you!"

"Wants to speak with me, does he?" said Saul. "I suppose I could give the old boy a few moments of my precious time. Ishvi, see that my wine stays cool, while I converse with the great prophet and demonstrate to him how his God must be pleased with us. Whether or not the shifty weasel himself will be pleased, well, we will see about that!"

And with a quick laugh, Saul ducked his head and emerged from the tent.

He found Samuel sitting painfully on the ground on a pile of colorful furs, in front of his familiar palanquin. His bearers and his servant—what was his name—were standing at firm attention around the miniature man. Saul smiled broadly and gave the prophet a deep bow; he felt he could afford a bow to Samuel and not appear some sort of underling. A military victory will afford that luxury. Besides, the blind prophet would not see it in any case.

"May YHWH bless you, Samuel. I have established the words of YHWH!"

Saul straightened and awaited the sure approbation of the harsh old man. He must now have the grace to agree that this time he had done precisely as he had been told, and that YHWH was pleased with his kingly servant. Samuel turned his blind eyes in the direction of Saul's voice and was silent. He then turned his face away from the king and shifted his body to the left in a contorted movement that must have cost the prophet considerable pain.

"So you have obeyed, have you? So you have established the word of your God?"

The words were bitter, the tone nasty, not at all what Saul had expected. The king braced himself, since he knew from the past with this smelly old monster that he could twist and turn words and actions in unexpected ways, could make the straight appear crooked, the large small. The smile was gone from Saul's face, and sweat beaded his brow as the silence stretched out after these initial words. What possibly could make the prophet angry this time? What problem could there possibly be now?

The twisted body slowly turned itself back in the direction of Saul, who was now standing less erect, now more bent over, as if he was shrinking down to the size of the prophet.

"What then is the sound of these sheep in my ears, the sound of the livestock I hear?"

The tone was quizzical, but there was within it an undercurrent of menace, like a snake at the bottom of a water hole filled with fish. But the question made Saul relax. So that was it! The prophet was merely surprised to hear the sound of livestock, because he had expected that all Amalekite people and goods had been destroyed on the field of battle; he had no way of knowing that Saul had decided to offer a grand holocaust of the animals he had saved as an unforgettable way to honor YHWH. He sighed in relief.

"I and the people have spared the very best of the sheep and the livestock in order to sacrifice them to YHWH, your God, here in Gilgal. All the very worthless animals, as well as all the people, men, women and children we have annihilated just as you and YHWH directed. The *cherem* demand has been fulfilled."

He decided to save the surprise of Agag for later, as a kind of dessert for the day of sacrifice to come. How could Samuel not be pleased with the promise of a great day of divine celebration, using only the purest of beasts, topped off with the immolation of the king of the destroyed people? YHWH's anger would be calmed, and Samuel would be deeply pleased and blessed by the rites on Gilgal.

Samuel raised himself up as well as his twisted spine allowed and spat a thick wad of spittle in the direction of Saul's voice. Saul was shocked at the gesture of public rudeness; spittle was not something that a donkey driver would direct at his most unworthy beast. How much more disgusting was this act in the presence of a king?

"Shut up!" shouted the croaking voice. " I have heard enough of your absurd words! Let me tell you what YHWH said to me last night!"

Saul knew that it was a hardly a request to him, asking if he wanted to hear what YHWH had spoken to Samuel; Samuel would speak on if a guard tore out his tongue, an action Saul contemplated for a brief time.

Instead, the king said simply, "Speak," and waited for the heated words he knew were on the way.

"Even though you may be little in your own eyes, are you not in fact the chief of the tribes of Israel?"

What in Sheol could that strange phrase mean, thought Saul?

"I hardly think that I am little in my own eyes; I have not been little in anyone's eyes since I was five years old; I am the tallest man in the land, and everyone knows it! And, yes, I am the head of all the tribes in Israel, because you, old man, anointed me to be so. The only time I ever feel little is when I am in your presence, Samuel. You have ever delighted in seeing me little, enjoying making me small in front of my sons and my general and my people."

While Saul was speaking, he stood up straighter and straighter until no one could fail to see his tremendous size, while the tiny shouting figure seated in front of him was barely noticeable, some sort of insect, a creature whom Saul could have squashed with one step of his sandals. But the creature was far from finished.

"Yes, it is true that YHWH, through me, anointed you king over Israel, and then sent you on a mission. Let me quote to you again what YHWH said. 'Go! Utterly annihilate the sinners, the Amalekites,' that is, perform the sacred *cherem*. Fight against them until they are completely consumed, swallowed into the great maw of the earth. Why did you not listen to the voice of YHWH? Why did you swoop down on the spoil and do what was evil in YHWH's eyes?"

Saul hardly knew where to begin in answering this infuriating speech. Just as he had the last time at Gilgal, Samuel was playing false with the demands he had made. When he had charged Saul with the destruction of the Amalekites, he had said nothing about "fighting against them until they were consumed." Those had not been YHWH's words. YHWH had merely said to perform *cherem*; it was Saul's decision to complete the *cherem* here at Gilgal. So he had not "swooped on the spoil," as if he were some sort of common thief. These accusations were absurd, and Saul would not let them stand as some sort of prophetic truth when they were in fact the lies of a cruel and jealous old man whose life should have ended many springs ago.

Saul spoke loudly enough so the dull ears of Samuel did not have to strain and so that all the people could witness the failed attempt of the prophet to humiliate Saul once again.

"I most certainly have obeyed the voice of YHWH. I have gone on the mission on which YHWH sent me. And, by the way, I have also spared Agag, king of the Amalekites, along with the very best of their livestock, for one purpose and one purpose only; to sacrifice to YHWH your God here at Gilgal. Once that sacrifice is ended, once the animals and the king have passed through the fire, the Amalekites will be no more, and *cherem* will be fulfilled. You may be astonishingly old, Samuel, but even your aged ears and mind can understand those facts."

Let the old man answer that, Saul thought. He may think that his way of thinking is the only way, but he will soon realize that it is not. I am king, and I have the right to do as I wish. That is what this infuriating man himself said the day of my private anointing: "Do whatever you see fit to do, for God is with you." Those were his very words, now etched in Saul's memory. Well, he has now seen fit to hold a great sacrifice to YHWH in order to complete the *cherem*. Who dares to contradict the plans of the king of Israel?

And suddenly, what Saul was only thinking, he blurted out loud. "Who dares to contradict the king of Israel?"

King Saul

In the silence, Samuel motioned for his servant to lift him up from the furs. Even standing, partially erect, Samuel barely came up to Saul's waist, but his sightless eyes were fixed on the king. His chest heaved with the painful effort of standing, his lungs squeezed by the twisted spine that forced him to turn his head upwards as far as it could go. His mouth opened to speak, and the foulness of his rotted teeth and reddened tongue, pocked with sores from years of rubbing over those craggy teeth, filled the air between them. Saul nearly gagged at the odor, but refused to yield the position of power over Samuel, whose size was made ridiculous by the gigantic king who had just issued the challenge. And from that foul mouth came the astonishing voice again, that voice dimmed by enormous age, now seemingly reborn, reenergized, renewed somehow by the challenge of the king. Amazement was all around, as Samuel dropped his years, almost one by one, and spoke his withering word again in the presence of all the people.

"Does YHWH care as much for burnt-offerings and sacrifices as in obedience to YHWH? To obey is far better than sacrifice! To listen is far better than fatted rams! Rebellion against God is just as evil as sorcery! Defiance of God's demands is just as evil as idolatry! Since you have rejected the word of YHWH, YHWH has rejected you as the king of Israel!"

The last words poured out in a strangled voice, but that voice was heard by everyone present. Samuel fell back on the furs, his fall only slightly cushioned by Etan. The great effort he had made in speaking these terrible words had exhausted him, and he lay on his side panting. The servant fanned his sweating face, then held a skin of wine to his lips. The sound of the panting filled the silence that the words had created. No one moved. No one talked, or even whispered. Saul was erect as before, but his face looked as if it had been slapped. His eyes were closed, the deep wrinkles of his forehead stood in sharp outline below his tangled graying hair. All were stunned. The king had been removed from his kingship by the prophet of God! He was in effect no longer king. But if that were so, then who was king? Jonathan? But Saul was still very much alive, very much present with them, very much the military leader of the people. How could he not be king?

Saul's eyes were closed, because he was carefully assessing what he had just heard from Samuel. He remembered each word of the outburst, and he was readying himself for a response. How should he respond? The enraged prophet had clearly misunderstood his intentions to sacrifice the spared beasts. Although he had twice said that that was what he had decided to do, the old man was so fixed in his ideas about *cherem* that he had not heard—or had not been willing to hear. It was clearer to Saul than it had ever been that Samuel's goal all along was to humiliate and depose him as king. And his actions here at Gilgal had offered the ancient soothsayer the chance he had been craving. His very words of condemnation made his intentions clearer than the stream Kishon where Deborah, the great judge, had mustered the forces of Israel against Sisera. Later the Canaanite general had been lured into the tent of Jael, wife of Heber the Kenite, and had, instead of required hospitality, received a tent peg in his skull. Saul felt today like Sisera, that unfortunate victim. He had expected thanks and praise from a pleased Samuel at last for his brilliant defeat of the Amalekites and his proposed grand sacrifice. What he had received instead was no better than a well-aimed tent peg. Yet, thought Saul, was this peg so well aimed?

Samuel had begun his assault by suggesting that YHWH preferred obedience to sacrifice. Well, Saul had been obedient, as he had said to Samuel twice. His intended sacrifice was not anything other than part of that obedience. The question was not one of obedience, however much Samuel claimed it was; the question was one of interpretation of the commands of YHWH. Did no one else, save Samuel, have the right to interpret what YHWH commanded? He had gone on to say that he, Saul, was a rebel against YHWH, one who defies YHWH's commands. Nothing could be further from the truth. He had gone to battle; he had been victorious; the Amalekites were annihilated. After the sacrifice to YHWH, their name would be expunged from the earth. No, this was not a matter of obedience or disobedience; it was a matter of interpretation, which was in the long run a matter of power. Just who had the power in Israel, Samuel or Saul? That was the real question of the prophet's claims about Saul's so-called disobedience. It all came down to power. He claimed I have "rejected the word of YHWH." That is plainly not true! What I have rejected is Samuel's claims to be the only one who knows the words of YHWH.

Saul opened his eyes and spoke into the heavy quiet of Gilgal. He chose his words very carefully.

"By your light I have sinned, Samuel. In the way you have understood the command of YHWH, I have been incorrect. I have indeed moved beyond your reading of that command, interpreted the command rather differently than you have. I have honored the people and listened to their voice. I do not blame them for my actions. They and I decided, at my initiative, to save the best for sacrifice. I can well imagine how you might think that I listened to their voice at the expense of listening to the voice of YHWH, but that is simply not true. My decision for sacrifice was an attempt to honor YHWH, and my people, in a way I felt fully fitting to the command and to the requirements of *cherem*. So, I ask you, Samuel, prophet of Israel, and my anointer, forgive my sin in your eyes, and come with me so that I may complete the sacrifice to YHWH that I have promised."

Saul said all this calmly, and in a reasoned tone. He felt that he had responded to the fury of the prophet in as fine a way as possible. He hoped against hope that the panting ancient one, lying on the furs at his feet, would at last calm and see reason, that he would make a public display of unity at the shrine with him. The last thing Israel needed now was a rift between the two most powerful men in the land. The Philistine threat was growing again, and the utter defeat of the Amalekites, and the subsequent unifying celebration, would go a long way toward the needed oneness for the struggles ahead. Perhaps Samuel would forget his worthless sons at last and pledge unity with the rightful king of the land. If not, Saul thought he might have to destroy the old man, as he perhaps should have done long ago.

With the help of Etan again, Samuel clambered up on his knees that popped with age. On his next words rested the future of Israel, and well he knew it.

Again he puffed out his bird-like chest and shouted as loudly as he could, "I will most certainly not worship with you. You have rejected the word of YHWH, and YHWH has rejected you as king over Israel!"

A slight movement of Samuel's head bid the bearers to come and lift him into the palanquin. They did so, but before he could be placed behind the curtains, Saul impulsively reached out to restrain the prophet's departure; there was still time to reason with him, Saul thought. He could not let him get away with the words of God's rejection resounding throughout the shrine as the last thing everyone would hear. But Saul's movement was too slow; instead of catching Samuel's arm, Saul grabbed only the sleeve of his filthy tunic. As the bearers continued to lift him into the palanquin, Saul's powerful grip did not let go, and the sound of ripping was heard as the tunic's sleeve tore away from Samuel's garment, that garment the prophet always wore when he appeared in public. A slight motion from the prophet stopped his progress into the palanquin. Once again, his sightless eyes turned to face the king whose right hand still held the sleeve of the tunic.

The foul mouth opened again, and he said, "YHWH has ripped the kingdom from you this day, just as surely as you have ripped my sacred tunic. Moreover, YHWH has given the kingdom into the hand of a neighbor of yours, who is far better than you. And believe this, Saul! YHWH will not deceive anyone nor will YHWH change anything; YHWH is no human being who changes!"

The word "change" hung in the air, as the prophet was placed back in the palanquin. The four bearers hoisted it to their shoulders and prepared to trot back to Ramah.

Saul shouted through the closed curtain, "I have already admitted that I have sinned in your eyes; what more can you want? You must honor me now publicly before these people, and before all Israel. It is important for us all, and for the future of the land, that you and I at least are seen to have a working relationship. Please, Samuel, I beg you. Go with me now to the sacrifice so that I may worship YHWH as I have promised!"

Saul heard a thump of the prophet's stick as he called for the palanquin to stop. The bearers placed it back on the ground, and Samuel poked his head through the curtains.

"Etan," he yelled, and the servant appeared as if by magic. "Carry me to the shrine!"

With great relief, Saul strode toward the large stone altar, and commanded that the pure Amalekite beasts be led to the place. One after the other, Saul slit the throats of the animals and hurled their carcasses onto the fire, all the while uttering the sacred words, fulfilling his promise for sacrifice. But his grand sacrifice, his hoped-for vindication by Samuel and YHWH and the people, had vanished like the smoke rising now into the sky. The prophet had spoiled his triumph! As he slit the final animal throat, Saul noted that Samuel sat mute in his palanquin, staring blindly into some place known only to him. He did not participate in the rites, did not even add an Amen at the appropriate places in the liturgy. His final humiliation of me! Well, mused Saul, at least he would have the satisfaction of burning the king, Agag, in the presence of Samuel, thus completing *cherem*, as he had promised and as Samuel had rejected. He motioned for Agag to be brought to the stone.

But even that satisfaction was not to be his. At the sound of the prisoner stumbling toward the altar, bound hand and foot, Samuel perked up in his palanquin, and demanded of his servant, "Who is that coming?"

Etan answered that it was Agag, king of the Amalekites.

"Bring him here," the prophet shouted.

The slaves who were in charge of the king did not know whose orders to follow, but they too had heard Samuel's rejection of Saul, so they quickly decided to obey the voice of Samuel. They dragged Agag toward the palanquin. As he approached the prophet, a small smile trembled on his lips, as he thought, "Ah, death's bitterness is turned aside! This ancient worthy and I will sort things out together, we will make a treaty one with the other, and I will get out of this mad house of insane men!"

But the closer Agag came to Samuel, the less certain he was of his hope for a future. The fantastically old man was horrid to see with his distorted body, milky white eyes, face furrowed like the land in the dry season, legs turned in ways they ought not go. And that mouth with those brown stubs that once were teeth! Agag nearly asked a slave nearby to bring him some wine, but remembered that this slave was not his own to command. The horrible mouth opened and the smell of death poured out. "Just as your sword has bereaved many a woman, so may your mother be bereaved more than them all!" Amazingly, the tiny prophet produced from his tunic a short sword, concealed in the folds, and managed to cut Agag's throat before he could utter a sound. The king fell to the ground, his blood gurgling, then spurting from his mouth and neck. He was probably dead before he hit the ground, his dreams of a new kingdom to rule stilled in dreadful death.

Saul watched him die, knowing that the grand finale of his sacrifice had been snatched from his grasp. The day of his supposed triumph had ended in complete disaster. The blood of the king of the Amalekites soaked into the soil, drained away into the ground around Gilgal, just as Saul's hopes had apparently disappeared that day. Was he king? Samuel twice had said no. Samuel had also said that YHWH had chosen a "neighbor" of Saul's. Just who was that? Had the crafty prophet been out pouring oil from his flask on someone else, keeping it secret until today? But why not say who it was? Why not bring the man to Gilgal and make a public spectacle of a coronation, while at the same time humiliating the first and real king of Israel?

King Saul

Was the old man bluffing? Did he really have someone else in mind for a new king? Saul watched Samuel's palanquin head back west for Ramah, and wondered what the future held for him. As far as he was concerned he was still king, no matter what that old has-been had claimed. He had won the victory, as he had been sent to do, and no one could deny that. It was his word against Samuel's, and Saul knew that in not many more days that old creature would find his way to Sheol at last. He had only to wait, since time was clearly on his side. But he must also be watchful, for if there were some new king already chosen, Saul would need to deal with him. The game was far from over, Samuel! You have not heard the last of Saul, I vow!

16

Samuel fumed in his palanquin as it bumped its steady way back to Ramah. Several times, he shouted for the bearers to slow their pace; his ancient bones could no longer take the pounding of a forced march, and he was really in no hurry to get home. He was more furious than he could ever remember being, since he had never been challenged so directly in public as he just had been. And by that dolt Saul of all people! By YHWH he had made the man, and he just as easily had thrown him away. But at what cost? The people's great joy at the victory over the Amalekites had turned into confusion and fear when they witnessed the public humiliation of their king. Then too Samuel had been so angry at the man that he had said something that was hardly true: YHWH, as far as he knew, and who would know what YHWH was about more than he, had not in fact chosen Saul's replacement from among Saul's neighbors or among anyone else. That idiot Saul had forced him into a lie, something he always tried to avoid; lies had this way of coming back later to cause trouble for the liar, and Samuel was in no mood for any more trouble. He had trouble enough as it was. Hence his foul feelings of dissatisfaction at the whole affair. Just as he had feared, Saul had made a mess of things and had dragged Samuel into the bog with him. If only the fool had simply done his duty, simply killed all the wretched Amalekites and their king in the field of battle, as Samuel had expected, and none of this would have happened.

But then again, if Saul had done the *cherem* in the way Samuel expected, there would have been no ready-made occasion for Samuel to upbraid the arrogant king, no occasion for public rejection and humiliation, and no occasion to try again to gain leadership for his aging sons, Joel and Abijah. Though he had heard nothing but bad reports about the two men from Beer Sheba for years, Samuel remained convinced that just a few months under his direct tutelage would straighten them out; they could be made leaders still.

But Saul was still very much alive, however cowed he might now feel. Unless there were really some new potential king to stand in Saul's place, someone who could hold power long enough for Samuel to groom his sons for the job, the imposing Saul remained a genuine thorn in the flesh, or in truth a sharp pain in the groin. Again, Samuel shouted for the bearers to slow their pace; he needed to think. But his anger was still overwhelming his clarity of thought. What could he do to remove this Saul once and for all? Murder could possibly be arranged, but the sheer size and power of the man would make the choice of assassin perhaps not so easy. And besides Saul's killing, so soon after Samuel's public assault on him, could look suspicious. Another humiliation? He could certainly arrange that, but twice was enough to break most men, and although Saul had been saddened and beaten down to an extent, he was still the king in reality, no matter what Samuel had proclaimed at Gilgal. No, there had to be another way, and again, rocking steadily to the now calming trot of the bearers, Samuel's mind returned again to the idea of another man. That just could work, he thought. But who? It would need to be someone extraordinary, someone little known, someone charismatic, but different than Saul. No gigantic warrior, no battle-hardened veteran. Someone younger perhaps, someone anxious for success and advancement, but not too difficult to control. But try as he might, Samuel could not stop the furious thoughts from invading again, pushing out the sharp vision he needed to solve the problem of Saul. Saul! Would to God he had never heard of the man! What could YHWH have been thinking to select such a miscreant to be the king of the people? Saul! Saul! What was YHWH thinking?

And suddenly YHWH spoke. Or at least Samuel was convinced that it was YHWH who spoke, which amounted to the same thing for him.

"How long will you waste your time in complaining about Saul? I have rejected him as king of Israel!"

YHWH as always was right; Samuel was spending too much time and energy worrying and wondering about the problem of Saul. He had rejected him as king, and YHWH had done so, too. But now what? YHWH continued, moving through Samuel's thoughts.

"Fill up your horn with the oil and go! I will send you to Jesse, the man of Bethlehem, because I have seen among his sons my king."

Bethlehem, thought Samuel. Who would guess that the new king would come from there? It was a very small village, a long day south of Ramah, in a green valley close to the heathen high mountain town of Jebus. It was surrounded by fertile fields, and there were more than a few large land owners there. But Jesse? He had never heard of the man, he did not think, but how else had the name appeared in his mind? He would have to ask after the location of his farm.

But the choice of a son of Jesse presented certain difficulties, and Samuel was initially reluctant and fearful.

"I am an old man, YHWH, and a marked one. You and I have just publicly rejected Saul as king. If I go to Bethlehem, and anoint his successor, and if Saul catches wind of it, he will kill me."

Samuel now was speaking to YHWH as if YHWH were really in dialogue with him. Perhaps YHWH was; Samuel had for so long been YHWH's mouthpiece, it was no longer easy for him to distinguish his words from the words of the God, if they were finally to be distinguished.

King Saul

YHWH, or Samuel, responded, "Take a calf with you, and announce, 'I have come to sacrifice to YHWH.' Then invite Jesse to join you, and I will show you what to do, and that is this: you will anoint for me the one I show you."

It was a good plan; Samuel of course was high priest in the land and regularly led sacrifices to YHWH in every town and village in Israel. No one would think twice about the priest appearing in Bethlehem for sacrifice.

Samuel shouted at the bearers to quicken their pace again for Ramah; he needed to collect his sacred horn of oil and to select a pure calf from the sacrificial stall for the ruse as suggested by YHWH. Yes, this was perfect. A replacement for the rejected Saul and from a place far enough away from Gibeah, and so little recognized or thought of, that no one would be aware of the anointing until several days afterward. By then Samuel would have had time to groom the man for his kingly duties and time to prepare the people of Israel to accept a new king. Samuel smiled again, and forgot about Saul as a problem and thought of him now as dead, dead to him and dead to YHWH and Israel. And he was rejuvenated! He was in power again, and making and deposing kings. He eagerly demanded that Etan fetch the sacred horn, and to make sure that it was full of oil. After only a brief break, the powerful bearers had the palanquin up on their shoulders and began to move straight south toward Bethlehem. They groaned inwardly, not looking forward to another long trot, but the one advantage of their burden's vast age was that he had become increasingly light with every passing year. It was almost as if the palanquin were empty when their master lay inside. They often joked at the expense of other bearers of important personages in the land, other aging men whose passing years brought extra folds around their middles and extra chins around their throats. One could always tell the weight of the burden by the depth of the grunts and the rivers of sweat pouring off the bearers. Samuel's men saw themselves as very lucky indeed and tended to overlook the sharp rebukes and disgusting breath of their master. They feared his death, for then they might find themselves bearing a man the size of a bear. In their dreams they saw Saul no longer able to walk and having to be carried the length and breadth of the land. Upon awakening, the sweat matched that of their more unfortunate friends.

So they trotted off, if not gladly, at least happy at the lightness of their master. Etan rode behind on Samuel's donkey with the calf tied securely to the donkey's rump, bleating sadly to be so confined. The tiny train reached Bethlehem and its low stone-walls just before the sun set. Several elders of the village came out to meet them, and they were visibly trembling. The news of Saul's humiliation by Samuel at Gilgal had reached them even here, and they, like nearly everyone else in Israel, did not know what to think about the confusing event. Was Saul still king, or not? Was Samuel still intent on replacing him with his own worthless sons, as rumor continued to have it? No one knew, but no one was willing to take any chances. Many had decided to stay out of the squabble between the men of power, to farm their land, to raise and protect their families, and to leave politics to those who did such things. But for the elders of Bethlehem, politics had just appeared.

"Do you come in peace?" they asked the prophet, and hoped he was here on a simple religious pilgrimage.

They noticed the bleating calf tied to his donkey, and though Bethlehem was hardly on any of the familiar pilgrimage routes, perhaps the high priest was merely looking for a place of retreat where he might escape the pressures of leadership. The one thing Bethlehem possessed in abundance was quiet, along with a very pleasant stream that watered the fields round about. Perhaps the great Samuel would choose one of the small huts dotting the stream to engage in prayer and fasting. It was said that other ancient ones, as they approached the end of their days, and faced the yawning maw of Sheol, had come to be alone with YHWH along their calm stream. They could always hope that was the reason for this visit.

"Yes, I come peaceably," croaked the prophet from his perch on the palanquin. "I have come for sacrifice, as I often do when I travel through the land I love and lead. Is the man Jesse here?"

A small, leather-faced farmer stepped forward, dressed in a dusty cloak, his feet bare, his beard something of a tangle around that deeply tanned face, weathered by years of work in the fields. Samuel wondered what the man looked like? He had been in the presence of so many insignificant men of the land in his long life that they now blended together in his mind, becoming nearly like one man.

"You are Jesse?" he said toward a sound the farmer had made.

"I am, my lord," the man replied in an oddly high-pitched voice, rather more like a slave girl's than a man's.

"You have sons, Jesse?" "I do indeed, my lord. YHWH has granted me eight fine sons, and they are the pride of an old man's life."

"So they must be," said Samuel, "so they must be," and the old pain of his own evil children struck him a harsh blow just below his heart.

"Consecrate them, my man, and bring them up to the sacrifice."

Jesse bowed as low as his aching back allowed, and hurried home to clean his sons up for the sacrifice. Consecration consisted of hand washing, an act done hardly more than once a day in normal times, brief prayers for YHWH's acceptance of them, uttered by the patriarch over each son, and vows from each that their coming participation in the rites be pleasing to the God. That done, Jesse and seven of his sons walked up to the high place, following Samuel in his palanquin and Etan and the squealing calf.

Jesse, his sons, and Etan, nine men encircled the puny altar, consisting of two medium size stones stacked haphazardly one on top of the other. Samuel was assisted in the rite by Etan, who held him up as the ritual progressed. As he spoke the prayers in a rote manner, hardly thinking at all about the words he had spoken times beyond counting, he moved his blind eyes in the directions of the voices of Jesse's sons. The booming voice of Eliab stood out from that of his brothers, and it sounded from a place high above the tiny prophet. "He must be a very tall man," thought Samuel. Surely YHWH's anointed is standing here right in front of me! His name that means 'my God is a father,' so right for a king, announces his fitness!" But at that same moment another thought clouded that first one. "A very tall man," it repeated. "No more tall men! Saul is very tall, and look what became of that! No! YHWH (now YHWH seemed to be talking again) does not see as human beings see. Human beings look only at the outward appearance, but YHWH looks right at the heart!" Samuel knew that this tall son was not to be king.

He concluded the sacrifice by slitting the throat of the calf, his hand guided by Etan, finally stilling his perpetual squeals, and asked that the servant pass him his horn.

"Jesse," he commanded, "have your sons pass in front of me in order of their ages, for sacrifice was not my only reason for coming here today."

Samuel was then helped to sit on his rich pile of furs. Jesse did not question the great Samuel, but lined his sons up from the oldest to the youngest.

"No need to send your tallest and first born over here; he is not the one."

Eliab frowned at the rejection, even though he had no idea what he was being rejected from.

Abinadab, the second son, walked in front of Samuel, but the prophet said, "YHWH has not chosen him either."

When Shammah, the third boy, walked in his turn, the prophet said the same phrase of rejection. And in their turn the other four sons present, down to the one just fourteen summers old, walked by Samuel and were rejected. Samuel was confused and frustrated, for he was convinced that his God had sent him to this paltry place to get a king, but none of these boys was the one, he was certain.

"Are all of your sons here, Jesse?" Samuel spoke with no little irritation in his voice.

"Well," Jesse hesitated before completing the thought. "Well, there is the youngest, barely thirteen winters, but he is keeping the sheep, which is the job he has been assigned. He has quite a way with sheep," he added, trying to offer partial explanation for this missing son's absence from the sacrifice.

"Ah," said Samuel. "Ah! Another son, heh? Well, bring him, man, bring him here! None of you may sit down until he comes!"

Jesse sent the youngest out to the fields to call his very youngest son to join them at the high place. While the other six boys waited for their brother, they all shifted uneasily on their feet and whispered quietly among themselves.

"What is all this about?" hissed Eliab. "What is the famous Samuel doing here in this backwater hole in the ground? And why does he keep saying that YHWH has rejected us? Rejected us from what? Perhaps the old man has become addled and hardly knows what he is saying or doing!"

King Saul

Etan overheard the whispered word, the last sentence of which had risen above the level of a whisper.

"I assure you all that my master has his wits fully about him, and that he has come here for a great purpose. I warn you not to speak ill of him, for though his eyes may be dark, there is little wrong with his ears."

This hushed even the brash Eliab, and they all waited in silence until their brother stepped up to the altar.

David was an extraordinary young boy in more ways than can easily be enumerated. He was not tall, nor especially muscular. But one did not look first at his arms or his height, or even at his strangely red hair and complexion. What captured all who first saw him were his eyes. Not only were they the deepest shade of blue, extremely rare in the land of Israel, but there were depths to those eyes, rich depths that drew the seer in. One felt that one could dive into those eyes and never surface again, so deep were they in color and faceted wealth. With eyes like these, David was always judged to be handsome, but calling him handsome was far too simple a description. Saul was handsome in a muscular and massive sort of way; even David's older brother Eliab was handsome, as any village girl would have said. But David. David was handsome beyond handsome. One did not merely stand apart from the lad and judge him handsome; one was drawn to him, whether man or woman, as arrows to their targets, as insects to the fire. YHWH might very well look at the inside of human beings, but no one could help but look at the outside of the magnificent David and his eyes.

And because that was so, his brothers never liked him much. Or better said, they were very jealous of David and his eyes. They were especially happy when their father had discovered that David was a fine shepherd, because that took him and his eyes away from them for much of each day. So as he entered the sacred circle of the altar, his brothers grumbled and muttered, some to themselves, some to the brother standing next to them. The blind Samuel sensed that the other son had appeared, and listened to the muttering of his brothers, and knew that the new king of Israel had just arrived. Without saying a word, but feeling YHWH's approval, Samuel nodded for Etan to lift him up and signaled for the newcomer to come close. Then, much to the unspoken horror of the seven brothers, and to the astonishment of his father, Jesse, the ancient prophet opened his horn, raised it over David's reddish curls, and poured a stream of sacred oil over his head. Though the word "king" was not said, all present knew that that is what had just happened. Samuel, prophet, priest, and kingmaker and king destroyer, had just anointed the thirteen-year-old shepherd boy, the eighth son of eight sons from Bethlehem, the new king of Israel.

And before anyone realized it, Samuel was leaving, his palanquin swaying on the bearers' shoulders, returning to his home city of Ramah. The brothers all looked at David, as the oil dripped down his clear face and puddled on his chin where one day whiskers would perhaps grow. They had no words for what they were feeling or thinking. Jesse walked over to his youngest boy and bowed before him but then grabbed him in a fatherly hug. The brothers said nothing. David walked away from the altar, moving back toward the flock. And everything returned to the way it was before Samuel came. But not really. David was king, yet he was a shepherd. David was king, but he was thirteen years old. Israel now had two kings, and no nation can have two kings for very long.

17

Saul sat day after day in a darkened tent. He brooded over the events of the past few months and could make no sense of them. He had won a stunning victory over the Amalekites at the express command of Samuel and YHWH. He knew he had followed that command to the letter; his desire to sacrifice publicly the remnants of the Amalekites was a legitimate way to perform *cherem*. He was convinced that once again the evil Samuel had thwarted him, humiliated him, reduced his power to nothing, reduced him to a little man, him, Saul, the biggest man in the land, the king of Israel! How had it all happened? Expecting triumph, vindication, adulation, Saul had been drowned in cracked oratory from a stupendously old man and an embarrassed snickering from his own soldiers. How could he face them again? How could he step into the light when his heart was darkened by that disgusting viper, the so-called prophet of Israel? The words that gushed from that nauseating mouth were not the words of YHWH, but the words of a bitter and frustrated father who should have died years and years ago. Samuel! Samuel had made him king, but he had done it only to use him as a tool, a tool to pound the people into accepting his own repugnant sons as leaders. If Saul was a failure, a complete utter failure as king, then perhaps Joel and Abijah would not appear to be so bad. It was all too much.

Saul ate little, and his skin grew sallow, his eyes sank back in his massive head, as deep crevices gouged his face. At first, the faithful Ahinoam came each day to attempt to cheer her husband, to rouse him with her still considerable charms, but even her voluptuous nudity, her woman's tricks learned over many years of conjugal satisfaction, were miserable failures, even driving the once-vibrant and sensuous man deeper into himself, reminding him as she did of finer days. Finally, she stopped coming into the dank and cheerless tent, and Saul now spent most days completely alone, alone with his hatred of Samuel, alone with his anger at what should have been, alone with a future denied and blunted and clouded. Saul sat silently, idly fingering his enormous spear, grasping it and letting it drop to the floor of the tent, strewn now with filthy rugs and furs. At times his eyes would widen in alarm as he imagined the sound of the dreaded palanquin padding its way toward him. Taking up his spear, he prepared to hurl it at the foul thing that was Samuel, hoping that his murder would end his suffering, would finally allow him to be the king. But the spear stayed in his hand, his fingers white around the huge shaft, his lower arm muscles tense with the effort.

For he suddenly realized that Samuel was not there, not in his rotting flesh, but in Ramah, anxious, he imagined, for Saul to self-destruct, to commit some other foolish act, some tiny religious transgression, as Samuel determined such things, perhaps finally to take his spear and thrust it into his own stomach, spilling his cursed guts on the rugs, ridding the prophet of the obstacle to his own dynasty.

But Saul would not oblige the old man. He was deeply saddened by the whole affair, but he would not give satisfaction to that hoary beast of a man, not yet. But he would brood and sit alone and not eat. And he would wait. Wait. For what, he did not know. Samuel's death? Perhaps. The appearance of Samuel's promised "neighbor better than Saul?" Well. The return of his spirit, the revitalization of his life. For that he would wait.

After more days than any could count, days of silent sadness, one just like another, Jonathan's servant, Ephron, had had enough of the torpor of the days.

In desperation, he shouted to his master, "My lord! How long must we wait for the king, your father, to cease this cursed brooding? The army grows lax and unprepared, and we know that the Philistines are again on the march. He must be made to listen to reason! I know that Samuel's humiliation still stings like a hive of maddened bees, but we cannot remain like this for long, else the heathen will drop upon us like the locusts they are, and devour us at a gulp!"

"Of course you are right, Ephron," responded Jonathan, "but if my mother could get no rise from him, either from his member or from his own soul, then how are we to effect a change in him?"

Just then another servant came up to Ephron and Jonathan, and said, "I know someone that might help our stricken king. Until recently, I was servant to a rich man in Bethlehem, a man who had sheep beyond the counting, and I made a friendship with an extraordinary young man, David by name. I think what the king needs, this boy has in abundance. Music is the way that whatever gods there be have chosen to soothe the most troubled spirit. God is obviously tormenting the king of Israel, but that same God has created the remedy. I tell you this David can play the harp like a god himself! He can put dancing in your step at one moment and fill your eyes with tears the next. When Saul falls to his brooding, he need only hear the wondrous David play, and the clouds of his spirit will part and he will return to himself and to us."

This seemed a hopeful plan, and Jonathan walked briskly into Saul's tent.

"My father, a servant has devised a plan for your healing!"

Saul looked balefully at his son, and said nothing, though he felt like rising and throwing him out of the tent. But that would have taken far more effort than he felt able to give. So he just listened with half an ear.

"He proposes that we find a superb musician—you know how much you love the fine strings of the harp well plucked—and when you are low in your spirit, the harpist will play and lift you from your gloom."

King Saul

Saul at first thought nothing at all of the idea. Rather than harps, he preferred Samuel roasting on a spit, screaming cries of pain out of his mouth rather than wild curses at Saul. But his second thought was of how much he in fact missed the sound of the harp. Saul himself played the harp a bit, had learned it to pass the lonely hours watching his animals back home at his farm in Gibeah, but his thick fingers were more suited to the hoisting of hatchets and spears than plucking the delicate strings of the harp. He had employed several harpists to urge him to sleep on those nights when sleep flew away into the night sky. One or two of them had been most pleasant to hear, and had provided a sure measure of comfort to him.

Saul rose up to his full height, his head nearly scraping the roof of the large tent, and said to Jonathan, "Very well, my son. Get me someone who can play well—very well in fact—and bring him here."

"At once, my father," said the grinning Jonathan as he rushed out of the tent.

"Get this David at once," he shouted to the man who spoke of the Bethlemite.

But before he began his run south to Bethlehem, he had something more to say.

"It is true, my lords, that this David can play the harp beyond all men I have ever heard, but there is much more to him. Though he is barely a youth, already he is known in his area as a courageous man, something of a warrior, though it is hard to credit that at his age, a fine speaker, and I would say very handsome for a youth. It should be said that YHWH is with him in a powerful way."

A frown crossed Jonathan's face. "He sounds a bit too good to be true. Will it not be potentially dangerous to bring such a man into contact with my father, who feels none too good about himself at this moment, thanks to the fulminations of Samuel?"

"Do not worry about that, my lord. Once you hear him play, you will forget all else, and Saul will be glad for the day that brought David to him."

Jonathan was less than convinced but asked that the servant go and bring David to Saul's tent.

The children of Jesse had settled back into a routine that was comfortable and familiar after the astonishing event of David's anointing by the prophet. Perhaps the old man had become senile and confused, imagining in his dotage that Israel needed another king when it still had the great Saul, however much Samuel imagined that he had sinned against YHWH in one way or another. Frankly, the whole affair was absurd, thought Jesse. Saul had annihilated the Amalekites, had lost very few Israelite soldiers, had brought back much booty, pure animals, and the heathen king, and Samuel had raged as if the army had been decimated and scattered in the deserts of the south. Then he rushes to Bethlehem, this pleasant but little-known pastoral place, and chooses his handsome boy, David, as some kind of king? One had to admit that it sounded like a kind of ancient mythical story: the king is not the king, and a boy takes his place due to some whim of the gods. Jesse and his older children had nearly forgotten the whole thing, and it seemed David had, too, spending his days with the sheep just as he had been told to do. In fact, it had become something of a joke among the brothers.

Whenever David would come in from the fields, his older siblings would bow humbly before him, in a mocking abject salute, and shout, "Long live the king! Long live our royal majesty!"

And then they would dissolve into gales of laughter, while David would smile and touch each of them on the head with his shepherd's staff, naming them general or prince or some other designation of power. Jesse himself laughed and was glad to see his sons enjoying themselves together.

But there was always much work to be done around the farm. Jesse's significant flocks needed constant attention, and David could not be expected to keep an eye on all of them. After all, sheep were close to the very stupidest of animals. When they failed to look where they were wandering in their never-ending search for grass, and they rarely did, they would stick their nose into the behinder parts of the sheep in front of them and move inexorably in that direction until a long line of them often found themselves hoof-deep in mud or clinging to a high ledge, bleating for help. More than once, several had fallen to their deaths or drowned face down in swollen streams. They could hardly be left on their own for more than the smallest amount of time. So when it was time in the late spring to move pasture from the valleys to the higher places, the winter snows having released their grip, all the boys would be necessary to assure a safe passage for the foolish animals. The day of pasture change had arrived, and four of Jesse's sons were picked to join David and the other three youngest boys in the lower fields to guide the flock to the rich green of the high pastures. They had just started to climb the hill behind the main house, when a servant unknown to any of them ran up to Jesse.

"My lord," the man panted, "I come with a command from the king."

For just a moment Jesse imagined that this was another joke about David's kingship, perpetrated on him by his eldest son, Eliab, who had ever been the chief jokester among them. But when no one laughed, Jesse decided that the king in mind was in fact the real king of Israel, Saul.

"King Saul commands that your son, David, the shepherd, be brought to him without delay."

Jesse waited for some explanation for this ridiculous request. Why in Sheol would Saul ask for David? Had he not numerous royal shepherds who tended his vast flocks? What need did he have of still another shepherd? And if David left, what would Jesse do with his own flocks? David had become indispensable to him over the years of his learning about sheep, and none of his other sons had the gentle yet firm way with the animals. Surely, this slave would explain himself further. But he did not; he waited for some reply from Jesse.

There was little that Jesse could do save respond to the command of his king; David would go to the king, and that was all there was to it. He asked the next youngest son to run to the field and call David. Jesse would simply have to make do without him. Since that was true, he wanted to demonstrate that he loved his king, and that he was more than a country bumpkin from an insignificant part of the king's domain. So as David and his brother ran down the hill toward their father, he selected his finest donkey, a large brown beast who could carry vast loads and walk for days without stopping, and loaded her down with many loaves of fresh bread, a large skin of wine, being careful to use his newest-made skin, and a large goat tethered to the back of the donkey by a stout cord. He bid his son goodbye, and wept a few tears at the farewell. His brothers did not weep, but they claimed they would miss their talented brother, because they loved his skill with the harp, as much as his way with the sheep. More-over, with David gone, the task of night watching of the flock would fall to one of them, and they looked at their father with apprehension each hoping he would choose some brother other than he. Then too that day when Samuel had come to anoint one of them still rankled, even if the whole business was a bit of foolishness, wrought by the muddled brain of a withered old man. They were not exactly devastated to see their brother head off north toward Gibeah.

Jesse had deep fears about David's future with the king. Saul was an impressive man, but had run afoul of the powerful Samuel on at least two public occasions. There was no telling how many more times the two had clashed privately, because there was obviously no devotion between the two of them. Word had gotten around that Saul was ill, or was at least hiding in his tent, without light, alone. What sort of king had he become, and why did he want my son? The thought of his tiny son, not yet three cubits tall, alone with the gigantic king who had become unpredictable in behavior as rumor had it, terrified Jesse. He had, upon hearing the command of the king from the servant, for just a moment thought of hiding his son in one of the caves that honeycombed the dry deserts of the south toward the salt sea. He would have done so, if he had had warning of the command. But it was too late now. David was gone to be with Saul. Jesse lifted a prayer to the great YHWH for his son's safety and for the king's return to wholeness. He included in the prayer the hope that David's service for Saul would be brief, and that soon he would find his way back home. But the flock still needed their attention, David or no David, so he urged his sons on to the lower pasture to gather the sheep for the move.

18

Just about the time that Jesse and his remaining seven sons had corralled the sheep and had moved them up the hill, David and the servant arrived at Saul's tent. No sound came from the large dwelling, but the servant urged David through the flap. It was as dark as night in the tent, and David's eyes took some time to adjust from the blazing sun of the late afternoon. He stood silently, his harp cradled in the crook of his arm, for the servant had said that he was to play for the king. The instrument was about two cubits tall and was shaped in something like a half-circle. Some said it looked rather like a letter of the Hebrew alphabet, a *caph* turned backwards, but since few could read the letters, only the priests or scribes spoke such things. Six strings were tightly strung from top to bottom of the half-circle. Each was of a different length so that a slightly different sound poured from each as they were plucked. An especially clever player could get multiple sounds from each of the strings by the different ways each string was pulled, and David was a very clever player, as Saul was about to discover.

David was framed in the light of the tent flap. He was dressed in his shepherd's tunic, a simple garment that covered his shoulders, chest and loins but left his legs bare. He wore rough sandals of hide that were worn thin by years of walking on rocks and wading through streams. He peered into the darkness, but at first thought he was alone. Then from the farthest corner of the tent, a muffled voice was heard, mumbling some words that David's sharp ears could not make out.

"My lord?" he said.

The voice sounded again, this time a bit more distinct.

"Close the flap, boy, and play your harp for me."

The voice contained anguish, deep sadness, only the smallest hint of command. David assumed it was the king, but if it was Saul, the voice gave little hint of royalty. Nevertheless, David turned and closed the flap of the tent, and plunged the tent back into near total darkness.

"My Lord, the king," he said in the cave-like blackness, "I cannot play well in this dark. Could we not open the flap just a bit, so that the light of God could illumine my strings the better to play them for you?"

Saul responded slowly to the request.

"Very well, but do not open so wide that the light might penetrate my corner of the tent."

"I shall take care, O king," and he opened the flap just enough to discern his strings but to keep the tent mostly dark.

David placed the harp against his left shoulder, and plucked one string, then two, then three all at once. The golden sound of the harp leapt from the strings like living things, like water dancing in the sun, like sheep gamboling among the hills, like the sweet sound of birds, heralding the bursting of the spring. Then he added words that had been passed down from the ages, words originally pagan, he had been told, but words that now were sung in the holy places and in pious homes throughout the land. He hoped that Saul would find them pleasing, since he knew that his king was a religious man.

> "Announce to YHWH, you children of the gods!
>> Announce YHWH's glory and power!
>> Announce YHWH's glorious name!
> Worship YHWH in holy splendor!
> The voice of YHWH is above the waters;
>> the glorious God thunders,
>> YHWH above the ancient seas!
> The voice of YHWH is powerful;
>> the voice of YHWH is filled with majesty.
> The voice of YHWH breaks the cedars;
>> YHWH breaks the cedars of Lebanon.
> YHWH makes Lebanon skip like a calf
>> and Sirion like a young wild ox!
> The voice of YHWH flashes flames of fire.
>> The voice of YHWH shakes the wilderness,
>> YHWH shakes the wilderness of Kadesh.
> The voice of YHWH causes deer to calve,
>> and strips the forest bare,
>> while at the holy place all cry, "Glory!"
> YHWH is enthroned over the great flood;
>> YHWH is enthroned as king forever.
> Let YHWH give strength to the people!
>> Let YHWH bless the people with peace!"

David had chosen this ancient song carefully. He sensed that the king needed to be reminded that YHWH was the king of Israel, thus taking final responsibility for the land off the shoulders of the earthly king. Then, too, the last word of the song was "peace," something the king keenly felt the lack of, but something that YHWH could always provide to those who listened for the divine voice. And that voice carried both awesome power and blessing and peace for the troubled spirit. The echoes of the song faded slowly in the tent, and David waited for the response of the king. From the dark corner came a quiet sob, emanating from the king's throat. David waited for some words.

Finally, Saul spoke.

"Wonderful, wonderful, my boy, I was told you played well, but your fingers are magic, your singing divine. You give honor to YHWH by such music, and YHWH is in your playing. Thank you. Thank you! I feel better than I have felt in weeks. Bless you, David, son of Jesse. You must stay with me always. Tell your father that you will not be coming home. You will now be my servant and play whenever I ask. Open the flap of the tent, open it wide. David the shepherd has brought light back to my life, and I sense that my darkness has flown away, never to return. Do not leave my side, David, for YHWH has given you to me for the comfort of my soul!"

And Saul grabbed the small youth in a huge hug of a bear and carried him through the tent flap, out into the light of the day. When the soldiers saw Saul standing in the light and smiling broadly, they all roared with delight and relief, for the king seemed restored, and in his restoration was their own restoration of hope and possibility for a winning future for the land. When Jesse was told that his son was not coming home, but had been enrolled as a servant of Saul, he was very sad, but also very proud that a boy of his had played a central role in the healing of the king.

And David stayed with Saul. Whenever the darkness would descend on the king, for it was not defeated by David's golden voice, only kept at bay for a time, like a caged beast ready to maim if given the chance, Saul called on David to play and find rest once again. And each time Saul would relapse, and David would play for him, it appeared that Saul became stronger, more like the great Saul of old, and the people were glad.

Saul was mad for the wondrous David, and even made him the bearer of his arms, though the great size of the weapons taxed the small David at first. But soon, David, who was a natural warrior, as the servant had said, could wield Saul's sword and brandish his battle ax nearly as well as his master. He regularly bested hardened soldiers in Saul's army in hand to hand combat drills, though they were much larger and much more experienced than he.

David's reputation in all things grew astonishingly, and as he gained years and muscle and size, women nearly swooned as he approached, and wondered which one of them would be chosen to share the rich delights that the handsome boy had to offer, or so their imaginations assumed and thrilled and hoped. David practiced his combat skills and played his harp for the king, and all was well in Israel. That is until the Philistines reared their heads and began another march to the east. And again Saul mustered his troops to meet their threat, confident that this time the heathen would be beaten just like the Amalekites before them. But this time the Philistines were not the most dangerous enemy that Saul would face; that enemy was much nearer the king than he knew.

19

Unlike their past incursions into Israel, the Philistines were this time more cautious. Rather than rush headlong into the hill country, where their chariots were worse than useless, merely hindrances to the hit-and-run fighting that the terrain necessitated, they marched out from Gath, the city furthest east in their collection of five great cities. They first overwhelmed the small Israelite border hamlet of Azekah, a place that had originally belonged to Philistia. The encampment was on the west side of the vale of Elah, and the Philistines saw the place as the perfect staging area for a more deliberate thrust into the heart of the Israelite highlands. The valley was two days' walk to the south and west of Gibeah, and if the Philistines were allowed to establish a strong presence in the valley, they could threaten the very heart of Saul's kingdom. He simply could not let that happen.

The territory where the battle was to be joined was known as Ephes-dammim, "Bloody Border." This lush river valley had been the site of numerous skirmishes between Philistine and Israelite over the years, since it was located right on the shifting border between the two realms. Saul already had a few soldiers on the east bank of the stream, lookouts with wary eyes trained on possible Philistine troop movements. When they saw a large enemy battalion leave Azekah, they quickly sent a message to Saul that the Philistines were on the move. Saul was ready for a rapid deployment, since he had expected his long-time foe to react to the uncertainties in Israel, created by the prophet Samuel and his public humiliation and rejection of the king. But, Saul thought, they had reacted too slowly, since he was once again in control of himself and the situation, thanks in no small part to the wonderful David. His army, several thousand strong, moved rapidly to the hills above the river on the east side of Elah. The valley was quite small, and the two armies could easily see the other across the stream.

Each group of soldiers performed similar pre-battle rituals. Each sharpened swords and battle axes with the help of the wandering smiths who were always to be found at the site of conflict. Artisans in both camps restrung sagging bows, refitted sharp arrow points on newly planed shafts of hard wood. Shields were strengthened with extra layers of animal hide, cured in the hot sun. Commanders donned leggings to cover vulnerable knees and ankles and checked their bronze helmets, hard enough to deflect weak blows of axes, but not finally able to resist a Philistine iron weapon. And here lay a significant difference in the two forces; the Philistine metal workers had the way of iron, and all of their weapons and armor were cast from this substance. Philistine ancestors had brought this knowledge with them from their original home-land in the midst of the Great Western Sea. The Israelites knew only bronze, an amal-gam of two metals, made stronger in the joining, but no real match for Philistine iron.

Common soldiers on both sides had no leg and ankle coverings, and usually pos-sessed only leather helmets that might deflect an arrow launched from a great distance, but did little to protect against any weapon employed at close range. In hand-to-hand battles such as these, many regular soldiers could expect a violent, bloody, and painful death by arrow, ax, or spear. Hence, all fighters on both sides made final preparation by ritual sacrifice to their respective gods. The Philistines worshipped Dagon, a corn and fish god, who gave them gifts from field and sea. Their priest regularly wore a huge head of a fish, crafted of leather with precious stones for eyes, as he performed the rites of the cult, burning an enormous fish on an altar of hewn stone, and shouting very loudly into the sky in the clipped tones of an ancient version of the Philistine tongue. Of course, most Israelites understood the language of the Philistines, since in the few peaceful times between the two peoples, they traded back and forth, and even on occasion married one to the other, though that was never fully countenanced by either side. But Hebrew words entered Philistine mouths as often as Philistine words poured out of Hebrews, as much as they each thought the other hateful and heathen.

Camp fires blazed, the sounds of metal on metal clashed, the harsh cries of com-mand echoed through the valley and bounced from hill to hill and back again, as the two armies prepared to try to obliterate the other. Excitement and fear rose in the hearts of nearly everyone, save those who had never smelled a battle before, its blood and rotting flesh and hopeless screams. Only the young ones yearned for the fight; the veterans made ready for a grisly death, fearing that their time may have come, since they had escaped death's demons in other fights. It was the veterans who were most fervent in their prayers, as Saul's priest invoked the power and presence of YHWH for the upcoming clash with burning goat and chanted word and music. He sang:

> Hear our prayer, great YHWH;
> > Let our cries come to you.
> Do not hide your face from us,
> > on the day of our distress.
> Incline your ear to us;
> > answer speedily on the day of our calling!

As often as many of the troops had heard that prayer in their places of worship, it had special power on this day, the day where many of their lives might well end. All watched the sacrificial smoke rise into the sky, noting carefully which way the smoke billowed and arched on its upward journey. It was said that movements of the smoke could tell much of the future if read aright, but no one saw very much no matter how hard they peered upwards; the priest said nothing save the familiar prayers. The soldiers left the sacrifice in silence, alone with their thoughts and their fears, hoping that YHWH was indeed listening and would stand as their champion in the coming battle. Few on either side of Elah slept much that night, for the morning would bring with it combat and certain death for many.

But the morning brought something completely unexpected. Before first light, the sentries of the night awoke the Israelite soldiers and bid them prepare for the struggle. But on the Philistine side, the camp was eerily quiet. The Israelite soldiers had already drawn up to their battle lines, rank upon rank, spearmen in the front, followed by wielders of the axes, backed up by the long-range archers who would launch their deadly missiles as a prelude to the running attack. The Philistine army awoke at the rustling sounds of the Israelite preparations, but they did not ready themselves for battle. Instead, they left their tents as if they had been camping with their families in the wilderness, slowly, sleepily, not putting on their armor or hoisting their weapons. They hardly glanced in the direction of the Israelites who were arrayed against them on the far side of the valley. The Israelite troops looked at one another, and then at their commanders for some signal to tell them what to do. Were the Philistines surrendering? It hardly appeared likely; they were not breaking camp but were only acting as if no war was imminent. But as the Israelites watched the Philistine camp with wonder and confusion, suddenly every Philistine eye turned toward the rear of their camp.

From the trees ringing the Philistine encampment there emerged the most enormous man anyone in the valley had ever seen. The Israelites were by now used to the gigantic presence of King Saul who towered over all of them, but this giant made even Saul appear ordinary. From the throats of all the Philistine soldiers the name "Goliath" roared as he stomped past each of their tents. He strode down onto the bank of the stream, his fantastically long legs covering twice the distance of an ordinary man at each step, his enormous shield, born by a normal man, completely hiding the one who carried it, his astonishing spear protruding above his head, his sword some figment of a madman's vision glinting in the morning sun. Who could say how tall this monster was? Six cubits and more most calculated, but no one imagined that they would dare to approach this Goliath to ask or measure. His bronze helmet covered a head impossibly large; he had obviously chosen bronze, instead of the readily available Philistine iron, to suggest that he feared no Israelite sword or ax or spear or arrow. His mammoth chest was protected by a coat of mail, a garment-like protective shield made up of iron circles linked together by hot fire and artistic skill. Its weight would have crushed any of the Israelite soldiers who dared try put it on, if they ever got such an opportunity, which all knew they would not. His lower legs and knees were covered with long bronze greaves, thick enough for protection, but polished and gleaming enough for ceremonial events. This Goliath was dressed not for battle but for show, for a public display, for the humiliation of the Israelites who stared at him in shock and horror.

King Saul

He paused at the brink of the stream, shoved his shield-bearer rudely away, spread his legs wide enough for a stable stance and began to speak. His voice was as his appearance, huge and dark and terrifying.

"Why in the name of Dagon have you sniveling Israelites arranged yourself for battle? Am I not a Philistine, and are you not Saul's slaves? Choose for yourself a man, and let him come down here to me! If he is able to fight with me and kill me, then we will be your slaves."

This sentence the monster said as if he could rather imagine a tree talking or a rat speaking Hebrew before he could imagine any Israelite besting him in single combat.

"But if I win the struggle with him, then you will be our slaves and serve us."

This was said with certainty and finality. The giant expected a quick victory or more likely a terrified Israelite retreat. The word "slave" rang through the valley, and every Israelite soldier envisioned a chained future, rowing Philistine galleys on the Great Sea, or building Philistine fortifications. Death would be preferable to these visions of horror, but no one made a move to contest the giant, and no one made a sound that might suggest he was interested in doing so.

"I defy the ranks of Israel," roared Goliath. "Give me a man to fight with now!" Goliath had announced the ancient call of single combat to decide the battle. This was done to prevent the slaughter of both Philistine and Israelite sons, and either side had the right to call for it. But who could answer such a call? The eyes of many of the soldiers searched for the king, the tallest man in the land and a hardened veteran of many battles. Surely, he would respond to the challenge. But those who found the king saw in him not courage, not willingness to confront the giant, but genuine fear. Some remembered the day long before when Saul had been found hiding in the baggage on the day of his coronation by Samuel, the Saul who had prompted some to say that he was no fit king. And now again doubts rose up in many minds as it became obvious that their huge king was cowed before this Goliath. Horror and abandonment infested every Israelite heart as Goliath waited in vain for an opponent.

After a long silence, the giant turned his back on the Israelites and strode back to the Philistine camp. Roars of approval for the enormous man followed his walk back to his tent, followed by hoots of derisive laughter directed at the Israelites, who one by one broke ranks and stumbled back to their tents in a sort of mock retreat. There was for a few a quiet relief for the lack of battle, but deep humiliation fell on all like stones hurled from the walls of a city on would-be attackers. Like the false king, Abimelech, felled by a woman's grinding stone from the walls of Thebez, so the Israelites longed to be put out of their misery as the worthless warriors they felt themselves to be. Saul went to his tent alone, shooing away any request for aid or comfort, feeling again the pang of failure that he thought he had banished forever. Sullen eyes followed him to the tent, eyes ringed in disappointment, suffused with resentment and fear. Saul fell onto his pile of furs in the darkened tent and wished for the soothing sound of David's harp.

King Saul

But the singer had visited his family, especially his aged and ailing father, Jesse, when the army had left for the valley of Elah. Though he was Saul's armor bearer, and had become something of a fighter himself, the king had decided that he would not join him in the battle, fearing that his favorite might be hurt in the fighting or, worse, killed. Thus, Saul had commanded David to remain in Gibeah with the women and children. But since David's three eldest brothers, Eliab, Abinadab, and Shammah, had joined the army at Elah, and left Jesse to run the farm in Bethlehem without his stoutest sons, David had begged Saul to allow him to visit the farm. It was well east of the fighting, David would be as safe there as he would be in Gibeah, so Saul relented and said he could go. Saul now wished that he had brought David with him, since he felt the darkness falling on his mind again; only the beauty of David's magical voice could lift the gloom. Just before Saul descended so far into his personal cave of night that he would be impotent and immobile, he thought he might call for a servant to fetch David from Bethlehem. But the intention was swept away as the veil of darkness fell over the king and he sat motionless in his tent for many days, and no one could rouse him either to eat or to converse or to join his troops.

Forty days passed. On several occasions, Jesse sent David to Elah to see how his oldest sons were faring and to bring a gift of food to the commanders of the army. Each time that David would come to the camp of Israel, no one mentioned that Saul had fallen under the canopy of evil that had gripped him before, and since David felt the great need to help his father with the sheep in Bethlehem, his trips to Elah were brief. But he did notice that each time he went that there was no sign of fighting, no tent for any wounded, no newly dug graves for the dead. The swords and spears were clean, the arrows fresh, the bows still tightly strung. He asked what was happening, but no one was willing to tell him the truth. And because each time he came, he feared that Jesse might die in his absence, he did not pursue the peculiar battle sight where there was, in fact, no battle being fought at all.

The truth was too ridiculous to be talked about, especially from an army supposedly ready to fight. It seems that the giant Goliath had come out every day, in the morning and again in the evening, every day for forty days, and had issued the identical challenge to the trembling Israelite army. In fact, he had shouted exactly the same words as he had on that first day each time that he had spoken. It became something of a joke in the camp of Israel, if there were anything funny to be found in an event of such humiliation for the people of YHWH. Every morning, the army would assemble for battle, spearmen, followed by axmen, followed by archers, and every morning Goliath would issue his unanswered challenge, the army would feel a renewed terror, and they and Goliath would, after a certain interval, retreat to their respective tents. It was a comedy of sorts, and all wondered whether it could be continued for much longer. Goliath, whose memorized speech seemed to be about all he was able to learn, his great size not being matched by his brain, appeared able to utter the speech indefinitely, while the Israelites seemed able to continue the game as long as he was ready to play. Meanwhile, Saul brooded in his tent.

But one afternoon David had been delayed in his departure from Bethlehem for Elah—his father had had a fall and needed some special attention—so that he arrived in the valley just as Goliath took his stand by the stream and prepared to announce his challenge for the eighty-first time. He could hardly believe his ears or his eyes—he had of course earlier been told very generally of Goliath's challenge, but this was the first time that he both heard and saw the giant. And it was the first time that he had witnessed the absolute terror of the army at the sight of the man. The army had shouted the familiar battle cries as they lined up in their ranks, as if they were about to engage the enemy, but at the first sound of Goliath's enormous voice, the Israelites became completely silent, stopping all martial movements. And were reduced to cowering cowards. David felt incalculable shame for them and for Israel and wondered aloud where the king was. But no one was listening to him; they were far too busy running headlong for their tents.

David caught sight of his brothers and urged them to stop.

"Eliab," he cried as his strapping brother hurtled passed him in craven flight. "Where are you going? Goliath is that way," pointing to the stream where the giant stood.

Eliab stopped, though his body still leaned in the direction of his tent, and his fear was plastered all over his face.

"Engage Goliath," he shouted incredulously. "Take on that monster? Have you gotten a good look at him? Not only is he supernaturally tall, his spear is longer than the trunk of a cedar of Lebanon, his metal coat is completely impenetrable with our puny weapons, and there is no way that any one of us could get by that massive shield that resembles the gate of a great city. No, David, I do not intend to engage Goliath, not now, not ever! And by the way," he added as he turned to run off," what are you doing here anyway? Where are your sheep? Have you left father alone? After that crazed Samuel poured his rancid oil over your head, and called you king, you have puffed yourself up beyond your station and your ability. Remember, you are a shepherd boy, not a warrior, however much that reputation has grown up around you. So, go back home to those scraggly sheep and leave the fighting to your betters!"

And before David could reply that he saw no fighting going on, nor evidence that any had gone on during the forty days of the confrontation, Eliab was gone, nearly diving into his tent and tying the flap up behind him.

The camp of Israel was now quiet. David went back to get a second look at Goliath, but the giant had turned his back on Israel and was lumbering toward the Philistine tents. David watched the massive warrior move slowly and carefully, picking his way through the stones and trees that formed the bank of the stream, placing his enormous sandals precisely so as to avoid falling. A man of his size had to be extra careful when walking on uneven terrain, and David watched him move gingerly, like a turtle picking its way over sand dunes near its seaside home. And David formed a plan.

After the echoes of the giant's voice had ceased rumbling through the valley, tent flaps were thrown back and warriors began to reappear into the sun, blinking their eyes at the sudden brightness. David approached a small group of soldiers as they emerged from their tent that was situated close to the king's tent in the center of the camp. Saul had not come out. David overheard pieces of their anxious conversation.

"I wish I had the courage," said one, "since the rewards are so tempting!"

"Easy enough to talk like that here, so far from the stream and that monster!" hooted another, "but no one with a grain of sense would challenge Goliath. Why, his sword by itself is longer than any one of us is tall!"

"True enough," said the first, "but have you seen Merab, Saul's daughter? She is a beauty, and the dowry she would bring would make all future work unnecessary. I would just loll about all day on an ivory couch while my wife Merab would feed me grapes and chilled wine and caress my body in ways only she would know and I would long to find out!"

His eyes closed and his mouth hummed in ecstasy as the vision of a naked Merab leapt into his mind.

The third soldier piped up. "Well, naked beauties and a future of rich idleness are pleasant prospects indeed, but what I would welcome is the tax-free life for my entire family for all the generations I can imagine. I would be the most important child our clan has had in all its long history in Israel. My name would be forever honored and never forgotten."

And he too dreamed a waking dream of indolence and honor, riches and fame.

And suddenly David strode up to the group and added his voice to the conversation.

"What did you say a person would get if he killed the Philistine and took away the shame from Israel? Just who does this uncircumcised brute think he is to defy the armies of the living God?"

There was a momentary silence as the soldiers took the measure of David who was at least a span shorter than the shortest one among them. Then their derisive laughter burst open like an exploding wineskin and echoed through the camp.

"So, you think you can fight the giant? Where are your sword and spear, your shield and armor? What do you propose to do, appear as you are, and hope that Goliath laughs himself to death? Or perhaps you could sing the brute to sleep with a golden melody from your harp!"

But before they could continue with more jokes at David's expense, he moved toward another collection of soldiers who had turned toward the first group, trying to discover the cause of the laughter. And David asked them the same question that he had asked the first group.

"What do you get if you kill Goliath?"

King Saul

And these soldiers made the offer clear: riches fit for a king, marriage to the king's daughter, a tax-free life for an entire clan forever. And their reiteration of Saul's offer was also followed by howls of laughter as they sized up the absurdly short youth who had asked the question.

"Perhaps Goliath will not be able to see this insect, so he might bite the giant in the ankle and thereby cause him to bleed to death!"

And David continued to ask other groups of warriors his question and he received the same answer accompanied by cackles and poor jokes. David was moving ever closer to the tent of Saul, and as the raucous laughter grew, the noise forced the curious king to appear into the light of day.

"What is this foul noise?" he bellowed, rubbing his temples in a vain attempt to rid himself of a terrible head ache that he feared would too soon become one of his dark times.

Saul's long shadow fell over David, obscuring him from the angry gaze of the disturbed king. The laughter in the camp had ceased the moment that Saul's voice had been heard. The small knots of men looked at their king and waited for him to command them into action. Forty days of inactivity and abject fear had brought many to the breaking point, and they hoped that their own giant would at last rouse himself to action.

One of Saul's bodyguards, who had overheard the conversation between David and a group of soldiers camped close to the tent of the king, broke the silence.

"Great king, live forever! Your musician and companion, David of Bethlehem, was asking several of your troops what the one who slew Goliath would receive when the deed was done. The laughter you heard was a response to David's request. He seems to think he can face the giant!"

As the guard concluded his speech to the king, he could barely stifle a chuckle at the absurdity of a three cubit and a span shepherd musician confronting the six cubit and a span giant warrior. Truly, as a lion is to a crow, so is Goliath to the miniscule David.

Saul stepped back the better to see his favorite harp player and smiled in a fatherly sort of way.

But David, fixing the king with a determined stare, said, "Do not any longer be afraid! I, your servant, will go out and fight this Philistine!"

And he took a step to head for the stream. If Saul was offended at David's announcement that he was afraid of the giant, he quickly covered over his possible shame.

"David, my good friend," thundered the vast voice of Saul, "you are obviously not ready to fight against this Philistine. I know you have trained with my troops, and are well skilled with bow and sword, but this monster has trained his whole life for fighting and killing. And his gods have given him unmatched size, creating in him a perfect fighter with gigantic weapons wielded by massive arms, supported by tree-like legs. I appreciate your fervor; would that your larger and older and more experienced brothers had more of it. But I simply cannot let you go to be devoured by this beast. I need your music more than I need your courage."

But David was not to be put off; the prizes promised by the king were far too tempting to miss the chance of winning them.

"My lord, your servant used to keep sheep for his father."

Of course, Saul knew this fact, and also knew that David still during the season of the birthing of lambs would return to Bethlehem to help his family at the farm. Yet, the king, as well as David's brothers, who had drawn close to listen to what their youngest sibling was saying to Saul, did not miss the way David had begun this speech. He had said that he "used to" keep sheep. Did he imagine that his shepherd days were over? Just why would he think that? They listened intently as the speech went on.

"Staying alone on the hillsides and dark ravines of the pastures at night was often dangerous business. Lions and bears lurked near the flock, waiting for their chance to snatch a straying lamb. Sometimes the hungry beasts would get a lamb in its jaws so quickly that I barely had time to react. But they were no match for me! My great running speed would catch them before they could get away; I would merely strike the animal with my staff, forcing it to release their prey unharmed. Hitting a lion or bear on its nose made them let go immediately. And if it turned against me, as it often did after losing its meal, I would grab it by its jaw and hit it in the face with my fist. Most times, I would kill it."

David spread his feet wider apart as he concluded this amazing tale of his astonishing prowess in lamb rescue, and thrust his jaw toward the sky. His deep blue eyes shone with the excitement of the story.

Of course, his brothers believed not a word of it! After all, they had grown up with David and had often listened to his wild tales of night hags, tree branches that shrieked, and stars with tails of fire. David always interpreted situations to show him in the very best light. But this time the lies were more than absurd! Snatching lambs from lions' mouths? Killing bears by hitting them bare-handed on the face? No one could possibly swallow such nonsense! Saul listened to his favorite with a bemused look, not revealing whether he believed the boy or not. He wanted to believe, because he needed a champion to kill the giant. Saul knew many of his people looked to him, Israel's tallest man, and sturdiest warrior, to face Goliath. But Saul also knew that he had already fought in several battles too many, and he feared that a one-on-one battle with the massive Philistine would be his last. He had for well more than a changing moon's time looked throughout his camp for a candidate to fight Goliath, but the camp did not yield one who remotely had a chance against him. And now came David. Was it not just possible that this melodious singer who was now well muscled and a master of sword and shield might give Goliath the fight of his life? Looks could always be very deceiving; he was short of stature but shrewd and clever. Anyone could see that. He might be the one.

King Saul

But David had not yet finished his speech. And he was not now speaking only to the king; he had swept his eyes over the soldiers who had gathered around Saul's tent.

"Your servant has killed both lions and bears, and this uncircumcised Philistine is no different from them. Just as they tried to steal my sheep, so has Goliath tried to steal the strength of the armies of Israel, the armies of the living God! YHWH, who saved me from the paw of the lion and the claws of the bear will save me from the power of this Philistine!"

David's red hair flashed and his ruddy cheeks flushed with energy as he invoked the presence and power of YHWH on his adventure with Goliath. And suddenly Saul's army was cheering wildly, and Saul, the king, joined in the clamor, lifting David off the ground in a great manly hug.

"Go," he roared right in the boy's ear, "and may YHWH be with you! But first, you must be properly prepared for the battle to come."

Saul turned back toward the tent and demanded that a servant bring to him his spare armor that he always kept in case of damage to his best. He called David to him and tied around his chest his coat of metal mail and placed his own helmet of bronze on his head. And after he had handed David his massive sword, David strapped it over the armor, around his waist on a belt he had tied there. Now the cheers of the army turned to howls of laughter again! Saul's helmet had fallen over David's eyes, his chain mail coat reached nearly to his knees, and the great sword was dragging on the ground. David tried to walk, but tripped over the sword, falling helplessly on his back in front of the king. He attempted to stand, but the weight of the armor and the helmet and the sword, now plunged into the earth at his side, made standing impossible; like a writhing beetle David wriggled and twisted in a vain attempt to get up. The laughter all around grew louder as the shepherd boy became increasingly tangled in the armor, the helmet now turned backwards on his head, completely obscuring his eyes, the sword twisted under his backside, threatening bodily harm if he moved just the wrong way. David could do little more than join the laughter. All that raucous laughter, bursting from everyone present, from king to lowest soldier, was the first real laughter that the camp had heard in a very long time. Many that day were reminded of the amazing birth of Isaac to the aged Abraham and Sarah, knowing full well that Isaac's name was in fact "Laughter," a name given to one born of one fantastically ancient. Such free and joyous laughter was long ago prized by the magical birth, and must have sounded like the laughter of relief sounded by the soldiers of Saul.

Finally, Saul bent down and lifted David to his feet. He quickly stepped out of the twisted coat of mail, tossed the huge helmet to the ground, and lifted the sword out of the belt, while continuing to laugh at the clownish vision he knew he was presenting. "I cannot move with these things draping my body! O king, we have both forgotten that you are the tallest man in Israel, and I am not!" Though Saul continued to laugh, he did not miss the implied rebuke in David's words; he was the tallest man in Israel, and should have been out fighting the tallest man any of them had ever seen, but here he was clothing a shepherd in his own armor, hoping that this boy would do the thing he himself was unwilling or unable to do. The laughter caught in his throat and turned to something like anger or fear or despair. Perhaps all three.

But the laughing David had grabbed his old shepherds' staff. With that familiar object, he turned toward the stream from which Goliath had just left. As he walked, many of the soldiers followed behind him, wondering what the boy was up to. When he reached the stream, he bent down into the water for some stones, smoothed by the rushing torrent. He dropped these into his small shepherd's pouch, that tiny bag that often held food for those long nights in the fields with the sheep. As he turned back to the soldiers, wiping his dripping hand on his tunic, all saw the sling that was in his hand.

With no further talk, David turned back to the stream, and shouted, "Goliath!"

It was the only sound in the valley, and it took little time to reach the ears of the giant, just as he was about to enter his tent. As his name came to him, he stopped and turned toward the sound, wondering who it was who was calling him. Goliath's eyesight was none too good, a fact he tried to hide from his fellow soldiers; it was important to him that he not in any way undercut the general conviction that he was an unbeatable force and that he had no weaknesses. So he did not squint in the direction of the voice; he had taught himself long ago never to squint and give away his secret. He merely glared in the direction of the sound.

And then he began to lumber back toward the stream. As he passed the Philistine tents, he broke into something that resembled a run, though his movement remained little more than a slow trot, eagerly searching for the voice that had summoned him. The voice was high-pitched, young sounding, yet demanding in a demeaning sort of way. Goliath worked on an angry response as his legs carried him, bear-like, back toward the stream.

"Who dares speak to me thus?" he tried, but that seemed too obvious.

"So, the cowardly Israelites do have voices after all?"

That was better, but still appeared weak.

"Who is this little man who speaks with the sound of a mouse?"

He liked that best and imagined himself saying that, with a rich disdain in his own voice, when he reached the stream. In his haste to return to his usual spot by the river, he had forgotten his armor-bearer, the much smaller warrior who had been chosen to carry the out-sized shield of the giant. That poor man—he was the third soldier who had received the "honor" of carrying the champion's shield, the other two having collapsed under its fantastic weight—was running after his lord, burdened by the shield, gasping for breath in the still, humid air of the valley. Goliath, hearing the man panting behind him, slowed his pace enough for him to catch up, and finally to lead him to the place of the voice. The shield-bearer reached the west bank of the river just before the shield threatened to crush him, scrambling out from under it before it hit the ground; he was just able to thrust it upright in the muddy soil, facing the stream. The shield of Goliath was magnificent, nearly three cubits through the middle, and four cubits tall. It was of leather, stretched over a large wooden frame, reinforced in the middle with several layers of animal hide. It weighed at least as much as Goliath's massive spear and could only be hefted and used in battle by the giant himself. Around its edges there was a beautifully wrought line of gleaming bronze that glinted as the sun caught its reflection.

Goliath arrived at his spot by the river, the place where eighty-one times before he had stood to defy Israel and Saul and their pitiful soldiers. At first, he could see nothing, his poor eyes unable to find the source of the voice. He scanned the far side of the water slowly and deliberately; everything Goliath did was slow and deliberate, his enormity defeating speed but threatening all who would confront the mountain that he was. At last his eyes fixed on a very small figure, a boy, red-complected, yet attractive as young boys often were, holding what looked like a shepherd's staff in his hand. Goliath shoved the shield-bearer out of the way, sending him sprawling into the mud.

"Am I a dog that you confront me with a stick?!"

He said this with a mixture of disdain and fury, sensing that the Israelites had sent this tiny boy to the river to humiliate him, the mightiest warrior in the world, by waving sticks at him with a jester's laugh. With a ferocious shout, Goliath lunged into the river, spewing curses in Dagon's name.

"May your shit-hole be closed up forever by the power of Dagon! May your arm drop from your shoulder with the corn god's angry arm! May the god of all fish swallow you into his angry waves!"

As Goliath drew nearer to the boy, he could finally make out his features. They were soft, so fair as to possess not the hint of a beard, so calm as to say that the world's tallest man was not in the least threatening to him. Goliath stopped mid-stream in shock. He had expected his movement toward the boy would result in a mad dash for safety, but the small figure hardly moved a muscle.

"Come here, boy, to me, and I will quickly feed your flesh to the birds of the air and the wild beasts of the field!"

The giant had stopped his movements toward David and stood knee-deep in the stream, his gigantic spear gripped in his right hand, his terrible sword still sheathed in his belt. The shield remained stuck in the mud on the bank; Goliath felt he had no need of sword or shield, since this puny boy would die quickly on the point of one spear-thrust. Goliath had only to wait for him to come a bit closer, within range of his weapon. The "battle" would be a brief one, and Goliath could picture himself moving slowly back to his tent and a well-deserved rest, made the more pleasant with wine, meat, and a woman or two to cap his triumph.

But the boy did not move either forward or back, staying well out of reach of sword and spear. Troops were gathering on both sides of the stream, drawing closer together than they had been since arriving at the valley nearly three moons ago. On the west, the Philistines were confident that their giant would dispatch this boy in one stroke. Men were betting money and armor, even land, on the timing of the boy's death—within ten heartbeats? Fifteen? On the Israelite side, grim-faced warriors looked in horror at the dripping giant, rooted in the river, and at the little boy David, standing at the river's edge, left hand grasping his staff, right hand slightly hidden behind him, fingering his sling. Silence gripped the assembled company, waiting for something to happen. The sounds of carrion birds, hopeful for a rich meal of bloody death, screamed on the air. A slight breeze rustled David's poor tunic and lifted his shock of red hair slightly from his head, ruffling it into a mass of curls.

And then David spoke, clearly and forcefully, without the hint of a tremor in his voice.

"You come to me with sword and spear and shield; but I come to you in the name of YHWH of battles, the God of Israel's armies whom you have insulted. This very day, YHWH will put you into my hand, and I will strike you down and take off your head. Then I will give your corpse and the corpses of the Philistine army to the birds of the sky and the wild beasts of the earth. And then all the earth will know that Israel has a God! And all of this company will know that YHWH does not deliver with sword and spear, for the battle is YHWH's, and YHWH will give all of you into our hand!"

As David ended his speech, he was looking not at Goliath, not even at the armies of the Philistines, but at his own fellow Israelites. It was quite clear that he had not been speaking to Goliath or to the Philistine warriors, however much his words seemed directed there. David was speaking only to Israel, convincing them that he was about to perform the impossible, rousing them to expect victory over the mightiest warrior in the world. He spoke of YHWH, but he also spoke of David, of David's skill, of David's assurance, of David's future. And Saul eyed David with fear and no little hatred as the boy glowed with the energy and light that Saul could not muster.

Saul's hatred was easily matched by Goliath's own hatred, as he still stood motionless in the river. This boy had stolen his thunder for the moment, freezing the giant's words in his throat. The time for words was over. With an animal roar the giant leapt from the river toward the tiny figure of David, moving as quickly as he could to get into spear range for the deathblow. But though Goliath thought his move a rapid one, all could see that his vast size made quick moves impossible. Easily David slipped to his right while Goliath was still some fifteen cubits distant from him. Goliath turned to face David squarely, taking one more huge step in his direction. Immediately, David placed a single stone, taken from his pouch, into his sling, hurled it over his head three times to gain momentum, and fired the stone at Goliath's head, at the place unprotected by his helmet, right above the bridge of his nose. The stone made a high-pitched whistling sound as it found its target, a finger's width above the giant's nose, and a finger's width below the helmet's rim. The stone sank deeply into Goliath's head.

The giant's movement toward David stopped; shock played through his eyes, as he fell head first into the mud of the river. The sound of Goliath's crash was the sound of a great boulder falling from high up a mountainside into water made slushy by melting snow. David rushed to the side of the giant, who still breathed shallowly, grabbed the giant's huge sword from his belt, and thrust the sword into Goliath's back, driving it as deeply as he could into his vitals. A great geyser of blood shot from the wound as the giant's lungs collapsed and his breathing stopped. David stood on the corpse, both feet firmly planted on the mountain of dead flesh, and with several great swings of Goliath's sword, he cut off the giant's head. Grabbing it by the hair, David held the head up to the sky and hurled a shout of victory into the air.

"As YHWH can see, and as all of you can see, I have defeated the giant. His great head drips blood into the ripples of the river, and his Philistines are shown to be what they always have been: heathen, thieves, cowards, prey ready to be plucked! Get up, my brothers, and take from them whatever you can!"

There was a slight hesitation as the two armies stared at the tiny warrior and at the grisly head of the champion, now severed from his bleeding trunk, lifted into the sky. With a joyous shout the Israelite soldiers grabbed their swords and shields and rushed toward the stream. At about the same moment the Philistines roared in horror and turned their backs on the dead Goliath, the cursed river, and the Israelite hoard rushing toward them like a hail of locusts. Saul was not in the lead of his warriors; his eyes were fixed on David, on his flashing blue eyes, on his boyish mouth, twisted upward in a terrifying glee. What manner of boy/man is this, thought Saul? I took him for a singer; now I see him a man, a champion, a soldier's soldier. Why does he stand there so long, motionless, with that foul thing thrust into the air? Does he not see that we all have witnessed the miracle of his victory over Goliath? What more does he want? What more can he want?

And David stood alone, balanced on the back of the headless giant, the trophy oozing gore down David's arms and hands, watching the Israelite army hurtle past him, seeking terrorized Philistines to rob and brutalize, now that the fearsome Goliath was no more. Had these bloodthirsty men, so timorous just a few moments before, now turned lions by David's act, heard what he said? Had they listened to his speech, a speech David had carefully composed before approaching Goliath? Yes, David knew he was fighting for YHWH, but he just as clearly knew that he was fighting for his own future. He had meant it when he had told Saul, cowering in his tent, that Goliath was to him no more than a lion or a bear, attacking his sheep. Oh, he had exaggerated his exploits then, but he had to get their attention. And besides, he took one look at Goliath and knew the giant was far from invincible. David was astonished that no other of the so-called warriors of Israel could see that the giant was slower than an early-spring fly and could just as easily be swatted and killed. David had the right weapon, a weapon designed for large slow-moving objects, a weapon that killed at a distance, at a distance beyond spear range, no matter how large the spear. David looked at Goliath and knew the giant was as good as dead. And David looked at Goliath and saw also that his death would astound his brothers, all the Israelite soldiers, and especially Saul whose eyes were on him even now.

King Saul

David turned slowly to face the king and saw the man's eyes fixed on him. His arm ached from holding the head aloft, but he would not put it down now. He remembered the story of Moses: the great prophet had kept his arms aloft long enough for the escaping Israelite slaves of Egypt to defeat those Amalekite beasts who attempted to impede their march toward this promised land of Israel. In that old story, well-known and often told to the young, even Moses had had to have help, as Aaron and Hur stood by his side to prop the old man's arms up as they began to sag. David vowed to himself that no one would need to help him with this oozing head! He forced his arm to push the head higher, as he peered at Saul. Suddenly, the giant Saul did not seem quite so tall, and the shepherd boy was no longer a shepherd. Standing on Goliath's back, David was nearly as tall as Saul himself. Nearly as tall as the king. The king. Why not, thought David, why not? And he pushed the gory head just a bit higher into the sky.

20

The Israelite army pursued the Philistine stragglers, those who survived the immediate onslaught in the valley, all the way to the gates of Ekron, one of the largest of their cities. Many Philistines fell along the way, even though they had left nearly all their goods in the camp in Elah's valley. When the Israelites returned joyfully to Elah, they looted the camp, taking everything they could carry: weapons of steel, arrows by the sackful, food for many days, tunics, blankets, fine Philistine pottery, decorated with burnished red design. David had finally lowered Goliath's head and had stuffed it into a large sack in order to take it to the tent of YHWH, that portable shrine in the center of the Israelite camp. And he commanded some soldiers to take Goliath's sword and spear and shield to the same place, as a suitable gift for YHWH's altar.

Saul and his general, Abner, stood silently as the enormous weaponry of the giant was lugged into the tent at David's direction. The hero himself followed the trophies into the tent, stepping proudly, still holding the sack with Goliath's head inside, a red and growing stain now marking the sack. Saul muttered something in the general direction of Abner, but the warrior did not hear what he said.

"What, my lord?" he asked.

"Can this be Jesse's son, Abner, the singer and harp-player?" murmured Saul in some wonderment. "I can hardly believe what my eyes have just seen: the giant vanquished, the army routing the Philistines, our victory nearly complete! And all because of a singing shepherd!"

"Hardly a shepherd any more, O king; now a hero sure enough, a wondrous man whose youth has washed away in Goliath's blood."

"True," said Saul, "true, but what now, Abner? What are we to do with a hero in Israel? Can there be king and hero at once in the land?"

"I know not, my lord," said the soldier, "but find out we must, it seems."

Just then both David and Jonathan, Saul's son, approached Saul and Abner. Saul noted that David had washed the blood from his arms and hands while he was in the tent of YHWH, and had changed his ragged shepherd's tunic for a more manly garment; a well-woven cloth coat now covered his body. And he had changed his sandals, too.

"Hail, O king Saul! Live forever! The battle is YHWH's, and the giant is dead. All I have done for YHWH and for Israel!"

King Saul

And David bowed a deep bow before the king, yet kept his face locked onto Saul's face all the while. Before the king could respond with an expected royal courtesy, Jonathan, without saying a word, began to take off his royal tunic, remove his weapons, both sword and bow, and hand them to the astonished David. And Jonathan, wearing now only an undergarment of the coarsest wool, stepped silently toward David and whispered something in his ear. Abner, who stood closest to the new hero of Israel, heard only one word from the few words that the son of the king said. That word was "covenant."

The word was familiar in the land. YHWH had long been said to have made a covenant with the people Israel, a sort of contract where the God promised protection and the people promised absolute loyalty. Of course, doubts about the success of this contract were always in the air, however carefully those doubts were expressed, especially around the deeply pious ones in the country. Where was the covenant protection, some asked, when the Philistines slaughtered Israelites with impunity in skirmish after skirmish? Where was the covenant when Israel spent hundreds of seasons, too many to count and remember, in the slave-holes of Egypt, sweating and dying for a succession of pagan pharaohs? At times, in the darkness and safety of the night and the desert, it was suggested by some bolder and riskier people that YHWH seemed to treat the covenant with less than consistent behavior, picking and choosing when to act, or not to act, on Israel's behalf.

But why would Jonathan, the successor to his father for Israel's throne, be speaking of covenant to David, flush from his improbable victory over the giant? Abner eyed David and Jonathan warily; they were standing much too close to one another, as if they had known one another for years, instead of just having a slight acquaintance, as least as far as Abner knew. The slight smile on the handsome face of the hero, in apparent response to Jonathan's whispered words, troubled the general, and a glance at the king revealed a similar disease at the unseemly familiarity on evidence between the prince and his new friend. It was a bizarre scene, a half-clad prince nearly embracing a much younger and much shorter man, whispering and smiling over unheard words. Saul's brow began to lower, his face visibly darkening. Abner, as much as David and Jonathan, knew what was sure to follow: that veil of darkness that could present itself as raging fury or grim-visaged despondence.

Abner quickly said, "My Lord! The news of this great victory wrought through you and the armies of Israel by YHWH of the Armies will surely spread throughout the land. Your people will be anxious to celebrate and will be honored to receive you and your great son to as many parties as your energy, and your bladders, can stand! Let us now leave Elah and return to Gibeah the better to receive the plaudits of those who love you!"

The flattering speech began to do its work.

Saul brightened, and responded, "You are right, Abner, to remind me of the need to celebrate. But we cannot join joyous parties of revelers without inviting the man of the moment, even David of Bethlehem, the shepherd become soldier, the singer become warrior! It is to him that we owe all this day!"

And with those words, Saul swept David up into his massive arms and hugged him to his chest with seeming affection.

Then, in an overt display of soldierly unity, all four men mounted their horses, David borrowing a fine stallion from one of Abner's captains, and rode out of the valley of Elah, heading east toward Gibeah. On the way, each in turn recounted their memories of the day's events, yet each also knew that David's deed far out-stripped his own. As men do, there was much joking and laughter in response to exaggerations of battle skills along with obscene jests about the size of Goliath's member. Saul especially asked David if he had chanced to get a look at the thing that hung between the giant's legs, and David replied that he had not had the time since he was too busy cutting off the thing that hung between the giant's shoulders. Jonathan said that it would have been far easier to cut off that thing than the head, but Saul shouted that if Goliath's member were even half the size of his own, as it surely must have been, David would have spent half the day sawing it off! And the air was filled with coarse laughter, a laughter made more ready and richer by the sweet odor of victory, and the at least momentary easing of fear of the enemy. But the laughter was tinged with its own kind of fear as each man wondered about his immediate future.

The loud sounds of raucous fun were heard in every village and hamlet they passed. And out of each one of any size, as was the custom, women rushed to the edges of the place, and with singing and dancing greeted their victorious king. In Israel, it was the women who were the trained singers and dancers, because they were the historians of the land, recording in song and remembering in dance the great deeds of their people. The women were dressed in their finest, in long skirts, dyed with flowered colors, billowing blouses barely covering their ample breasts, flaxen wreathes entwined in their glossy hair. Some were veterans of the dances and left the wilder steps to their younger performers, while adding their rich lower voices to the swelling sound of the song. And some, older still, played drums and three-stringed harps to accompany the song and the dance. The younger dancers' eyes flashed dark and sensuous, as they fell on the glorious warriors passing in their parade of victory. And the four mounted men gazed down from their horses with greedy appreciation of the beauty displayed before them. David could hardly avoid assessing the harp-playing of the women, knowing well the difficulty of the instrument in its tuning and the skill it took to undergird the sinuous melody of the song.

The song they sang had passed quickly from town to hamlet to village. By the fourth time of its repetition, the four could have sung the song for themselves, if they had desired, but at least one of their number became increasingly irritated as the song rose up from the women's throats over and over again. It was a familiar tune, known by nearly everyone in the land. It was "A Dove on Far-Off Terebinths," a tune usually employed in services of religious devotion, led by priests and professional singers. But it was a popular tune now, and could be used for any new song that fit the tune's shape. And these new words fit the old tune well. The women sang with strength and energy, straining with all their might to please their king and the new hero of the land.

> Saul has struck down his thousands
> and David his ten thousands!

It was a traditional way to write a song. To honor victors in battle the poem must praise those responsible in grand and glowing phrase. Saul, the king, had struck down thousands, they sang, and indeed he had, albeit his thousands were perhaps in reality more like hundreds and that over many battles. Still, of course, this was poetry after all. And then the real victor of the day was praised in the final line, and given the poetic conventions of the day, his exploits must be sung to exceed those of the warrior hymned in line one. There was no intent in the happy poem to compare warriors, not really. The intent was to celebrate the deeds of all those named in order that all may join the party and receive the plaudits of all.

But, if one heard just the words of the poem, just the literal meaning of the words, one could not help but think that David had outdone the king and in an astonishing manner. If Saul's victories were wondrous, David's were glorious, if Saul was a fine warrior, David was beyond compare. And after hearing choir after women's choir sing this same song again and again and again, the numbers "thousand" and "ten thousand" began to echo in Saul's head, and his laughter and joy faded into shadows, his face's deep lines appeared prominently on his blood-filled countenance, as the lowering darkness descended on his life once more.

Just before the shadow gripped him completely, he thought to himself, "To that shepherd boy they have given tens of thousands and to me they have given merely thousands. The next thing he will have is the kingship!"

And somewhere in Saul's mind he knew that the jump from one-day hero to king was too large a leap to be likely at all; his fine son, Jonathan, was sure to be king after him. He still had years of kingship in his own strong body; but the darkening shadows of his cursed illness made clear thinking impossible. While Abner and Jonathan and David continued to soak in the pleasures of the adulation of town after town, Saul plodded along behind them, anxious to reach Gibeah and his own shrouded bed. And all along the rest of the journey, Saul rested his hooded eyes squarely on David, this shepherd who thought himself a king.

And Saul thought, "There are ways to deal with would be kings."

After what seemed an unending trip, the horses finally crossed into Gibeah and Saul lurched, like a drunken man, for his house and his bed. Ahinoam tried to embrace her husband, to congratulate him for his victory, to welcome him home with wine and food and the sensuous pleasures of the marriage bed, but Saul did not even look at his wife. He headed alone into the bedchamber, demanding her to stay away from him and to keep all others out, too. She took one step toward the room, but stopped, remembering other times when her man was strangely distant and angry. Just before Saul disappeared into the chamber, she asked gently if she might invite David to come and sing for him, and soothe his troubled spirit. Saul turned abruptly to face his wife and fixed a stare of such hatred and loathing on her that she thought she might faint under its power. Tears sprang to her eyes as she hastily left the house.

21

Saul was no better the next day, and had slept little in his cold and lonely bed. It was as if an evil spirit from the great YHWH had flown into his life to torment him. His foul mood this time was as terrifying as Ahinoam could remember, and in desperation she summoned David who in the past had been Saul's best medicine. She urged him to bring his beautiful harp with him and to come as quickly as he could. David entered the house and could hear Saul raving like some beast in his room, shouting unintelligibly and roaring at the shadows on the walls. David slipped into the room, fearful that the madman would attack him or would try to harm himself in some way.

The chamber was so dark that David could not see Saul well, but only glimpsed an outline of the king, silhouetted by one flickering lamp against the far wall of the room. He writhed as if possessed, moaned as if being mauled by some invisible creature. David could just discern great beads of sweat on his face, mixed with blood, the result of a self-induced series of cuts made by the gleaming knife in Saul's hand. In fear, David sat as far from the king as he could and began to play. He played whatever came to his mind, tunes from his shepherd days, composed during those long hours on the hillsides near Bethlehem, soothing his sheep against the terrors of the night. David thought that Saul had become little more than a beast himself and now needed soothing against the terrors of his own dark night. David played and played, tunes like "The Hind of the Dawn," "The Lilies," well known tunes of Asaph and Korah.

Hour after hour, after the moon had risen and set, after the sun was high in the sky, David continued to play. He was no longer looking at Saul, even when Saul quieted his roaring and ceased his movement and became calm. Saul in fact had nearly fallen asleep, when with no thought at all, David began to play the tune, "A Dove on Far-Off Terebinths." Saul's eyes started open as the words he had nearly forgotten sprang back into his mind. "Thousands" and "Ten Thousands," Thousands" and "Ten Thousands." Suddenly, Saul's enormous spear was in his hand, and he looked at David, outlined against the far wall of the chamber by the bright light of the sun. With a roar, Saul hurled the spear at David with the clear intent of pinning his body to the wall of the room.

Looking back later on the terrible scene, David could never quite imagine how he had eluded the deadly spear. The king was known as one of the great spear-throwers in the land, and if he had wanted to kill David in fact, David would have died that very moment. But the spear buried its point into the wall just above David's head, and before Saul could pull it out and try again, the harpist had rushed from the room and burst into the sunlight, running away as fast as he could go. Many people in the city witnessed David's mad dash from the house of the king and also witnessed the king himself, the wildest of looks in his fevered eyes, framed in the large doorway of his house, spear in his hand ready to throw at the retreating figure of the new hero of Israel.

And all that day were confused. Why would their king try to murder David, the one who had brought victory over the fearsome Goliath, a victory that had lead to a rout of the enemy? All of course knew all too well of the king's unexpected moods, but they also knew that it was this same David who had in the past calmed the king with his music, and had thereby become the king's closest confidant. What was happening in the land of Israel? After the defeat of the obvious enemies of the land, could it be that the land itself was now generating its own internal enemies? No one who saw the scene ever forgot it, because it led to an appalling series of further events that would change Israel's life forever.

Saul could hardly imagine why he had tried to kill the boy. He remembered the jealousy that had swallowed him when those accursed women had sung their song about his victories and David's still greater victories. The song had become stuck in his head as songs do, and even as that terrible familiar darkness fell on him, the song did not fly away with his wits. He knew he had been raging—his wife and servants had often enough recounted the sounds and movements he made while under the influence of the darkness, sounds and movements he never could recall when the light had broken through—but that song had stayed alive within him. Even when David had played many other tunes—exactly when he had slipped into the room, Saul could not tell—the song was still there, its fading echo ricocheting in his brain. Just before it disappeared, the tune again poured out of David's harp, and Saul, now fully conscious, had grabbed the spear to stop the tune once and for all! To kill the harpist would kill the tune!

But something had blunted his aim. At ten feet, Saul had not missed a target since he was a boy. If he had wanted to kill David, really, the boy would now be pinned against the wall, Saul's huge spear quivering in his chest, his blood congealing on the floor beneath his limp body. No! Something, someone, had turned the king's arm. YHWH? Had the God of Israel, that same God who dropped Saul into those pits of darkness, now in increasing intervals, interfered with his aim, foiled his murderous intent, saved the God's favorite, the shepherd boy of Bethlehem? Or was it the king himself who had saved David from certain impalement? After all, David was Saul's friend, was he not? Had he not pulled Saul out of the darkness too many times to count with patient and loving playing and singing? Was not his victory over Goliath a sign of his love for Israel and for its king? Or was his victory over Goliath a sign of his ambition and not-so-secret desire to usurp the kingship by humiliating Saul and finally deposing him? Was it possible that David was in fact YHWH's favorite? Had the God of Israel turned the divine face away from the king, who was chosen by YHWH as king over the people? Was David that cursed Samuel's "other man, better than you?"

Saul could not make up his mind about David or YHWH. His victory over the Ammonites so long before was fading in the mind of the people and in his own mind. The sight of the shepherd holding the bloody head of the giant high enough so the whole army had clearly seen was still vivid behind his eyes, while his defeat of Nahash, the Ammonite king, had become vague, unfocused, fast disappearing into history. What did YHWH want of him? How could he be king with this powerful and handsome young man haunting his dreams and his days? Saul emptied his scrambled mind long enough to see more clearly what he felt about David. He was afraid. He feared him, because it seemed that YHWH was somehow with him, somehow protecting him, while YHWH had somehow left Saul, left him alone, displaced him for another. Saul may be king of Israel, but this David was a thorn in his flesh, a burr under his armor, an insect burrowed in his beard. And like thorns, and burrs, and insects, he needed to be removed.

Saul retreated into his room and demanded that Ahinoam, as ever standing fearfully nearby, anxious to serve the man she so deeply loved, leave him.

"But, my love," she cried, "you have so soon escaped one of your evil times; I would now bring you food and drink. I would cradle you in my arms, for you are the lord of my life and the king of Israel. You know well that I love you and would hope that my love will soothe your pain."

And she reached out to embrace her husband, but Saul roughly pushed her from him, and shouted, "Leave me now, woman!"

Tears glistened in Ahinoam's eyes as she ran from the room. Her food had too often become her tears in these troubled times.

Saul did not mean to act so rudely with her; he did love her dearly, not the least for her steadfastness in the face of his towering rages and terrifying moods. But he now needed solitude, for he wanted absolute quiet the better to plan David's demise. What would be the best way to remove this boil from his person? Obviously, his direct attempt at murder had failed, either through the agency of YHWH or through his own unwillingness to have such blood on his hands. There were surely other ways, more subtle ways that would not directly implicate the king. Soldiers, for example, died all the time in one battle or another. Enemies of Israel were legion, eager to steal livestock or women or goods of various kinds. If David were made a soldier, something he clearly had a knack for in any case, death might very well come to him as it did for so many in the army.

Yet, the king could hardly make David a common soldier; his fame was already far beyond that lowly status. Why not make him a commander of a thousand men, responsible for tactics and equipment and provisions? That way, if he did not die at the hands of some enemy or other, perhaps his own men would become dissatisfied with his leadership and rise up against him. Such mutinies happened all the time, and when the offending commander had been dealt with, another man would take his place. A brief funeral, a few tears of some women who had hoped to attract the eye of the handsome David, and the land would quickly return to normal with King Saul once again in control. The king smiled to himself, and was greatly pleased at the plan that he had devised.

"For the great work of killing the giant, I hereby reward the mighty David with the leadership of my finest soldiers."

As he uttered the command to the assembled forces of Israel, another delightful thought came to him. He knew well that several seasoned soldiers in this cohort of a thousand fully expected to be rewarded by their king for long days of service with the command that he now had given to David, the nobody from Bethlehem. Perhaps the murder of David would come from one of them; disgruntled soldiers had for centuries taken perceived slights into their own hands and slipped a knife between the ribs of rivals to better their own chances for advancement. Saul heard muttering from several corners of the troops assembled, and imagined that David's death was as good as done.

But it simply had not happened. Nothing had worked, and Saul's careful plans had come to nothing. David had led the troops into battle and skirmish and ambush and had been successful wherever he had gone. Instead of resentment against him, his men loved him with a fierce abandon. Instead of enemies killing him, his men had again and again thrown themselves in front of knives and spears and stones to protect their commander; more than a few had died saving David. And for each death, David had wept, had declared fasts and sacrifices and psalms, and had himself led the services for his fallen comrades. Rather than his death, Saul's naming David commander had raised his stature in the land to even greater heights. Rather than lance the boil that was David, Saul's fear of him grew, as throughout the land, both north and south, David, the shepherd, David the singer, David the warrior, was loved, because he it was who gained victory after victory in battle, and always led his troops into the heart of the struggle. Saul had unwittingly made David even greater and known everywhere as a hero without equal. And the king felt the darkness descend on him again just as the light of his rival burned ever brighter.

22

Saul was sick to the teeth of the reports of David's greatness, of his victories, of his enormous piles of spoils, of the devotion that the troops, the people, especially the women, heaped upon his shoulders. The king could not now think of the harpist without his brow darkening, the deep lines of his forehead turning into dry stream beds, the frown lines around his huge mouth stretching down into his grey beard. This ant must be destroyed! But how? There must be a way.

One day, Merab, Saul and Ahinoam's eldest daughter, brought her father a late afternoon snack of dates, figs and wine, cooled by mountain snows. Saul was only half awake when Merab brought the treat quietly into the room, took the food off the tray, and prepared to exit, not expecting Saul to speak to her. But the king's eyes suddenly brightened as an idea formed in his skull. Merab was surely of a marriageable age. She was pretty enough with hips more than adequate to birth numerous babies with minimum risk and little pain. Various suitors had been sniffing around her, bees to the hive, but she had not made a move toward any of them, as far as Saul knew. Of course, no suitor would dare take any liberties with the daughter of the king without the king's expressed approval, and Merab's desires in the matter of marriage had little to do with her choice in any case. And, Saul thought with bitterness, once he dangled David in front of his daughter, the girl would probably faint with anticipation of the champion in her bed, between her eager thighs. Every other woman in Israel would die with jealousy, thinking of Merab and David going at it night after night, trying positions little used, sweating and moaning aloud for all to hear. Here at last was the way to destroy David. After all, the king had promised the slayer of Goliath would marry one of the king's daughters. Who better than Merab? What better time than now?

"Merab," Saul called out calmly, disguising the evil beneath fatherly solicitation.

"Yes, father, " the girl replied, slightly stunned that he would speak to her at all, since he often went days without uttering a word to her.

She waited for some command or other, about the food, or the cleanliness of the bed sheets, or the wood for the fire.

"What would you say to a husband?"

Merab immediately thought of the men who had seemed interested in her, and her heart sank. Each of them were men who drank too much and became violent, or who ate such food as to make their mouths and breath rank, or who smelled in their bodies and clothes more like open graves than living men. But she knew not to cross her father; he made the choices, and as a woman of Israel, she had to obey, even if he were not her king as well as her father. She waited in horror for him to name someone, as her mind ran through a list of the men whom he may have picked, hoping against hope that it would not be one too violent, too rank, or too foul.

"What would you say to David for husband?" her father said.

Merab nearly shrieked aloud at the name! She attempted to appear calm, but inside her guts boiled fiercely and her loins grew hot and eager. David! O YHWH, she thought; what woman in Israel would not commit crimes to gain the attention and the body of David? To have such a one as husband! To care for him, to love him, to share his bed! Merab calmed her voice as well as she could.

"I would be pleased, father, if it is your will."

"It is indeed," said Saul, "And I am very glad you appear to approve of my choice for you."

Approve, thought Merab? I will surely die if it is anyone else but David! She moved deliberately from the king's room, but the moment she escaped his gaze, she gathered up her tunic, and skipped all the way to the room of her sister, Michal, to tell her the astonishing news that she was soon to wed the great David, hero of Israel!

"Sister," she shouted. "Michal! You will never guess in a thousand suns what is about to happen to me! Michal, come here now!"

Merab was impatient to tell Michal, and was irritated that her sister was not immediately within earshot, but Michal was out in the family garden, pulling the darnel from the healthy plants, a never-ending and back-breaking job, usually given to the younger children in the house. In the field, she heard her sister calling, demanding, but she was less than eager to hear what she had to announce. It would inevitably be some new accolade or gift offered to Merab, another suitor after her beauty—she was quite lovely, even Michal had to admit—another new dress or robe, another prize for her vegetables which were always larger, more succulent, more delicious than Michal's own. Very reluctantly, Michal stood erect, her back creaking in the way of a much older woman. She wiped the sweat from her filthy brow and turned her attention toward the shouts of her sister.

"I'm out in my garden, Merab. I'll wait for you here!"

Michal knew that Merab preferred to meet people inside to avoid the scorching sun; she was always fearful that the bloom in her cheeks would turn to red and after the red would come those lines, permanently tracked on her face, announcing that age was coming on her. But the news was too wondrous to wait any longer. Merab hurried to the garden of her sister, and spoke in a flood of words before she saw Michal clearly.

"I am going to be married, and my husband will be…"

But she stopped in mid –word, realizing that some fun could be had with Michal, who was in the main not a fun-loving girl.

"Guess, Michal. Go on, guess!"

Michal hated these games, so she made a ridiculous guess.

"Abner," she said.

Merab hooted with derisive laughter.

"No, silly. Not that dried up old soldier. Besides, he has more wives than I can remember already! Try again!"

"The prophet Samuel," Michal guessed, knowing such an absurd name could hardly be true.

The wizened man was older than the mountains and the sea, and was hardly a fit companion for a goat, let alone a young and eager woman.

"Oh, all right," said Merab, "since you do not want to play, I will tell you. Ready?"

Michal nodded, but half-turned back to her plants, feigning little interest, though her mind began to experience a sense of dread.

"David," said Merab. "David, the wonderful one, is father's choice for me! Who would ever have thought it possible!"

Merab uttered these last words with an exultant cry, looking high into the blue sky. She did not see the look that passed over the face of her sister, a look of shock and horror and astonishment and anger all at once. David! Michal was madly in love with the man, and had been since she first laid eyes on him some months ago. When her father had promised Goliath's killer the hand of his daughter, Michal had longed only for it to be her hand that he meant. At his name, she weakened. In the night, on her bed, she dreamed awake about entwining her body with his, of feeling his member reach deep within her, of bearing his children, all of which would be as glorious as he. In a puff of smoke, her dreams disappeared. With Merab's words, her breath stopped; she was struck mute with fury. She gathered her emotions as well as she could.

"David? But Merab, how could this be?" she said, hoping that the intense jealousy she was feeling was hidden deep in her words. "I have never seen David near your house, and certainly have never seen him looking in our direction," though Michal thought she had looked often enough in his direction with her body yearning for his touch, even just for a glance.

"Of course not," said Merab. "He would not wish to reveal his desire for me openly; his soldiers would see him as weak. He obviously has kept his desire for me secret, only sharing the news with our father when the time was right. Oh, I hope the wedding is soon! The sooner we wed, the sooner to bed!" And she laughed a lascivious cackle with a lusty gleam in her eye, as she ran back to the house.

Michal was appalled, astounded, and very suspicious. Of course Merab was the eldest daughter of the king, but why should David decide now to marry her sister? If he were ambitious, and everyone knew he was very ambitious, why not wait a bit longer? Saul was increasingly disturbed; it was only a matter of time until Israel's people would be clamoring for another king, and who else would they want but the former shepherd of Bethlehem? She had heard that her brother Jonathan and David already had some sort of agreement about which of them would be the next king. If he married Merab now, it could be seen as a naked grab for power, rather than any sort of a love match. Merab had always been ruled by her loins rather than her head, but Michal was by far the more clever one, though she felt her own soft spot stir when David floated into her head. Still, she was nobody's fool. She wondered in fact if David knew anything at all of this proposed marriage to Merab. She resolved to find out.

She dropped her gardening stick, washed as much of the dirt off her face, hands, and arms as she was able, and strode directly toward the house of the king. Saul's large house was only fifty paces or so from her own smaller dwelling, and she made the distance in a short time, nearly running at times but maintaining her dignity as a daughter of the king by striding only. She headed straight toward the front opening when she saw the object of her visit enter the portal. David had gone into the king's house! So, it was true! Michal was sure that David had not seen her, but had gone straight into the king's house. She gave him time to enter fully and then hurried to the door and quietly went in. She tiptoed up to the door of the king's private chamber, being careful not to be heard or seen, and listened to the conversation she knew was about to begin. It was brief and direct.

The king spoke first, as was only right.

"Here is my daughter, Merab," he began.

So Merab was right and had hurried at the summons of their father to meet David. Michal's insides froze as if she were trapped in the snows on Hermon.

"I will give her to you as wife," Saul continued, and tears sprang to Michal's eyes when she thought of David in Merab's arms.

But the king had one more thing to say.

"Just be valiant as we all know you to be, David, and fight the battles of YHWH."

Michal waited for her father to say something about the marriage, about where the couple would live, about his hope for a fruitful issue of many children. But Saul said nothing more and that forced the hidden woman to weigh his words more carefully.

Just why would Saul end an announcement of his blessing on the marriage of his daughter with the most eligible man in the whole land with a charge for the man to fight YHWH's battles? Why focus on David's battle prowess on this day of all days? And Michal was suspicious. She knew, as did all the people, that Saul had tried to kill David with his massive spear. Though he had missed, something he rarely did, that attack was surely some sort of warning to David, a kind of announcement that Saul felt considerable discomfort in the presence of the killer of Goliath. So, she reasoned, why marriage now? Why the charge for David to fight YHWH's battles? It came to her in a flash. Saul wanted David dead, but did not want to bloody his own hands with the deed! Of course! She wondered she had not seen the plan before. David may or may not have been attracted to Merab—who could know?—but Merab was the bait for Saul's hook. Marry my daughter, valiant David, but be certain that you fight and fight hard for me and for YHWH. In the bloody face-to-face struggles, it was more than likely that some Philistine or Amorite or Ammonite sword or ax or spear would find its way into David's lovely flesh. And Saul would be rid of the upstart forever.

There was a brief silence from the room, but David then spoke.

"Who am I, and who are my relatives, that I should be the son-in-law of the king?"

And with no further words, David left the room, leaving behind an astonished and furious Saul and a devastated and weeping Merab. He went by Michal so quickly, he did not catch sight of her, but she watched his comely form leave the house just as quickly as he had come. Michal was elated! David had rejected Merab with one scathing sentence. Oh, he had sounded polite, but such politeness did not fool Michal. He wanted no part of a marriage that demanded of him the cost of fierce and dangerous fighting; he had clearly seen right through Saul's supposed trickery, but had covered his knowledge by feigning humility, a poor man from a poor family. How ridiculous! No father and no woman in Israel would hold David's humble Bethlehemite origins against him, not after that magnificent event in the valley of Elah.

But something else was clear to Michal as well, and this fact caused her spirit to surge within her. David had not thought Merab worthy of dangerous fighting, thus proving he bore no love for her. There was still a chance for her! She too was the daughter of a king, and had yet to have her chance with the man. And Saul's final words to the distraught Merab lifted Michal even higher.

"So, the young warrior will not have you? Well, you look good enough to me for marriage, so I will give you instead to…"

Here Saul paused for a moment, as he searched for a name.

"Adriel, the Meholathite! Yes, he is the husband for you, Merab, and I will hear nothing more about it."

Adriel! Oh, he was rich, all right, but the man had hardly a tooth left in his misshapen head and reeked of beer and onions. This marriage would be dreadful, unthinkable, and as the announcement sank into the room, Merab bolted for the door, wailing in horror. Michal barely had time to get out of her sister's way as she careened outside, flinging her arms wildly in the air, grabbing handfuls of dirt to plaster her head with, and tearing her best robes in deep mourning. Well, thought Michal, the thought of a lifetime with Adriel could do that to a woman, and she stifled a chuckle at the fate of her sister. But, she felt enough for Merab to go slowly to her side to provide what comfort she could, though she knew that a full night of her sister's weeping lay ahead of her.

And she had been right. Merab screamed and shouted, her incoherent sounds punctuated with "David" and with "Adriel" in equal parts, but the former said with an anguished loss and the latter with unbridled disgust. Finally, just before dawn, Merab fell into an exhausted sleep, and Michal crept back to her own room and collapsed on her bed.

King Saul

But as she slept, events were happening that would change her life forever, would bring her at the first the greatest joys and at the last the most profound anguish and pain. For what she did not know is that Saul had been watching her more closely than she had thought, and had determined, quite rightly, that his youngest daughter was in love with David. It was quite rare for the warrior Saul to be so perceptive about other humans, but this time he had been exactly right. However, his plan to use Merab as snare for David had failed, but there was no sense in letting such a good plan go to waste. He just needed the right bait, and Michal's love for the shepherd would be just the thing. After all, Michal was nearly as beautiful as Merab and was so much more clever, a more obvious match for the handsome and witty David. But this time, Saul brought rather more sophistication to the plot.

23

Saul invited David to return to the king's house, looked him square in his deep blue eyes, and said, "You can be my son-in-law through my second daughter. Now, before you say no, as you did before, think a bit longer. You are a worthy match for any woman—all say that—and my Michal is a sprightly one, eager and clever and fair enough. So take some time and consider my offer."

And David did. He spent several days thinking of a life with Michal who was pleasing to the eye and who was without doubt the daughter of the king and could become another stepping stone to the kingship, if David were so inclined—and he certainly was. While David was reflecting on the advisability of the marriage, Saul had prompted some of his closest servants, those entrusted with his very person, to go to David and tell him just how much Saul loved him, and how much all of Saul's servants and friends loved him, and, just so he was clear, how much Michal doted on him and longed for him. The servants met David in a house where the beer was rich and flowed freely.

"Mighty David," said Elhanan, a very tall man, though not as tall as his master, "my Lord the king urges you to consider his offer of marriage to the princess very carefully. He is eager to have you in the royal family." Elhanan drank heavily from his tankard of beer, smiling at the young man with his best smile, and since he, unlike many of his fellow servants, had most of his teeth, at least the ones in front, that smile was especially winning. Naharai, who would later bear the armor of the great Joab, general of David's army, added, "And great David, you have no idea how smitten the princess is with you; she swoons each day on her couch with love for you, running her hands over her lithe and nubile body in anticipation of your hands doing the same. She is eager, my man, eager for you!" And Naharai fell on the floor in a feigned swoon to show to David just how eager Michal really was. The servants all laughed at the show, but David merely watched and weighed the idea of a marriage with Michal.

David then said to Saul's servants, knowing full well that his words would quickly find their way into Saul's ears, "Is it a light thing in your eyes to become son-in-law to the king, since I am a poor man and thus am not worth much?" David had begun to warm to the idea of Michal as his bedmate, and his entrée to a possible kingship of his own, but he needed Saul to know that all of his battle success had yet to translate itself into wealth. How could he really afford the bride price needed for a king's daughter?

He said this, of course, hoping that Saul would not ask of him more than he could offer.

Dutifully, the servants reported all this to Saul, but Saul knew full well that this would-be son-in-law of a king would have little money or goods to offer; his spies had kept him informed of David's profligate use of booty. All of this made Saul's plan absolutely perfect. He now saw at last a way to rid himself of the pest. So he sent his servants back to David and asked them to say something like this.

"In fact, David, the king requires no marriage present at all! At least nothing like a traditional present, silver or cattle or booty from some battle or other. No, the king has another sort of price in mind. You know well his hatred of the Philistines. Their constant pressures on our land are insufferable to him and to us, and we are sure to you. What he wants from you is this: bring to him in a bloody bag one hundred foreskins of those uncircumcised heathen, and thus you will humiliate them, and our king can have a laugh at their expense. There is little enough opportunity for laughter in Israel these days."

David was more than a little shocked at this horrendous request. He liked Philistines as little as did the next Israelite, but how in Sheol was he to grab one hundred of their men and perform the act of circumcision on them? Should they have this done to them while they were still alive? Far easier if they were dead, of course. But the humiliation would be much greater if they went on living as men with members like Israelites. But the thing was risky. David was no fool. He imagined that Saul had dreamt up this grisly plan with the hope that one of those Philistine soldiers would spear him or mutilate him, perhaps even cut off his own member entirely once he saw what the Israelites were trying to do. He weighed the chances of success. Keeping them alive might be better, but too dangerous. David resolved to kill them and then to perform the cutting. But perhaps Saul would be disappointed if the enemy were all dead rather than alive in humiliation, so why not give him double the number? Two hundred foreskins from dead soldiers would be the equivalent of one hundred from live ones. And David could not deny that the mutilation of two hundred of the repulsive Philistines would be a most satisfactory several days' work.

Not only had David decided to increase the number of the skins to two hundred, he had also determined to do the bloody thing in as short a time as possible, thus amazing Saul with his prowess as warrior, and to demonstrate the eagerness with which he desired Michal. Well, she was comely enough, with rounded buttocks and high and pointed breasts to match. And behind those flashing eyes, David could see a woman worthy of his own power and wit. She would indeed make a delightful wife, and, at the last, a fitting queen. As David's mind roamed pleasantly over his imagined future as husband and son-in-law to the king, he noted how much longer he mused on the time of his own kingship. With those thoughts, thoughts of a king David, the face of Michal became less and less distinct as the image of a throne swam clearly into the vision of his inner sight. And David knew that his motives for marriage with Saul's younger daughter had much less to do with lust for her than lust for that throne.

But David was in no mood now for such idle daydreaming. If all his desires were to find fulfillment, he had to act quickly and well. He demanded that his closest friend, Joab, the greatest of his soldiers, muster fifty of his hardiest fighters to join him on an interesting quest. Joab did what David had asked and within the time of the sun's movement from half up in the east to half down in the west, the fifty stood in front of their commander.

"Men of Israel," shouted David in that peculiarly high-pitched voice.

Though David's chest was large and muscled well, as rippled as any of his men, yet from his throat poured not thunder but something rather more like the piercing cry of an eagle, at times cracking in the wind. Still, the man could be heard all right, by all who stood silently before him. Each of them had heard David speak often enough, but that odd sound never failed to provide a moment's shock before they settled in to listen.

"Our king has set before us a great task. We are to kill exactly two hundred Philistine men, no women and no children. And the larger these men are, the easier our ultimate job will be. I command each of you to slaughter four of them. But simple killing is not our work this day. I know that you will do the killing well enough, since all of you hate our mortal enemies as much as do I. But this time, killing will be followed by special mutilation."

At that word, some muttering arose from the men, as they turned to a neighbor and remembered other demands for mutilation: ears, noses, hands and feet. Each man there had done one or more of these things in his time. Sometimes killing was not the goal of a fight, but humiliation through maiming and disabling was requested. In that way the soldiers were no longer dangerous, but in addition they were public displays of Israelite power and an enemy's pathetic weakness. Many of these young soldiers had heard of Saul's saving of the doomed people of Jabesh Gilead, how the evil toad, Nahash, had determined to gouge out all of their right eyes to effect such humiliation.

And there had been times when the mutilation had followed killing, though some soldiers found this somehow less glorious than reducing an enemy to a living object of scorn and ridicule, a beggar on some Israelite street. David raised his arms for silence.

"Be careful that your killing does not affect that member that hangs inside those Philistine tunics, the one that swings below the belt, the rod that gives life, rather than the sword that takes it!"

This last phrase David had shouted, his high-pitch moving even higher as his mouth broke into a raucous laughter. Most of the men joined in the gales of ribaldry, but a few held back, wondering what the leader had in mind. At their puzzled looks, David howled again.

King Saul

"You don't understand? Well, let me be blunt. I want you to cut their pizzles off, and take their stones with it, if you like! I want you to make them look like women! Is that clear enough for you?"

It was, and the men all shrieked with smutty pleasure at the prospect.

"But that's not all," screamed David, through his cackling that had now brought tears to his eyes. "The king does not actually want bags full of such stuff, though YHWH knows what fine sacrifices a crackling bonfire of Philistine pizzles might be. No, all the king wants is the tips, the foreskins, the little crown of skin that separates our men from theirs. First, make them like women, and then make them like us! And take those little flaps of bloody flesh and stick them in a bag. Be careful! I want exactly 200 flaps, so make your cuts neat and tidy. It would be easier to count stones than flaps, but I have my orders and now you have them, too. So go, my fine cutters, and may YHWH be with your arrow's aim and your sword's thrust. But most importantly, may YHWH steady your knife's careful blade! Remember! Four each, but in case one or more of you does not return from the fight—may YHWH protect you all—then one or two extra would not hurt the king's cause!"

And with a final burst of manly laughter, Joab led the fifty warriors out of the camp and into the wilderness.

David stayed in the rear of the convoy to observe whether the men were fulfilling his command. They camped that night, and at first light, went west in groups of ten in search of any under-protected Philistine encampments. That first day two groups of Israelites surprised some sleeping and unwatchful Philistines and began the work that David had announced. Fifteen were easily killed, with no Israelite casualties, and fifteen Philistine foreskins were pushed into a bag, a dark stain of brownish blood oozing from its bottom. The next day twenty-six more were murdered, but this time two careless Israelites were attacked by several Philistine warriors who had escaped the skirmish and had hidden behind some trees near the camp. The Israelites had died, but the Philistines too had been killed by an enraged group of Israelites who had heard the screams of their comrades. After six days the five bags of skins contained more than the required two hundred, though eight Israelite soldiers had been killed and their bodies had been exposed in the wilderness as meals for the carrion creatures that after all were YHWH's own creations just as they had been.

The remaining forty-two soldiers, along with Joab and David, assembled back at the base camp, bringing their foul booty with them. David himself took the five bags of skins, and reaching into each one, quickly counted the skins, and transferred each flap of skin into one new bag brought for the purpose. He made sure that this bag contained exactly two hundred flaps. Some of the men had been much more careful than others, their flaps resembling little caps like a woman's breast nipples. Others were more like unrecognizable lumps of flesh, not like caps at all but at least obvious enough to serve the purpose. The extra flaps of skin, those so crudely cut as to appear like lumps of any body part, he hurled into the darkness. With a triumphant shout, David held the bag over his head, to remind his men of the defeat of Goliath.

But there was more than a little discomfort among the men when they saw David raise that bag to the sky. Why foreskins? What did David plan to do with them? Were they part of some sort of magic ritual that Saul, their sometimes mad king, had planned to perform for YHWH, or, YHWH forbid, for some other god unknown to them? They had asked Joab, but he either did not know, or was not going to tell any of them. They could hardly ask David, since he was the commander whose orders were to be obeyed without question; any soldier knew that.

Of course, David had not told them the reason for the bloody bag of skins. He could not have predicted what they might have felt if they had known that the skins were a kind of bizarre bride price for him, and that they were risking their lives so that he could bed Michal and become son-in-law to the king. For that, eight of their friends had died. Would they have imagined that sacrifice worthy? Would the shades of their comrades rest easily in Sheol after such deaths? Better they remained ignorant for now; they would find the truth soon enough when they got back to Gibeah.

But all needed a night of rest after nearly a week of slaughter and mutilation. So the living soldiers spent the night in raucous revelry, emptying uncounted skins of wine after feasting on several succulent animals of the wilderness, a wild ox, a foolish ostrich, and a small badger of the rocks, great hunks of all tossed together into a huge clay pot always at the ready for a stew. And all the men howled out increasingly low jokes about stones and pizzles, finally collapsing into random jumbles of drunken piles.

David, however, drank far less than his men, as was often his custom. He hated for his teeming mind to be clouded with drink or his gut to be overfull of food. He had spent too many lonely nights on hillsides, watching for the straying of too many ridiculous sheep, to allow himself to fall prey to the weaknesses of food and drink. As his men calmed into a snoring mass, David thought deeply about what had happened and what he was certain was about to happen. More specifically, he thought about how his life was taking much the same turns and twists as had the life of the great patriarch of the people, Jacob, who in fact had become Israel, so renamed by the mysterious wrestler at the Jabbok stream. Like Jacob, David had been offered two sisters in marriage, and had ended up marrying the one not first intended, since he was now convinced that he would soon marry Michal, as Jacob had ended up first with Leah, but later with his beloved Rachel. Also, Jacob had had to pay a very unlikely bride price, demanded by Laban, to wed first Leah and finally Rachel. Jacob, like David, had had no money, so he had worked for a total of fourteen years for his wily uncle to pay for what turned out to be both sisters. David wondered whether fourteen years of hard labor on Laban's ranches were somehow equal to a bag full of foreskins, and decided that he had gotten the better bargain, though that gruesome bag, so near the place of his sleeping, had begun to reek with the smell of human death. And, David mused, would he, like Jacob, have in the end to run from his father-in-law, with the help of his wife, to find his own way in the world? Only time, or the hidden YHWH, would tell, but David would not be surprised if that part of his story would also mirror the patriarch's. As he finally fell into sleep, the picture of Jacob swam into his dreams, that tricky man who had won riches and fame by the strength of his own wits, and, to be sure, the blessing of YHWH. Not a bad model, that, thought David, as blackness fell upon him.

Just as the sun was rising, David awoke with a start. In a dream, not filled with the successes of Jacob as he had hoped, he saw himself winding up a valley toward a city, set high in the hills. He was leading some sort of procession, and behind him were trumpeters, singers, dancers, while he himself sang and danced in front of them all—completely naked! His ruddy cheek reddened at the memory, even after he knew it had been a dream only. No male Israelite would ever appear in public without his privates covered. The act of procreation, and especially the member that performed it, was not to be shown to anyone but the woman for whom it was intended. Of course, all men knew that on occasion, when only men were together on long battle campaigns, a man would comfort a man with certain actions that were expected but seldom discussed. David had been comforted this way himself more than once. But even in such circumstances the sexual member was never displayed to more than one other person. In this dream David was whirling and dancing for all to see, his pizzle flying in time with his wild movements. He looked up and saw Michal, daughter of Saul, pointing to him and laughing and jeering him from the wall of the unknown city. Then, to his horror, she pointed toward a soldier who notched an arrow and aimed it at David, and launched it directly toward his member—but then he had awakened, sweat streaming from his face, his throat raw from apparent screaming.

What sort of dream was this? The terrible smell of the bag of foreskins jerked him back to reality, the sack crusted now with congealed Philistine blood. Perhaps the previous days' focus on foreskins had caused this filthy dream to rise into his head from that murky place whence dreams were born. Dreams had been known to tell the truth of a life, either the present or future. Everyone knew of the great Joseph's way with dreams, how his wondrous abilities to tell them and understand them had saved the people of Egypt from famine, and at the same time, had preserved the lives of the ancestors of Israel. Without Joseph's way with dreams there would be no Israel at all. David resolved to remember this dream; it might be valuable in his future, however uncertain that future might now be.

But there was nothing confusing about his immediate future. He had to get the sack of bloody foreskins to Saul in order to gain his wife. He good-naturedly kicked his sandals into the backs of several of his soldiers whose wine-soaked sleep threatened to keep them inert for many hours still. Grumpily, the remaining soldiers stirred, stretched, and grabbed their aching heads that felt much too large for their aching bodies.

"Let's get moving," he commanded. "This stinking sack holds the key to many surprises for each of you and untold wonders for me, your leader."

Joab replied, "Do you plan to sell these things to some men who wish they had theirs back? Do you plan to sell them some tar to keep them on, too?"

At this, many of the soldiers snickered, the picture of men smearing tar on their members, and carefully placing a Philistine flap of skin on the end providing an image too ridiculous to summon, yet somehow deliciously difficult to avoid.

"Just wait," shouted David, snatching up the sack and tying it to the rope around the middle of his donkey, as far from his nose as he could manage.

When all the captains had mounted and all the walkers were ready, the column moved back toward Gibeah. They were in high spirits, laughing and joking, stories of members and stones flying back and forth, up and down the column. It was generally assumed that the taller the man, the longer the pizzle, so Saul must have the grandest one in Israel. It was to many all the more strange that he had only two wives. But another soldier claimed to have known a very short man—he could not remember his name—who had a member nearly magical in length. So long it was, he said, that this man could balance a sack of wine on its end and still have room for a man's two hands to encircle the rest. Most scoffed at this, but David, leading the raucous group, just smiled, knowing that very soon he would be employing his member, however long or short it may be, in delicious ways with the comely Michal.

Soon, the walls of Gibeah appeared before them, and David shouted for the guards to open the gates. The scrape of wood on wood announced that the gates would soon be swinging back, and David and his jovial men rode and walked into the city. They were met by delirious crowds of men and women, shouting and laughing, quickly counting the troops and seeing that most of the men had returned. Only the widows of the eight who had died dampened the mood with their hooded and tear-filled eyes. Saul strode out to the center of the square, leading Michal who was dressed as if for a wedding. Messengers had run from David's camp and had brought the news that the men had indeed defeated several groups of Philistines, and had brought the demanded bag of trophies with him back to the king. Saul's face betrayed his anger and frustration that another plan to be rid of this David had failed, and as a result, he was going to have to give his daughter to this man, making him one step closer to the kingship of the land.

Yet, Saul outwardly tried to display pleasure at his soon-to-be son-in-law.

"Great David! Again you have done the impossible. This deed has outstripped the killing of the great Goliath! Where are the "things" I asked you to bring to me? Have you actually done it?"

"Without fail, my king! The treasure bag is here!"

And with a flourish David hoisted the sack of foreskins over his head and hurled them in the direction of Saul. Instinctively, the king reached out to catch the bag, and found his huge hands suddenly covered in sticky blood, while his nose wrinkled in disgust at the terrible smell of death rising from the sack. The great crowd shouted and laughed at their king, finding it very funny that Saul was now the bearer of Philistine blood and stink. And they hailed the victorious David, picking up the now-familiar chant "Saul has struck down his thousands, and David his ten thousands!" And as the chant grew louder and louder, Saul's face grew darker and darker. Michal saw this transformation with alarm, and raised her arms for quiet.

"My fellow Israelites! David has given us a great victory, but he has done so because my father, the king, sent him out to do so. Today's victory is Saul's as much as it is David's. Long live King Saul! Long live the king!"

Some in the crowd picked up that chant, but many still shouted the other, and the tension in the square rose higher. David went to the well at the town's center and washed his hands of the bloody bag, and moved toward Saul and Michal.

"My lord, the king! You hold in your hands what is left of 200 Philistine heathen; as you can see, they smell just as bad in death as they do in life!"

As he spoke, Saul noted that everyone in the crowd hung on his every word, every woman lusted after David with their eyes, every man leaned toward him with the hopes of catching his gaze. And Saul realized that he was disappearing in the blinding light of this insufferably powerful shepherd boy.

"David, you have indeed performed the deed I called on you to do, and you have done it well. I congratulate you, even though I had hoped that you would have brought two hundred live and humiliated Philistines to us for our pleasure, rather than a grotesque bag of their tiny remains to stain our fingers and offend our noses!"

This last was said with sarcasm with a clear intent to lessen the thrill of the victory. The crowd quieted, recognizing the king's verbal attack on their champion; uncomfortable muttering rose from many parts of the crowd. Saul was momentarily convinced that his words had diminished the delight of the people for this upstart.

"Still, this smelly sack is proof that you have done the king the service he requested, so now I give you your promised reward—my daughter Michal."

Michal stepped forward toward David, and he grabbed her in a great hug and kissed her full on the lips. As their mouths parted, there was a loud smack, followed by David's great laugh. The crowd cheered, while Michal reddened with shock. Public displays were not the thing in Israel, and to embrace the daughter of the king so openly was an astounding display of arrogance. If it had been anyone other than David, the slayer of Goliath and the champion of the people, Saul's guards might have separated his red head from his muscled body. But because it was David, Saul restrained his guards with a nod, forced a brief smile, and shouted to the people.

"We will go to the high place and join these two passionate lovers as one. It appears that there is no time to lose! Let us act quickly before they consummate the match in front of all of us!"

Saul laughed when he said this, and many in the crowd laughed too, but there was little joy in his laughter. David had won again, despite Saul's excellent plan to rid himself of the rodent. And now he really was going to be his son-in-law. The people loved him to distraction; he was victorious wherever he turned. And worst of all, YHWH had obviously marked him for greatness.

Yet, Saul was still king, and had the power of the kingship on his side. There were surely other ways to deal with the boy. Now that he and Michal were to be married, he would necessarily be closer to Saul on a more regular basis. Perhaps such close proximity would yield opportunities not yet conceived? Poison in the food? A hunt gone awry? Michal could help trap him in some foul deed or other, aiding the enemies, stealing some booty? Saul's mind filled with possibilities, and his mood lightened as he savored the end of David once and for all. Laugh now, boy, and enjoy the fleshly pleasures of my daughter, but I am still king, and you are my servant, to do with as I please. One of our poets wrote that YHWH delighted to turn our mourning into dancing. Well, David, if I have anything to do with it, your laughter will become wailing one of these days. One of these days. His head filled with murder, Saul joined the crowd moving toward the high place of Gibeah to bless the marriage of David and Michal before YHWH, the God of the armies of Israel.

24

After the wedding, David and Michal went to Bethlehem to spend some time with Jesse and some of David's brothers. It was always seen as important to introduce a new bride to the family to demonstrate the wisdom of the choice of the woman. Was she clever? Was she beautiful? Most importantly, could she bear sons for the ongoing health of the family? And since David was the secret king of Israel—his brothers and father had witnessed his crowning by Samuel in their own house, though they scarce still could believe it—it was especially important that his choice of queen, now secret but one day public, be approved. Michal seemed to the family clever enough, and comely enough, and of course was daughter to Saul. But whether she could bear children was not so certain. She was surprisingly small for the daughter of the tallest man in the land, but women far smaller had born large broods of children. Time alone would tell if this woman were worthy of David.

But back in Gibeah David, not Michal, filled the mind of the king, as he continued to plot ways to dispose of him. On certain occasions, Saul would remember how David had first come to him, to soothe his dark moods with the beauty of his playing and singing. But those memories were increasingly vague, nearly wiped out by the enormous acclaim David had received from Israel at his defeat of Goliath and his continuous victories over Israel's enemies. When Saul looked at David now, he seldom saw the sweet singer, the faithful friend and help. He saw the rival, the upstart shepherd, the ruddy boy who would stop at nothing to depose the rightful king of the land and seize the throne for himself. David, son-in-law to the king, was not to be trusted; he must be destroyed, and plans flitted in and out of Saul's head to do just that.

Just as Saul had first noticed Michal's infatuation with David, an infatuation that apparently had blossomed into love, and now marriage, so too had Saul observed his eldest son, Jonathan's, very close relationship to the man. Who could have missed Jonathan's actions right after David's defeat of Goliath, when Saul's son, smitten with the greatness of David, had handed him his tunic, his sword and shield, had nearly stripped himself naked in front of YHWH and the people? Saul had eyed Jonathan's behavior very closely since that day, fearing that the boy's hero worship might slip over into something unseemly, something unmanly, something that could never be acceptable for the son of a king. So he resolved to test his son, to see if his love of David was rather more than it should be. He invited Jonathan to join him in the house.

King Saul

"My son. Though David has married your sister and has done wonderful things on the fields of battle against the enemies of Israel, I admit that I do not fully trust the man. That day he killed the giant, for example: did you hear his boasting, even before he hurled that miraculous stone at Goliath's head, that he was going to show all of us how great he was by the killing? Oh, I grant that he got the name of YHWH on his lips at the end, but the first thing he said referred only to himself. Did you hear him, Jonathan?"

"I did hear that day, father, as we all did. But my memory is unlike yours. I heard David call on the power of God before he killed the giant, and I heard him give God praise after the deed was done. In fact, I have never heard David do or say anything without first praising or thanking YHWH for the deeds and the words. I simply cannot imagine why you do not trust him; I find him exemplary in every way, the very finest man I have ever met, brilliant at everything he does, music, battle, love. Who could not devote one's very soul to a man like that?"

And, thought Saul, who indeed has devoted his very soul to the man: you, my son!

"I must disagree," replied Saul with more heat than he intended. "You have been taken in by David, as have so many others. He is devious, clever, interested only in himself. Make no mistake; this David wants to be king of my land and is scheming even now to accomplish it. Do you actually believe that he loves your sister? Have you ever heard the word "love" from his lips, unless he is speaking of some new piece of music or a just-forged spear? Does David at the last love any other person save himself? Men like David are the most dangerous men of all; they feign love, but they plot conquest. They pretend the care of others but care only for themselves and their vast ambitions. Mark my words, Jonathan! David wants only power, and you and I stand in his way. He plots to destroy us, so we must strike first before he kills us and our loved ones. I say, we kill David now!"

Saul bellowed this last phrase so loudly that the guards heard him clearly as did any who happened to be walking thirty paces from the house.

Jonathan ran from the house without saying another word and headed toward Bethlehem on his best mule to warn his friend. As it happened, David and Michal, and their retinue of guards and baggage handlers were returning to Gibeah, having concluded their visit with David's family. Jonathan saw the train from a distance and spurred his mount to gallop faster to meet it. He reined in the donkey, jumped off, and rushed up to his friend.

"David! My father is trying to find ways to kill you!"

"Surely you are mistaken, Jonathan. I and Michal, the king's daughter, have just married. I have fought many battles for Israel at Saul's request, and have been successful at every turn. When the king's moods darken, he always asks for me to come sing and play for him, to lighten the burden, and I have never failed to do so. Why in the name of YHWH would he want to kill me?"

195

"Truly, I cannot imagine why, but I can only say that it is more than true; he has your death on his mind. But I have a plan to find reconciliation between the two of you. When you get back to Gibeah, do not return to your house; he may have sent soldiers there for the killing already. Rather, hide behind the large stone in the king's barley field early tomorrow. The king and I will go for our weekly inspection of the progress of the grain, and there I will speak well of you to him. You listen to the conversation and see if you can detect in him the murderous intent I mention. I will attempt to change his mind about this foolish act, and if I can, you may come back into the good graces of the king and live in peace with him."

As was the custom, the king and his first-born son met early to inspect the grain fields that supplied the coffers of the king and his family. The fall rains had been unusually plentiful, and the barley was green and high enough to wave in the slight wind like waves of the great sea. It was always a blessing to see such abundance in a land where famine was all too common. Saul paused to thank YHWH for the sight, while Jonathan added a prayer to the gods of the grain who had been praised in the land long before the arrival of Israel. It never hurt to keep contact with whatever gods there may be, he thought. But his prayer was short, since he had David's life on his mind.

"My father, I have been thinking much about our conversation yesterday about David, my brother-in-law. I am still surprised that you wish to kill him, he of all men the most devoted to Michal, to Israel, and to you. Such talk is deeply offensive, when he has in no way offended you. You have dreamed that he hates you and wants to kill you. He has never indicated anything like that to me and has certainly never acted like it toward you. He has always acted for Israel and for you. He took his own life in his hands and killed the huge Philistine that led to a great victory for YHWH and for Israel. You yourself witnessed these things, and you rejoiced and were glad. I urge you not to kill this great man, and thereby shed innocent blood, for there is no reason at all to murder David, the savior of Israel."

And Saul listened to the speech of his son, while David, hiding behind the stone, listened, too. And Saul was torn in his mind between his fear of the rival, David, and his love of the singer, David. He was mightily sick of being reminded over and over that David had killed the giant, Goliath, since he, Saul, as Israel's tallest warrior and king, should by rights have done the deed. And when Jonathan had called David "great," it was as though he had thrown a spear at his own father whom Jonathan had never called great, nor ever would after Saul's murderous threats at Mizpah. If he could just be rid of David, his life would be so much simpler, but his son was right; shedding innocent blood was a heinous crime in Israel. Look what had happened to the ancestor Cain after he had murdered his innocent brother, Abel, over some problem of sacrifice: he had been banished from the land and the soil and spent the rest of his days wandering from place to place, always fearing that he in turn would be killed by someone or other. And without the mysterious mark of YHWH on him, he undoubtedly would have been. Saul shuddered. It was more than enough that the cruel Samuel had twice humiliated him in front of his people, claiming he was no longer king over the land. To add banishment and the actual end of his rule and dynasty would be too much.

"All right, my son. I have heard your voice. By the life of YHWH, David shall not be put to death."

But Saul said the command carefully; he said David shall not be killed. He did not say that he, Saul, might not do the killing himself at some opportune time in the future. Nevertheless, at those words, David left his hiding place, and bowed low before his king. "My Lord, I have never meant you any harm; my life is yours to do with as you wish. You are my king, and I am your servant. Give me any task, any task at all, and I will gladly do it." And Saul bid David rise from before him, and he grabbed him in the hug of a bear. But whether the hug was one of play or one of another sort was not clear, especially in the mind of the king. Nevertheless, for the moment David was once again welcome in the court of Saul. And, as before, he went out to fight the king's battles, and when he had returned he played his harp and sang his songs for Saul. And Jonathan and Michal were glad to see the two men again together and at peace.

But the peace did not last long.

25

David's extraordinary victories over the enemies of Israel continued, and became so expected that any small setback was met with shock and surprise. But before any real fear could grow that the Philistines were poised to take the offensive, David would rally the troops and drive them back again. With the increase of Israelite victories came an increase in the reputation of their author; David was without doubt now the most famous man in all the land and was as deeply feared among the Philistines as he was richly loved among many of the people of Israel.

And as this love for him increased, Saul grew more wary and short-tempered. His loving wife, Ahinoam, every day found herself berated for bad food, unclean blankets, unkempt hair, improper speech. She could now do nothing right in her husband's eyes, and she soon tried to be with him as little as common wifely duty demanded. Jonathan was no better used. His devotion to David, and his stern defense of him after the affair of the Philistine foreskins and the marriage of Michal, did little to endear him to his father. And Michal, once Saul's favorite, now became only the wife of David, and hence little better in her father's eyes than a whore, sleeping with a man despised. Saul was seen less and less by his people, spending the bulk of his time alone, brooding in his house, hiding from the light. Those closest to him, Ahinoam and Jonathan and Michal and Merab, his nearly forgotten daughter, the wife of the aged Adriel, remembered that time some years ago when Saul had first suffered his dark mood and how only David could banish that mood with his sweet voice and magical playing. But now that that very David was the cause of this mood, for reasons none could understand fully, not one of them could see just how the troubled king could be helped.

But surprisingly, it was David himself who offered to try to soothe the king once again. He had returned from still another victory, and had been told that Saul would not receive him in the throne room. But David could see how the people of the land were unable to celebrate his triumphs adequately, because their king would not join them. And since David's rise to power depended in part on the public acclamation of his military prowess, it would hardly do that there were no cheering crowds, no wine-soaked parties, no massive sacrifices in Gibeah. In short, he was very tired of Saul stealing his thunder by his perpetual bad mood.

So, David demanded to see the king.

King Saul

"My lord David," shouted Saul's imposing guard, "the king is not to be disturbed—by anyone," as he pointed his spear at David's vitals.

"I will not be denied by you, whatever your cowardly name may be," thundered David. "I am son-in-law to the king, and I am the leader of his armies. The time has come to celebrate another defeat of the heathen, and I insist that the king lead the victory party and parade. I demand to see him, so stand aside!"

As the noise of the confrontation increased, the guard that stood inside the room where Saul was, stepped through the door and joined his comrade to face the furious David. Blood was sure to flow, since David's sword was now drawn, and the two guards had their orders not to disturb their king. Their hugely muscled arms and thighs tensed, ready to disarm the warrior if they could and kill him if they must.

David moved toward them, fully prepared to kill them both, when Saul's enormous form appeared at the door.

"Stand aside, you dogs," he shouted, and grabbed both of the guards by their sweaty necks, shoving each of them into the wall.

A tight smile was on his face.

"David, David, my wondrous son-in-law! I apologize for the actions of these two fools. I did say for them to bar the door, but surely they knew the face of David. Everyone knows the face of David, the wise and brilliant and talented and ever-trustful David!"

David could see that the king was unwell, either by too much drink or too much of something not as easy to perceive. But he stood his ground.

"My lord, the king, father of my beloved Michal, I come to urge you to join us in celebration of the defeat of the pagans. The people want to shout and sing and dance, but they want to see their king lead them in the fun. Please, my father, come out of the house, put off your sadness, and enter into the joy of the day!"

"Sing for me now," Saul said quietly, and moved back into the darkened room.

David hesitated, but could see that he had little choice but to grab his harp, now always hanging near Saul's door, and sing for the troubled man. Saul would not join in public celebration until his mysterious mood had lifted. And so David sang. He sang of the snows of Hermon, the rushing streams of the far north, the fearsome bears of the mountains, the foolish ostrich of the steppe. Song after song poured from his lips and filled the pitch-black room with sound. He could not see the look on the king's face, as he sang, could not see that his eyes remained hooded, his mouth tight, his left fist clenched, his huge spear held at the ready in his right hand. But the warrior, keenly alert to the sounds of any movement in darkness, learned from his shepherd days and honed by countless night skirmishes against human enemies, sensed the slightest rustling from the spot where he imagined the king was sitting. David could not see that Saul was rising up on his left knee just enough in order to hurl his spear at the singer, but he knew that something was happening, and knew he needed to move as quickly as he could. He dove down toward the floor, tossing his harp from him as he hit the rugs, just as the king's spear whistled by his head and stuck trembling into the wall. The force of the cast caused the spear to sing as it vibrated rapidly in the wall, but before David could hear any of its deadly tune, he was gone from the room.

"Your father has tried yet again to murder me at the point of his spear," he cried to Michal, having rushed home to his wife in complete terror. "The first time he threw his spear at me, I imagined that it was a kind of warning, but this was no warning. I could not see his face in the darkness, but that spear cast was designed to slaughter your husband. Your father has plainly gone mad! There is no doubt that he wants me dead, though I cannot think why exactly. He knows I want to be king; I have not lied to him or to anyone about my ambition. But he also must know that I will wait my time. He will not live forever, and Jonathan and I have an agreement that I mean him no harm if he succeeds his father. What am I to do, Michal? Help me!"

David fell on their bed, shaking and crying in fear.

Michal looked out of the window and noticed that four large men, clearly sent by Saul, were running toward their house. They were heavily armed with shields and swords, full battle gear. But rather than break down the door, they stationed themselves two at the door and one each at the corners of the front of the house. Fools, she thought. They have left the rear of the house unguarded. Apparently, they intended to prevent David from leaving the house, but were told not to kill him in the night. Why her father had given such peculiar orders were unknown to her, but it was still another sign that the king was not well. A plan quickly formed in her mind.

"If you do not leave tonight, you will not see another sunrise. Here. Put on one of my best tunics and cover your hair with this piece of cloth. I will lower you down from this rear window. When you reach the ground, move quietly but quickly out of the city. Say nothing to anyone."

"But Saul will surely come to the house and will demand to see me. When it is seen I am gone, they will pursue me with a hundred soldiers, and I will easily be caught."

"Leave that to me," said Michal. "I have a way to buy you some time. They will not discover that you have left for many hours; by that time you will be safe. Now hurry, my husband!"

David put on his wife's best tunic, her most loose-fitting one, since she was far smaller than her heavily muscled man, and covered his copper hair with a beautiful piece of cloth, a gift he had given her after some raid or other. A pair of her finest sandals completed the disguise; fortunately her feet were rather large for her small frame. At a distance the battle-hardened warrior could easily be mistaken for a lovely maiden. The night and the clothes would perform the trick. Michal grabbed her husband in a fierce hug and kissed him long and deeply on his lovely mouth. Tears sprang to her eyes as she whispered loudly that he should go now. He grabbed onto the rope she had produced, sprang to the sill of the window, and disappeared over the side of the house and into the night. Through her tears, Michal watched her lover walk easily but quickly toward the city gates. She knew that the gatekeeper would recognize her tunic and would ask no questions when "she" asked to be allowed to leave the city.

What Michal could not see, nor did she sense, that her passionate kiss was not returned by David, nor was her fierce hug given back to her. And her tears blinded her to the fact that there were no tears of a lover's leave-taking in his eyes. Michal loved David with a recklessness that bordered on self-abandonment, and she had convinced herself that her husband felt the same sort of love for her. Their lovemaking was wild enough, though it was true that its frequency was not to her complete satisfaction and was usually confined to those times following her blood flow. She had wanted a child desperately, and David had said that he too longed to make a baby with her. But she had not become pregnant, and her flat belly was becoming the source of some tension between them.

But why was she brooding about all this now! She had to put her plan into action. And it was a fine plan indeed! She chuckled to herself as she prepared to deceive the idiot guards of her father. The idea was hardly original with her. Her mother, Ahinoam, had told her the old story often enough. When their ancestor Jacob had gone to Haran, across the Jordan River, to escape the fury of his brother, Esau, he had married both Leah and Rachel after being hilariously tricked by his uncle, Laban, into doing so. But after twenty years in Laban's employ, Jacob and his family had grown very rich and had decided to leave Haran and return to the land of promise. During those years, Laban had treated Jacob and his own daughters more like slaves than family, so when Jacob's family left Haran—they in fact slipped away without telling Laban at all—Rachel, to get even with her father, stole his teraphim, his tiny and beloved household gods. These were little images of divine women with large bottoms and pendulous breasts and divine men with engorged and protruding members, all designed to ensure healthy flocks and large crops of grain. Such objects would surely be useful when they got back to Israel, and their theft would just as surely make the old goat Laban furious. Rachel had laughed as she held them in her saddlebags.

When Laban discovered that Jacob had left, who in addition to growing very rich himself had in the process made Laban far more wealthy, he rushed after him, hoping he could convince him to return and thus continue his own increasingly comfortable life style. And when he found that his little, much-loved teraphim were gone, those objects that in his mind were a significant part of his success, he pursued Jacob with even more energy. When he overtook the slow-moving caravan, he accused Jacob of stealing his gods. Jacob became very indignant at this accusation, since he had no idea that his beautiful Rachel had in fact stolen the things. Laban looked throughout the camp, but could not discover where the teraphim were. Finally, he barged into Rachel's private tent. When he accused her of the theft, she roundly denied it, and bid him search wherever his suspicious nose would take him.

However, she said, (and here was the great fun of the story), "Forgive me, my father, for not standing in your exalted presence, but the way of women is upon me! Well, I suppose you could look under me if you wish."

Of course, no self-respecting man of that or any time would in a thousand suns place his hand anywhere close to a bleeding woman, so Laban declined the offer and hurriedly left the tent. Of course, under Rachel is precisely where the teraphim were all the time!

Michal chortled with glee when she remembered this rowdy tale, and was grateful to her mother for telling it to her; it now offered an idea that would save her husband's life. For Israelites still had teraphim that they consulted on occasions when YHWH was strangely silent, though her teraphim were a good deal larger than the ones in Rachel's story. In fact, they were nearly life-sized, formed in the shape of a man, made of leather and cloth, stuffed with the dust and chaff left after the winnowing of the grain. Michal grabbed the largest of her teraphim, dropped it on the bed she shared with David, and covered it with the blankets they always used on cool nights. Just to add to the deception, she added a crown of goat's hair to the top of the teraphim, the reddest hair she could find to attempt to match David's very distinctive color.

Just as she finished arranging the teraphim with the goat's hair to resemble a sleeping David, Saul's guards, anxious to get this night's work done, burst through her front door and demanded to see the sleeping man.

"I regret to say that my husband is too sick to rise from his bed. If you care to see him, you will note that his color is none too good. (Michal saw that she was enjoying this ruse a good deal.) Perhaps you can return tomorrow and see whether he has improved."

The guards left in confusion, not knowing quite what to do. When they returned to Saul, he was enraged, since he had expected to see David dragged before him, preparing himself for death.

"Well, you fools, where is the man? Sick? Sick in bed? Pick up the bed and bring him here still in it! He can die in his bed for all I care. I want that wretch here before me, and I want him now! And to make sure I get what I want, I will go with you myself to get the man. It appears that I am the only one in Israel who can see that this man must be dealt with before he executes his mad desire to become king of the land."

Saul and the guards returned to David's house, and, brushing by a protesting Michal, surged up to David's chamber.

Saul roared, "Get up, you conniving weasel, and face your doom!"

And with that Saul ripped the blankets off the reclining figure, and found a teraphim with a goat hair top!

"Where is he? Who dares trick the king of Israel?"

Michal stood silently, a slight smirk on her face. She knew now how Rachel felt in the presence of her father, Laban.

"You, my daughter, my own flesh? Why have you done this and allowed my enemy to escape?"

"What was I to do, father? Who better than you know of David's terrors? He threatened me with death if I did not help him escape. Do not roar your rage at me, father. Do you not love your daughter still? That man I married is powerful and not to be argued with. Rather than accuse me of something, why do you not show me some fatherly comfort?"

And at that, Michal dissolved in tears, some of which were real, for she did fear her father, but most of which were for his benefit and for her safety. As she crumpled to the floor, Saul stormed from the room, muttering threats and demands that no one could understand or fulfill.

26

And Saul thought, Where would the man go? Bethlehem? Not likely, since his relationship with his family appeared tenuous at best, his brothers' jealousy obvious. To the wilderness? He would not survive a week in the wilds of Ein Gedi alone, without water or weapons, for Saul was almost sure that he had fled ill equipped. Ramah! Of course. He will go to that ancient man of power, Samuel, for he knows that the prophet and I bear no love for one another. But he does not know that even Samuel, YHWH's so-called mouthpiece, will not stop me from ending the life of this upstart shepherd boy. Before I go myself to Ramah, I will send some men to be certain that David really has gone there.

"Abner!" The sleepy man rushed into Saul's room, adjusting his tunic and wiping sleep slobber from his mouth.

"My Lord King!"

"Take ten of your sturdiest and deadliest warriors and run to Naioth, that puny village in the vicinity of Ramah. I think that bastard David has fled the city and has gone to the place of Samuel. Watch out! He is a very clever man, and I believe him to be a traitor to our throne and rule. I want him captured and I want him alive in my presence this time tomorrow. Do you understand—alive? However, if he resists taking—well, you know what to do with traitors, I assume?"

Saul said this with a sneer and a wicked chuckle. Abner rushed from the room in no little confusion. David, the hero of Israel, killer of the giant, lord of battles, a traitor? He knew there was hatred of the man by the king, but how could David, of all people, be traitor? Still, he had his orders, and he was a soldier.

Abner ran to the barracks and commanded ten volunteers to act for the king. He knew six of the ones who responded well, hardened men of the wars against the Philistines who would follow orders without question. The other four were not known to him, but their eager response to his call spoke well of them.

"Follow me, and quick march! We go to Naioth, due north, a half day."

The 11 soldiers left the tent and broke into a warrior's trot, a pace they could sustain for a full day and more. They held their spears in their right hands, their shields in their left. Their short swords were fastened into their leather belts on their left sides, and their skins of water were on the their right sides. As they fell into the rhythm of the run, no man spoke the better to save their wind; the only sound was the steady slap of sword against thigh, sandals against rocky ground, the drum-like heavy breathing of muscled chests.

As the 11 approached the village of Naioth, no more than a few scattered clay huts, unprotected by any walls or guards, the warriors slowed their pace and came to a halt. Abner called for them to take a short breather and to check their weapons. Only now did he reveal the mission they were on.

"Our lord the king, the mighty Saul, has called us to bring the foul traitor David back alive to his house to answer for his crimes against the throne of our master."

At this, several of the men muttered darkly into their beards; David's name was whispered as surprise and shock registered on several faces.

"Are you prepared to follow the king's command? If not, come here and face my sword!"

Abner had been chosen as intimate to the king, because he was known as the greatest swordsman in Israel; it would take a fool or an arrogant newcomer to face him in single combat. Among these ten, there were no fools and no newcomers arrogant enough to confront the mighty Abner. There was now silence among them.

"Divide yourselves into two groups of five, and separate one group from the other some twenty paces. I will lead you toward Naioth; if we are lucky David may, as servant to the king, come easily with us. But, you all know him to be a superb fighter, and if he chooses to resist, be ready for a dangerous struggle. He is but one man, and we are eleven; we have our orders. Do your best to take him alive, but if he threatens your life or the life of your comrades, do what you must to survive."

With swords drawn and jaws set in grim determination, the soldiers advanced on Naioth, five to the right and five to the left, with Abner striding fearlessly in the middle, alone and exposed.

At first, there was no sign of life in the village, no cooking fires, no cry of children, no sounds at all. Only the steady breathing of Saul's men rode the desert air. Suddenly, as if they had been conjured from the dust of the ground, some twenty ragged men rushed to confront the eleven heavily armed soldiers. But these ghostly apparitions held no weapons, brandished no shields. They were shouting, dancing, writhing, in a frenetic ecstasy, beating their shriveled chests, tossing dirt in the air and grinding it into their grimy hair. And in their midst sat the prophet Samuel, wizened like a grape too long in the sun, his scrawny arms raised in bizarre benediction of these men. It looked to Saul's men as if the maw of Sheol had disgorged its latest victims as too foul even for its capacious appetite.

The men fell back in horror at these monstrous wraiths, and tried to run back toward Gibeah. But suddenly they were seized with the same frenzy of the wild men, and Saul's men soon found themselves on the ground, shouting and writhing uncontrollably, tearing their tunics, and tossing their useless weapons aside. Just as Abner fell into darkness, trying to resist the unseen force that was sapping his will, he saw Samuel smiling what could only be called an evil smile, calmly presiding over the melee. And he also thought he glimpsed the form of David, standing behind the prophet, gazing quietly on the scene. But then there was only screaming and crying and dancing and darkness.

One of the warriors escaped the place of madness and rushed back to tell Saul. He burst into the throne room, unannounced, surging past the guard. He fell to his knees before Saul.

"My lord king! We went at your command to capture the great traitor, David, and to return him to my Lord. But the awesome Samuel commanded a band of holy men to come out to us, screaming and dancing in religious frenzy. My Lord, we could not kill these holy ones, since you, my lord, gave us no command to do so, nor did we wish to risk our own spirits by staining our hands with the blood of such men. My Lord, that terrible spirit of abandon and ecstasy soon fell on us, but I escaped before I was swallowed up with it, like the prey of a great eagle. But I fear all of your other men, even the great Abner, have succumbed to the power of this thing and have gone mad in the deserts of Naioth!"

Who better than Saul himself knew of the power of this spirit of frenzy? Had he not fallen under its sway when first he had been called by Samuel to lead Israel? He remembered with a shudder how foolish he had felt, sweating and writhing on the ground for most of a day and a night, sharing a soiled blanket with some of those evil-smelling holy men who spent all their days in such absurd ways. Saul had healthy respect for all things holy, but he often questioned the sincerity of these ecstatics; he wondered if their wild motions were more designed for regular meals, prepared by faithful men and women in awe of such things, rather than for genuine devotion to YHWH of the armies. And the fact that Samuel remained their leader made them even more suspect to the king. The wily Samuel! He had no soldiers, but this holy rabble had thwarted his attempts to capture his rival.

"Get off your knees!" Saul spoke roughly to the very frightened man. "Gather twenty soldiers this time, and run back to Naioth. Capture that foul traitor this very day or face my wrath!"

Saul's voice boomed through the room and poured out into the square of Gibeah. Twenty men were quickly assembled and ran off north. But after an anxious wait of nearly another whole day, two stragglers from the twenty returned to Gibeah, announcing that their comrades had also fallen under the spell of the terrible Samuel and were even now cloaked in madness at Naioth.

Saul had had enough of these failures and decided that he now would lead another force to Naioth to deal with David once and for all. He hid his reluctance from the men he chose to go with him; the early memory of his own madness under Samuel's influence was still fresh, how he had trembled and thrashed in the filthy dirt, embarrassing himself in front of many of those he had known from his youth. But the traitor, David, had to be dealt with!

King Saul

"Come, you cowards! You need not fear one aged man! I am king; that man himself made me so! I will lead you to capture this upstart shepherd!"

Several soldiers rallied to Saul's side, but many more remembered that awful day at Gilgal when the terrible Samuel had rejected Saul's kingship, calling on YHWH to do so, and had butchered the king of the Amalekites with his own bloody hands. Samuel may be older than anyone had ever imagined a man could be, but he was still God's prophet, and was not to be trifled with. Only a fool would stand toe to toe with such a one as Samuel. But Saul was even now running toward Naioth, some fifteen soldiers with him.

The group approached the large cistern at Secu, a brief run from Naioth, and Saul demanded to know where Samuel and David were, roughly grabbing a herdsman who had come to water his flock.

"As far as I know, great Saul, both are here in Naioth, if they have not returned to Ramah."

The man was terrified to be accosted by the king and his words spilled from him in a jumble.

"Show me where you last saw them," shouted Saul, but as his lips formed the last word of his command suddenly he found himself no longer able to speak at all.

His feet were planted in the dirt, his arms were flailing the air uncontrollably, spittle was flying from his lips, and his great torso was falling forward. As he hit the ground, his legs began to writhe and twist, his head swiveled on his neck from side to side, and his bowels released inside his tunic with a mighty rush, followed by a putrid smell. Saul was in ecstasy once again, and those who had come with him were soon beside themselves, shouting and crying and tearing their robes in wild abandon. Saul and his men were all naked as the day they were born; none of them saw Samuel carried toward them with a satisfied grimace, observing them completely helpless before him and before YHWH.

The prophet demanded to be brought closer to the king so he could look down at his twisting body.

"So, O mighty king Saul. You think you still have power in this land? The power is still mine, and I am still YHWH's representative here and everywhere! Do kings of any land fall on the filthy ground and twist and turn and behave like brute beasts? You are no king of this land or of any land. You are barely a man at all. You are nothing but a broken vessel, a pathetic weed fit only for the trash heap or the fire! YHWH has rejected you, as I have already said, and waits only for your death. Sheol will soon gain a once royal inhabitant. So go, Saul, reign in Sheol, and command your subjects there, because you have no more power among the living!"

As Samuel shouted these last words, his ancient body attempted to straighten, so that what was left of his voice could be heard by those who stood near the wriggling forms. Among them was David, who looked on the scene in wonder, observing Saul, the man who had twice tried to murder him, now reduced to an infant in the presence of Samuel.

YHWH's power is astounding, he thought, and Samuel is the right friend to have. Surely, my lord Saul cannot be long for the land of the living. Who would ever have imagined that Samuel, the ageless one, would outlive the first king of Israel? And could it be that my time to rule Israel has come so soon?

Saul and his men lay on the ground naked all day and all night, and many who heard of it came by to hoot and laugh at the king, bellowing that old proverb, "Is Saul among the prophets?"

Well, they thought, perhaps Saul is among these sorts of prophets, wild men of the mountains, who have no power, no reason, no standing in the world. But in the face of Samuel, the real prophet of YHWH, Saul was no prophet at all, but a bumbling fool, a religious mountebank, a soldier of great physical size, but a size unmatched by wisdom. Surely, they imagined, this could not be the king of Israel. And Saul raved on, unaware of these shouts and these thoughts, and soon he and his men were alone at the cistern of Secu, sending their wordless cries into the empty air.

27

David stood for a few moments and watched Saul twist foolishly on the ground near Naioth, wondering how this man could ever have become the king of the land. What had possessed Samuel to make it so? And why exactly was this writhing brute trying to murder me? I have no intent whatever to murder him. Why should I want to begin a precedent of the killing of YHWH's anointed ones, since I too am one of YHWH's anointed? Yet, his murderous desires are clear enough, and I must try to stay out of his way.

"Samuel," shouted David, over the howling gibberish pouring from the throats of Saul and his warriors, "I am grateful for your help against the king, but I know he will not stop his attempts to kill me. Where can I go to keep from dying at his hands? Michal, my wife, has saved me once, and now you too have come to my aid. But Israel is a small land with no easy place to disappear into. What should I do?"

And ancient Samuel shouted back, "My son, you are the new king of the land, for this man has been rejected by YHWH as well you know. I have seen that Jonathan, the king's eldest son, is your friend. Go now to him, and he will perhaps find a way to help you. But you should leave Naioth, since the king will soon throw off the ecstasy that grips him now."

So David rushed back toward Gibeah and met Jonathan near the gate of the city. Now David was not certain exactly why Samuel had urged him to seek out Jonathan, though he was convinced that Jonathan was smitten with him, having earlier offered to him quite publicly his own clothes and armor after David's defeat of the giant. It was an embarrassing act, announcing to all who saw that Jonathan had resolved to be with David even in the face of his father's fury. So perhaps the king's son could find a way to protect David against the rampaging Saul. But it was important for Jonathan to be convinced that his father was in fact mad, and had determined to kill David. That way David would know for certain that Jonathan was fully on his side. So David put all of his energies into convincing the king's son of Saul's complete and unchangeable lunacy.

As he approached Jonathan near the city gate, he cried out, "What have I done? What is my crime that your father continues to track me down to try and kill me?"

King Saul

"Heaven forbid!" shouted Jonathan in horror. "You will not die! Look, my father will do nothing, however tiny or great, without telling me first. He has said nothing to me about desiring your death."

Jonathan was, of course, lying by saying this; he knew all too well his father's fervent desire to kill David. But he strangely still had hope of a reconciliation between all of them.

"Why would he have allowed you to marry my sister, if all he wanted was for you to die?"

"You are naïve, Jonathan, my friend. The king hoped I would die at the hands of the enemy when he sent me out to gather those Philistine foreskins, but I was able to perform the disgusting command and he had to offer me Michal as reward for the deed. She has just saved my life from him by allowing me to escape the assault of his guards on our very bedroom. And Samuel, the prophet, has also protected me against Saul by causing a prophetic frenzy to fall on him, permitting me escape to find you. Your father of course will not tell you of his murderous plans, because he knows you are my friend and would try to protect me. The fact is that there is only a small step between me and Sheol! You must now help me as they have against your own father!"

Just for a moment, David wondered if Jonathan were actually going to help him, or if his filial responsibility were about to drive him back to the aid of Saul.

But Jonathan responded to David immediately.

"Whatever you ask, I will do."

Looking into his eyes, David knew that the king's son was with him, even against his father.

"Thank you, Jonathan. Here is what I need from you. The festival of the new moon is tomorrow, and as you well know, all the family of the king are expected to join him at the evening meal to celebrate and to praise YHWH for the gift of another month of life. It may be possible that Saul's rages, which ebb and flow like waves of the Great Sea, have again cooled and I would once again be welcome in his presence. But I cannot risk simply coming to the table. So here is my plan. I will hide in this field both tonight and tomorrow. You go to the feast tonight and when my absence is noted, say, 'David has been called to Bethlehem to celebrate the festival with his own family, since Jesse is old and ailing and may have few celebrations left before he is gathered to his ancestors.' If Saul responds to this statement calmly and without anger, I will know that I can safely return to his house. But if he becomes furious, come back to the field and tell me. And if you discover from him that I have in fact done some deed worthy of death, you may kill me yourself, for I would rather die at the hands of a friend than be murdered by that man!"

"Heaven forbid that you talk of my killing of you! I could under no circumstances conceive of such a thing! If Saul had resolved to kill you, do you not think I would tell you? I have made a covenant with you, David, that shall never be broken. I know for certain that it is your destiny, and not mine, to sit on the throne of Israel after my father's death. I only ask, by the love I bear you and by the covenant we have made, that you will not forget my family when you have attained your power in the land."

David heard these magic words from Jonathan in some surprise, since he had assumed that the king's eldest son would deeply desire to follow his father to power. But of course David knew, what Jonathan could not know, that he, David, was already king in Israel, having been made so by Samuel himself. So Jonathan was even more right than he knew, but David was grateful that one more obstacle had been removed from his path. Yet, he had to be sure of Jonathan's absolute loyalty.

"Will you really tell me if your father becomes furious at my absence?"

"Come over here," said Jonathan, and he led David to the middle of the field. "If my father becomes enraged at your absence tonight or tomorrow night, at the final meal of the festival, I will return to this field, to the place you are hiding, and I will tell you the results. If Saul rages against you, I will shoot three arrows to the north side of this great stone. But if he appears calm and is unmoved by your absence, I will shoot three arrows to the south of the stone, and you will know that it is safe to return to the king's house. Trust me, David my friend. YHWH is witness this day that the covenant I have made with you is as fixed as the stars in the sky, as the sand on the shore of the sea."

And with that, Jonathan grabbed David in a great embrace, so great was his feeling for him. He little noticed that David's embrace was far less fervent than his own.

"Camp here this night and tomorrow, and after the feast I will return, and you will know where things stand between you and my father. I pray that YHWH will soften his heart, and he will see you as I do."

And with tears in his eyes, Jonathan left the field and went to the feast in the house of Saul.

David watched the king's son's retreating form and wondered what would happen. Jonathan was certainly a faithful friend who was now risking his relationship with Saul, and hence any opportunity for a future as king, to help David survive. David wished he could reciprocate Jonathan's graceful gift of himself, but he found himself far too interested in his own future as king to give much time for the future of anyone else. Perhaps when he became king, he could find a worthy place for a man like Jonathan in his court. But then again it might not pay to keep any relatives of Saul too close since kingly rivalries could be a problem. Well, he thought, there would be time enough to think of these things when he finally and at last was king of Israel, a time that might not be so far off now. With such pleasant thoughts, he drifted off toward sleep, hiding behind the large stone of the field. The night was cool, the breeze delightful, the quiet sounds of the sheep, pastured nearby, a reminder of David's shepherding days, now gone forever. Soon he would be shepherd of Israel, he thought, as blessed sleep closed his eyes.

King Saul

Jonathan entered Saul's large eating room, and saw that everyone else was there. His brothers, Ishvi and Malchishua, were seated close to Saul at the head of the table, Merab and Adriel, her too old husband, were on the other side of the king, next to Ahinoam and Rizpah. He noted with some surprise that Abner, Saul's longtime warrior leader, and one of his wives—he could never remember her name among the seven or eight women Abner called wife—was at the table. Michal, Saul's youngest daughter, David's wife, was seated at the other end of the table, as far from her father as possible. He remained furious at her for thwarting his plans to kill her husband, but her very presence suggested that she might still have a place in her father's heart, however small. The seat next to her was conspicuously empty. Saul glanced at the empty chair of his son-in-law and said nothing. The meal and celebration were generally light-hearted, the good food, beautifully cooked as always by Ahinoam and Rizpah, accompanied by humor and jests. Laughter, sounds rare in this house, were welcome noises this night. All ate, and laughed, and joked, and went to their beds satisfied.

The second night of the festival all were seated in the same places, and David's chair remained empty. But this night Saul was full of questions.

"Jonathan, why has the son of Jesse not come to the feast last night or this?"

Instantly, the tension rose in the room. No one missed the fact that Saul had named the absent David, "son of Jesse," rather than "son-in-law," or "husband of Michal," as if to question his connection to the family.

"My father, O king, David asked me to say that he has been called by his brothers to attend a family sacrifice in Bethlehem. He bid me to ask you to excuse him from this feast in order that he could see his ailing father and his brothers. That is why he is not here. I am sure you understand, my lord."

Jonathan had practiced this speech several times so that he could say it calmly. The effect was not what he expected.

Saul stood up in an immediate and violent rage, upsetting his chair and his glass of wine, and shouted at his eldest.

"You son of a perverse and faithless woman!"

Ahinoam, seated next to her husband, recoiled from the slight as if slapped.

"I know perfectly well, as we all do here, that you have chosen the son of Jesse to your own shame and to the shame of your mother's own sacred nakedness! As long as this son of Jesse lives on this earth, your future as king is far from assured. Surely you cannot be so stupid as not to realize that? Since you love the bastard so much, go now and fetch him, for I am certain you know where he is hiding. But know one thing, my son; he is a dead man!"

But Jonathan stood up from his own seat, and stared directly, unblinkingly at his father.

"Why should David be put to death? What in the name of YHWH has he done?"

After a brief and painful silence, suddenly Saul grabbed his huge spear and threw it at his son to kill him. It whizzed by his left ear and stuck in the wall behind him, its shaft making the only sound in the room, vibrating furiously as if it was trying to extricate itself for another attempt at murder. Ahinoam cried out, and Ishvi and Malchishua stood up, not knowing whether to defend their brother or help their father, who had obviously gone mad. Jonathan looked at his father with horror and some pity, glanced briefly at his mother and brothers, and left the room.

He was furious and horrified and humiliated all at the same time. He now knew without any doubt that his father was both mad and intent on killing his friend. As he ran past his house, he shouted for Ephron to join him and to bring his bow and some arrows with him. Ephron quickly fell into step with his master, having grabbed the first bow he could find. Jonathan fought back tears as he ran to the field where David was hiding. As he reached the field's edge, he quickly notched an arrow in the bow and fired the first arrow to the north side of the great stone. After he had launched two more arrows in the same direction, David arose from behind the stone and looked at Jonathan, who ran quickly to meet him. Both men were grim, since both knew that David was no longer safe in Israel. In silence, they grabbed one another in a long embrace and offered one another a kiss of peace. Large tears appeared in both their eyes, as the truth of their respective situations became clear.

"My father hates me as much as he hates you, David. He just tried to kill me with his spear, and called me the most repulsive names in front of all of our family, accusing me of being a bastard or of having some sort of disgusting relationship with you. He wanted me both humiliated and dead. Well, he failed at the last, in truth, but I am now dead to him in fact. But you must leave Israel as soon as you can."

David was crying hard now, sobbing in fact, not able to control his emotions. His dreams of kingship, of real power in the land, appeared to have ended. His rising fame as warrior and leader, his marriage to the king's daughter, all pointing to a future of greatness, were disappearing into the air like sacrificial smoke. But unlike that smoke, the result of its rise was not ambiguous to read: David's rise to power was over. He was alone, his friend, son of the king, was now hated by Saul as he was, the door to the throne had closed against him forever. Jonathan's tears may have been for the loss of his friend, while the tears of David were in the main for the loss of his dreams.

"Go in peace, my friend, for the two of us have sworn in the name of YHWH, and have said, 'YHWH is witness between me and you, and between my descendants and yours, forever.'"

Thus did Jonathan bid goodbye to David and told him that he would do whatever he could to help him slip from the country.

Then David said, "Where will I go? To the west there are only the hated Philistines, while in the deserts of the south I will find only Samuel's disreputable sons in Beer Sheba. In the north the Canaanites still hold sway over their ancient cities. Perhaps I should run to the east, but the town of Jabesh is of course completely loyal to Saul after his rescue of them from the Ammonites. I know nothing of the southern deserts near the Great Salt Sea, but I can think of nowhere else to go. Jonathan, do what you can to throw your father and his men off my scent; give me some to time to fade into the wilderness. YHWH willing, I can survive alone in the dry lands of Ein Gedi."

But he was not certain that Jonathan had heard his desperate plans, hatched only on the spot in the field of the arrows. The king's son, still weeping copious tears, was trudging back toward Gibeah and his house. David now found himself really alone. He gathered up the arrows and the bow that Jonathan had dropped and ran southward, not knowing quite where he was going, not having any clear notion of what he was to do, fearing that this night might be his last in Israel if not the last of his very life.

28

David moved slowly and carefully, skirting the outposts of the forces of Saul that ringed Gibeah at all hours of the day and night. He knew the places well; since he had himself established the protective perimeter not two moons ago. As he passed the southern guards' small encampment, he noted in disgust that all three of the fools were sleeping soundly.

In earlier days, David would have drawn his sword, slipped up behind the louts and given them the scare of their worthless lives. But those days were over, and stealth meant letting them sleep as he moved out of range of their responsibility. May YHWH provide better guards on Saul's western flank near the camps of the Philistines!

Soon the sacred village of Nob, its one continuous temple fire illuminating the moonless night, appeared. David walked toward that fire, having hidden his bow and arrows behind a large stone. Better to come to the holy place unarmed, and not arouse suspicion. As he approached the tiny temple, one room surrounded by animal pens dotted with pure beasts of the usual kinds, he saw the old priest, Ahimelech, was still awake. His shoulders were stooped, what hair that still existed on his liver-spotted head was gray and thin, and it was with very gnarled hands that he reached up to add fuel to the torch in the wall's sconce.

David slipped through the dark temple doorway but stumbled slightly on the threshold. Ahimelech started and dropped his jar of oil; it shattered in a shower of wet shards.

"Who is there? Who dares enter the holy place of YHWH without leave from me, YHWH's priest?"

"It is only I, old man, David, the slayer of the giant, son-in-law to the king of Israel, mighty Saul."

"Why have you come alone?" Ahimelech asked.

The priest obviously was surprised to find the most talked-about man in the kingdom entering his small temple in the middle of the night.

"Where are your soldiers, your weapons? What is the news of your lovely wife, Michal, daughter of the king?"

David thought quickly, and replied, "The king himself has charged me with something, and has commanded me quite clearly, 'Let no one know of this thing you are doing.' I have left my men someplace close by."

The responses were lame and very vague, but it was the best he could come up with for the suspicious priest.

"What sort of food do you have on hand, some loaves of bread? Give them to me, or whatever else you have."

David was famished and resisted the urge to grab a bone off the altar to suck its marrow.

"My son, I have no ordinary bread on hand, but only the holy bread, baked each day and laid on YHWH's altar. I could give that to you, but only if your young men, not to mention you yourself, have not slept in the arms of women the previous day." David knew these older priests were sticklers for ancient law and custom, but Ahimelech would have little way of checking on the sexual habits of the giant killer. By the time he might find out something, David would be well away from this pathetic temple in Nob.

"Holy father, whenever my men and I sally forth to fight the enemies of YHWH, we always follow the old ways and avoid sapping our strength through the blandishments of women. Why, how much more is this true when we are on a mission for the king himself?"

David's lies were flowing so freely now that he could not resist leading the old man around a bit by his sanctified nose.

"Well, in that case, please take the bread, my son, and may YHWH bless your task, whatever it is the king has asked you to do."

Ahimelech was not quite the doddering old fool David had made him out to be. He had heard the vagueness of the reply from the famous man, and had concluded that something was not quite right in the entire dialogue he had just had with him. But he had also decided to get rid of him as fast as he could, because who did not know of the deep antipathy between Saul and David, not to mention the outright hatred that Samuel felt for the king. It was no easy time in Israel, and Ahimelech's small priestly post was a good place to stay out of the way of the clashes between these powerful men.

But during the strange conversation, Ahimelech and David did not notice a third figure sliding noiselessly into the temple. It was Doeg, a herdsman originally from the villages of Edom, south and east of Israel, just across the Salt Sea. The man had moved from Edom to Gibeah many suns before, and became a member of the council of Gibeah, after his surprising act of valor that saved some in the city from would-be thieves. After Saul had been made king, Doeg, among other foreigners, had naturally looked for work in the new court, since he was a citizen of the same city as the new king. Though he was a silent, rather surly man, living with a woman who may or may not have been his wife, Doeg had always had a good way with pastured beasts and had quickly proven his skills to the obvious satisfaction of Saul's chief keeper of the flocks. Doeg had been sent to Nob by that man to sacrifice to YHWH for safe passage for the flocks from winter to summer pasturage. Other trustworthy herdsmen had been dispatched to sacrifice in all the small shrines that ringed Gibeah. Unfortunately, Doeg had been detained at Nob, because the sacrificial animal he had brought to the altar had been judged by Ahimelech not pure enough for the task, so Doeg had, with a muttered grumble, pulled the wretched thing out of the temple and had gone to buy another animal for the purpose. He had decided to get the sacrifice done as quickly as possible the sooner to get out of Nob, there being no place to get a decent cup of beer or joint of meat.

So he had come by night to offer to this YHWH, whoever that God was. Being an Edomite, Doeg knew little about the strange ways of the Israelites, though he had lived with them for many moons; he simply did as he was told. As he had approached the temple, he had heard voices and had tethered the small goat he had purchased well away from the temple's door. He had entered just as Ahimelech had handed David the holy bread straight off the altar. He stayed deep in the shadows and heard David's next request.

"Do you happen to have a spear or sword at hand? Saul's mission was so urgent I had no time to grab sword, shield, or knife."

"We have but one weapon here, my son. It is the huge sword of the giant Goliath whom you slaughtered in the vale of Elah those years ago. We got it from some of your men soon after the victory and have kept it wrapped carefully in cloth, placing it near the holy ephod, the image next to the altar, over there. You are free to take it if you will. In a sense it is yours in any case."

David had often wondered what had happened to that enormous weapon, the one he had sawed off Goliath's head with. The old thrill of that amazing victory flooded back to him, but the good feeling was soon dashed by the recognition that now he had been reduced to sneaking around by night, and hiding in a backwater hole of a temple, conversing with a useless priest.

"Well, there is surely none like it. Give it to me."

So Ahimelech reached his gnarled hands behind the altar and started to haul the thing out of its hiding place, but he could not. David walked over and the two men tugged the sword into the light of the fire. David had forgotten the weight of the sword—five hundred bronze shekels at least—and laughed as he tried to imagine how he had lifted the thing to do its grisly work. It was often said that great victory leads to great strength, beyond one's own thought, and it must have been so that day. Of course, David was older now, and battle hardened in Saul's service. He would never have chosen this sword as his own—it was absurdly long, perhaps three cubits—but his muscled arms could wield it now with little problem. He held the sword in his right hand, and the bag of bread in his left, and moved out of the temple, followed by Ahimelech who offered him YHWH's blessing for the mission of Saul. Neither he nor the priest saw Doeg in the shadows, but the Edomite waited in silence for the two men to leave and then he crept from the temple, his sacrificial goat forgotten. He had heard all and had seen Goliath's sword and the holy bread in the hands of David. He imagined one who would pay well for such information, and he broke into a run to share the news in Gibeah.

29

As Doeg hurried to tell Saul that he had seen David at Nob, and that old Ahimelech had given him a weapon and food, David rushed westward toward the cities of the Philistines. Exactly why he was headed toward the very heart of Israel's implacable enemies he could not have told. He only knew that he was unsafe at Saul's court, unsafe at his home, where he imagined even now his wife was undergoing close questioning as to his whereabouts, basically unsafe in any place in Israel. So why not the Philistines? Surely, they would welcome a powerful warrior who was now in ill favor with their great enemies, the Israelites. Of course, they would all remember how he had vanquished their giant champion, but that was some time ago. Besides, the war-mad Philistines held special awe for a mighty fighter, and who was mightier than David? So he hoped that he might find at least a temporary refuge from the maddened king among the pagans. David had no illusions about the Philistines; he hated them with a deep hatred, but he saw them as he saw most of his own people, as persons who could be useful at the right time for the right reasons.

He headed for Gath, the greatest of the cities of the plain, a hard day and a half run from Nob. As he neared the place, he nearly ran into a force of chariots, practicing battle runs outside the walls of the city. David crouched behind a large stone and watched in wonder as some twenty battle wagons wheeled and danced around the flat plain, turning one way and then another in perfect formations, their drivers directing the horses with consummate skill and the archers, one standing in each chariot, hitting their targets, placed all over the practice field, with remarkable accuracy. He thought not for the first time how fortunate Israel was not to have to face these terrible weapons in the rugged and uneven ground of the hill country.

He waited until the chariots stopped their maneuvers and headed back into the city. David, now merely one more unarmed traveler (he had left the great sword and his bow and arrows at a place he knew he could find them again), walked into the city and asked to see the king of the place, Achish. All Israel knew Achish as a vain, soft, and probably foolish man who appeared to enjoy good beer more than fighting and fine statuary rather than great victories. If any Philistine leader would be open to hiding David for a time, it was Achish.

Since David was not dressed in a typically Israelite way, no distinctive headdress of the mountains or deserts, no familiar brightly colored tunic that would have identified a particular tribe or locale, he was ushered into the outer room of the palace to wait for an audience with the king along with many other nameless suppliants who were eager for the help, legal or monetary, that only a king could give. He was not completely certain what he wanted from this pagan king, but he trusted that his God, and his quick wits, would give him the right words and actions when he confronted him.

The sun had nearly set over the Great Sea before David was at last summoned before Achish. The king was grossly fat—too much ease and too much food and beer, thought the trim warrior—as he approached the elaborate throne chair on which Achish had dropped his mountain of jiggling flesh. But just as David was about to commence the elaborate ritual of self-introduction, preceded by the necessary flattery and lies for the king, a tall and beautifully dressed courtier shouted.

"Is not this man David, the king of our enemy, Israel? I have heard, as have many of you, the song they are singing of this man, the song that accompanies their recent ritual dances: 'Saul has struck down his thousands, and David his ten thousands!' How often have I overheard this tune in the camps of their warriors. Yes, this is that same David, I am sure. What brings him to the court of the great and wise Achish?"

There was a long silence, as the king looked intently at David, as several body-guards of the king reached for their short knives, while others drew their swords, moving toward this man who had killed many of their warriors and friends. David's heart leapt toward his throat and his stomach lurched as he dropped into a defensive stance, hoping somehow to survive the many weapons all pointed in his direction. But instead of rushing at his would-be killers in attack, he quickly shouted loudly with some incomprehensible words, let his tongue loll out between his teeth, and filled the air with a stream of his spit. He dropped onto all fours and crawled slowly toward the door that he had just entered, scraping his finger nails up and down the frame of that door, and staining his reddish beard with foaming yellow liquid, retched up from his steaming vitals. While he moved closer to escape, the king stood up, shoving his enormous belly out from under his tree trunk legs to do so, and shouted for all of his defenders to sheathe their knives and swords. His great paunch shook with laughter.

"Can't you see that this man is a raving lunatic! He can hardly be David, though I grant he resembles the man I have several times seen leading the forces of Israel. But no matter. Why is this madman here, staining the dignity and calm of my court? Who let him in in the first place? Don't I have enough madmen in my court as it is without adding to their number with one more wild ass of a man from the desert?"

And again Achish howled a high-pitched squeal of laughter, and looking around at his court filled with indolent and sycophantic men, demanded that they join in the king's laughter, too, if they knew what was good for them. They did, and filled their mouths with hoots and beer.

While the chaos continued, David slipped out of the palace and out of the city, running toward his cache of weapons, very glad indeed to be alive.

"That cursed song nearly got me slaughtered," he said aloud to the desert, after he had put distance between himself and the city. "It is a good thing I had witnessed the madness of Saul so many times to get the trickery just right. Thank you, my Lord the king of Israel, O mighty Saul, for saving my life today, though in reality you had hoped to take it instead! And thank you, my lord King Achish, for being the fool I had heard you were. I can now quite easily see that being a king will be no difficult task if Saul and Achish are models in the thing!"

And with that, David, king of Israel, at least in his own mind and in the mind of Samuel, shouted his own laughter of triumph, a laughter that echoed off the walls of the hills and resounded into and out of the caves of the wilderness of Maon, beyond which one found the strongholds of Ein-Gedi, the forbidding place where he had decided to go.

30

David ran overnight and gathered Goliath's sword and his own bow where he had left them near the cave of Adullam, south and east of Gath. He knew this area of the southern deserts like his own hand, having pastured many a sheep here in those few times when the rain had been plentiful enough to create lush grass. He had to keep much distance between himself and Achish and between himself and Saul. There was no better hiding place than these wilderness areas, ribboned with countless hills and dark valleys and pocked with hundreds of caves. Saul would need many more soldiers than he had to root David from these natural fortresses, so David felt quite free to hatch his plan to gain power over the land.

He first had to protect his family. An enraged Saul might already have targeted them for revenge due to his failure to capture or kill his rival. He bribed a messenger to take word of his safety and his location at Adullam's cave. David remembered with a wicked pleasure the story his mother used to tell him of the woman of this place who had married his ancestor, Judah, and had had three sons with her. The first two of these sons in turn had married Tamar, but each in their turn had died under peculiar circumstances, until only his youngest son, Shelah, was still alive. Naturally, Judah had refused to marry Tamar to this son, for fear that he too would die, though the law and custom demanded that he must do so. Finally, the widow Tamar, who had no legal and social rights at all unless she were protected by the power of a man, had grown tired of waiting for her marriage to Judah's final son. She had disguised herself as a common prostitute, had seduced her father-in-law, and had become pregnant by him. To make certain he was the father of her child, she had demanded from him a token before she would lie with him, his own signet ring along with his distinctive staff.

Her pregnancy had caused a scandal, and as her belly swelled, old Judah demanded that she should be burned for shaming his family so. But the clever Tamar then quite publicly had produced the ring and the staff, and had asked the lecher whether he recognized them since the father of her child had given them to her before he had tumbled with her in the fresh field of Adullam, right in front of this very cave. David had always liked that last scene, how the randy Judah had been shown up by the woman, Tamar. He wished he had been there to see the look on Judah's face when his ring and staff were produced for all to see. David had learned from that story that women could be very clever indeed and he had resolved never to be taken in by one as Samson and then Judah had been. And he had also learned that it was more than possible to live by one's wits, that a sword was not always the best weapon to survive in this world. It was exactly right that David begin his rise toward kingship at this very cave.

His mother and his brothers soon joined him in the cave, and they made arrangements to take her and his father, Jesse, who was so old as to make any travel difficult, to the king of Moab, across the Salt Sea. David himself implored the king to shelter his parents "until I learn what my God will do with me." It was a deeply religious idea, his openness to the mysterious workings of YHWH, and the Moabite king was dutifully impressed. In fact, he had little love for Saul or for any strong Israelite leader, since they stood in the way of Moab's rise to power in the southern deserts. He was thus only too glad to help David, since a strong David made for an occupied Saul, opening the way for Moab's brighter future. He graciously, at least outwardly so, agreed to protect Jesse and his wife while David hoped to prosper in the wilderness, hiding from the fury of Saul.

As usual, David was only partly open to the ways of his God, because in fact he had a definite plan in mind as he established his stronghold at Adullam. He soon made it known in the area that he was available for counsel to anyone who felt threatened by the unstable king and his warriors, who was in debt to that central authority in Gibeah, or who was simply bitter about the general mood of the land. It did not take long for nearly four hundred men to gather around David at the cave and with his natural leadership skills he was quickly seen as their captain. Not all of these men were soldiers, though many had fought for the land in previous battles while others had skills of various kinds, from shepherds to farmers to a few who could even read or write a bit. One was known as a prophet of one sort or another, Gad by name, and he urged David to move away from the Adullam cave, since it was too close both to Philistia and to Gibeah of Saul. So David moved deeper into the territory of Judah, into the very heart of the wilderness of Ein-Gedi. Though the place was nearly three long days from David's Bethlehem home, these people were his people. He knew them and their needs, and they trusted and respected him as the talented fighter and artist that he was. He knew that this southern desert would be the base of his ultimate kingship over the whole land.

As news of David's leadership in the south flashed north, Saul again found himself threatened by the one he experienced as his bitter rival. Saul had taken to sit, usually alone, under a huge single tamarisk tree, growing on one of the highest spots looking down on Gibeah. Always now, after David's escape from death, the king held his massive spear in his right hand, as if poised to fling it at any threat, real or otherwise. His brows were low over his eyes, his grey hair tangled in tufts hanging over his face, his shoulders slumped wearily. Some ten warriors were in attendance on the king to guard him against attack, but they stood at a distance from him, partly to offer space for his royal person and partly in fear of his sudden rages.

Saul abruptly started and stood up to his vast height. Thunderclouds appeared in his eyes.

"Pay attention, you worthless sons of Benjamin! Do you imagine that this bastard son of Jesse will give each of you fields and vineyards? Do you suppose he will make you captains of thousands or leaders of hundreds? I know you are all conspiring against me. Do you think me feeble of mind and blind that I am unaware of your plotting to make that cur king in my place? Why has not a one of you camel drivers told me that David, the shepherd boy, is even at this moment lying in wait somewhere to slaughter me and that he has made a pact with my own son, that bastard Jonathan, to make himself king?"

There was no answer to these fantastic charges, but all there knew that there were shreds of truth resting among them.

Then Doeg, the Edomite, walked up to the king, and bowed low before him.

"Mighty Saul, I myself saw the son of Jesse coming to Nob, the small sanctuary near here, to consult with Ahimelech, son of Ahitub. The priest inquired of YHWH for him, then gave food to him and even the sword of Goliath."

At the mention of the giant's name, Saul flinched in pain, remembering the cursed day in the valley of Elah and the terrible events that followed.

"Send me Ahimelech and all of his motley priests!" Saul bellowed, and he sat down, tightly fingering his spear.

Two warriors ran to Nob and rounded up the cohort of holy men who served the tiny temple. The warriors were too afraid to bind the priests but rather begged them to follow them at the king's summons. They came willingly and without fuss, since they all felt they had nothing to hide from their master. There were eighty-five of them, including the high priest, and Ahimelech was first to attend Saul. Once again, the king stood up, towering over the man.

"Listen, son of Ahitub."

Saul respected the office of priest, but his opening request was tinged with fury. Ahimelech did not miss the barely hidden anger of the king, and noted that Saul had not called him by name. Still, his life as priest had been beyond reproach; he had nothing to fear from the unpredictable king; or so he thought.

"I have come, my king. What is it you wish from me?" he said calmly.

Saul exploded.

"Why have you plotted against me, you and the son of Jesse, giving him food, the sword of the pagan Goliath, and even an oracle from YHWH, the great God, so that he is even now lurking near to destroy me and take my kingship?"

Ahimelech's worst fears about his meeting with David were coming true, and his heart leapt into his throat. But, he felt that there was still a way out.

King Saul

"O king! Who is like David among all your servants, fully loyal to you, your own son-in-law, captain of your armies, deeply honored in your own household? Was this the first time that I cast an oracle of YHWH for him? Hardly! I have prayed to our God again and again for him and for you, my king. Do not accuse me of conspiracy against you, O Saul. I treated David as your loyal servant, the loyal servant and hero of Israel. Of course I would provision him, since he himself said to me that you had sent him on a mission for you and the kingdom."

The priest just then realized that David had lied to him about everything, and he felt completely naked before the furious king. Still he looked outwardly calm.

But the king was not calm. He burst forth like a weakened wine skin, spewing its liquor into the air.

"You are a dead man, you lying priest, you and your family and all these so-called holy men with you!"

Saul's eyes flashed with storm, his words flew from his mouth like the roaring winds of creation, and his spear pointed right at the priest's heart, prodding his priestly robe, anxious to draw the old man's blood. But he withdrew the spear point and whirled on his warriors.

"Kill all these disgusting men, priests of YHWH, for they are David's men, all of them. They knew he was running from me but said nothing of it. Their own mouths condemn them to death!"

One or two of the warriors took a step toward the priests with their swords drawn, but finally not a one of them wanted to kill the holy men, representatives of the mighty YHWH, God of battles and grain and wine and oil. To murder a priest of God could lead to YHWH's lack of protection for the killer when next a warrior faced the enemy. No man moved to follow Saul's demand for death.

"You, then," Saul shouted to Doeg, "You stab these wretches!"

The Edmomite, who knew little of YHWH and even less of those who served the God, saw the priests only as vermin for extermination, things that could lead to greater honors from the king of Israel. So, without a word, the shepherd quietly and quickly moved from priest to priest, stabbing each one expertly through the heart. Doeg had often enough slaughtered sheep for sacrifice; these priests were finally no different. Eighty-four men died without protest, giving up their lives for the God they had vowed to serve. But while Saul's warriors watched in horror the near-silent massacre, one priest escaped without notice. He was Abiathar, Ahimelech's son, and he ran for his life from Saul and Doeg and the mad killing at Gibeah. It was not difficult to learn the whereabouts of David, since his fame was spreading rapidly in the wilderness of Ein-Gedi.

"Great David," Abiathar gasped out to him after his dash to safety, "Doeg, at the command of Saul, has butchered all the priests of YHWH who served at Nob. My father, Ahimelech is among the dead."

And as he uttered the name of his father, Abiathar sobbed, his voice catching in his throat. David grabbed the young man in his arms and held him close while tears stained his tunic.

After Abiathar had gathered himself a bit, David said to him, "I knew Doeg, that Edomite dog, was there in the temple that day, and I knew that he would surely tell Saul all that had gone on. By YHWH, it was I who was the cause of these murders. So, Abiathar, stay with me, since you and I are now both under threat of death. Be my own priest, and I will protect you always."

From that day forward, Abiathar served David as priest, and David did protect him even when the elderly Abiathar chose the wrong royal son to follow, Adonijah rather than Solomon, when David died, many years later.

David's confession of responsibility for the death of the priests of Nob to Abiathar was remembered long after it was uttered. The reason for its memory was that it added to the confusion about just what sort of man David was. He was always seen as the most clever of men, lying with skill when needing to, dissembling again and again to get what he wanted. But he had these rare moments of candor, of looking deep within himself, probing for truth beyond what most men did. Later, in the most important event of his life, he slept with one of his general's wives, getting her with child. He then had the man murdered in battle, and had lied brazenly and cruelly about the entire affair. When confronted by the prophet, Nathan, he had finally confessed the whole thing to him. And even later, when his traitorous son, Absalom, was murdered by general Joab, David wept cupfuls of tears, sobbing that he wished he had died rather than that arrogant and beautiful son who wanted nothing more than to see his own father dead.

The fact was that David may not have known at all that Doeg was in the temple that day in Nob. Yet, when he heard of the slaughter of the priests from the only survivor, he took the blame for it. Well, it was true that he was ultimately to blame, but did he need to accept blame when he thought he and Ahimelech were alone? A complex man, this David, who would later become a complex king. But that kingship was in the future; now David sought merely to survive in the wilderness.

31

While David was moving from hill to hill and cave to cave in the wilderness of Ein-Gedi, hiding from Saul and his warriors, the Philistines took the opportunity of Israelite confusion to invade the land again. David, still loyal to Israel if not to its king, raided several Philistine strongholds, most especially the large village of Keilah, a brief walk south of Adullam, but several days' forced march west of Ein-Gedi. He captured the village and made camp inside of its fairly strong walls. Saul's spies saw the victory over Keilah and alerted their master that David was now trapped inside the city.

"YHWH has at last handed the man over to me, since he is now caught inside a walled town. I have only to surround the place, and he will be mine to do with as I please."

But before Saul and his troops could march to Keilah, Abiathar, David's priest, warned him that YHWH had revealed that David should leave the apparent safety of Keilah lest he be trapped like a bird in a net. So David took his men back toward Ein-Gedi, and when Saul came to Keilah he discovered that his bird had flown away.

Yet, David's men had left clear traces of their route of escape, toward the southeast, so Saul continued his hunt. As David passed through the territory of Ziph, Jonathan came to meet him. "David, my dearest friend, my father is close behind you, but I vow he shall not capture you. For I know that you will be king, and I will rule with you as viceroy. But my father fears that this is a true portrait of the future, and he is right to be fearful, but I will do all to keep you safe from him." So Jonathan went back to Saul's army.

"David has divided his forces in two, and while some are heading back toward Ein-Gedi, David himself is going north to his home village of Bethlehem."

He did not of course say any of this to Saul who knew his son to be a traitor to him, but he told Abner, Saul's general. Abner then convinced Saul to turn the army northward to pursue David there. But Saul remained convinced that David was in fact heading back to the southern wilderness, so kept some of his troops with him in pursuit, while Abner and the rest of the army headed north.

David was now sheltered somewhere in the caves of the wilderness of Ein-Gedi, overlooking the Salt Sea. He and his men had chosen a large cave in which to make their camp. The entrance to the cave looked directly at the Sea, its brackish water spewing a salty mist into the air, causing the sky to gleam with brightness and making the mountains of the Moabites on the far side of the Sea seem to float, as if unattached to the earth. Little grew in this ground and no fish lived in the Salt Sea. It was thought that the evil of the cities, Sodom and Gomorrah, their lack of hospitality and strange female and male sexual desires, had caused YHWH to curse the place with a perpetual death, burning the entire area around the Sea with a heavenly fire and killing all life in the process.

But since nothing lived in the immediate area, and since hundreds of caves dotted the many low hills, the place was ideal for hiding. It would take months to discover people secreted in one of the caves around the Salt Sea. So David and his men felt quite safe in their cave. The men set up regular guards to watch for the possible coming of Saul's forces or the dangerous roaming wild animals, lions and bears especially, that lived in the wilderness to the west, but whose feeding territories extended for miles in many directions. The few women who followed their husbands into the wilderness to live rough with them and to supply the needed food and clothing for the men surrounding David, established the cooking fires deep in the cave's heart, at the place where the ceiling was highest to prevent excess smoke from choking those who spent most of their time in the cave. No children had yet been born, but one or two of the wives had begun to show signs that they would in time produce young ones for their men. The cave soon became rather like a village although a small, easily defensible one.

Life in the cave settled into a routine. Each morning, after the women had cooked the meat stew over the fire, after they had mended various torn garments, after the guards at the entrance had been changed and the sleepy night guards had settled for their rest, patrols ventured into the wilderness to watch for Saul's approach and to hunt for food for the next meals. The cave dwellers had swelled to over eight hundred, and feeding and clothing them was no easy matter. On many occasions, David himself would lead the patrols. He had grown bored with this cave life, and hoped that some real fighting would occur soon. He did not relish a fight with Saul, but if it came to that he and his men were ready.

One day, during one of the patrols, David and his band of ten soldiers sought shelter in a small cave some distance from their own cave home. The day was wilting with heat, and the caves always provided pleasant cool shade for the sweltering troops. David and his men went to the back of the cave to rest and perhaps to sleep a bit before returning to the larger cave, a half-day journey to the east. They had had a good morning hunt and were carrying a large deer, two foxes and several squirrels that would help feed the increasingly large company back at their home.

Just as sleep was overtaking them, a small sound at the mouth of the cave forced their eyes to open, and their hands grasped their weapons, ready for a fight. A solitary figure entered the cave in silence. By his shadow they could see that it was a man, and a very large man at that. In fact, the man was enormous, and David's men all quickly concluded that the huge man was none other than the king of Israel, come to the cave to relieve himself. They watched as he turned his back to them, gazing out at the sunlight dappling the rugged hills of Ein-Gedi. He then lifted his tunic, displaying his giant cheeks and grunting in the usual way. Joab, David's greatest fighter and most loyal man, could hardly contain his joy. He whispered with excitement.

"By YHWH, David, look at what prey God has dropped into our net. YHWH has given your enemy right into your hands, and you can do with him whatever you want! Why not slip the point of your sword into his squatting back; he will die in his own dung, as he so richly deserves!"

This he said with an evil grin; Joab was a man with no interest in subtlety. He did what he did to protect David and himself and cared nothing for social niceties.

All the while the king continued his necessities, completely unaware of the mortal danger that lurked in the back of the cave. But David gave Joab a look of genuine disgust, covering his mouth with his hand to silence him. With no words and little sound, he seized his short knife, crept over to where Saul crouched, and carefully, ever so carefully, cut off a piece of his tunic, and slipped back to the rear of the cave. He waved the piece of the tunic so his men could see, and each stifled a laugh, though Joab was furious that his sound military advice had gone unheeded. Saul completed his defecation, stood up with a satisfied sigh of pleasure, and strode from the cave.

David and his men waited until the king had moved out of earshot and then exploded in laughter.

"Did you see the king's hairy cheeks; they could block out the sun," one shouted, while another said, "And the size of that cock, dangling to the ground, could kill a horse! No wonder Ahinoam always has that satisfied look on her face!"

The chortling men did not look at their commander, who was not joining in the fun of the moment. Though he had humiliated the king, cutting his royal tunic as an announcement of his power over him, David now felt he had gone too far. He had laid his hands on the anointed of YHWH, and though Saul had left the cave unharmed in his body, he left the cave far less of a king than when he came in. And David thought to himself, "If I can do such a thing to the current king of Israel, what is to prevent others from doing such things to me, who also is the anointed of YHWH?" And so he spoke out loud to his still laughing men.

"Be silent, you fools! YHWH forbid that I have done this thing to my master, YHWH's anointed, that I have reached out my soiled hand and have humiliated Saul, who remains the anointed one of YHWH!"

The laughter of the men caught in their throats, and they were puzzled by their leader. Why would he pull a prank one moment and feel that he had done something foul the next? And why did he not kill the mad king when he had the chance?

While they speculated about David's peculiar behavior, he ran to the entrance of the cave, and shouted after Saul's retreating figure.

"My lord, the king!"

King Saul

Saul stopped in his tracks and turned around to see who had shouted his name. He saw his bitter rival, the killer of the giant, spread on the ground in the position of honor, his face in the dirt. The supplicant lifted his head enough to speak to the king.

"Why, mighty Saul, should you listen to people's words, those who are trying to convince you that I want your harm? Look, O king. YHWH handed you right into my grasp today in that cave. My men said to me, 'Kill him now,' but I had compassion for you and said, 'I will not reach out my hand against my master, for he is YHWH's anointed.' And, my father, look, yes, look at the piece of your tunic I have in my hand. I cut it off instead of killing you, which I easily could have done. That is proof that there is no evil, no guilt, in me. Yet, you continue to stalk me to take away my life. May YHWH judge between me and you! YHWH may avenge me against you, but I will never lift a hand against you! Remember the old proverb: 'From wicked ones does wickedness come forth.' But not me, my king, not me. Who am I that you bring your warriors against me? A dead dog? A single flea? YHWH will judge between us; YHWH will plead my case and take judgment against you!"

As he finished, David thrust his face back into the dirt to await the king's reply.

As David had spoken, Joab and the other eight men had come to the mouth of the cave to witness the scene. Also, many of Saul's troops, at least fifty, had rushed toward the cave when they heard the familiar high-pitched voice of the man they had been hunting for so long. An eerie silence was broken only by bird sounds and the small rush of the wind, whistling into the cave. Joab imagined that he and his fighters were dead men, as he looked at the swelling force that stood just behind the king. And he cursed David's foolishness in his refusal to murder Saul and his idiot revelation of himself, and all of them, to the king. What game was David playing now, he thought? Well, this game will likely be his last; David killed one giant in the valley of Elah, but he will surely die at the hands of this giant in the wilderness of Ein-Gedi. Saul's soldiers grabbed at their weapons and gawked eagerly at David and his puny band; blood rose into their eyes.

But the silence was shattered not by battle cries, but with the sound of weeping.

"Is it really your voice, my son, David?" And the king sobbed and sobbed, great tears falling down his face. His men were astounded. Why is the king weeping like a woman at the sight of his bitterest enemy? Can he not see that YHWH has at last heard his cries, and has handed the cur into his clutches? This was no time for weeping! It was time for swords and arrows. David's death would solve everything! And with those thoughts, several of Saul's sturdiest men advanced on David and his warriors, swords drawn and arrows notched. But Saul stopped them with an enormous shout.

"Stop, you beasts! What do you think you are doing? This man has done nothing but good to me, and you would kill him?"

And Joab thought, "The man is mad indeed! David has done nothing but good? He has maneuvered and lied and twisted his way toward the kingship since the day he killed the giant, and you, king, can see only good. What sort of a man are you?"

King Saul

And Saul moved to David and said, "You are more in the right than I am, because you did a good thing today by not killing me when you had the chance, while I would have killed you if I could. When someone discovers an enemy, does he ever send him off unharmed? Hardly! YHWH will give you many good things for this deed today. David, my son, I know that you will be king in the land one day, and that the kingship will remain in your hands and the hands of your descendants. And now, please swear to me by YHWH that you will not cut off all my seed after me and that you will not blot out my name from the house of my father."

"My lord, I do swear it," answered David, and Saul grabbed him up in his arms like a child and wept again.

But Saul's men were speechless. And Joab and David's men were mute. All tried to fathom what they had just seen. David, claiming some sort of remorse for cutting a bit of Saul's robe, had risked his own life and the lives of all of his men, by confronting the king with the act and by claiming that he, David, was in the right in the sight of YHWH, and that King Saul was wrong to pursue him. And then Saul, instead of slaughtering the arrogant little piece of dung and his men for humiliating him and for accusing him of evil behavior against David, had agreed with David that he, Saul, had been wrong all this time by assuming David was a usurper and traitor to the throne. But more than that! Saul had just said that he knew David was going to be king, and that his family would rule the land forever, and he had begged David to rescue his own family from shame and oblivion in Israel! Was Saul a king at all? Was he not a toady to the red-haired shepherd? And all who were there that day knew that Saul's days were numbered, and that any with wisdom would sense the freshening breeze that blew the giant-killer toward the throne.

But for the moment, Saul was still, in name at least, king of the land. David and his few men headed back to their large cave, and Saul and his large army moved out of the wilderness and headed for Gibeah and home. But more than a few of Saul's men stayed behind in the wilderness, hiding in several caves until the bulk of the army had gone. These men then joined David in the large cave and followed him whom they now saw as the certain king who was coming to rule the land of Israel.

32

Samuel had for the past weeks felt at last just how ancient he was. His failed body had shrunk into itself so far that he could no longer stand at all, nor could he sit or lie without pain. His voice, that glorious thing that had made and unmade kings and had ruled the land of YHWH for more years than any could number, was now only a toad's croak, the sound creeping through a toothless mouth, cursed by death-like breath. He was gasping out the last days of an outlandishly long life. He knew he was at the end, but he hated with a fierce hatred leaving life now.

He was sick of the monstrous Saul, that hulking nincompoop who should long past have been dead or at least rendered powerless as Samuel had proclaimed publicly more than once. David, the matchless warrior, should already be king, replacing the fool currently on the throne, but he was at the moment running around in the southern wilderness, camping in caves, living by his considerable wits. All the while, the beloved Israel was under constant threat from the heathen Philistines. If only he were forty years younger! The land would have peace; the constant bickering between David and Saul would never have happened at all. Why had YHWH forced me to crown that overgrown fool in the first place?

And then there were his sons, still playing out their wasted lives in the deserts of the far south. Just like that blind and obese priest, Eli, I, too, have been cursed by disgusting offspring, I, the greatest man in the history of Israel, scarred, weighted down, crushed with two failed sons! Why? Why? Samuel tried to shift from one shriveled rear cheek to the other, but could make no movements at all. He croaked for Etan to attend him, the faithful boy, now himself old, who had been with him for so long. It is good I am so light now, thought Samuel, or he could hardly lift me, given his own failing strength. The servant reached down to shift Samuel on his palette, an act he did frequently in the vain attempt to prevent the noxious sores that covered the prophet's body where he lay too long. Samuel smelled like death from his foul feet to his wheezing breath, but Etan seemed not to notice as he lovingly struggled to move the old man. Perhaps his sense of smell was failing, thought Samuel; lucky man, not to have to inhale such a fragrance!

YHWH! YHWH? Was the God listening? Did the God care about the death of those who had given their lives in divine service? Did YHWH care about the death of any of God's creations? Samuel never was fully convinced of the answers to any of these questions, though he had never voiced his doubts out loud. He was YHWH's prophet; it would hardly do to present doubts about the one called by YHWH to speak God's word! But Samuel could doubt now, as he looked back over a life that had gone beyond anyone's ever had. Prophet called by YHWH; priest, advisor, judge, military leader. All that was surely a sign of YHWH's presence with him. But now at the end of it all; a foolish king, useless sons, internal Israelite power struggles, a wasted body, good for nothing but lifting, smelling, painful evacuation. Samuel had been reduced to a child again. Was YHWH gone from him? Was he YHWH's prophet or YHWH's mewling infant?

One thing he did know and believe with every dying part of him: he was on his way to Sheol. All went to Sheol when they died, whether rich or poor, good or bad, short or tall or fat or thin. They descended to the dark cave beneath the earth and became shadows, ghosts passing through air and space and time, without pain or responsibility. Slaves were free from masters there, because all were one, mute, rested, without conflict or struggle. As Samuel thought of the place, long dreaded by every living man or woman, he found himself longing for it, wishing he could dig for it like buried treasure, could at this very moment see the earth split underneath him and swallow him into its waiting maw. And at the thought, a smile creased his thin lips, a smile of hope, a smile of surprise, a smile of wonder, a smile of…Etan could not guess what that last smile meant, nor could anyone else who saw it. Those final witnesses knew only that the great Samuel was dead, and their loud shrieks alerted those in Ramah and finally throughout the land that an era had ended in Israel. The prophet Samuel was on his way to the place of no return to join all those who had gone before.

Saul was immediately told of Samuel's passing, and he too smiled. But his smile was a smirk of triumph. He had finally outlived the devious old monster! Perhaps it was at last a sign of YHWH's blessing for him and his kingship. The loud and cock-sure prophet had humiliated him and commanded him and confused him for the last time. Saul at first felt free, free from the withering voice that rang ever in his ears, free from those surprise visits that led only to baffling demands and then crushing public abuse and scorn. He prepared for the lavish funeral by dressing in his finest tunic, fitting his best sandals on his horned feet, made hard from many years of walking on the packed soil of numerous grain fields and fields of battle. He picked up his shield, reworked with fresh leather, and grabbed his famous spear, that shaft he had hurled at both enemy and son and rival. He stood as straight as his advancing years allowed and strode from his tent, looking every span a king, well-nigh like a god.

The solemn cortege walked ceremoniously from Ramah due south to Gibeah where Saul and his troops waited. Samuel's well-known palanquin had its top removed, and the ancient prophet lay on the floor of the cart, now become his bier, carried by the latest cadre of four powerful bearers. Samuel was wrapped in his tunic, that garment that had covered his holy frame each time he had made a public appearance. It was that tunic that he had worn when he first took control of the land; it was that tunic that Saul had torn that terrible day at Gilgal when Samuel had ripped the kingdom from him—or so he had thought to do. Saul looked at the dead man without expression, remembering particularly that day after his utter defeat of the Amalekites and how victory had turned to ashes in his mouth.

"And so, old man," thought the king, "It comes to this as it always does. Even you, arrogant man of God, could not shout down death. You pronounced my kingship ended, but I am still king, and you are now in Sheol!"

Saul resisted the desire to shout this last sentence aloud, but his expression remained the same.

Saul followed the procession at a respectful distance as it moved out of Gibeah toward the north, back toward Ramah, the holy place in the mountains outside the city of Samuel. The usually brief journey would take all day, since the pace was slow and solemn. Several hundred picked troops, polished and clean, with swords sharpened and shields shined, followed the king. Priests from several surrounding shrines walked directly in front and behind the bier, chanting psalms, hoping to ease Samuel's way to Sheol. Saul noted bitterly that these priests had conspired to leave a large space in their devotion where priests of Nob would have been, reminding all present that those priests had been murdered at the express orders of the king. *Even in death, the old man finds a way to mock me.*

33

David had of course heard of Samuel's death, and he had thought to sneak into a place from which he might see the burial and the festival to follow, but he was at the very time of Samuel's passing engaged in the far southern deserts with a brute of a man named Nabal, "fool" in Hebrew. He had threatened this Nabal with death if he did not pay him for guarding his flocks and herds from desert bandits. Nabal quite naturally had seen this demand as extortion, since he had not hired David or any of his men for the job. The upshot of the whole affair was that Nabal had died a sudden death, and his wife, a very beautiful and clever woman, Abigail by name, had become David's wife. All knew that she was well rid of that churl, Nabal, whom she had been forced to marry, and was happily joined with the handsome and fast-rising David, whom she grew very quickly to love to distraction. David made it very clear to Abigail that his first wife, Michal, meant little, if anything, to him, and that Abigail was more than welcome to his bed. She readily agreed, and they shared many a fine and sweaty tumble during the succeeding nights.

Of course, it was no small matter that along with Abigail, David also got all of Nabal's many fine flocks and herds, his many servants, his copious storehouses filled with grain and fruit, and his house and lands. Yes, David's confrontation with the rich Nabal had turned out very well for his future prospects. The very last thing on his mind at this time was death or prophets or solemnity. Abigail was a hot-blooded woman and kept his mind off everything but her comely self. At least for a time. Though it was whispered about that even during the languorous nights with Abigail, David's mind did occasionally turn toward how all these delightful events would aid his inexorable movement toward the throne. Abigail would make a fine queen, he thought, as he watched her sleep. Michal had helped my escape, but there was something about her that rankled; her status as daughter of Saul had been helpful at the beginning, but Saul's waning power and support in the land considerably lessened that value. Besides, Abigail was indeed beautiful, thought David, as he reached for her breast, lying so coyly near his wandering fingers.

But just before he touched the lovely, single-peaked, half-moon, a touch that would lead to such wondrous pleasures, he did think, however, briefly, of the dead Samuel. Well, the old man had made him king, however secretly, and he had at a crucial time in his life, protected him from a rampaging Saul with his mysterious powers of ecstatic behavior. He was of course grateful to Samuel, and he was sorry that death had seized him at last. But, gazing at Abigail, he saw again how beautiful the woman was, and forcing the dead prophet from his mind, he grabbed the waiting breast with a playful tug, and Abigail rose to greet his caress with several pleasing pinches of her own.

34

Samuel had been buried at the high place of Ramah with all the honor and dignity that the people of Israel could muster. Thousands of them had come, nearly filling the plain that lay below the mountain's flattop. Saul himself had played a central role in the rites, since he was king, however many of those witnesses wondered at the truth of it, given Samuel's very public rebukes of the man. He had deftly sacrificed the pure goat, had powerfully lifted the bleeding and dying creature over his head, and had dropped the dead thing on the blazing altar. The smell of the roasting meat had wafted far down the mountain, while the smoke had risen lazily into the windless sky. As Saul offered sacrifice for Samuel's death, the prophet's wasted body was being laid in the earth, bringing him closer to his final destination in Sheol. He was buried in his prophetic tunic, of course, so that those dead ones who welcomed him would instantly know who he was. The goat had served its purpose as the goat of guilt; if Samuel had done any foul deeds while alive—and he surely had, since all do—, those deeds would fall on the sacrificed goat, thus making Samuel's own self pure. Even if one became merely a shadow in Sheol, it was always good to purify the dead before they entered their last home.

The feast that followed had been raucous, filled with food, beer, dancing, and other pleasures of the night. Saul had had his fill of meat and beer, but took no interest in the dance. Even when his faithful Ahinoam had approached him lovingly—she was of course nearly as old as he but still beautiful to him—he had quietly indicated that he was uninterested in love making this night. He kissed her with fondness and thanked her for her attention, but moved away from her toward Samuel's fresh-dug grave.

He paused at the grave and looked down at the mound of earth and the stones that lay in piles at the place of the feet and the head. All who visited left a stone by way of long custom as a sign that the person lying underneath the ground had not been forgotten. Of course, Saul knew that no one would ever forget the great Samuel. "Yes, the great Samuel," he thought. "revered by all as the very mouth of YHWH. The very rear end of YHWH, more like! The arrogant, foul-breathed, beast who had made my life miserable! The disgustingly loud and sanctimonious so-called holy man who demanded of me actions, sanctioned by YHWH, and then, when I had done them, told me I was a sinner because I had not done them at all. He spoke less for YHWH than for himself and his odious sons, who could not and will not rule a nest of scorpions, let alone a kingdom!"

King Saul

Saul fell to his knees before the grave, and he prayed. He had prayed so little recently, and was surprised to do so now, here. But, he thought, perhaps YHWH would listen to him now that his nemesis, his mentor, was no longer able to get in his way. "YHWH," Saul prayed, "Creator of Sky and Earth, Commander of the Armies, Giver of Life and Death, listen to your servant, Saul, king of your chosen people. Tell me what I should do! David is my son-in-law, my friend, my tormentor, my rival, my hero, all of these things and more. Is he to be king after me? But what of my son, Jonathan, who is blinded by his love for the man, and has turned against his own family and me, his father? Where shall I turn? I ask your priests to reveal your will to me by the sacred bones, Urim and Thummim, but they claim the bones say nothing, or that you do not speak through them in any way they can understand. I sleep fitfully, trying to find you in my dreams, but my dreams are forgotten when my eyes open or do not appear to me in sleep at all. The raving prophets of the mountains, whom you used and taught, have nothing to say. It is as if you have grown silent, or have disappeared, or have gone off elsewhere to choose another people far away and unknown to us.

YHWH! YHWH! What am I to do? Should I continue to try to kill David? Should I welcome him as my successor and return to my beloved farm? Speak to me, YHWH! Now! I am your king! I am your servant, YHWH! Speak! Are you there? Have you ever been there? Are you God in Israel? Prove yourself! Show me some sort of sign! I beg you! I beg you!"

But the only sounds came from the few who still danced, who shouted out drunkenly, who rutted loudly in the bushes. The skies and its stars were still. The moon, half its full size, gazed down impassively on the kneeling figure at the grave of the prophet. The wind freshened from the Great Sea. A lone birdcall sounded from far away. But there was no sign. Saul sharpened his ears and eyes, probing the darkness, peering at the sky, sweeping the night with his anxious and desperate face. Nothing. YHWH had nothing to say, nothing to reveal, no apparent interest in the king YHWH had called.

Saul stood up, his aging bones creaking. Just one year ago, he had expelled all those from the land who claimed to be able to communicate with the dead, who said they could turn stone to bread, who claimed all manner of magic arts. Saul was convinced they were rivals to the power of YHWH, and in a burst of religious devotion, he had decreed that any who dared traffic with such people would face death at his own hands. He had done this as a gift to YHWH. YHWH, the silent God. YHWH, who refused to respond to his urgent cries for help.

At least when Samuel was alive, he could depend on a word from YHWH, however twisted and crabbed it came out of the old man. But Samuel was dead; there would be no more word from YHWH by way of Samuel. Or would there not be? Was such a powerful and astonishingly ancient man really and truly gone from the earth and from YHWH? One of the holy songs Saul knew well said, "The dead no longer praise YHWH." Was Samuel in Sheol, cut off from YHWH forever? Was his mighty voice really stilled for all time? Was there no way to hear from him once again?

King Saul

Could he still speak for YHWH, the now silent God, as he claimed to have done for so many years? Another song proclaimed that there was no place that could escape the presence of YHWH, neither the sky above nor Sheol below. Saul wondered and was confused since one song said one thing and another something else. He wanted to know. He must find out. He needed to find out. He needed…he needed someone who could help him. Someone who could do what he could not. He needed to hear once again from Samuel. Saul walked quickly from the grave of the old man and demanded that his servants find for him someone who could help him, now. He would hear from YHWH, and he would talk again to the one to whom the God had spoken for so long. Samuel, the dead prophet, must speak again!

35

The first few of his servants claimed not to know where Saul could find such a person, one who knew how to conjure, how to speak with the dead, how to do things ordinary people could not do or dared not try. He knew they were lying. The people of Israel for years had gone after those who made great claims for their occult skills. Lovers had long needed curses placed on rivals, or potions to make a woman love, or make a man weak with desire. Of course, there were acceptable holy men, trained to read the smoke, or the guts of sacrificed beasts, but when such recognized arts failed, and they too often did, people turned to more heathenish practitioners, strange men with one eye, living in trees or alone on rocky crags, women who knew the ways of herbs and foul-smelling liquids. It was these that Saul had thrown out of Israel, but now he needed such a one.

He finally found an old retainer, the washer of his feet, one of the meanest of jobs, to tell him what he wanted to know.

"Mighty Saul," the old man stuttered to his master, "I know of one that can do what you want."

He looked around him wildly, hoping no one could hear. But it was Saul himself who was the supposed danger, since he it was who had outlawed what the man was about to do.

"Do not be afraid, my friend"—Saul could not remember his name, though he had seen him often enough, trusting the royal feet to his care for many years—" Just take your time, and give me the name of one who has dealings with the dead."

"Rufah," the man said, "Her name is Rufah. She previously practiced her art not far from here, but since the command that her kind were no longer welcome in Israel,"—here the old man looked up at Saul, hoping the king would not become furious at the mention of the decree—"she moved to the far north, to En-Dor, near Mt. Tabor, many days walk from Gibeah. Whether she can or will help you, O king, I cannot say."

"Can you lead me to her, old man? I will pay you well, and will release you from your foot-washing work for the remainder of your life."

He smiled a toothless smile, and readily agreed to the bargain. Saul handed him a small sack of gold, and shouted for his body servant to join them at once.

"Get ready for a long trip, my man. We are heading north."

"Where are we going, great Saul?"

King Saul

"You will know when we arrive," Saul snapped. "Now no more questions. Prepare to leave immediately."

The servant hurried off to get ready. Saul put off his royal clothes, his beautiful tunic, his fine sandals. He threw over his shoulders a rude piece of cloth, not fit for a camel, and he decided to go barefoot, as so many of his subjects did. Obviously, it was necessary for him to disguise himself; he had forbidden his subjects to do what he was about to do. But he had no choice; he had to hear from the only man who had all his life heard from the great YHWH. His enormous height could not be disguised, but he felt if he stooped over enough, he would be seen merely as a very tall man and not the gigantic king of the land. He covered his face in a filthy rag and looked like any number of peasants who made their difficult livings herding animals, throwing pots, or growing grain.

Two of his most trusted men joined Saul, Abner, leader of his armies, Abner's servant, a wonderful fighter too, the old man, and Saul's body servant, making a party of five. As night fell, they headed north, moving as fast as the old man was able. Saul was eager to meet this Rufah. If she was as skilled in dealing with the dead as the man said, the silence of YHWH would soon be over, and Saul would be told what he should do. Without YHWH, and the spokesman of YHWH, Samuel, Saul was frozen. He just could not make a decision concerning David and the course of his life as king.

They slept little on the five-day journey, small bits of time intermittently snatched from long periods of fast walking. The old man winded easily, but since he knew the way, he had to keep up. At times, Abner and his man carried the old man on their shoulders to maintain the pace. At dusk on the fifth day they arrived near the village of En-Dor, which sat at the base of one of the great mountains in the land, wondrous Tabor, countless cubits in height.

Saul's servant urged him to go into the village for a night of real rest, but Saul demanded that they push on to see the woman. The old man then led them away from the village gate, which was barely the height of a man, and up the near-by slope of Tabor. Some distance from the gate, on the side of the mountain away from the village, there was the mouth of a cave. A dim light in the bowels of the cave invited their entrance. Saul sent the men in first to see if the place was safe and not some kind of trap for the disguised king. They soon returned to the cave's mouth and ushered their master in.

The place was thick with smoke that rose from a roaring fire set in the middle of the cave floor. The cave was not large, barely large enough for a few people to inhabit at one time, and the very large Saul soon found himself crowded too near the fire for comfort. He demanded that two of his warriors and the old servant leave immediately but urged Abner to stay. He handed the servant some extra gold, and warned him to say nothing to anyone about this night. The servant bowed low before the king, but Saul whispered rather loudly for him to straighten up at once; he did not want the woman to know who it was who had come to her place of magic. Saul remained,

240

peering through the smoke, to discover the woman who would do the deed of darkness he needed done. Abner stood quietly against the wall of the cave.

Finally, the king's eyes had adjusted enough to the darkness and haze of the room to perceive the silhouette of a small person. Whether it was man or woman was at first not clear. He first noted the filthy rag it wore, the wild tangle of the black hair streaked with gray, the gnarled feet, encrusted with the grime of many years' walking and work. The face was not easy to discern, but as some of the smoke cleared, an outline of a woman showed itself. She was surprisingly soft featured, with a full mouth, a small nose, and very bright greenish eyes, hooded by black brows that nearly joined together on her broad forehead. Saul instinctively bowed to this small woman, sensing the power that radiated from her tiny form. She was at least a cubit and a span shorter than he, but her shadow, cast on the back wall by the fire, was enormous, and hovered above the head of the king.

"Welcome," she said in a hollow voice, practiced, Saul imagined, in numerous night encounters with people who, like himself, came to her out of desperation, wishing to speak to departed lovers and fathers and friends. "Who are you, friend?"

"My name of is of no importance, woman," Saul snapped. "I have a job for you, and I am told you are the only one who may be able to do it. They call you Rufah, do they not?"

"They do indeed call me that, and if you prefer you may use that name. But my real name is known only to those who live in the realm of the dead."

"So, you do communicate with the denizens of Sheol, as I have been told?" Her response was not immediate.

"Friend," she finally answered, "You must know that King Saul has decreed that no one may have concourse with the departed ones, on pain of death. You may have heard that Rufah can do such things, but I cannot say whether or not she can do it in fact."

Saul advanced toward her, skirting the fire. He now towered over her, his huge shadow merging with hers in the firelight.

"As YHWH lives, woman, no harm shall come to you if you perform your art this night. And I give you my word that you will be safe from Saul and from any others who claim to have power in these matters."

"Very well," she muttered, "Very well. I will do what you ask, though you must promise never to say anything of what you are about to witness. Tell your man to leave now."

Saul waved his hand toward Abner, dismissing him from the cave. He bowed only slightly and left.

"Come over here," said Rufah, leading him to the dark recesses of the cave.

Saul's heart hammered in his chest as if he were about to enter a battle. The smoke and the blackness recalled more than a few skirmishes he had fought in his long life, and he faced this struggle with the same fear and resolve as before. The woman at last arrived at the back of the cave and stood on the edge of a very deep crevasse, running the whole length of the cavern. Into the crevasse, a bottomless split in the earth, Saul peered down but could see no end but only heard the dripping of an unseen liquid source. The part he could see was green with moss and shiny with rivulets of water. He also saw some small white insects scurrying in and out of the hole. Rufah was now removing her filthy tunic and stood before the gash completely naked. The king watched in wonder as her eyes first closed and then opened again as wide as eyes can open, and she raised her arms high, beginning to wail sounds in an unknown tongue. Her withered breasts, sagging stomach, and white-haired thighs began to quiver, then shake, as she fell into a trance. Suddenly, Saul heard words he could at least partially understand.

"I am the ghost wife who stands at the entrance to the home of the dead. Hear me, you shades, you who dwell in the perpetual dark of eternity. Human seeker, whom do you want me to summon for you?"

Saul found his tongue thick with fear but managed to blurt out, "I want to see Samuel, the prophet!"

At the sound of the name of the prophet, the woman's shaking became violent, her eyes rolled back in her head, her arms began to move slowly up and down as if she intended to fly to Sheol and bear the man back to the cave on her back. Her voice grew impossibly loud; she shouted, "Samuel, Samuel, Samuel," over and again, calling and calling beyond time and space for the ghost to appear.

Saul looked fixedly at the hole in the cave floor, hoping on the one hand to see the old prophet reappear and on the other hand hoping that the woman was a clever but impressive fraud who would soon faint and later demand a few gold coins for her performance. The king's rapid thoughts were broken by a tremendous shriek from Rufah. Her eyes were fixed on the crevasse where, much to Saul's wonder and horror, a form was taking shape, rising from the hole, congealing within the smoke of the room.

"You have tricked me! You are Saul," she bellowed.

"Never mind that," Saul shouted. "What do you see, woman?"

Saul looked hard at the emerging form, but could make little of what he was seeing.

"I see a ghost pouring out of the earth," she said.

"I can see something like that, too, you fool, but what does it look like?"

"It is an old man, rising and forming before my eyes, and he is dressed in the tunic of a prophet. Welcome, O dead one, great prophet."

And with that greeting Rufah fell back from the mist creature that continued to shape itself into Samuel. It was not the wasted and shriveled prophet who had been buried recently; this was the mighty and powerful prophet of long ago, the one who had controlled the land nearly for his whole life.

Saul finally saw the tunic and knew that it was the dead Samuel, brought back by the wonderful power of the ghost wife, Rufah. He praised the day that her name had been given to him. He could once again ask Samuel what it was he was supposed to do in his life. The king fell on his face in the dirt floor of the cave and offered worship to Samuel, who if he was not now a god, surely was as close to one as Saul would ever see. But first, the apparition spoke; it was the familiar massive voice of Samuel of Israel.

"Why have you disturbed my eternal rest by summoning me back to this terrible world?"

Samuel's tone was harsh, severe, as if he had not died after all.

"Saul, your idiocy appears to know no bounds! You have thrown all magicians out of our land and then you rush headlong to a heathen woman to break my well-earned repose in the depths of Sheol. You have once again defied YHWH as you have done repeatedly in your worthless life."

The thing that appeared to be Samuel hovered above the crevasse, its stern features, especially its scornful mouth and half-opened eyes, set squarely on the huge man cowering on the floor.

Saul lifted his face, fearing to look directly at the ghost, and stammered, "I am in dire straights, and the Philistines are fighting against me and God has turned away from me and no longer answers me, not through prophets or dreams, and I called to you to let me know what I should do."

Then he pushed his face once more into the dirt.

"And why by all the darkness of Sheol, would you ask me such things, since YHWH has turned away from you and become your enemy? YHWH has done to you exactly what I said; ripped the kingdom from you and given it to David, that man you think you can eliminate from the land. Must I say all this again? You did not listen to the voice of YHWH; you did not carry out YHWH's fierce wrath against Amalek, so YHWH has led you here to be humiliated by me! But now YHWH shall give Israel, along with you, into the power of the Philistines, so that tomorrow you and your sons will be with me in the place of darkness. This night, Saul, will be your last upon this earth!"

And as the word "earth" echoed around the walls of the cave, the ghost began to dissipate, becoming ever less distinct. As Saul lifted his face from the floor, he could see only Samuel's scornful mouth, drifting in the air, unattached to the rest of the form. But soon it too melted into the smoke, and there was a profound silence. Saul tried to lift himself from the floor of the cave, but found he could not. His body was weak, his arms unable to bear his weight. He collapsed again and lay still, conscious but unaware of where he was. His lips and tongue moved but no words issued from his mouth; he babbled like a helpless child and thought he would never rise up again.

Rufah, who had left the cave in terror, imagining that Saul would now kill her for transgressing his own command, crept back into her home and saw the king lying immoveable on the cave floor. But instead of seeing her king, her potential judge and executioner, she saw only a man, weak and helpless, who had just heard that his life was at an end. She felt her heart soften in the face of Saul's desperation, so she pulled another tunic over her head, and rushed to his side. She bent down toward his ears and whispered.

"My lord, your servant has listened to your command and done what you asked, calling forth the ghost of the prophet. I took my life in my hands to do this, but I acted as you demanded of me. Now, let me command you, my lord. I will bring a bit of bread and a cup of beer for you to eat and drink to strengthen you for your task ahead."

But Saul, like a petulant child, replied, "I will not eat, woman."

But his refusal was not said in anger. He sensed the kindness of Rufah; it was one of the few kind things anyone had done for him in a very long time.

Saul raised himself up to a sitting position and gratefully took the offered bread and cup and ate and drank. And as he chewed the somewhat stale bread and sipped the flat beer, he revived a bit, and he thought about what he must now do. The death of the prophet had changed nothing; the old man was only capable of spewing out hatred for anyone who did not act as he assumed all should act, namely to do precisely and without fail all that only the prophet saw was right. He had some time ago rejected Saul, and he had, even as a shade from Sheol, done it once again. But the dead man had even extended his evil curse. Now all of Saul's sons were to die, and the land of Israel was to be handed over to the hated Philistines. All because Saul and Samuel had disagreed about the means of the destruction of the Amalekites! Such madness! A disputed interpretation of the command of YHWH will now lead to the end of Saul, his family, his reputation, and his life, and the life of his beloved people.

And what of David, his rival? Saul loved the boy but at the same time hated him with deep hatred. All the things Saul had hoped to do as king he was certain David would now do. The king had heard that while he was being pressed hard by the Philistines, the would-be king was in fact living with Philistines! And was prospering in the bargain! His spies spoke of David's western raids against what remained of the Amalekites and his complete slaughter of all those he met. However, the clever man was lying to that fool, Achish, king of Gath, telling him that he was in fact slaughtering Judeans, his own people, and plundering their camps to provide splendid goods for Achish's lavish tastes. What he was doing in reality, Saul had on the best authority, was giving Achish a few Amalekite baubles, and was at the same time supplying the Judeans with the choice part of the Amalekite spoils. Oh, David was clever all right! When Saul and his sons were killed in battle tomorrow, as Samuel had affirmed, David would be ready to mount his final drive to become king, using his base in a friendly Judah and soon convincing the remainder of the people, who would be by then near slaves of the Philistines, that only he could save them. Yes, the slayer of the Philistine giant would convince them that only he could defeat the Philistine army and save the people of Israel! He would be king, and Saul and Jonathan and the rest of his sons would be with the scornful Samuel in Sheol. Saul feared that Samuel would berate him for all eternity, and hoped that the Sheol ghosts could only speak when summoned by the sorcerers of this world, as many of his priests had taught.

King Saul

Rufah broke into his musings with a wonderful meal she had prepared for him and his men, a succulent calf well cooked and delicious flat bread, fresh from the oven. She even served a sharp beer, taken from a sack buried in the floor of the cavern. Saul called his men who had been on guard outside to join him in this feast. The warriors came gladly, but looked warily at their king, wondering how he could eat so heartily, even toss a few jokes into the conversation, after having heard that this meal would almost certainly be his last.

After they had eaten, and had thanked Rufah for her unexpected great kindness, Saul rose again to his full height among them.

"My men! You few have been always faithful to me, while I have raged in sickness, while I have tried to kill my ambitious son-in-law, David, while the prophet Samuel humiliated me over and over. I have done what I thought YHWH called me to do, and when the God grew silent to my cries, I acted as well for my people as I could discern on my own. YHWH has now appeared to have rejected me and my family from the rule of Israel and has chosen David, the shepherd boy to shepherd the land. I say to you openly that I do not understand the actions of YHWH nor can I fully accept what YHWH has decreed for Israel, a land I love as much or more as David or any of you.

As for the prophet Samuel, I reject his fulminations against me, claiming he was speaking for YHWH when again and again he was speaking only for himself and for his appalling sons. I accept his claims to speak for YHWH, but I am convinced that I had a right to speak for YHWH, too, if only YHWH had listened to my voice as YHWH was listening to the voice of David."

And then the king of Israel, mighty Saul, the son of Kish, lifted his arms to the ceiling of the cave, and shouted in his enormous voice.

"I now curse Samuel as a false prophet of YHWH! And I curse David, as a traitor and ambitious toad, who has wheedled his way into the hearts of so many!" Then his voice grew even louder. "And I curse YHWH, a God who listens only on whim, a God who makes choices of human beings for no clear reason, a God who calls and then rejects. I curse such an abuse of divine power, and I go out to fight Israel's enemies despite YHWH's silence and whims and unreasoned choices. Would that YHWH were in Sheol along with Samuel and all the other fools who have worshipped and bowed and scraped to YHWH too long. Come, men. We fight for Israel's future and YHWH be damned!"

Rufah and Saul's men listened in horrified shock to the king's tirade. He had said things no Israelite had ever said aloud, though surely some had said such things in whispers after excessive drink or in silent sobs after a grievous loss. But despite the astonishing words, words rejecting so much of what Israel had held to for years and years, those who witnessed and remembered the speech saw their king illuminated with a light of power and freedom they had not seen since his long ago defeat of the Ammonites and his saving of the village of Jabesh. They could all see that Saul was still king, and though he stood alone, he still stood. There was a greatness in the man, however soon has greatness would be snuffed out. They remembered the way Saul looked, but no one ever repeated what the king had said that night in the cave; the horrific words were never recorded.

Just then a soldier rushed into the cave.

"O king, the Philistines have gathered all their armies and are rushing into our land from three places in the west. We must move quickly or we will be annihilated!"

"Is that wretch David, our so-called friend, among them?"

"I do not know," replied the man, "but I cannot imagine that he would fight against us with our enemies; I will not believe such a thing."

"No matter," said Saul, "he has his destiny and we have ours. Assemble all of our troops at the mountain of Gilboa! We will face the heathen there!" "May YHWH grant us victory!" shouted the soldier, but Saul merely smiled, glancing briefly at the sky as he rushed from the cave.

36

A thick fog coiled around Mount Gilboa and cloaked the horrors of night. By the probing light of the full moon, struggling to pierce the swirling haze, the mist appeared red, a bloody miasma streaking the silver. The battle had been brutal, sword-to-sword, foot-to-groin, head-to-head. Fingers, arms, hands, eyes, ears, teeth littered the hill. Battles began with screams of victory and dreams of glory and ended in shattered bodies, severed limbs, pooling blood, and further screams – screams this time of agony, hopelessness, loss, despair, the terror of death.

In some way he could not have explained, Saul even now knew what had happened. He floated over Gilboa, a ghostly figure, somehow seeing his own end, witnessing with something like disgust the remains of his life. He had no idea just how he was seeing anything, since he knew past doubting that he was dead. There was no beat of his heart; he felt no blood coursing through him. Breath had stopped. Still, he clearly saw what he had become, what it had become, that thing that lay just below.

Saul, he who had been the king, lay dead on his back, mouth slack, eyes crusted and closed with gore, the whole a huge mass of bloody flesh, spears prickling his chest and legs, arrows protruding from his shattered skull. He had cried to his God at the last, but his cries had come to nothing. He remembered that his enemies, the Philistines, worshippers of false gods, gods of fish and grain, gods made with hands, had lunged toward him with their iron spears. He was God's anointed king, chosen by the prophet Samuel; he had known beyond doubt that he was fighting YHWH's battles. But the heathen swine had hacked him to death in spite of all that. The mysterious YHWH had been outrageously silent.

Where had the God been? Why had not the mighty YHWH put in an appearance? His priests had regularly hymned the battle prowess of YHWH who always came to claim victory over Israel's foes. When Deborah had lead Barak to Mt. Tabor, had not YHWH appeared to confound Sisera and his nine hundred chariots? When pharaoh had threatened the destruction of the escaping Israelites, had not YHWH been present in the pillars of cloud and fire, urging the great Moses to lift his magic rod over the sea first to divide and finally to drown the enemy in its waves? That God had often come in dreams, but his nights before the battle had been dreamless. His imperious priest had cast his sacred bones, the Urim and Thummim, that he kept in the pouch of his ornate robe, in a rattling search for God. But he had claimed the dice did

247

not speak, their message at best cloudy and opaque. He could not tell the king what they were saying, he said in that oily righteous voice Saul had hated, because they said nothing. Saul's mass murder of priests at Nob had at the end made any priest reluctant to be of much help to the king. The ghost thought that those priests had deserved death, since they were all traitors, in thrall to the wily David. But after the massacre no priest ever again looked the king in the face. No priest performed the sacred sacrifice for his king. No priest sought the will of God for him. No priest, no priest, no foul sniveling purveyor of things sacred lifted a supposedly pious hand for Saul.

The ghostly Saul thought again of the wretched concubine, that story used to scare the young and dispirit Israelites of any age. If a spirit could shudder, Saul shuddered, as he thought of the dismembered body of the concubine, her bloody parts carted throughout the land as a signal for revenge. Would his once grand body face such humiliation, and if so, what would it signify for Israel—joy at the demise and mortification of the strange king, probably. Would any weep for the death of Saul?

And what of Samuel, the prophet? Though he, too, was dead at a fantastic old age, and had anointed him king, the spirit knew that Samuel had detested him, had barely abided his presence, had accused him of apostasy and blasphemy on two separate occasions; he had humiliated the king publicly, insisting that he, Samuel, had the power to determine what God wanted and didn't want. Even though he had outlived the furious old man, and secretly rejoiced when death had snatched him, he had thought that his freedom from the raging, unyielding prophet would make his life somehow better. He was wrong.

At least Samuel had continued to speak to Saul. At least he had served Saul as a living antagonist. At least with Samuel Saul knew he was still alive. But when the prophet had died—well, Saul had felt a sort of death, too. With the death of Samuel had come the final severance from God, for without Samuel God had withdrawn into a disquieting hush that left Saul alone and trapped and haunted by his memories, dreamless, prophetless, Godless. So now he was dead, just like the old man. Now he would join Samuel in that place he dared not imagine, but the place he knew all too well was real. Yes, the spirit knew where he was headed after he had had his fill of Gilboa and its horrors. YHWH perhaps had a sense of humor after all, sending Saul to endure Samuel forever. If the God had had anything to do with it after all. That withered psalmist may have been right; "the dead do not praise YHWH!" she had croaked. Well, thought the ghost with a brittle bitterness, YHWH should expect no praise out of him, since an eternity of Samuels' jibes should be more than enough to drive all thoughts of YHWH far away.

And now he was doomed to join him in Sheol! To be forced to listen to that voice for eternity! To be unable to escape the sound of the prophet until the end of the world! If a ghost could tremble, what remained of King Saul trembled, as it faced an interminable existence with Samuel. But not yet. The spirit loomed above the hill and remembered more of the end.

King Saul

He had had to fight; the Philistines were not going to give up their push into his land, and he could not put off the battle forever. He and his sons and his army had fought that day on Gilboa. And they had lost—everything, sons, army, the cities where they had lived. And he had died, as Samuel had said. He had battled bravely, as he always had, but the enemy was too many and too much for him. He had taken several of the uncircumcised with him as he fell; there was satisfaction in that. But they had wounded him in too many places to number. Falling for the last time, he had noticed his personal bodyguard—the one who had replaced that double-dealing David-- defending him as well as he was able, but he too had been at the end of his life. With his last breath he shouted for the man to kill him; he was not going to be murdered by those irreligious scum! As the bodyguard had staggered under the pressure of enemy swords and flailing fists, he had hurled his short sword at the dying king, certain that it had found its mark. His last thought had been that his great king had at least not been murdered by the foul Philistines!

But he had been wrong. His sword had in fact missed, and missed badly. The king had been within seconds of being slaughtered by his enemies. With a final cry to the indifferent YHWH, he had crammed the hilt of his sword into the ground in front of him, and fallen onto its bloody point. He had died instantly, the sword cutting his heart in two, just before the Philistines' spears slammed into his lifeless body. Saul's spirit recalled his last words to his God; only his killers heard them. The spirit imagined that YHWH had not heard, since the God had stopped listening to him long ago. Those last words:

> "YHWH! You have won, you silent monster! May my final spurts of blood
> spatter a curse on your foul heavens!"

The floating spirit spoke the words again through what had been its clenched teeth. The spirit felt satisfaction in their bitterness.

Even the repulsive Philistines had been shocked by the blasphemous words, and they were repeated among them in whispers of horror, uttered with furtive glances at the sky. It never paid to attack any of the world's gods, they thought! Whoever this YHWH was, if he was at all, best let sleeping gods lie. The spirit chuckled as it listened to the heathen; it well knew that even if YHWH did exist, and who finally could know, YHWH was probably not paying attention to anything out of the mouth of Saul, God's so-called king.

The spirit hovered another moment over the scene, and then began to dissolve into the mist. It did not see the desecration of the body, though it had feared it. Just as well. Even a spirit would not have welcomed such a scene. The Philistine soldiers in a blood lust of exaltation, severed the arms and legs off the massive trunk of the dead king, and sawed off his proud head, shouting that the tallest man in all Israel was not so tall now! Their thuggish laughter added to the howls and screams of the dying, as their comrades looted Israelite corpses for anything of value. The last thing the spirit heard on its final trip to Sheol was that insane victorious laughter. But now, it thought, Samuel awaits. The cruelty of YHWH knows no bounds, it thought, if the God has anything to do with it at all, as its vanishing vapor seeped into the earth.

The living winners grabbed bronze armlets, tiny gold rings, bits of lapis jewelry, mostly inferior work; the Israelites were a poor and backward people, shown especially by their crude art. They even found a small idol of one god or another in several of the tunics of the dead. The Philistines chortled that these very religious people, claiming a single-minded devotion to the mysterious YHWH, had hedged their bets and had carried other gods with them into battle, just in case their own great god was otherwise occupied. Fat lot of good any of these gods had done them this day! The Philistines fell on the bodies like beasts and stripped them clean.

But not quite. With victory came sacks of wine, looted from the Israelite camp. Speech slurred, and ransacking became haphazard as the wine disarmed the army. Soon, the loud sounds of drunken sleep were joined to the weakening cries of the dying. And as night fell, and the fog thickened, the silence of the gods was matched by a silence on Gilboa.

Another ghostly figure appeared at the edge of the carnage, but this ghost was still very much alive. The mountain was still held in night and fog; the figure was obscured. The moon was down. He moved with the ease of one who had spent much time on battle sites, not to fight, but to plunder what was left of the mangled bodies and shattered swords and spears. He knew that victorious armies were better at killing than at taking care with what was left. He knew well what they cared so little about; broken swords can be sold in order to make new ones. Torn shields can be repaired. Bits of jewelry, half-decent pieces of art, are often missed by the clumsy oafs whom this man had long despised.

He was an Amalekite, a group cursed to be playthings of the powerful. His people had become the special toy of the fast-rising star of the land, the charismatic David, who had robbed them repeatedly when he was living with the Philistines, while lying to his own masters that he was actually stealing from Israelite Judeans. But the Amalekite knew that David was taking stolen Amalekite goods and giving them to those same Judeans, not the other way around. You had to hand it to David. While his own king, Saul, was being destroyed on Gilboa, David was living the high life in Philistine Ziklag, lolling on Amalekite rugs, drinking Amalekite wine from Amalekite cups, raiding Amalekite encampments unimpeded, and duping the foolish Philistine king Achish, claiming that the lavish goods had come from Judeans! Oh, David was clever, all right; the Amalekite admired him greatly as a man after his own heart, one who lived by his wits, who played those around him like an Amorite drum. The Amalekite had plans for David, plans that would end his dangerous life as a scavenger of battle sites once and for all. If only he had that one piece of luck.

Carefully, he padded around the dregs of the battle, stepping over dead and dying bodies, avoiding the piles of limbs and digits that littered the ground, well-hidden by the pooling fog. When he had heard the Philistine soldiers' discovery of an Israelite stash of wine, he knew that his chances of luck had increased. He had only to wait for an hour or two as the wonder of the wine worked its magic, as the soldiers' attempts to search for booty turned into a series of grisly jokes about the dead, and drunken struggles over a ring or an image. When the alcoholic snoring began, his time would come. They will surely have missed something important, something valuable, something beyond spear shards and ripped shields.

He searched for what seemed a long time. The sun was coming soon, and he would need to be well away before its light revealed him at his work. And then he saw it. He could hardly believe his eyes, but it was true. There in the mud, nearly covered in dark clay and blood, and wet by the blanket of fog, lay a crown. It wasn't much of a crown as crowns went. He had heard of the fabled double-crowns of Egypt that the pharaohs had worn since the world was young. The jewel-encrusted crowns of the many kings of the land between the great rivers in the east were legendary in size and allure. This leather band, inlaid with several poor pieces of chipped lapis, festooned with tiny bits of colored cloth now caked with mud, would hardly rival those wonders, but the Amalekite was not one to be dazzled by shiny bits of stone or cheap material. Like any good thief, he saw more when he saw this humble crown. It was the crown of Saul, king of Israel, he was sure of it! Absurdly overlooked by the Philistine brutes that had murdered him, it lay poking its muddy edge out of the soil of Gilboa. A crooked smile formed itself on the Amalekite's thin lips. He stifled a cry of triumph, reaching out to lift the prize closer to his eyes to be certain it was what he was sure it was.

Saul's own crown! He had been there the day that old Samuel had tried to place this object on the massive and shaggy head of the new king. Even Amalekites had been welcome to the coronation of the first king of Israel. The prophet had had to stand on a very large rock to reach Saul's head that had towered further into the sky than any other head in the land. Many had laughed aloud to see the old man stand on the very tips of his toes to attempt to fix this thing on the king, but he at the last could not reach so far up. Finally, Saul himself, like some headstrong boy, had grabbed the crown out of Samuel's hand and plopped it on his own head. Even louder laughter followed that act, while Saul grinned broadly and performed a small dance for his subjects, as if he were mocking the tiny man who had come to make him king. The Amalekite remembered that at least one person that day had found the scene not the least amusing; the prophet had scowled through the whole thing, as if he was doing something he desperately wished he did not have to do. Funny or not, that day had led to this day.

The Amalekite looked at the headless trunk of the colossal Saul, lying like just another mound of earth near by. The common phrase "dust to dust" came into his head as he gazed at the desecrated thing that used to be Saul. He knew of the immense size of the man, as had all the people of the area, but his imposing bulk meant little now. There was something obscene about this thing Saul had become, this lump of bruised and battered flesh. But the obscenity was not the death of the king. Saul was known to be a very strange man, and his size was somehow not matched by his will. Or so the Amalekite had heard. No, it was obscene, because a vital and living human being could be so easily turned into such a mounded thing, strewn and forgotten on a fog-shrouded hill.

The Amalekite thought very little of humanity in any case, but this discovery of what remained of the mighty Saul fixed that view more firmly in his mind. Still, there was no time to be wasted, reflecting on the fate of mortals. The thing that was Saul, and his pathetic little crown, energized the Amalekite to quicker action. As the thick fog began to brighten with the rising sun, and as patches of the ground began to appear, he rushed away from Gilboa, choosing a path that would hide him well as he escaped. He started his loping stride, long-practiced after his actions of theft, but abruptly stopped in mid-step. His sharp eyes lit on another object of value. It was an armlet, a band of some sort of metal, perhaps bronze, yet well worked by a fine artisan (probably Philistine, he thought; he knew of no Israelite capable of this quality!) into a matched pair of snakes, coiled and angry and encircling the severed arm of a soldier of significance. Whose arm it was was not in the least important. It could have been the arm of one of Saul's own sons, perhaps even the proud Jonathan, but the Amalekite did not care. Eagerly, he picked up the arm so as to see the armlet more closely and to decide whether the piece was worth his time to tear it off. It was not Saul's arm, he was sure, since the loutish Philistines had certainly given the king's limbs and head, not to mention his probably enormous member, to some Philistine leader or other for public display, the better to ridicule the defeated enemy and to serve as the source of crude Philistine jokes. It may not have been the king's object, but it was worthy of a king, and the person he had in mind to see now would not know the difference. He tugged the piece off the arm, and grasping it eagerly in his right hand, tossed the mangled length of flesh away with his left.

As the Amalekite ran, the plan solidified in his mind. He would take this crown, cleaned-up and shining of course, and the snake armlet, to the one man in the whole land who would most find value in them. This would be proof that that man would need: that his rival was dead at last, that his Philistine dupes had done his dirty work for him, just as he had hoped. They had killed Saul, and his successor, who several times had refused to murder the murderous Saul, though he had had every right to do so by any tribal law, was completely innocent of the death. Oh, all had worked to that man's great advantage!

But then the thief had another thought, his long strides bringing him ever closer to the one who would make his fortune. The Philistines had clearly killed Saul, and the Israelites would be thirsting for Philistine blood. The new king would be saddled with the need for revenge; his soldiers would demand it. He would have no time to consolidate his power over the land. Would it not be better for the new king if the Amalekite himself took credit for Saul's killing? That way the Philistines would be partially exonerated in that act of regicide, thus lessening the need for immediate revenge. Then the new king could turn his full attention to the rigors of politics, could publicly reprimand the Amalekite for the murder, thus proving his anger at such an outrage, but privately could reward the man for his helpful deed and for the gift of crown and armlet, symbols of the old regime gone forever. The strategy was risky, but promised even greater, more long-term, reward.

All he had to do was dream up a lively story about Saul's murder. His excellent imagination soon was working on the details of the dramatic, if entirely fabricated, events that led him to the necessity of killing the king of Israel. A smile of satisfaction crossed his lips as he ran. Who knows? David's hatred of his own Amalekite brothers might be ameliorated by these events. Not only would he be secretly honored by the new king of Israel; he could also become a fabled Amalekite hero, feted and loved by an adoring populace once he found his triumphant way home. Many nubile Amalekite women would turn their lascivious eyes on him, their new national hero, and he would allow one or two or three to join him in his immense bed, the first thing he would ask from his king, whoever that king happened to be at the moment. After the public and bloody slaughter of the former monarch by that mad Samuel, he had not heard who had ascended the throne of Amalek. Well, whoever it was, this Amalekite would never again sleep under the cold stars after a long night of searching for castoffs from wretched soldiers. Luxury was in his future and caresses and wine and delights unnamed and yet unknown. The rising sun announced a new beginning, and he lifted his arms and shouted for the sheer joy of the day and for his hopes!

But first things first. He needed to focus on the means to that glorious expectation. The story of Saul's killing had to be the best he could create. Only then would honor and glory, both Israelite and Amalekite, follow. He picked up his pace, running now to his future destiny, anxious to face the new king of Israel, the clever and handsome and mercurial David.

37

David had lived in the pathetic village of Ziklag for nearly sixteen moons. He had come there first right after the hamlet had been given to him by Achish, the king of Gath. It had been ridiculously easy to fool Achish about the real reasons why David had fled to the Philistine city. The aging king had been amazingly gullible, overly eager to have a powerful Israelite friend to help him defeat his eastern enemies. David of course knew that loyalties shifted quickly in the lands he planned to rule, but if Achish thought he could in any way control his actions, he was the very fool David knew him to be. And he had actually fooled the foolish Achish twice.

The first time, many summers ago, he had been running away from Saul, more madman than king, and in desperation he had come to Gath and sheepishly requested an audience with Achish. In those days he had been naïve enough to imagine that the Philistine would not know who he was. How wrong he had been! Achish's retainers took one look at David and sang to the king the song that everyone in the countryside was singing: "Saul has struck down his thousands and David his ten thousands!" The king was enough of a poet to realize immediately that such a poem should have caused no particular upset: when one added a second line to a poem, that line said the same thing as the first line, albeit with a slight twist. Well, it was more than obvious that Saul was no poet, because he had heard the lines as an attack on his prowess as a warrior when compared to the much shorter and much younger David. He had gone into a near-homicidal rage. Saul and he were less than close, but David had known even then that he was clearly on the rise in the land; his day was coming. Achish knew that he bore watching, both as possible powerful friend and as powerful enemy, but David realized that Achish's heart was far less subtle than his own.

So when David had entered the throne room in Gath that first time, he had not received the welcome he had imagined. He had to act quickly; he pretended to be insane, using Saul as his model; he had often enough seen King Saul raving and delusional, calling out in desperation for the soothing sounds of David's harp. So he had scratched crazily at the doorframe of the throne room's entrance, and worked up enough spit to allow it to drip down his red and matted beard.

King Achish took one look at this seeming mad fellow and had shouted, "Am I short of madmen that you wish to add one more to my idiot stable? Throw this fool out!" He could easily have been killed, but David was not one to be bested by a heathen Philistine. His agile heart snapped and whirled, while their thoughts moved like winter rivers. He had escaped safely enough and had had a huge laugh with his men. This of course was after he had gathered some men to him in the wilderness, some moons after his first confrontation with Achish.

David later delighted in recounting the hilarious scene for his ogling mercenaries, their eyes crinkling in drunken pleasure. He hopped about the fire, roaring in feigned idiocy, shouting in his attempt to be understood in a poorly mouthed Philistine. But since the point was *not* really to be understood, he had found it easy to use his bad linguistic gifts for the purpose. "A king's rat," he yelled, "the queen's bum!" "Fire's a hot one, and the stars will fall," and other such nonsense. He did not know what he was saying, but that was good. All the while spittle was sluicing down his face into his beard. And then David became Achish and made his voice kingly and pompous. "Send this man away; I have idiots enough!" And David would add, "No doubt that was true," and the men laughed and shouted, since they never missed a chance to make fun of their enemies. David was a grand mimic, and his men loved him for it.

After some time had passed, and Saul's madness and fury grew beyond all bounds, David had again to escape to Gath. Saul had several times tried to kill David himself with his deadly spear. Amazingly, he had missed each time, though Saul was a fabled master of the spear. David had long wondered whether Saul had, deep down, not wanted to kill him after all. Nevertheless, David was tired of dodging Saul's attacks and so returned to Gath one more time. This time he had tried another tactic. Of course, he had not come alone that time. He had a hardy group of six hundred warriors now, and though many of them were not the most trustworthy of men, they were loyal to David and were survivors of the difficult life their lord had been living in the wilderness of Ein Gedi, some two day's hard march east of Gath. The Philistines, who knew that territory well, admired anyone who could live there, let alone thrive there. So, this time David was received rather more warmly as a potential ally of Achish against the increasingly unstable Saul.

But David's subtlety was far superior to that of the simple Achish; the king was as slow as he had ever been. A few days after his arrival, his men had stabled their horses and had been given simple places to stay in the city. David, now a significant chieftain, had found suitable lodgings for his two wives, Abigail and Ahinoam, Saul's former wife. Michal he had nearly forgotten, hardly considering her wife at all. He then requested an audience with Achish. He dressed as well as his difficult wilderness existence allowed and confronted the Philistine king.

"My lord," he began, "if I have found favor with you (as he knew he had this time!), please give me one of your country hamlets to call my own; why should your servant live in the capital with you?" Why indeed, thought Achish? The man has burnt his bridges with Saul; there can be no going back there. He will be my servant for life, and his cutthroat gang of six hundred will add nicely to my increasing armies as we move deeper into Israelite territory. Why not give him his own place? His family is growing, his men need a place to call home. If David is happy, then I will be happy, and he will be happy to serve me all his days. Why not?

"Why not take Ziklag as your own? It is a short trip south of here, but has good sources of water and fairly fertile soil. You can flourish there with hard work and pluck. I give it to you freely." And with a magnanimous gesture of an open hand, Ziklag became the first city of David. It was not to be the last.

Upon arriving at Ziklag (it was hardly as salubrious as Achish had made it out to be, more sand than soil with scant sources of fresh water), David put his well-laid plans into immediate effect. He had no intention of making the pathetic city into a permanent residence, so had not ordered any plowing of the ground for agriculture. David knew he could steal what he needed for his expanding army from the small communities that lay a day's ride or so from Ziklag. He established a number of raiding parties, dividing his rag-tag army into three groups. Group one was responsible for the Geshurites, group two for the Girzites and group three, which David himself headed, for the Amalekites. David knew little about any of these puny groups of people, but he had no intention of knowing them; he only wanted what they had in order to sustain his people.

The charge he gave each group was simple: "Fall on them without mercy! Kill both men and women; leave no one alive! Take everything they have: sheep, oxen, donkeys, camels, clothing, jewelry, art objects, everything, and bring them all back to Ziklag." The demand he made to kill all the men and women had little to do with religion, though some among his men believed that YHWH commanded such complete annihilation as a sign of perfect devotion. Every army had its share of the deeply pious. But though David was a religious man, at least as religious as the next ambitious warrior, he did not demand their deaths as a way to avoid pagan contamination or as a sacrifice to his God, however much his religious men imagined or desired his commands to mean. Still, David was not averse to allowing his men to believe what they pleased about his motives, and if they found religious devotion in the slaughter, so much the better. But the real reasons for these slaughters in David's heart lay elsewhere.

After the raids were performed, the huge pile of booty was carefully stacked and sorted and brought to Achish in the capital. Achish looked at the fine animals and the stacks of stolen objects, and asked, "Against whom have you been raiding to gain such a lovely haul?" Achish was always on the lookout for new objects or finer animals that would increase the power of his image. And David would respond differently each time to this question.

One time he would say, "Against the Judean wilderness of the Negev." And he would spin a fine story of the raid; David was a good teller of tales. "My Lord, you should have seen the dung-covered half-wits run at our approach! We surrounded them before they could pull on their tunics, and their members bobbed up and down and their backsides jiggled just before our swords and arrows cut them down like wheat at the harvest. Oh, I tell you it was grand fun! I wish you had been there, my Lord Achish. I know well what joy you find in a safe slaughter of fools!" And Achish would howl with laughter (David could imitate that braying laugh almost exactly when the king was not around), spraying his beer down his kingly robe and on the grain-covered floor.

Or another time he would reply, "Against the Jerahmeelite desert places of the Negev." And another tale would ensue. "We caught them all asleep, and turned them into women, if you know what I mean!" And Achish would bray like the jackass he was, and hold onto David to prevent his falling down. David rarely laughed, though his beautiful eyes would gleam with pleasure, pleasure at the story, pleasure at the beer, pleasure at his own cleverness.

Or one time he even said, "Against the Negev of the Kenites." And bloody stories would follow, punctuated with crass butchery and crude decimations. For all the ribaldry and mayhem and blood lust, the stories were all lies. Well, the blood and death were not lies; David murdered well and with relish. But he was always careful to tell Achish that he had been raiding east, into territory controlled by Israel, into the Negev, into Judah, his home place. In fact, Geshur and Girz and the place of the Amalekites were all west and south of Ziklag, on the way to Egypt. But since there were no living witnesses to the locations of David's attacks, no one, save the raiders themselves, knew where they had been. David had sworn his men to secrecy, on pain of death, never to reveal just where they performed their savage thefts. Thus was Achish fooled into thinking that David was stealing from and murdering Israelites to provide gifts for him, when in reality he was raiding against others and offering gifts to his fellow Judeans, along with enough booty to keep Achish himself satisfied.

And Achish was more than satisfied. With each gift of well-wrought urn and cup, or bronze armlet, or thick-bossed shield, he was increasingly convinced that David was now his lackey for life. By robbing Judeans, he has made himself disgusting to his own people; he must stay with me, and be my ferocious and most useful slave, forever, thought Achish. More than once he had said, "Well done, my faithful servant," while David had submissively lowered his head and bowed his knee before the king in supposed obeisance. Achish at these moments never saw David's eyes, hooded in mock obedience, his lovely mouth thin-lipped with false subservience. The king's own eyes flashed as they took in the fine presents his new slave had brought and his own lips curled in glee as he dreamt of David's future conquests on his behalf. "It was a glad day when you stumbled into my city these moons ago," he said, "And a gladder day that I took you in, as needy and poor as you were. But it is well that a true king show mercy to the downtrodden. I have heard, David, that your own God is big on mercy to the poor. Still, I am glad that your devotion to that God does not prevent you from separating these fine gifts from their rightful owners!" And the braying laugh would fill the hall, and David would smile his own smile, as he withdrew, prettily backwards, from the presence of the king.

King Saul

With such a friend, such an ally, mused Achish, such a willing and steadfast slave, there is no reason that I, Achish, should not eventually become king of all five cities of the Philistine federation and eventually—why not?—king of the entire land of both Philistia and Israel. And with such pleasant dreams flowering in his heart, Achish began to compose the speech he would give on the day of his coronation over his vast kingdom. And the design of his crown would be important, too, so he headed off in the direction of Gath's finest jeweler to discuss it, to be certain that it would have no rival, just as he would have none.

And so it was to Ziklag that the Amalekite came to see David, the supposed slave of Achish, king of Gath. David had recently returned from another successful raid on the Amalekites, had stolen much lovely spoil, both livestock and personal goods, and had slaughtered every person in the village. There had been one unfortunate incident to mar the success of this raid. He had seen a sole survivor running out of the camp. He ran after the escapee, grabbed him, and slit his throat with a single stroke. He then called to him the leader of the group responsible for complete extermination. His name was Asher.

"Did you not hear my strict orders that all must every time be destroyed in the camps where we raid?"

"I did, my lord," Asher managed to get out of his violently trembling lips. "Then why was this man still alive? Why did I have to kill him myself? You know that I do not enjoy killing, and do not want to gain any sort of reputation as a killer. Do you have any explanation you can give?" Asher stifled a crude laugh at David's claim not to be a killer, since he had been a consummate killer from the day he had run to the wilderness.

"None, my lord," he almost said, but the word "lord" caught in his throat as, at a small signal from David, Asher was garroted from behind by a certain Shem, his windpipe instantly crushed, using a recently plundered camel rope.

David's men threw the corpse onto the pile of dead villagers, some to be burned and some to be exposed to the carrion birds, ever hungry for a fresh meal in the harsh desert. Clean human bones were numerous in the deserts south and west of Ziklag during David's time there.

It was to this David that the Amalekite, fresh from Gilboa, came on that warm spring morning. He begged audience with the chieftain and presented to him a pitiful sight. In addition to the careful speech he had prepared, he had added to his appearance two important visual items. First, he had torn his outer garment. This had been hard, since it was his only cloak. But he imagined after his conversation with David he would have more cloaks than he could manage. And second he had covered his head with fresh soil. The thieving Amalekite hated the feeling of dirt in his hair, but he knew that his news was at least publicly mournful, and torn clothes and a headful of dirt were necessary to announce the seriousness of his mourning. The fact that he

258

had run all night, and had not slept in many hours, added to the pathetic portrait he presented David.

As he approached the warrior, he wanted him to be certain of the vast esteem in which he was held. The Amalekite hurled himself, nose down, at David's feet in abject humility and honor. And he waited for the great man to speak. The words were slow in coming, for David was sizing up this stranger, so pitifully sad in appearance, so eager to show proper deference.

From his prone position, the hopeful Amalekite peered up at David through slits of his eyes. The stories were true about the man! He was absurdly handsome, with long and lustrous reddish hair tumbling beguilingly around his deeply tanned and rugged face, pierced by penetrating ice-blue eyes. He was shorter than the Amalekite had imagined, but his torso was thick with muscle, his arms like fat tree branches, matched by legs like trunks. He sat on a campstool like any common wilderness wanderer and gazed at the adoring man at his feet with curiosity. A long silence. Two burly guards stood like giant statues on each side of David, each lightly touching a sheathed dagger. Though appearing not to move, the coiled energy of trained killers throbbed in the muscles of their limbs. The Amalekite worked hard to stay still, to wait, to have patience. But his discomfort increased as the only sounds continued to be the heavy breathing of one of the guards, the slight rustling of a lizard on the ceiling of the tent, the small puffs of air that moved fitfully to provide a hint of cool in the stifling heat. Sweat broke out on his face, his left leg, forced by his impulsive dive to the ground under his body, ached to be released. If only the man would say something! Just what is he waiting for? My future is now in his hands, thought the Amalekite. Let's get on with it!

Finally David spoke. His voice was rather high-pitched for such a thickly muscled man, but his words came out slowly, carefully ordered. He had clearly thought before he had uttered a word. Had he delayed his speech for effect? Was he trying to intimidate the postulant before him? The Amalekite listened to the words as carefully as he could, given the painful position he occupied on the floor of the tent.

"Where in the name of Sheol have you come from?"

There was a slight, almost imperceptible, emphasis on the "you," as if David somehow knew the man, or perhaps had expected someone else to grovel at his feet. And that rough language, using the name of the place of the dead in such an off-handed, slangy sort of way. It seemed a bit beneath this obviously intelligent and charismatic man, thought the Amalekite, but he could not deny that the mention of Sheol, the realm of the dead, made him shudder. He had spent his life around the dead and had little desire to join their ranks any sooner than he absolutely had to. And today was not going to be that day, because what he was about to do would make his future honors and luxury secure and his life pleasantly long.

Since the great man had spoken, the Amalekite scrambled to his knees, brushing off some of the tent floor's dirt, combing some of the filth from his hair with his

long fingers. As he reached to rub his aching knees, the two guards with swift movements half unsheathed their long knives, but a glance from David forced them to push
them back into their scabbards. The Amalekite noted that the massive one on the left
showed just a hint of disappointment as his master stopped what might have been a
small pleasure of killing in the boring duty of guarding David.

Quickly returning his eyes to the tent floor, he answered. "From the camp of
Israel, I have escaped." His work as battle thief had made the Amalekite the master
of many tongues--a thief had to be quick to escape many a tight spot-- and he spoke
David's Hebrew very well, if with a slight western twang.

The word the Amalekite used, "escape," could also mean "flee away," but he hoped
that David would not catch that nuance and conclude that he had fled in terror from
the clash on Gilboa. He had "escaped," that is he was right in the thick of things and
had with luck gotten away with his life, running straight here to tell the mighty David
the truth of what had happened there. He felt his brevity and careful word choice at
this early stage of the dialogue would serve him well.

David again was silent, but far more briefly this time.

"Go on. What is the thing?"

It was a most peculiar sentence and uttered with more force than the Amalekite
expected. "What "thing" did the man mean? Did David know more than he let on?
He tamed his rising fear, and assumed that David meant something very general like
"What happened?" He took that as his cue to begin the speech he had practiced well
on the journey.

"The people fled from the battle, " he began.

He wanted to make it clear that the struggle quickly had become a rout and that
escape was the only route to survival; he had hardly been the only person to flee Gilboa. He did not want David to think he was a coward, but a shrewd judge of situations,
one, like David himself, who knew how to find a way to live when death seemed a
real possibility. We are two of a kind, you and I, the Amalekite thought, as his speech
plunged on.

"Still many of the people fell during the rout and many died."

Now came the important announcement, nicely delayed for maximum impact.
"Saul and his son Jonathan were among the dead."

He had struggled with the right way to reveal this news, but he finally decided
that the warrior David would like it quick and sharp without embellishment.

David showed no outward emotion at the news. He kept his eyes on the young
Amalekite, hardly changing his expression.

Then, with a slight lifting of one eyebrow, David asked, "How do you know that
Saul and his son Jonathan are dead?"

With that question, the Amalekite now had a choice. He could have responded
simply, just relaying facts, allowing David to act on those facts in whatever way he
wanted to. But that would not serve his grand plan well. If he answered, "They are

dead, because I myself saw the bodies." there would be scant reward for such bald realities. No! The Amalekite had to have had a hand in the death, had to have been directly involved so that David could be fully aware of the great service that had been performed for him, the next king of Israel. So the well-rehearsed tissue of lies began.

"I just happened to be on Mt. Gilboa," he said.

He did not want David to think he was one of those battle scavengers, a thieving low-life who lived off the carnage of heroic combatants, especially since that is exactly what he was. He found himself on the mountain of the last battle between Saul and the hated Philistines purely by accident. Of course, the Amalekite said nothing in his speech about the Philistines being hated, since he was delivering it in a Philistine city, however much the city was really David's. David's relationship to the Philistines was the subject of much rumor and supposition, and there was no use taking sides when the sides were not so clearly known.

Now the Amalekite began to employ his most dramatic gestures as he continued his address.

"Why, there right in front of me was Saul himself, leaning precariously on his famous spear."

He thought he would emphasize his recognition of the spear of Saul, since practically everybody knew the stories of Saul's multiple attempts to kill David with it. Surely Saul's death and the final impotence of that huge spear as a result would bring David some sense of relief. He went on to paint the scene.

"Why, there were chariots (well, perhaps not too many chariots, given the hill country's hardscrabble ground) and many horsemen drawing closer to the obviously helpless Saul. Suddenly, to my surprise, he glanced behind him, taking his eyes off the fast-approaching Philistine warriors, and saw me. Those kingly eyes were bloodshot, rheumy, half-closed with anguish and terror, and he laid them on me, calling out, 'Who are you?' I responded as sympathetically as I could and said, 'I am an Amalekite!' I had to shout over the din of the fast-charging warriors and the squeaking armor."

The speaker did not notice, in the midst of his great performance, that as he revealed himself as an Amalekite, David's eyes narrowed, his lips grew taut, his jaw hardened.

"Then the mighty Saul, reduced to the final words of his life, sobbed loudly, 'Stand close to me; kill me, because the death-throes have seized me, but I somehow am still alive.'"

At the utterance of the word "death," David shuddered ever so slightly and laid his hand on his sword. At that movement, his two guards became more alert, laying their hands on their daggers. But the Amalekite saw none of these actions, since he was near the end of his drama. His voice rose in pitch and volume, as he rushed to the conclusion.

"So I stood close to him and killed him, for I knew that he could not live after he had fallen."

King Saul

No use making up how the killing occurred; just the facts of the killing itself will make its mark. And now for the clinching demonstration. With a sweeping flourish, the Amalekite produced his precious finds.

"I took the crown that was on his head and this exquisite armlet that was on his arm, and I have brought them here to my lord."

This final sentence was spoken from his knees, eyes downcast, the crown and armlet held up at eye level.

The speech and its accompanying visuals had the perfect impact. With a loud cry that quickly turned to wracking sobs, David took hold of his robe and ripped it raggedly in half. Immediately his two statue-like guards did the same to their tunics, pulling them apart in a paroxysm of grief. And as the massive sounds escaped the leader's tent, all who heard it did the same until the entire camp was convulsed with howls and screams and clothes were everywhere left in tatters.

The Amalekite looked on in bemused astonishment, not knowing quite what to think. He, of course, could work up no passion or tears for the death of Saul, and it was somehow highly unseemly that David, Saul's bitter enemy, whom the enraged and mad king had attempted to kill again and again, should go out of his own head at the news of his death. But then the Amalekite thought: of course! David has to put on a great public show of sadness in order to demonstrate that he really loved Saul in the end, and that his death is a great loss to the people of Israel. Very clever of the young warrior, although the loss of all those perfectly good robes does seem a bit excessive! Well, let them all rage and roar as long as they like, he thought, as long as I get what is coming to me for making the kingship now available for the taking. Even though the Amalekite had of course not killed Saul, his story was so good that for a moment he imagined he actually had!

The Amalekite had to wait until evening to be dealt with, because David and his men just would not quit their mourning. They wept jars of tears and refused all food until late, shouting out from all over the camp first about Saul and Jonathan, then about the other members of the fallen army, and finally for the dark fate of the house of Israel, all dead by the power of Philistine swords.

The Amalekite grew impatient, wondering if this sordid charade would ever end. Finally, the screams and cries grew softer, then died out. The smells of roasting meat clogged the soggy air, and the Amalekite sat up in David's tent in eager anticipation of the rewards now finally to be given. Now that David had put on his show, he could re-turn to the tent and thank him privately for his service to the new king. Perhaps some gold would be offered. David was reputed to have vast quantities of gold, compiled from his numerous raids during his days in Ziklag. The Amalekite thought, with considerable bitterness, that much of that gold had come from his own people. It would be a small sense of justice to receive some Amalekite gold in return for the killing of Saul—even though he did not in fact kill him. Well, just as David had made a career duping that fool Achish, it would be lovely when he, the Amalekite, duped David out of some gold for a killing he did not do! Rough justice in a rough world. It was no more or less than the young warrior deserved. And when the Amalekite returned to his people, or what remained of them after David's murderous raids, he would show them their own gold, and they would hail him as a hero, all laughing uproariously at the clever murderer who had finally been bested at the game of deception. A smug smile played over the lips of the Amalekite.

David stepped into the tent. His blue eyes were red from weeping, his red hair a mass of tangled strands, his torn robe loosely tattered over his massive chest. He looked at the Amalekite.

"Where do you come from?" he asked with real brutality, a nasty edge in his raspy voice, made hoarse by hours of shouting and crying.

Perhaps David had missed his nationality, so he said, "I am the son of an immigrant, living in this land. Amalekite, as I said before."

David stalked back to his campstool and sat down heavily.

He then looked squarely at the Amalekite and said with a snarl, " How were you not afraid to raise your hand and destroy the Lord's chosen one?" These shocking words hit the Amalekite like thunder on a day of storm, like a battle club from a hidden place.

David turned easily to one of his huge guards, and said, without emotion, "Come here and smash him."

And before the Amalekite could think once more of his hopes for a bright future of honor and favor, the guard's club fell on his skull, crushing his dreams and his hopes. David watched the murder quietly, then waved the guards out of the tent. Slowly he rose and walked over to the dead messenger and watched the red pool eddy out from what was left of his head. He stood over him, straddling the corpse and shouted loud enough for the whole camp to hear.

"Your blood be on your own head, because your own mouth has spoken against you when you said, 'I have killed the Lord's chosen one.'"

He laughed coldly to himself, after the words shouted to the camp had ceased their echoing. Well, his blood is even now on his own head! Just look at it oozing out all over my floor. He had to be killed. We simply cannot have in Israel the idea that anyone can kill the Lord's chosen ones whenever the thought comes into their heads. After all, thought David, I am also the Lord's chosen one; I too was crowned by the prophet Samuel. If anyone dares to raise a hand against the Lord's chosen one, the penalty must be death. I refused to kill Saul, and now this pathetic Amalekite has done it for me, or so he says. Well, whether he did or didn't is quite irrelevant to me. Saul is at last dead, and I will be king.

And with those thoughts in mind, David sat down to compose a song, something he loved to do and was known for in all parts of the land. He grabbed his harp, and plucking at the six strings, he began:

King Saul

Your glory, O Israel, has been slaughtered upon your high places;
> How the warriors have fallen!

Do not tell the story in Gath,
> nor proclaim it in the streets of Ashkelon,
> or the daughters of the Philistines will celebrate,
> the daughters of the uncircumcised will shout for joy!

Mountains of Gilboa,
> let there be no dew or rain upon you,
> nor abundant fields!

Because there the shields of the warriors have rolled away,
> the shield of Saul no longer anointed with oil.

From the blood of the slaughtered,
> from the warrior's flesh,
> the bow of Jonathan did not cease
> nor did the sword of Saul return empty.

Saul and Jonathan, loved and lovely!
> In life and in death they were not divided;
> swifter than eagles, more powerful than lions!

Daughters of Israel, weep for Saul,
> who dressed you with crimson luxury,
> who placed golden ornaments on your clothing.

How the warriors have fallen in the midst of the battle!
Jonathan is slaughtered on the high places.

I am devastated because of you, my brother Jonathan;
> greatly beloved you were to me;
> your love to me was marvelous,
> even more than the love of women!

How are the warriors fallen,
> and the war weapons perished!

David sang for hours, far into the night, searching for just the right word, just the right tone for his lament for Saul and Jonathan. It was necessary that the funeral for the two warriors be both dignified and at the same time set the right mood for the coming of David's own kingship. He must show that he never hated Saul. He must show that Saul and Jonathan, father and son, were never really divided, all appearances to the contrary. He must show that Jonathan and he were great friends, though it was clear to David that Jonathan loved him far more than he ever loved Jonathan. Jonathan always was a bit too cloying, he thought, a bit too close for comfort. Still, he was a great fighter, and was much loved by many of Saul's followers. It was important that all recognize the close relationship that David had with Jonathan.

And then there was Saul, that crazy and sad old man. He never really was a king, David thought. Oh, he tried, but he was doomed somehow. It never was quite clear to David why it had all gone so wrong. He and Saul had initially been close, almost as if

King Saul

Saul were a surrogate father for David. But Saul was unpredictable. Many called him insane, but David was not so sure. Still, as he composed his lament, his mind wondered back to the beginning of Saul's kingship. He had heard various accounts of this beginning, from Saul himself, of course. From Jonathan. From Ahinoam, Saul's wife, now married to David. And later he would hear other tales from Michal and Merab, Saul's daughters, the first of whom had become another of David's wives. From Abner, general of Saul's army, before he was murdered by that bloody-minded Joab. Saul's story had been told again and again. But even after all those tellings, David, along with so many in Israel, was still not certain just who exactly the first king of Israel had been. Well, at last he was dead. The time for wonder and speculation was over. David stood up from his singing, fully ready to assume his rightful place as the king of Israel.

39

David very soon heard the reports of the complete defeat of the armies of Israel at the hands of the Philistines, and of the death of Saul and his sons on Mt. Gilboa. He further heard how the remnants of the army rushed in terror across the Jordan River, eastward and southward, hiding in caves and rocks and holes in the earth, fleeing headlong from the victorious heathen. He imagined that a few probably stumbled into some of the caves that had housed him and his men when Saul was trying to kill him. Well, he thought, I have seen my last cave for a home. I will now live only in well-appointed houses in my own land, and as king of that land. Samuel was dead and now Saul and all his sons, save that lame boy Mephibosheth, who was surely no threat to become king, had joined the prophet in Sheol. It was all too clear who now was king. But David had to react to Saul's death in the right way.

He needed to show sorrow, but also needed to begin immediately to consolidate his power over the land. When the Amalekite wanderer had come to his camp, bearing the news of Saul's death, he could not be sure whether the messenger was lying for his own gain or had in fact killed the king at his request. It made no difference what the truth was: David needed to kill the Amalekite and he had done so with as much brutality as his guards could muster. It was crucial not to set a pattern of killing YHWH's chosen ones, since David was one of those himself. So, as much as he disliked the king, his father-in-law and would-be murderer, he needed to announce, by word and action, that Saul and he had not really been enemies, and that his death was a terrible loss to the land. And furthermore it was important that all knew that Saul and Jonathan were never quite the antagonists that they appeared to be. David, of course, knew that they in fact detested one another, but it was necessary that a story of their final reconciliation be well known. Had they not died together, defending Israel?

Hence, David's killing of the Amalekite had been quickly followed by a state funeral for Saul, though his body unfortunately had been stolen off the mountain by unknown thieves. David wrote one of his finest poems for the occasion, lauding Saul and Jonathan's greatness and calling for weeping at the enormous loss of the first king of Israel. And also there were the poetic attacks against the nasty Philistines. The fact that the new king had been living with them while Israel was being decimated on the mountains by their armies had circulated quickly throughout the land, so it was important that David say publicly and loudly that he bore no love for those heathens.

He had been duping them all the while, supporting the southern Judean Israelites while claiming, most cleverly, that he was really a Philistine collaborator. Yes, thought David, all was working out beautifully for his steady rise to be king.

He left the pathetic village of Ziklag and led his entire company toward Hebron, the chief town of the Judeans. He himself was of Judean stock, Bethlehem being a village of Judah. The funeral had been splendid with many Israelites in attendance, those who were not hiding from the Philistines. David had little real fear of the Philistines. He had lived among them for nearly two years and well knew their many weaknesses. Once he consolidated his southern community, making his capital in Hebron, he would deal with the Philistines.

As he rode comfortably and slowly toward Hebron, he gazed at the beginnings of what he knew was going to be an inexorable rise to complete power. He nodded at his beloved Abigail, and their son, Chileab, whom she carried in the cart. This wife was a beauty, and the wisest woman David had yet met, and she had given birth to a strapping son whom David hoped would one day himself be king. He thought very briefly of Michal, Saul's daughter and his first wife, still living in Gibeah he imagined, though he could not be sure she had survived the assault of the Philistines. He in truth did not much care; Michal had served her purpose, and since she had no children played little if any role in David's future. He then nodded at faithful Joab, his chief warrior, riding by on his fine horse. Joab would be general of my armies, he thought. He was stolid but fiercely loyal and would serve without question.

And then David thought of the great YHWH, the God who had chosen him, through the mouth of Samuel, from among his brothers in Bethlehem. YHWH was a mysterious God, no doubt, but David trusted in any being who was wise enough to bring him to power. Saul had of course been huge and imposing, but he had also been mad, or at least something like mad, and YHWH had deposed him and chosen David. What could be more reasonable? David was clearly the better man; had not Samuel himself said so? Size did not insure success; it took cleverness, confidence, assurance, certainty of one's skill, one's destiny, one's greatness. As David watched his company plod toward Hebron, he was more convinced than ever that his time of power had at last come.

And so, before he joined the procession again, he paused to pray and to thank YHWH for all that had happened and for all that was about to happen. "O great and glorious YHWH," he began. "You are the only God in all the world. Your fingers have made all that is, and your hands are open to supply our every need. And you are especially wise in the ways you order our lives, choosing the right people to do your will and rejecting those who do not or cannot advance your holy work in the world. I praise you, O YHWH, for you have chosen me to be your king in Israel, I, David, who is wise as you are wise. Grant me your power, O God, that I may rule your people well and may vanquish your enemies at last, so that peace may be established in the land, and so that my descendants may reign for as long as the sun rises in the east, and that my name may never be forgotten in all the earth. Thank you, thank you, for your many gifts to me. Make me great, as you are great, and I will honor your glorious name forever. Amen."

And David felt that YHWH had heard his prayer. A swell of power filled his heart as he hurried to join the line moving to Hebron. David's destiny was, he felt, now certain to be fulfilled.

40

The news of Saul's death and mutilation at the hands of the Philistines reached the village of Jabesh very soon after those grotesque things had happened. After the king of Israel had saved the village from the Ammonites and their freakish king, several villagers had joined Saul's army and had been among his most faithful servants. It was one of them who had run all night to the village to announce that Saul and his sons had been slain on the mountain of Gilboa, and that the drunken Philistines had cut off the arms, legs, and head of the mighty Saul and had taken the trunk that was left and nailed it on the walls of one of their military outposts, a remote place called Beth-Shan. The men of the village resolved immediately to rescue what was left of Saul's glorious body and bring it back to Jabesh for proper burial. The tiny outpost was just on the west side of the Jordan, so the small group of courageous villagers, some twenty in number, had merely an overnight journey to the place.

They approached the fortress just before dawn, when they imagined the guards would be listless and not too vigilant. When they saw what was left of their hero, just visible by the light of the rising sun, several wept while others stared in horror. Saul's torso had been impaled on the wall of the place, near the gate. The place where his head, arms, and legs had been were now ragged gashes of congealed blood and torn flesh. Some Philistine lout with more cruelty than knowledge of Hebrew had incised a small tablet with the words "*melet* Israel," which means something like "bald one of Israel." Of course, the first word was very close to the word "*melek*," "king" in the language, so perhaps the Philistine had known more about the language than first thought, and had punned darkly as the tablet suggested.

The Jabeshites needed to act quickly before the sun rose full. They were right that the guards were sound asleep after the joy of their complete victory and the drunken celebrations that followed. The villagers had brought a hand-held cart to carry the body in, so after two of them had stood on the shoulders of the tallest men in order to unfasten the large mound of flesh from its place on the wall, they very quietly loaded it onto the cart, and four of them shouldered the long poles; and they moved back toward Jabesh. They quickly reached the Jordan and moved downhill until they came to their town. They doubted the Philistines had heard anything and were probably still asleep in any case.

King Saul

As they carried Saul's remains, all thought of that wonderful day, now so many years ago, when the giant young and handsome one had appeared on the horizon, prepared to obliterate Nahash, the king of the Ammonites, who had threatened their whole village with torture and humiliation. The man had appeared like an avenging angel as he swooped down from the mountains and fell on the Ammonites like a great eagle. How they had cheered when the king had been slain by Saul himself as easily as he might have swatted a fly in the spring. The Ammonites had been routed before the sun was straight overhead, and the Jabeshites had had a celebration that all would long remember. Saul had stayed for the party and had laughed and sung and drunk well into the night and into the morning. His future as king of the land on the west of the Jordan seemed certain and bright.

Now it had come to this, an unrecognizable mound of torn and bloody flesh, carried by a few forgotten villagers toward a tiny hamlet. But the Jabeshites had never forgotten their savior and had watched in dismay as his kingship over Israel had spiraled down to disaster, to defeat and terrible death and dismemberment. Still, they planned to bury him properly. Though they knew little of the Israelite God, YHWH, that One of the unpronounceable and mysterious name, they resolved to do their best to honor Saul. They were like most people of that time; they respected the gods others worshipped, though they could not always imagine how certain kinds of worship of particular gods had taken hold.

This YHWH was a good example. Of course, over the years, those who were raised in Jabesh in Gilead, had had dealings with worshippers of this YHWH and had learned from them certain facets of the belief and practice. Sacrifice was of course important, as it was for all religions of the region; they knew the gods of whatever name enjoyed sacrifice whether for the smell or for the sustenance it gave them as they lived in their lofty places in the sky or on mountains.

But what troubled the people of Jabesh especially about this YHWH, the god of Israel and presumably the god of Saul, was that god's whimsical nature, the god's unpredictability. They had all heard that the god had chosen Saul to be king, but then they heard that the god's mouthpiece, the aged Samuel, had claimed that YHWH had changed the divine mind and had rejected Saul and had chosen another, the shepherd David, who had killed the fearsome Goliath. Apparently, this David was even now on his way to claim the kingship in Hebron, but what would prevent this YHWH from changing course yet again and choosing someone else and deposing David? Just why would anyone worship a god who could not decide from one day to the next who was the right choice to rule? And how exactly could anyone finally know what the "right" choice of the god was?

The religion of Jabesh was so much simpler. The "god" was actually the world in which they lived. It was the fields and flocks, the soft breeze from the west and the wilder winds of the east, the trees, the rocks, the grasses and wheat, the dependable dyings and risings of growth in winter and summer. How much easier all that seemed.

King Saul

Rather than leave Saul as a misshapen mass, they burned his monstrous trunk until all that was left were the bones, those white things that were firm and made a man or woman able to stand erect. Saul's bones were extraordinarily large, of course, and they were gathered up in several tunics—his had been torn to shreds on Gilboa—and were buried underneath a sacred tamarisk tree just beyond the village walls. Out of respect the villagers fasted for seven long days, far longer than ever they had, and the tree became for some years a place of pilgrimage for many in the area. And instead of the obscene sign they had found on Saul's body at Beth-Shan, one of the literate ones among them scratched into a tablet of stone the words "*melek* Israel," "king of Israel," for so the man was. And he added, this unknown scribe, "*ish* YHWH," "man of YHWH," in order to honor Saul's god.

And the people of Jabesh kept the shrine for many years and continued their memory of the hero of Jabesh, Saul, son of Kish, king of Israel. But whether or not YHWH remembered, or even cared, no one knew.